Table of Contents

Foreword by Mike Rother

Back when Western companies used to try to copy Toyota's production system, I think Toyota's leaders may have shaken their heads a bit and wondered: "Why are these people trying to copy our solutions to our specific problems, rather than how we develop solutions?"

One of the things that sets Toyota apart is its ability to improve faster than the rest of the market and to continue doing so. It took a few years to uncover the routines of thinking and acting that enable Toyota to keep improvement and innovation going (Rother, 2009). After that, the even-more-interesting question became: How can other companies develop such skills and mindsets in their organizations? That led us to develop practice routines – called "Starter Kata" – that any team or organization can use to develop its own continuous improvement and innovation routines (Rother, 2018).

Today it is a pleasure to see how the Toyota Kata topic has experienced many adaptations in different organizations and business sectors. Now, in this book, Jesper Boeg shows us a version of Toyota Kata from and for the world of software development. Jesper describes how to get started and how you can adjust Toyota Kata to your context while staying true to its core patterns and principles. I find myself paying attention and learning again, and I encourage you to do so too.

Best wishes for your practice!

Mike Rother

Foreword by Diana Larsen

"Getting Better–it's the whole point of changing how we work–becoming more productive, higher performing, more profitable, more effective; meeting higher quality standards; and forging mutually beneficial relationships with customers and users." This is how I began the foreword I wrote for Jesper's previous book, Real Life Scrum. Upon review, my opinion on this matter hasn't changed since Jesper published that book in 2012.

In fact, our sense of this mutual alignment of the purpose and potential of Agile approaches created a bond between Jesper and me over ten years ago. Neither of us has wavered in our focus on helping teams and organizations become the best they can be. (Have you noticed? When we connect with people who share our values and intentions, we create a strong bond.) Since Jesper and I first collaborated, our professional inquiries have continued to lead us along separate yet very similar paths. Each time we reconnect, we are eager to hear what the other has learned about approaches to "getting better" and what new line of inquiry each is following.

Working in different parts of the world for different clients, as we do, Jesper and I spend long periods out of touch. As a result, the email in which Jesper invited me to read his most recent book was a delightful and intriguing surprise. From my perspective as co-creator of the Agile Fluency™ Model, I was well-positioned and eager to read his latest ideas about coaching and consulting with organizational leaders to help them reach their businesses' goals.

Jesper's previous books (Priming Kanban and Real Life Scrum) and other writings about Kanban, Lean, Agile, and Scrum have placed him firmly on the logical path to a deep exploration of Toyota Kata. His work with clients gives him new opportunities to apply and learn from his exploring. I am grateful that he is sharing his experiences with us.

He hooked me with his introduction to the book, laying out Toyota's rationale for a relentless focus on continuous improvement and providing a powerful set of statistics to support his thesis. "In general, you might say that we talk about Agile and implement Agile tools and practices, but that most organizations fail to deliver on the very basic elements." Improvement comes from centering our attention on the "Process Vision." The flow of this book leads us on a systematic progression toward increased understanding of the potential in his approach. The text combines practical steps to complete along with illuminating case studies and executive summaries to consolidate our insights.

In the Agile Fluency Model, James Shore and I describe the observable behaviors of teams and the benefits organizations can harvest by investing in them. The techniques in this book also rely on what is observable. There is no reliance on hand-waving theory here. In our model, James and I also

2

emphasize the applicability of learning or adopting any of the Agile/Lean methodologies and practices as tools that support improvement. The key steps come by discovering and unlocking the best fit for the organization's strategic direction and culture. As outlined in Jesper's book, applying Toyota Kata could support and strengthen the investment plans that leaders choose.

It may have been obvious that I would find many complementary elements between Jesper's Toyota Kata and my thinking on Retrospectives for continuous improvement. However, there is also a clear link between the intentions and effects of Toyota Kata and reaching target zones in the Agile Fluency Model. One of the early stories Jesper tells of using Toyota Kata with a team provides a wonderful description of a not-quite-agile team stepping up into Agile Fluency "Focusing" zone proficiency. From Liftoff, Agile Chartering's Purpose contains similar elements to Toyota Kata's Vision, Challenge, and Target Conditions by emphasizing the importance of clarifying the current state while moving toward "a desirable future state."

My electronic copy of the book is full of marginal commentary and highlighted sections. I found so much here to absorb and apply. As Jesper describes it, I could incorporate Toyota Kata as part of my solution set when helping organizations achieve the Agile Fluency zone proficiencies for greatest benefit. It's another technique in my consulting "toolkit" for getting managers and senior leaders more directly involved in continuous improvement efforts for "Focusing," "Delivering," and "Optimizing" zone investments. Through their participation in the Kata analysis and activity, leaders will more effectively perceive the small successes along their journey. Our Agile Fluency Improvement Cycle relies on experiments and feedback loops which are analogous to the series of team-level Challenges. Accomplishing multiple Challenges strengthens a team on its way to repeating its Diagnostic workshop and demonstrating its improvements.

The emphasis on improvement also appears in a quote from a manager speaking to their team: "In general, we expect teams to use between 10% and 20% of their capacity on improvements, but naturally we would rather see you create amazing results in an hour than spending 100 hours getting nowhere."

This book proposes another important step toward extending and improving our practice of Agile approaches for team and organizational benefit as we continue to borrow from the broad base of knowledge from other fields (Lean, DevOps, Organization Design, Socio-Technical Systems, Complexity Science, and more) and from authors (Mike Rother, Steve Bell, Eliyahu Goldratt, Gene Kim, Jez Humble, Nicole Forsgren, Elizabeth Keogh, Paul Tolchinsky, Glenda Eoyang, David Snowden, and many more). I was also delighted to find a "shout out" to two of my hometown colleagues, Adam Light and Kathy Iberle.

In the core Agile community, we are working toward a world in which building software solutions becomes "more effective, humane, and sustainable" (Agile Alliance) and in which individuals and organizations can reach their "full potential and deliver innovative solutions." I'm honored to be on that path with Jesper.

Diana Larsen

Co-Founder & Chief Connector, Agile Fluency Project LLC

Portland, Oregon, USA

Co-author, The Agile Fluency Model: A Brief Guide to Success with Agile (with James Shore)

Co-author, Agile Retrospectives: Making Good Teams Great (with Esther Derby)

Co-author, Liftoff: Start and Sustain Successful Agile Teams (with Ainsley Nies)

Co-author, Five Rules for Accelerated Learning (with Willem Larsen)

Acknowledgements

This book would not have been possible without the great people in the organizations with which I have worked and the reviewers and thought leaders who have helped frame the book's content and structure, making it much better than I could ever have done on my own.

Of the many people with whom I have had a chance to work during the past years, I am especially indebted to CIO Flemming Krath Engedal and CDO Christian Wiese at Bankdata for supporting the Toyota Kata initiative and exploring new frontiers of continuous improvement across the organization. I would also like to thank Director Berit Doormann Kuhr at Bankdata for her ability to constantly challenge my mindset as well as the mindsets of others, as well as for insisting that anything is possible despite setbacks and problems. In addition, I would like to extend a special thanks to the Agile Coaches at Bankdata—Bente Pedersen, Annica Berggrern, Lars Behn-Segall, Pia Thimsen, Anita Nissen, Rasmus Kaae and Anita Mortensen—for their feedback and help in turning theory into practice and for working with me throughout our many successful and not-so-successful experiments.

I also would like to thank Martin Rosén-Lidholm and Johannes Klose Andersen for their support and help in exploring the use of Toyota Kata to integrate Kanban principles in their organization. That was truly an inspiring journey and I hope to continue discussing the use of Toyota Kata, Kanban, Lean and Agile with you guys in the years to come.

Diana Larsen and Mike Rother deserve a special thanks for writing the forewords of this book. Both of you are thought leaders in your fields and this book is very much the result of standing on the shoulders of giants. Thank you, Mike, for welcoming me into your network of Toyota Kata practitioners and for sharing your thoughts and perspectives on Toyota Kata, as well as continuous improvement through your books and website. I know you are both busy people and I appreciate that you took the time to support my work.

To my friend Ulrik Møller Christensen, who is partner at the management consulting firm Hildebrandt & Brandi, I am truly indebted. We have been friends for most of our lives, and I can think of no other person with whom I share more, both privately and professionally. Your thought-provoking ideas about organizational change, culture and improvement are constant sources of inspiration, and I am honored to count you among my closest friends. This book and probably my entire career would not have been the same without you. I look forward to many great experiences, professionally and privately, in the years to come and to working on the shared goal of using Toyota Kata to build Agile organizations inside and outside the world of IT.

Many people have helped review both early and late versions of the manuscript for this book. Among those, Adam Light, Johannes Klose Andersen, Tomas Eilsø, Håkan Forss and Michael Blaha deserve special thanks. The amount of time you put into providing both detailed comments and high-level reflections is truly amazing. Without you, this would have been a very different book. Your unique perspectives have helped make the book much more accessible to a wider range of people. Additionally, I would like to thank Adam for letting me use his case-study and success-card concept in the book and to Michael for coming up with the idea for the book's title.

I would also like to thank reviewers: Thomas AC Kofoed, Klaus Bucha-Lassen, Troels Richter, Lars Andersen, Mikkel Jensen, Anders Nygaard, Bente Pedersen, Rasmus Kaae, Alexandra Lundbæk and Magdalena Houska. You have each provided great comments and reflections that improved both the content and the structure of the book.

Finally, I would like to thank my wife, Line, and our two kids, Noah and Vitus, for supporting me through the bad moods, doubts and writer's blocks that I am sure most authors experience throughout the process of writing a book. Without family, professional success is an empty shell, so I count myself lucky to be successful in both areas and with enough free time to enjoy it.

Introduction

The first time I heard about Toyota Kata was at a Kanban leadership retreat in Mayerhofen, Austria back in 2012. There, Håkan Forrs gave a presentation on the subject. It sounded interesting, but I had trouble relating the manufacturing principles to my usual context of IT development and innovation. Needing something to read for the summer holiday, I downloaded *Toyota Kata* by Mike Rother on a whim (Rother, 2009).

Within the first chapter, my interest had turned to excitement and the feeling that this would not only affect my daily work but potentially my entire career and approach toward helping organizations succeed with Lean and Agile. From the many great points in Mike´s book, to me the most important ones were:

- Problem-focused continuous improvement is reactive and will keep us anchored in our current situation. Improvement should be guided by a clear and desirable Future State.
- True continuous improvement is not something you "wake up" to every two or four weeks, but part of daily work.
- Leaders' and managers' primary job should be to drive continuous improvement – from having their own improvement targets to coaching teams and Process Leads.
- Real improvement comes not from the number of improvement tasks you complete but rather from focusing on the few changes that will make a real impact.
- Improvement is not a straight road from A to B. It requires an iterative approach of setting measurable goals and validating the results of experiments toward them.
- Solutions are context-specific and we cannot copy our way to success. Improvement should be driven by a focus on core Lean/Agile principles and not specific roles, events and practices.

It was a bit like getting a punch in the gut. I was starting to realize not only how organizations could improve much more effectively, but also how I might have been guilty of leading people and organizations down the "wrong" path in the past. Looking at the world from the perspective of Toyota Kata, it is no surprise that organizations struggle to move beyond Agile mechanics. If we seriously believe that continuous improvement is the major differentiator in the marketplace, we need to treat it as such and not as a second-class citizen who might get what little time is left when we are done with the "real work". If we continue to allow ourselves to look at continuous improvement from the narrow perspective of what can be done within a single iteration, if we focus on copying specific solutions and if improvement is happening only at the team level, we should not be surprised if it is not delivering the results we want.

I can readily recall all the situations in which I have asked people to forget the past and look at their biggest current impediment, but truth be told, I knew deep down that we were more in the "reactive problem-solving" space than gaining a real competitive advantage. But because I did not have an alternative and found that people around me were doing the same, I convinced myself that it was good enough.

Continuous improvement as the major differentiator

At Toyota, it is a core belief that success does not come from current capabilities but from the ability to continuously evolve and improve faster than the rest of the market. This means that all leaders and managers are measured primarily on their ability to drive continuous improvement (Rother, 2009). It is in the very DNA of the entire organization and the reason why Toyota has been so successful in the last 60 years, why it has bounced back quicker than anyone imagined from the financial crisis and the 2011 earthquakes in Japan and why it remains the most profitable car manufacturer worldwide.

If we agree that the ability to improve is crucial in an ever-changing world, we might ask ourselves how well we do this. Are our leaders and managers proactively driving improvement or primarily concerned with budgets and reactive firefighting? Do our Process Leads, Scrum Masters or other formal or informal leaders inspire, guide and coach in the adoption of Lean and Agile or are they just facilitators? Are team members complaining about the dependencies on centralized platforms, shared deployments or outdated structures but nothing seems to be done about it? In my experience, most larger organizations will find themselves less-than-ideally set up to handle improvement effectively.

The Toyota Kata framework enables you to establish a culture of continuous improvement across the organization, from directors to the team level. Directed, measurable improvements allow you to deliver better services to your customers and end users at a lower cost with happier employees. Improvement grounded in core Lean/Agile principles like delegation of decision authority and small batches will set a shared direction but still give areas, departments and teams the freedom to develop or find specific solutions and methods that match their context. That is the potential of Toyota Kata and I hope you will find it as great and inspiring a prospect as I do.

Getting there is not easy, and it requires a fundamental shift in how we perceive Process improvement and management. Through this book, I hope you will discover that the potential is so great that it is indeed worth striving for. I am convinced that until now we have just been scratching the surface of what continuous improvement truly means in the Agile community.

Who is this book for and why should you read it?

This book is for CxOs, managers, leaders, team members and consultants interested in establishing a culture of continuous improvement. 83% of large organizations in Western Europe are adopting Agile methods, but 45% are lacking management support. 63% have a culture that is not aligned with Agile and 43% are experiencing resistance to change (Cappelli & Tavis, 2018).

In general, you might say that we talk about Agile and implement Agile tools and practices, but that most organizations fail to deliver on the very basic elements. From a delivery perspective, we are also a far cry from the Lean/Agile notion of a smooth flow of customer-recognized value as there are 94 restarts for every 100 started projects and over 30% of projects are canceled. Only 24% of project investment decisions are made using any kind of financial modeling (Humble, 2018). Even though business value is a primary economic risk, we spend our time tracking only the cost which has a much lower information value (Hubbard, 2009). A basic Agile principle like user involvement is rated as the primary deciding factor for success while the lack of it is regarded as the second biggest cause of failure. On top of that, over 50% of all delivered features are rarely or never used and thus not really great proof of a capability to take a customer-centric and early feedback approach (Standish Group Chaos Report, 2014).

Those are not easy challenges to overcome, so the need for a systematic way of driving aligned, measurable improvement across all layers is more relevant than ever. Not as an add-on but as an integrated and natural part of daily work. Initial Agile training and workshops have proven to be a great starter kit but unable to deal with the powerful forces of culture, habits and a structure that might no longer be "fit for purpose" in today's world.

When I give presentations at local meetups or at a company, I often ask people to raise their hands if they experience well-known anti-patterns like part-time team allocation, task switching, constantly changing priorities, missing feedback loops, lack of transparency, inside-out focus, forecasting based on wishful thinking and centralized decision authority. It always surprises me that the very companies I have seen giving presentations on the success of their Agile transition are often still experiencing some or all of these. It is not that they do not recognize the anti-patterns, but they are simply unable to deal with them effectively.

This book covers all aspects of introducing Toyota Kata in an Agile setting, from high-level principles to specific roles, events and practices as well as cases and examples showing how theory has been turned into real-life results at all levels of the organization.

You do not have to be an Agile expert to read the book, though a basic knowledge of Agile principles and frameworks like Scrum and SAFe is expected. If you do not possess this knowledge, I would recommend that you read along and seek additional knowledge online when you come across a concept or principle that you do not feel is explained in enough detail.

We will cover the aspect of defining Agile organizational capabilities in much more detail in Chapter 9 "The vision", but for now, it is enough to state that we optimize for business Agility using a combination of the four value statements and 12 principles from the Agile Manifesto and core Lean principles of pull, flow, feedback and visualization.

The structure of the book

The book consists of five major parts:

- **Part 1. Toyota Kata Basics**, introducing the overall framework (6 chapters)
- **Part 2. The Starter Kata Roles, Events and Concepts**, introducing the details of the individual Toyota Kata elements in an Agile context (9 chapters)
- **Part 3. Toyota Kata in the Wider Organization**, introducing the aspects of collaboration as well as roll-out in the wider organization (5 chapters)
- **Part 4. Using Other Models with Toyota Kata**, diving into the specifics of Value Stream Mapping, Kanban and the very interesting topic of using Toyota Kata for product development instead of Process improvement (3 chapters)
- **Part 5. Examples and Cases**, providing specific examples of Challenges, Target Conditions and 5 case studies (2 Chapters)

You will get the most out of this book by reading Parts 1-2 in that order, as you will find a lot of references to content that was covered in previous chapters. The chapters included in Part 3, 4 and 5 may be read in any order. I think you will find that Part 5 serves as a great inspiration catalog that you can keep going back to when you start applying Toyota Kata in real life.

Looking at the organization, I will refer to the different levels using these terms:

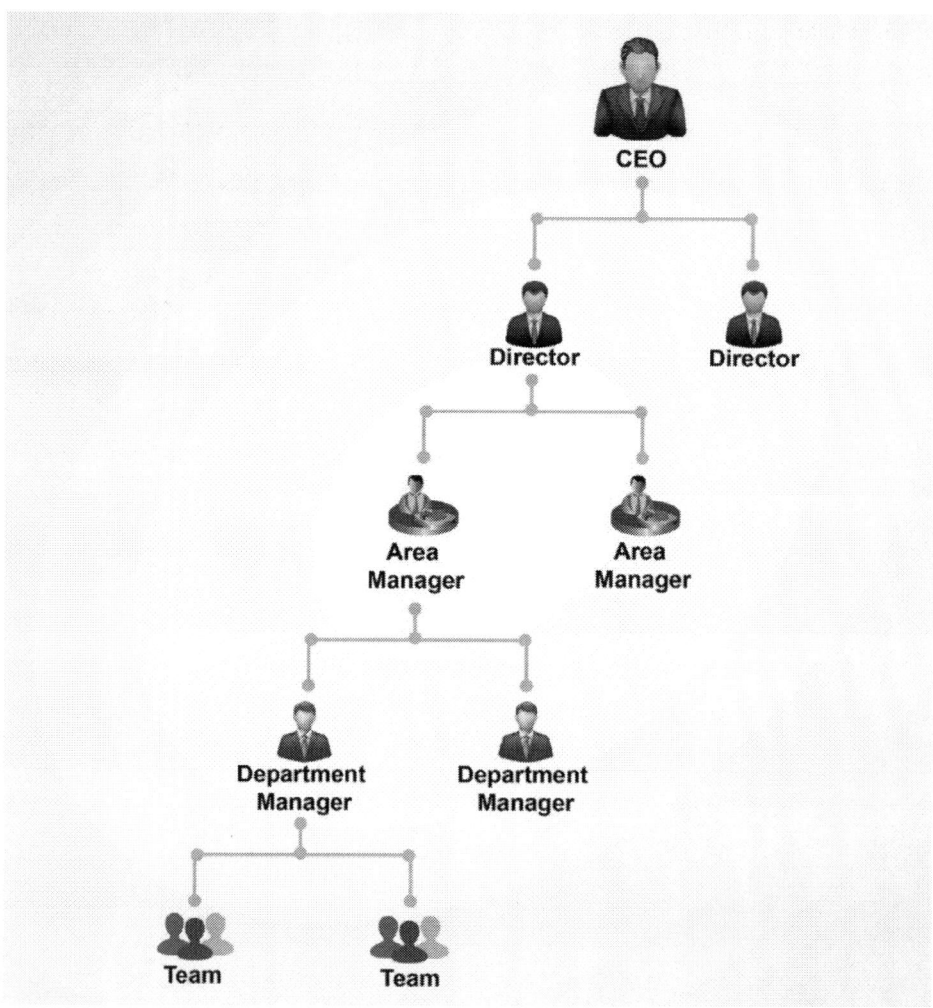

Figure 1: Naming of organizational layers

There are many versions of the structure above. Before moving on, I encourage you to write them down and match them to your organizational structure on a piece of paper. You may find that you have fewer or more levels. I will leave it as an exercise for you to match the examples in the book with your own situation.

Throughout the book, I will switch between "I" and "we" when referring to specific elements, concepts and adjustments. That is because I had the help of many talented internal coaches, directors, managers, team leads, Scrum Masters and team members in implementing Toyota Kata across the organizations I have worked with. Their immense feedback helped frame both the roll-out concept as well as training material and processes. It was a joint effort to navigate the unclear territory of making Toyota Kata work in an Agile setting.

Method-specific wording and concepts

Since 2001, when the Agile Manifesto was written, people have included a lot of roles, principles and practices in the Agile vocabulary. Some are general concepts and some are specific to, e.g., Scrum, Extreme Programming or The Lean Startup movement. Because this book is about Agile I will try to use words that are not tied to specific methods. Instead, I will be explicit when I refer to, e.g., specific Scrum roles like Scrum Master or Product Owner and XP practices like Test Driven Development (TDD) or Pair Programming. I will use the terms "throughput" instead of "Velocity" and "work items" instead of "User Stories" and will talk about "delegation of product decision authority" rather than the explicit interpretation of that principle through a single person being the Product Owner. By doing this, I hope to both avoid alienating people from various schools of thought and bring the focus back to core Agile and Lean principles instead of framework-specific solutions.

Executive Summary

"Toyota Kata" is a name coined by Mike Rother and his research team after years spent studying Toyota's ability to improve faster than its competitors (Rother, 2009). Understanding the fact that competitive advantage does not come from current but future capabilities is the key to recognizing that continuous improvement should be treated as a first-class citizen and not one that gets what little time is left once important work items or deadlines have been completed/reached.

Toyota Kata is based on directed improvement toward a desirable Future State. This is a radically different way of driving improvement, as most other approaches are based on reactive problem-solving, effectively anchoring the team or organization in the current context. Removing what you do not want does not get you what you do want. Using Toyota Kata in an Agile setting, you must agree on the direction beyond vague terms like, e.g., "iterative and adaptive". This book argues that core Agile/Lean capabilities can be framed as the ability to deliver on:

- Strategic alignment
- Empowered, self-organizing teams
- Stable end-to-end teams with 100% allocation
- Always releasable – all code, any time, fully automated on demand
- Small batches (MVP, MVF), always outside-in approach
- Visual Management – full transparency
- Continuous qualitative and quantitative customer and end-user feedback
- One-by-one flow (Limit WIP)

We call this list the Lean/Agile "Process Vision", as they are the capabilities we must establish across all layers of the organization to deliver at our optimal performance. One essential point this book makes is that we should aim to deliver on those deeper capabilities and introduce methods like Scrum and SAFe only to support them, not as the end goal. Another key point is that you cannot just tell people to trust each other, show acts of leadership, experiment or take larger risks; however, you can build the capabilities to support and evolve these behaviors.

To take systematic steps in the direction of the Vision, all organizational layers must set measurable Process improvement goals and work iteratively to achieve them. This involves getting a detailed picture of current processes and setting objective metrics that indicate whether we are moving closer to our desired Future State. Moving toward a realistic, ambitious goal involves daily experimentation as well as the ability to validate results against the target metrics. Continuous improvement is, thus, not something teams and managers "wake up" to once every few weeks or at the end of a project, but a natural part of daily work.

This process of directed continuous improvement goes on at all layers of the organization. A key element of Toyota Kata is for managers to recognize that systematically creating a better environment for people to succeed and coaching their direct report in the aspects of Process improvement are their core responsibilities (Rother & Aulinger, 2017). Systems thinking teaches us that you cannot improve the whole by focusing on the individual interdependent parts.

A Kata is used in martial arts to practice behaviors so that they become routine and so we can free up our cognitive load to focus on the situation. Toyota Kata uses two Kata to enable effective improvement: the "Improvement Kata" and the "Coaching Kata". The Improvement Kata enables us to iteratively work our way toward our measurable goals by identifying Obstacles and validating the results of experiments. The Coaching Kata establishes Coach/Learner relationships with the purpose of developing the improvement skills of the Learner. Put together, the two Kata form a Starter Kata that enables organizations to practice the core skills of directed continuous improvement before adapting to the individual context (Rother, 2009). This book presents a version of the Starter Kata suited for IT organizations to begin that journey.

Applying the Toyota Kata framework to an Agile context in which flow is measured in days or weeks, it is necessary to use tools and practices like Value Stream Mapping as well as to adjust the cadences of Toyota Kata events. The result is still very much aligned with the original framework and has proven to be a very effective improvement driver on both the team and organizational levels.

Rolling out Toyota Kata in the organization requires building a team of internal coaches and getting buy-in from the top level. You may start small but even a pilot initiative should include more than just the team level to gain real experience. Toyota Kata is not an add-on or a small adjustment to existing practices but a fundamental change of mindset toward Process improvement and with the potential to deliver great results.

Perspectives on the use of Toyota Kata include a powerful combination of The Kanban Method invented by David Anderson (Anderson, 2010), driving Agile transitions, using it to scale Agile more effectively, as well as the use of Toyota Kata outside the field of Process improvement by applying it to product development. Toyota Kata functions as a keystone on which other Lean-based methods like Kanban become energized. Toyota Kata does this by acting as a foundation for building a culture of discipline and decision-making based on the scientific method.

To get started with Toyota Kata, it is necessary to understand what constitutes good and actionable metrics for improvement work in an Agile context. Therefore, a considerable part of this book is reserved for introducing the concepts of leading and lagging metrics as well as a large inspiration catalog with examples and case studies.

Part 1. Toyota Kata Basics

This part of the book introduces my initial experiences with Toyota Kata as well as the overall Toyota Kata framework and the included events, roles and practices. The goal is to introduce the context, so the remaining parts and chapters won't seem like fragmented individual elements but part of a bigger whole. You will learn about the two major Kata which serve as the foundation, as well as the specific cadences adapted to the context of Agile. The last chapter in this part includes an example of applying Toyota Kata to provide context for the many new words, principles and concepts. Note that this part of the book is only an overview – details will follow later.

Unless otherwise stated, any reference to the Toyota Kata body of knowledge outside the scope of Agile organizations is based on the work by Mike Rother:

- Toyota Kata: Managing People for Improvement, Adaptiveness and Superior Results (Rother, 2009)
- Toyota Kata Culture: Building Organizational Capability and Mindset through Kata Coaching (Rother & Aulinger, 2017)
- The Toyota Kata Practice Guide: Practicing Scientific Thinking Skills for Superior Results in 20 Minutes a Day (Rother, 2018)
- Mike Rother's website "PRACTICE SCIENTIFIC THINKING" with lots of available resources: http://www-personal.umich.edu/~mrother/Homepage.html

It is not required reading to benefit from the content in this book but especially "The Toyota Kata Practice Guide" is highly recommended to get a deeper understanding of the underlying framework. It does not share the hardcore manufacturing focus of the first two books and is therefore much easier to relate to if you find yourself in the context of innovation and knowledge work.

1. A different context

Had I known how much trial and error would be involved in getting real, directed, continuous improvement with Toyota Kata to work in the context of IT and Agile organization, I might not have dared embark on the journey. However, because the time machine has yet to be invented, that is not a question I need to answer.

Reading Mike Rother's books, you quickly realize that examples are from a different context. There are many new concepts and words, like Target Condition, Coaching Kata, Improvement Kata and Process characteristic, as well as a very different notion of a team leader and manager. Had I not already been familiar with Lean, I probably also would have struggled with concepts like tact-time, cycle time, PDCA Cycles and Japanese phrases like "Kaizen", "Andon buttons", "Kanban systems", "Poka-yoke" and "Heijunka". But what do these terms mean? How do they translate from a manufacturing context in which completion time and flow are counted in seconds and minutes to an IT context of hours, days or even weeks? What is the difference between an outcome and process metric and is it even possible to work with improvement daily in such a different context?

	Manufacturing	Knowledge Work
Cycle-Time	Sec./Min	Days/Weeks
Variability	Low	High
Accuracy	High	Low

Figure 2: Manufacturing vs. Knowledge work

When I first tried looking for answers, I watched conference presentations and spent hours googling, hoping to find examples from an Agile or IT context. What I found was, unfortunately, only vague statements and quotes, short-term initiatives in which a single team had experimented for a few weeks, or purely theoretical discussions. It seemed that a lot of people liked the theory behind Toyota Kata and the Improvement Kata, but that specific examples of applying it in real life were largely missing from the equation. That is what I hope to change with this book by providing lots of examples from the past six years, five organizations, 30 departments and nearly 80 teams involved.

This book is the one I wish I'd had six years ago. You learn a lot from mistakes but not all mistakes need to be repeated by everybody. My goal is that you will become as excited about the potential of Toyota Kata as I am and that you will find it considerably easier to get started. You should, however, realize that Toyota Kata represents a fundamentally different approach to continuous improvement and, to some, a considerable shift in mindset from more traditional approaches like Scrum Retrospectives.

The content of this book is based on six years of working with Toyota Kata, from the first experiments in a single team back in 2012 to including it as an element of Agile transitions and Kanban implementations until finally getting the chance to work with Toyota Kata as an organization-wide initiative across all layers in the 700-person bank cooperative "Bankdata" in Denmark from 2016 to 2018.

2. Why do we need Toyota Kata?

Through the introduction of Scrum, retrospectives have by now become almost an industry standard. If you are doing it well and can answer "yes" to the following questions, there is a chance that Toyota Kata will not be a game changer, as you are already consciously or unconsciously using the principles:

- You set ambitious improvement targets aligned with core Lean/Agile principles and systematically work to achieve them.
- Improvements are measurable, and numbers are moving in the right direction on a frequent basis.
- Each step is validated using scientific thinking, taking an iterative and experimental approach to Process improvement.
- Improvement is part of daily work and both teams and managers work together to achieve the targets.
- Improvement targets point to an ambitious Future State rather than a focus on reactive problem-solving.

9 symptoms that you need Toyota Kata

If you experience one or more of the following symptoms, Toyota Kata could very well be the framework that will provide you with improvement capability beyond what you thought possible. Remember that all the listed symptoms are organizational issues and not the fault of the individual leader, manager or team member. It is not because someone did something intentionally wrong but rather that we failed to provide the processes and structures to do better. It is a rather long list and I have selected only the most important, so bear with me as we discover the many issues with traditional improvement approaches. Solutions will follow later.

1. You are avoiding the "big stuff".

Are you focusing on what is easy to change instead of what is most important? Are you being constrained by a two- or three-week Process improvement focus to the extent that you avoid the bigger and more important issues? Are people focusing more on experiments that are fun rather than on what has the most potential? Do teams "wipe the slate clean" after each iteration, allowing themselves to move on to the next issue when they have reached a challenging problem? Have you talked about real end-user feedback, continuous delivery, outcome focus and measuring end-user engagement numerous times but been too daunted by possible obstacles and the size of the task ahead to do something about it?

2. You are focusing on actions and forgetting the effect.

Do you focus on your ability to complete retrospective SMART goals, but little time evaluating whether they changed things for the better? Are you missing the knowledge, framework or experience to judge it, even if you had the time available to follow up on your actions? Are you skipping the evaluation of previous actions because deep down you know that they were not the success you hoped for and you find it easier to move on to something new?

3. Managers are not focused on driving improvement.

Are managers busy handling budgets and administrative tasks, but left with little time to be proactive? Are they given neither the time, skills nor responsibility to drive improvement? Have organizational structures made them so distant from the actual work that they might not even understand how they can help and make decisions that are counterproductive without knowing it? Were managers given a one-day introduction to Agile and Agile leadership but never really received the time, focus and coaching to understand Agile or how they fit in that context? Are teams getting stuck in their improvement efforts because department-level managers fail to engage in continuous improvement and help remove Obstacles to flow and feedback?

4. The Daily Whirlwind takes over.

Do User Stories, defects and deadlines often take precedence over improvement work? Are they connected to critical deadlines to the extent that teams are reminded several times a week about how crucial it is to get a User Story or defect fix deployed? In the book "4 Disciplines of Execution" (Covey S. , 2015), "The Daily Whirlwind" is mentioned as a constant and fierce competitor threatening to consume 100% of our capacity and leaving little room for improving our long-term production capability. Are you able to fight your Daily Whirlwind of important User Stories and defects, or do you often face the fact that improvement initiatives become too small to truly make a difference?

5. Improvements are lacking in direction.

Do your improvement initiatives lack direction? Are they guided by today's, yesterday's or last week's problem and not any real ambition in terms of where you want to be? Are you overwhelmed by problems you could solve but lacking the ability to know which will make a difference? Do retrospectives revolve around reactive problem-solving, focusing more on what can be improved rather than what should be improved? Are you looking back six months thinking, 'What have we really improved?' Are you using terms like "high-performance team", "learning organization" and "adaptive/iterative development" but failing to define what they really mean and whether you are getting closer to delivering on those goals?

6. The Scrum Master is reduced to a facilitator with the ability to ask "What do you think?"

Does your organization not recognize Scrum Masters as drivers of improvement and are they given little or no actual decision authority? Are Scrum Masters not taking responsibility for coaching and guiding the team and organization in the adoption of Scrum, Lean and Agile, but seeing themselves as facilitators at the mercy of the organization? Are Scrum Masters relying entirely on the input from the team, asking "What do you think?" in terms of identifying both improvement potential and how to get there? Do Scrum Masters have a huge and untapped potential, but the organization is not set up to provide them with the "leading" part of the "Servant Leader" and, therefore, they offer the organization and team little expertise, coaching and direction beyond the role of a facilitator?

7. There is too much improvement WIP (Work In Progress).

Have you started five, 10 or 15 improvement initiatives in the team or department or across the organization but failed to follow up on their progress, their effect or whether they were truly started or completed? Do your improvement priorities change before you get the chance to finish existing initiatives?

8. Improvements are slow and often on hold.

Are you finding that retrospectives begin with the sentence "The previous SMART goal was not reached because…."? If SMART goals fail, are you waiting two or three weeks to plan the next step, effectively losing two weeks of improvement capacity and slowing down both feedback and execution? Do people think of improvement as a straight road from A to B and fail to recognize the iterative nature of the task?

9. The escalation of impediments brings continuous improvement to a grinding halt.

Are teams and managers spending most retrospectives discussing what outside structures, teams, specialists or managers should change? Do they point to all the problems in the rest of the organization and conclude that it is something they should do rather than asking the more important questions of: "How can we work around that obstacle?" or "How might we facilitate or influence the process of finding a solution?" Are impediments escalated to a series of Impediment Boards but with no capacity or overall prioritization mechanisms to get them solved?

Are you prepared to invest time and energy to get the results you want?

If the answer to one or more of the above statements is yes, Toyota Kata could very well be the remedy that will make your improvement work more fun, engaging and effective. Yet establishing a culture of true directed improvement is not easy. It is a bold Challenge with the potential for great rewards; however, make sure you are prepared to invest real time and energy before you start so that you can quickly navigate to the positive side of the J-curve. As with any other change initiative, Toyota Kata requires an upfront investment:

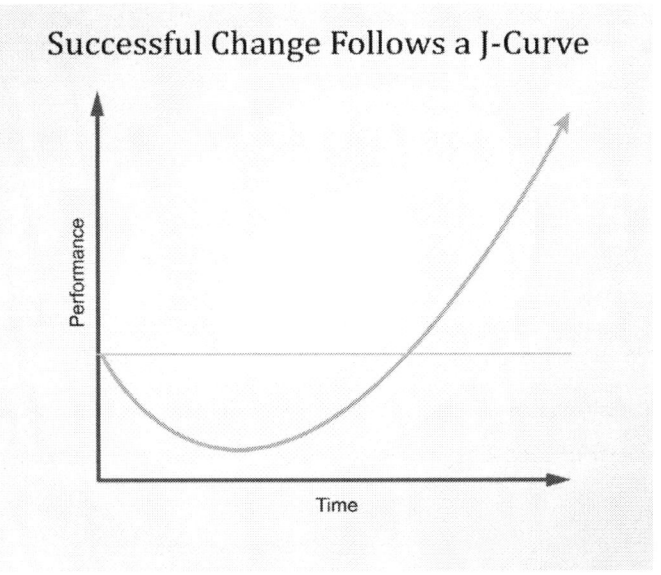

Figure 3: Change J-Curve

But as W. Edwards Deming pointed out, "Learning is not compulsory... neither is survival" and research papers now offer hard proof of the value of investment in continuous improvement in IT delivery (Nicole Forsgren, 2017).

What can you expect to get with Toyota Kata?

To truly understand and appreciate the effect of Toyota Kata, we must gain a better understanding of what successful Process improvement means. In the following chapters, you will learn about Process Visions, Challenges and Target Conditions, leading and lagging indicators, process and outcome metrics, how to get a good understanding of your Current Condition to see whether your experiments are generating the expected results and many more aspects of Toyota Kata.

Toyota Kata makes it possible for you to reach for the stars and deliver on the full potential of your organization by setting targets and reaching them through relentless daily improvement. We all talk about continuous delivery, automated deployment, the potential of fast feedback and decision authority delegated to the team level. With Toyota Kata, we are no longer talking and trying but doing! The key is to take small iterative steps in your chosen direction and allow yourself to experiment and fail, not on a bi-weekly basis but every day in very short experimentation cycles. This means that even in the short term you can observe improvements that make a difference which drives both the motivation to continue and the actual results. Examples of short-term results include:

- Work not getting blocked during execution, resulting in faster flow and higher throughput
- Focused periods of work without meetings or external interruptions, resulting in higher throughput and job satisfaction
- Lower Work in Progress (WIP), resulting in faster feedback and shorter cycle time
- Ability to solve things in order of business priority and not according to individual skill sets, resulting in higher value and stakeholder happiness
- Avoidance of re-occurring defects resulting in less failure demand, higher throughput and higher job satisfaction
- Automated deployment pipelines resulting in higher throughput and higher deployment frequency
- Transparent visualization of priorities and ongoing work in one place, resulting in lower WIP, higher throughput and less stress
- Test automation, resulting in fewer manual regression tests, higher throughput and better quality
- Better quantitative and qualitative feedback loops resulting in higher value and better quality

We will dive much more into the details and metrics behind both ambitious Challenges and these types of short-term results later. However, already you might start to realize that Toyota Kata enables you to reach ambitious process goals and earn the resulting benefits.

3. A short story illustrating how this works

Because we have yet to introduce the basic elements of the Toyota Kata framework, I will avoid using Toyota Kata-specific terms in this short story. Still, it should provide you with a general idea of what Toyota Kata is and how it differs from our more traditional Process improvement initiatives. It is based on an example of a team failing to deliver on one of the most basic capabilities of an Agile team – namely, the ability of a cross-functional team to effectively deliver work items in order of business priority.

Meet the team

The team in question had been using a Scrum-like process for about two years. They knew each other well and had been supporting their main product for a long time. On the surface, things looked alright but a re-occurring problem at their retrospectives had been that the completion of individual work items was highly dependent on a single senior developer who would do most of the initial solution design as well as help complete work items when other team members ran into problems. The result was that:

- Work items would often not get finished during the Sprint, as they were waiting for input from the senior developer.
- Prioritization of new work was mostly done by trying to match the capabilities of the team rather than in order of business priority.

To compensate, they allowed themselves to start new work when they could not finish so that all team members would not be "idle" while waiting for the senior developer's input. Naturally, this meant that a lot of work was in-progress and often in-progress work would be put on hold for weeks or months because more important issues had arisen. Some of their retrospective SMART goals had included:

- Prioritizing work items to match the capabilities of the team
- Knowledge sharing sessions/workshops with the senior developer
- Pairing work with the senior developer
- Splitting work items in functional deliveries (front-end, back-end, test etc.)
- Starting new work when things got blocked to keep the rest of the team busy

By now, you might imagine a senior developer clinging desperately to knowledge. However, with the stress of an ever-present bottleneck, the situation was the exact opposite. The senior developer was, in fact, very motivated to share knowledge with the rest of the team. He would enjoy being able to take a day off without feeling as though he was letting down the rest of the team.

However, despite all the good intentions, the situation had remained unchanged for at least 12 months. A single knowledge-sharing workshop would be held, and team members would pair with the senior developer on one feature but then the next would be canceled. Despite the intention of pair work, there seemed to always be an important deadline or delivery, making it impossible to take the time to do it on a more consistent basis. The Product Owner had, at this time, acknowledged the situation and before even considering the priority from a business perspective, gone directly to the consideration of keeping the team busy.

Introducing Toyota Kata

Upon the introduction of Toyota Kata to the team, things fortunately started to change. Looking at the core Lean/Agile of a customer-centric perspective, limiting Work in Progress (WIP) and flow, it was clear that they had moved further from the core principles. They took a detailed look at their Value Stream and identified actual numbers to support their intuitive grasp of the situation. Looking toward a better Future State, they defined the following goals for themselves for the next three months:

- From 20% to 80% solved in order of business priority
- From 37 to 15 User Stories in progress
- From 5% to 80% of User Stories written from an end-user perspective

This goal changed the whole approach to their improvement efforts. Not only were they able to measure their progress but they did it from the perspective of the true process capabilities they wanted to build. They identified obstacles to the goal, including pressure to deliver on short-term results and a misguided focus on "being busy" rather than delivering value. Having a measurable goal, they were able to both set up experiments and validate results and they learned that failure is just a chance to do better tomorrow.

Process improvement is as much an iterative path as product development. Their manager acted as coach and helped them follow up on their ability to reach the goal twice a week. Through this process, she became aware of the fact that she was sometimes a major contributor to the problem of focusing on near-term deliveries at the expense of longer-term Process optimization. Thus, specific experiments included changing the way work items were negotiated and prioritized in the team.

In the end, they delivered on most of their goal. At the end of the three months, they had gone:

- From 20% to 70% solved in order of business priority
- From 37 to 13 User Stories in progress

- From 5% to 75% of User Stories written from an end-user perspective

To do this, they had to face many of the obstacles they had struggled with previously. By now, both pair work on bottleneck topics and joint reviews on new features had become second nature and part of the process. Another apparent effect was that due to the focus on end-user value, the Product Owner was now taking on a much more proactive role, as they had moved from a utilization and technical focus to a value focus.

This is just one of many results achieved using directed and measurable Process improvement with small daily experiments. Through this short team-level example, we have introduced many of the concepts you will learn about in detail in the next chapters, so you can use the power of Toyota Kata to achieve similar results.

Traditional Approach	Toyota Kata
Problem focus	Goal focus
Improvement workshops	Daily focus
Team involvement	Team + Management involvement
Good intentions	Measurable capabilities
Actions/SMART goals	Validated experiments
Assumes success	Iterative approach

Figure 4: Traditional Approach vs. Toyota Kata

Learning objectives and questions for real-life application

Having covered the first two chapters, it is time to reflect on the learning objectives so far. By now you should have realized that:

- Real continuous improvement is a part of daily life and as essential to success as the operation and maintenance of your products. It is not an add-on or something you wake up to once every two or three weeks.

- Continuous improvement is a joint organizational responsibility covering all organizational levels, including managers as essential drivers.

- Most companies are not ideally set up to effectively deliver on improvement and struggle with many aspects, including a focus on reactive problem-solving and falling prey to the pressure of the Daily Whirlwind.

- Measurable improvement goals provide a way to validate hypotheses iteratively and establish sustainable change that "sticks".

Before you continue, write your answers to the following questions to the best of your ability:

- Do you believe your current improvement initiative is focusing on the thing that will have the biggest positive effect? If not, why?

- Are you able to allocate enough time for improvement to stay competitive? If not, why?

- Can you validate the successes or failures of your improvement initiatives and use that feedback to make better improvement steps? If not, why?

- Is continuous improvement a daily focus? If not, why?

- Are continuous improvement initiatives a joint focus across all organizational layers? If not, why?

4. Introducing the Toyota Kata framework

The next few chapters will introduce the Toyota Kata framework and the terms and concepts involved. We will begin with a chapter providing a short introduction and then later dive into the details of applying it in an Agile context. In this chapter, you will get an introduction to the two primary elements of the Toyota Kata framework: "The Improvement Kata" which helps us reach the current improvement goal and "The Coaching Kata" which helps us improve our general continuous improvement capabilities.

"Toyota" and "Kata"

I assume that you have already guessed that Toyota Kata originates from Toyota. With Toyota's ability to achieve higher quality and profitability than its competitors, it is not surprising that its production system is among the most researched in the world and is the keystone behind the entire Lean movement (Ahlstrom & Modig, 2012). As with many other concepts from the Toyota Production System (TPS), Toyota Kata is so much a part of the DNA and daily life at Toyota that it took years of study by Mike Rother and his team to find out what was truly going on beneath the surface (Rother, 2009).

For years, companies have been trying to copy Lean tools and practices observed at Toyota but are failing to copy the culture, principles and practices that developed those solutions. Thus, many Lean initiatives have plateaued because they managed only to copy solution-specific mechanics and not the ability to drive continuous improvement. The result is a focus on specific tools and practices but one lacking the deeper understanding of the underlying Lean principles of pull, flow and feedback.

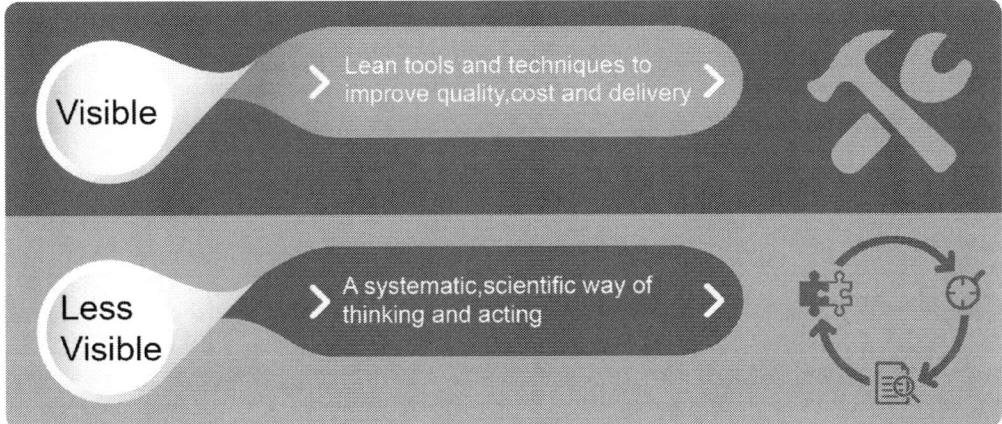

Figure 5: Tool vs. scientific thinking focus. Adapted from the Toyota Kata Practice Guide (ROTHER, 2018)

Over the years much the same has happened in the Agile context. The core values of self-organizing teams, delegation of authority, fast flow, close collaboration and integrated feedback loops have given way to specific tools and practices like Scrum Masters, Backlogs, User Stories, Product Owners, Sprints and Scaling Frameworks offering a single answer to all your context-specific problems. All those tools, roles and practices have great value in a specific context but instead of supporting the underlying principles, they often become the goal. Over the last 12 years, I have seen countless teams and organizations stuffed with Agile roles, tools and practices but with very little local decision authority, feedback and iterative flow of value. This is not surprising, as practices, roles and events are tangible and easy to implement. Thus, it is tempting to focus on these instead of on the underlying capabilities and value drivers.

What is a "Kata"?

The second word "Kata" is a knowledge transfer method based on repetitive actions that are practiced again and again. The most familiar application is probably martial arts. Teaching martial arts to new Learners, the teacher often uses a series of movements put together in a "Kata" that you practice to build muscle memory. This will free up your cognitive load so you can focus more attention on your opponent.

Figure 6: Building muscle memory

When I started training Karate many years ago, I was at first frustrated by the time required to go through the same patterns. However, if you are in a sparring fight and you must consciously recognize the opponent moving his foot, evaluating whether that will turn into a kick and what kind of block and counterattack you should use, you are already lying on the floor in pain and with a lost point.

Kata is, thus, about building muscle memory so that it becomes a recognized pattern that your brain can follow without conscious effort. With Toyota Kata, the aim is to build muscle memory of continuous improvement/learning so that it becomes part of your daily work and not something that "surprises" your brain once every two to four weeks or at the end of a successful or not-so-successful project. Process improvement should be as much a part of your daily work as working on new features, maintaining your systems and having lunch.

In this section, we will take a brief look at the basics. Though not a prerequisite for reading this book, I strongly encourage you to also familiarize yourself with Mike Rother's work to get a deeper understanding of the origin. If you don't feel like going through it all the first half of "The Toyota Kata Practice Guide" (Rother, 2018) is highly recommended as an introduction to the original framework.

Please note that a large part of this book and the material provided by Mike deals with what is now known as a "Starter Kata" – a way of developing scientific thinking and skill sets to drive effective continuous improvement. It is expected that once you have gained a thorough understanding of those concepts by practicing them in real life, you will adapt and improve them to fit your context. As with any new skill set, you will need to learn the basics before you can make the right choices for adaptation. I have seen teams, departments and organizations that have remained stuck too long in the Starter Kata or that have adjusted too quickly before they truly understood the essentials of taking an experimental approach toward improvement using scientific thinking.

The two Kata

At its core, Toyota Kata consists of two main elements: The Improvement Kata and the Coaching Kata.

Improvement Kata

The Improvement Kata is a systematic way of setting an ambitious and measurable Challenge and moving toward it in short experimentation cycles. For each cycle, the Experiment hypothesis is tested against the actual result to provide fast feedback and learning. Based on that, the next experiment is run until you meet the Challenge or decide to pivot to a new Challenge. This is basically the core concept of scientific thinking.

In Toyota Kata, you always work from your Current Condition toward a desirable Future State. Future States are divided into three elements: Vision, Challenge and Target Condition. The Vision is the ultimate "True North" which might be years into the future or even unobtainable. A Challenge represents one step toward the Vision – typically, months into the future. The Target Condition is a short-term step toward the current Challenge. Both Challenges and Targets are ambitious – engaging the organization, team or individual to move out of the comfort zone and dare to strive for excellence.

Element	Description
Vision	The True North which might be years into the future or even unobtainable
Challenge	Ambitious goal aligned with the Vision - typically months into the future
Target Condition	A short-term ambitious goal - 1 step toward the current Challenge

Figure 7: Vision, Challenge and Target Condition

Both Challenges and Target conditions should be objective, measurable and grounded in a firm understanding of the Current Condition. It is important to realize that from a Toyota Kata perspective, the Current Condition is not good or bad. There is no judgment or blame – the Current Condition simply "is". If we start prettifying our Current Condition, we will not be able to judge what constitutes an ambitious goal, and actual progress might seem less than it truly is. If you are starting from zero, you have a much greater potential for improvement – and that is a good thing. We will cover Vision, Challenge, Target and Current Condition, including many examples, in much more detail later.

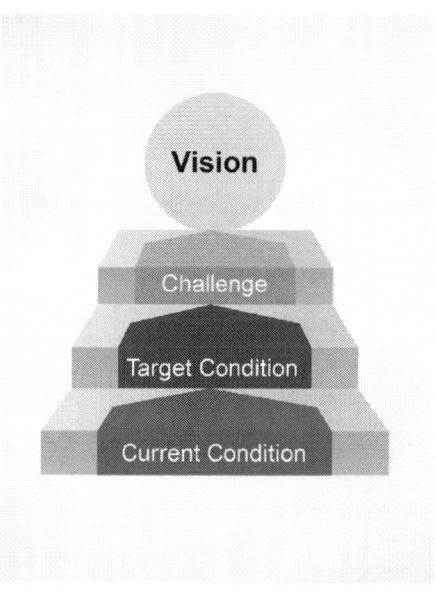

Figure 8: Current Condition, Target Condition, Challenge and Vision relationship

The Improvement Kata follows an iterative sequence. You start by understanding the "True North" Process Vision and setting a Challenge that aligns with that (Understand the Direction). Then you get a thorough understanding of your current process (Grasp the Current Condition). From there, you decide on a Target Condition before you start working in short Experiment Cycles to achieve it.

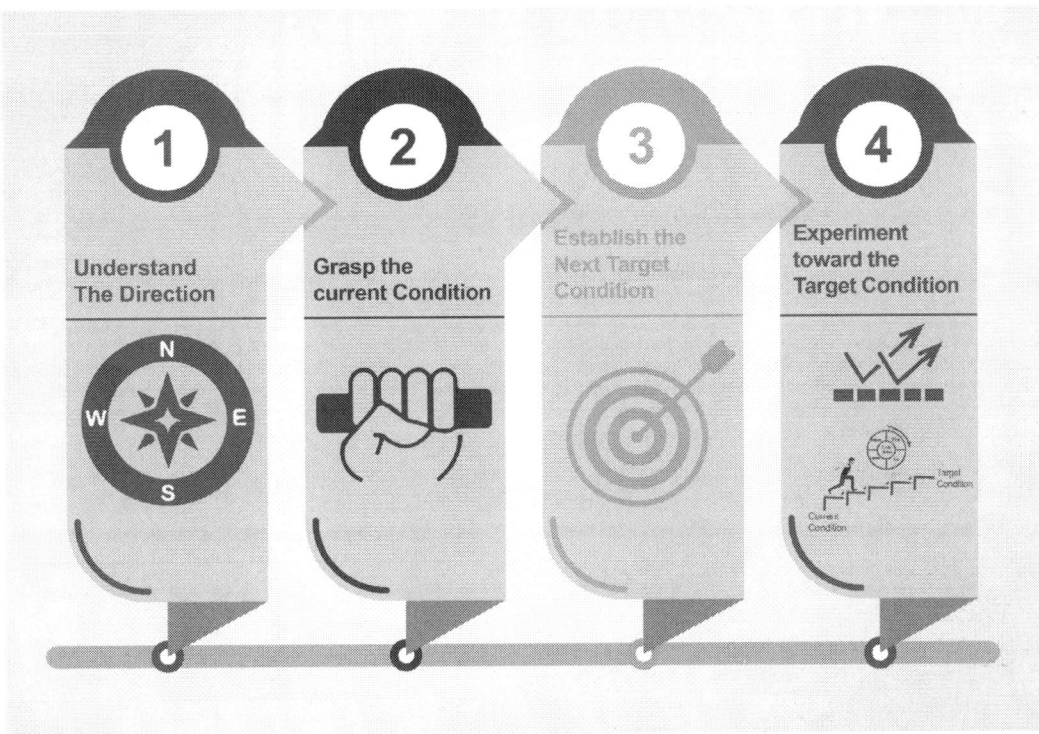

Figure 9: Toyota Kata process overview, adapted from the Toyota Kata Practice Guide (ROTHER, 2018)

It looks a bit more sequential than it is in real life. You must understand the Current Condition to set a Challenge, and several Target Conditions will be required to reach it.

A key point is that both Challenges and Target Conditions should be realistically ambitious. They should be ambitious so that they force you to think outside the box but still something you believe you can achieve. This is a subtle difference from the stretch goals used in methods like Objectives and Key results (OKR), where achieving over 70% of your target is perceived as a sign that your target wasn't ambitious enough. In Toyota Kata, we call the iterative process of reaching ambitious goals "navigating unclear territory".

As an Agile practitioner, you should be very familiar with this concept from a product perspective. Instead of trying to plan all details upfront on a product and feature level, we set a goal and work iteratively to achieve it. It is the same with Challenges and Target Conditions in Toyota Kata. Why create a plan from the beginning when we know that after taking the first step, we will have more information available to plan a better way forward the next day? Anyone who has worked with Process improvement will recognize that, as with our products, it is rarely a straight road from A to B. Habits, technology, communication patterns and processes are difficult to change, and we should expect some experiments to fail. The following figure shows how we are navigating the unclear territory in small steps toward our Target Condition.

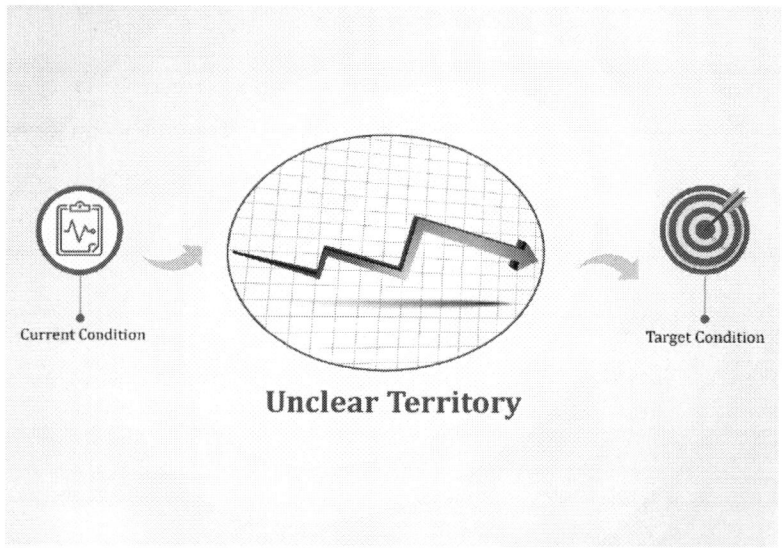

Unclear Territory

Figure 10: Iterative path through the Unclear Territory, adapted from the Toyota Kata Practice Guide (ROTHER, 2018)

Coaching Kata

The Coaching Kata is a coaching dialogue with the goal of improving the Learner's ability to execute the Improvement Kata. The cadence may vary from context to context, but the important point is that the Coaching Kata offers a space to discuss the current progress toward the Target Condition and for the coach to provide reflections and learning opportunities for the Learner. The coach supports the Learner by asking a series of questions designed to explore the knowledge threshold. A common pattern in Lean organizations is that the manager will act as coach, while the manager's direct reports will be the Learners. This design will engage all layers of the organization in improvement work. Managers will also get a clear picture of both the maturity level of their direct reports as well as current opportunities and obstacles in the organization.

Later, we will introduce the six Coaching Kata questions that help ensure that both Target Condition, Current Condition, Obstacles and Experiments are covered. The follow-up questions are the real benefit, as they challenge the Learner to move beyond his or her current improvement capabilities. If the Coaching Kata did not provide a learning opportunity for the Learner, it should be considered a wasted opportunity. "If the learner did not learn – the teacher did not teach" is a central mantra at Toyota.

But how do we translate this concept into an IT context in which managers are not operational experts? How can Scrum Masters or Process Leads take ownership of Process improvement while still allowing the creativity and participation of the entire team to flourish? How do we work with daily continuous improvement in an Agile context in which experiments cannot always be validated right away? The following chapters will provide the answers to those questions.

Some chapters close with a section comparing the Agile setting to the manufacturing setup and a brief explanation of which elements have been adjusted and why. If you do not find the original Toyota Kata body of work interesting but simply want to get a picture of how it looks in an Agile environment, feel free to skip sections with the headline "How is this different from the original Starter Kata?"

As you have probably already realized at this point, Toyota Kata looks simple at a glance. However, as you gain more experience, you will find that complexity and opportunities arise for each layer of the onion you peel off.

5. Toyota Kata events and cadences in an Agile context

When you introduce a framework like Toyota Kata in a different context, you must make some adjustments to ensure that it fits. The problem is that if you adjust too much, you risk losing the key principles, culture and mindset behind the framework. Therefore, we have tried to stay as true to the original principles as we possibly could. The current result is a Starter Kata which can work in an Agile setting and which is still highly aligned with the original mindset and principles.

This chapter will provide a brief introduction to the events and cadences we have adapted to fit the context of Agile teams and organizations. My hope is that a high-level overview will make it easier for you to place the specific details of the following chapters in the right context.

Because Toyota Kata is fractal, all processes are repeated at each level with small adjustments in terms of cadences. We will initially focus on the team level for the following reasons:

1. In an Agile organization, top-down command and control is replaced by team-level empowerment and small end-to-end Value Streams. This means that much decision authority, and often the entire Value Stream, are found at the team level. Ideally, it is where customer value is identified, implemented and validated. If we cannot enable Toyota Kata at the team level, it becomes very difficult for the rest of the organization.

2. The team level is also the largest part of the Agile organization and, therefore, where Toyota Kata will influence the biggest number of people.

3. The empowered self-organizing, cross-functional team is arguably where the Agile organization differs most from more traditional structures and, thus, where we have had to make the biggest adjustments to make Toyota Kata fit the context.

4. By creating a firm understanding of Toyota Kata at the team level, I hope to make it easier to understand how this relates to the rest of the organization in the following chapters.

You might say that small end-to-end teams redefine the notion of a "system" as we aim for each part (team) to deliver value separately. This brings a different perspective to systems thinking and Process improvement.

Yet this does not mean that it is not important to implement Toyota Kata at the other levels of an Agile organization. If, e.g., department-level managers do not actively engage in using Toyota Kata, teams have a limited chance of success. Many improvement opportunities involve the broader organization and large programs challenge the notion of end-to-end teams. If you have not yet succeeded in forming end-to-end teams or delegating decision authority to the team level, there is much to gain from establishing that as a management-level Challenge. Therefore, Chapter 17 focuses exclusively on the potential and Challenges when scaling it to the other layers of the organization and the Catch-ball element when a shared focus is established across organizational levels. Note that this first section is an overview, so do not expect all the details to be included.

Cadences

We have found that in most cases, a successful team-level Challenge has a timeframe of two to six months with a preference for the shorter end of the timescale. Two to six months is long enough to dare set a high ambition level and strive for the important but difficult goals while still short enough to be relevant and maintain a sense of urgency.

On the Target Condition level, four weeks is typically a good tradeoff, which means that each Challenge will include two to six Target Conditions. Four weeks is enough to achieve a substantial result and a big step toward the Challenge, while still being short enough to be close and relevant.

To reach the Target Condition, we must navigate the unclear territory mentioned previously. We call this four-week timebox of setting a Target Condition and iteratively working toward it through experimentation "The Improvement Kata".

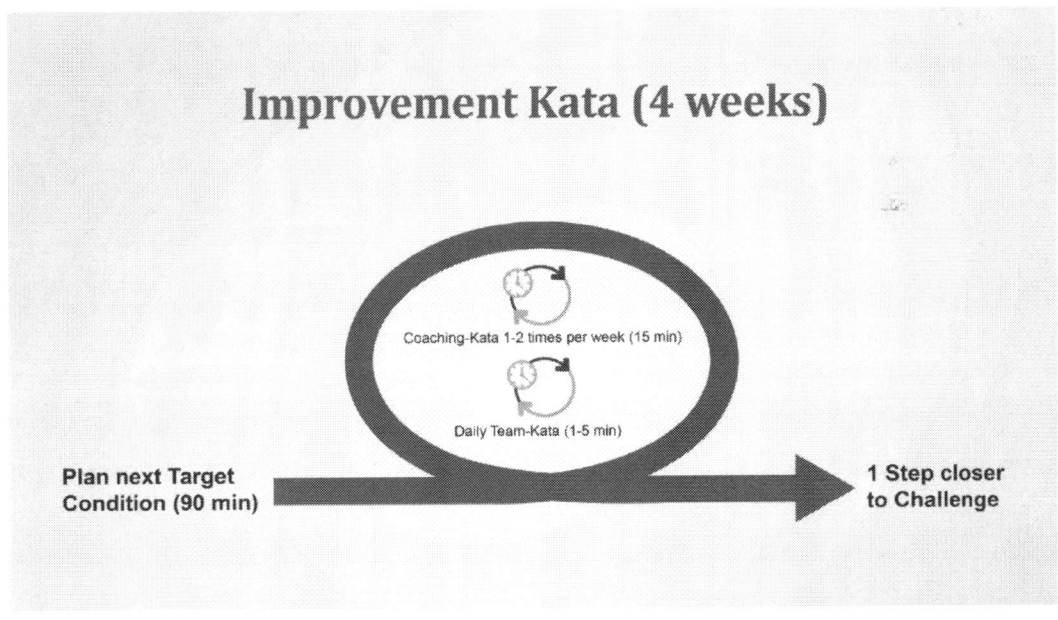

Figure 11: Team-level events and cadence overview

As in the case of a Scrum Sprint, we start the Improvement Kata with an Improvement Kata Planning meeting. We book 90 minutes for this but mature teams are typically able to do it quicker. At this meeting, a specific and measurable Target Condition is identified which should bring the team one step closer to the Challenge. As with a Sprint Planning meeting, this requires refinement and preparation to be done effectively, but instead of the Product Owner being responsible, process ownership belongs to the Process Lead (the Scrum Master in a Scrum context). Naturally, the refinement work involved in enabling a successful and effective Improvement Kata Planning meeting is greater when you are approaching a new Challenge, as shown in the figure below.

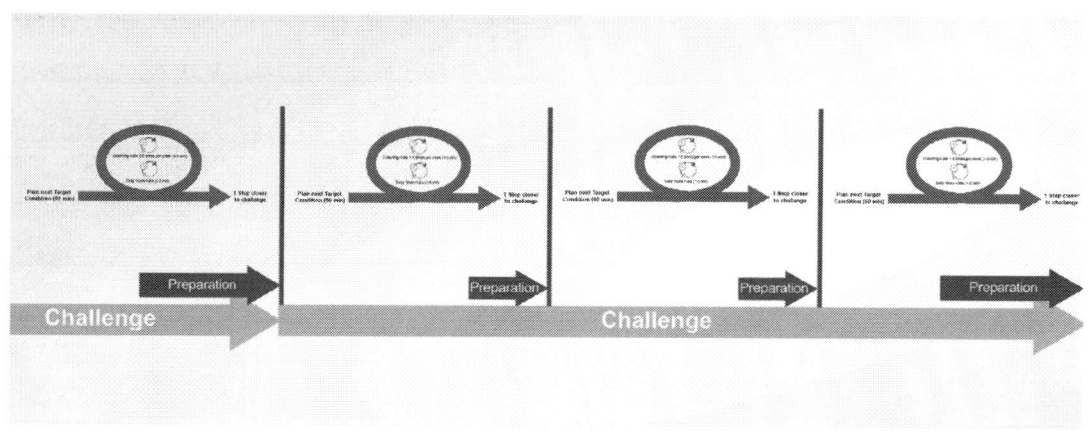

Figure 12: Target Condition preparation time is depended on the status of the Challenge

We have found that having Coaching Kata one or two times a week is a good fit in most situations, with a strong preference for two times a week. As maturity increases, teams become better at framing short experiments and once a week is not enough, but on the other hand, we have yet to see a single team that had more than two for longer periods of time.

The Daily Team Kata (or just Daily Kata) is a quick one- to five-minute session at the end of the Daily Stand-up meeting. In the Daily Kata completed, ongoing or planned experiments are evaluated and the team ensures that they get the full potential of their efforts and adjust if necessary. If no experiments have been completed and no adjustments to ongoing experiments are necessary, this meeting may last just one minute. We will cover the Daily Team Kata in detail later, but for now, it is important to understand that this event has proven to be an essential aspect of making continuous improvement a natural part of the daily work in an Agile setup and battling the ever-present pressure to focus exclusively on finishing User Stories and meeting deadlines. As previously mentioned, in 4DX they call this battling the "Daily Whirlwind", which I think is a great metaphor.

The paradox of the two- to six-month improvement focus

But wait a minute – two to six months instead of adjusting every two weeks in traditional Scrum retrospective sessions? That sounds an awful lot like batching and moving closer to a tradition of long-term planning and not the inspect-and-adapt nature of Agile. Does a two-week period not force us to be creative about getting quick results instead of waiting for a bigger batch of work? That is a valid point but there are a couple of points to remember regarding this aspect:

- We are building process capabilities for the longer term. Once an improvement is in place, we can expect to reap the benefit for all future User Stories. Naturally, improvements are context-specific but because we bring work to the people and not people to the work, we can expect to use our improvements for a long time.

- Though our improvement strategy is long-term, the results are immediate. Through our Experiments, we aim to generate real day-to-day improvements. On the Process improvement level, we aim for a culture of true continuous improvement in which even a two-week cycle would be considered too long.

- There is not a direct relationship between effort and benefit, but our experience is that the things that truly matter also require considerable effort. Deployment pipelines, staged roll-outs, automation, T-profiles and an effective feedback loop with real stakeholders and an early adopter are not things you establish in a day or two.

We have numerous examples of teams that have been wanting to improve certain areas for months or even years without daring to take on the Challenge in their retrospectives. Only when they got the chance to work with Toyota Kata did they finally deliver on it. We will dive into some of these cases in Chapter 25 but to name just a few, those topics included:

- o Automation of difficult manual tasks
- o Developing T-profiles to balance the team against customer demand
- o Aligning input channels
- o Automating test and deployment
- o Stakeholder feedback
- o Stakeholder response time

How much capacity does Toyota Kata require?

To battle the "Daily Whirlwind", it is important to recognize that you must set aside real capacity. That means we must answer the very difficult question "How much time/capacity?" Though we can all agree that we are more interested in getting results than spending time, I strongly suggest that senior management use this chance to show their support and commitment by indicating a real number and not just vague statements like "what it takes", "real capacity" or even worse, "what our deadlines and other commitments permit". When asked this question, one director in charge of the Toyota Kata initiative gave the following answer:

"I expect it to be more than 0% and less than 50%."

He said this with a smile. Fortunately, he continued with the more specific statement

"In general, we expect teams to use between 10% and 20% of their capacity on improvement, but naturally we would rather see you create amazing results in an hour than spend 100 hours getting nowhere".

In retrospect, it is hard to underestimate the importance of this statement to the success of Toyota Kata. It showed the entire organization that this was serious stuff and that senior managers were prepared to invest real time and energy into the improvement capability of the organization. In the breaks during training sessions and workshops, I heard people talking about this using statements like "Wow, they really mean it" and "I never thought they would have the guts to do this; this will really make a difference".

How is this different from the original Starter Kata?

The observant reader will recognize that we have made a change to the concept of the Improvement Kata. In Mike Rother's original version, it includes the entire loop from looking at the Challenge to identifying the next Target condition and iteratively performing experiments (PDCA cycles) to reach it. Teaching Toyota Kata in an Agile context, we have found it beneficial to exclude the Vision and Challenge from the concept, as the Improvement Kata then resembles the notion of a Scrum Sprint, which is a familiar concept to most Agile practitioners.

We found that Toyota Kata introduces many new concepts and requires a considerable mindset shift on Process improvement. Relating one aspect to Scrum made it possible to use this reference throughout training, workshops and coaching and also made it easier for people to understand the framework. I hope you will excuse this slight adaption of the Toyota Kata framework. After all, it is "just" a Starter Kata. We still include the Vision and Challenge elements in the Toyota Kata framework, but we move them out of the notion of the Improvement Kata for teaching purposes.

In a manufacturing context, Coaching Kata might be done several times a day to evaluate the success or failures of experiments and to coach and guide the Learner. Unfortunately, our cycle time in Agile is not measured in seconds and minutes. Thus, setting up experiments and validating the results often takes considerably longer. With that in mind, we must adjust the frequency of Coaching Kata accordingly. We found that one or two times a week is a good fit in most situations.

At Toyota, a Challenge often has a duration of between six months and three years, but in the fast-moving world of IT, we found that to be problematic. Not only do conditions change so that a two-year goal might have become irrelevant by the time we reached it but we are also able to change faster. A shorter attention span could also be a valid explanation, but the two- to six-month time horizon was found to be a better fit.

The Daily Kata is not part of the original Toyota Kata framework. When you are doing Coaching Kata daily or even several times a day, you already have a frequent feedback loop in which you reflect on experiments and learning. To build a true culture of continuous improvement but with a narrower focus, we have found it necessary to introduce an additional event, "The Daily Team Kata", which you will learn more about in Chapter 8.

6. A personal health example

In our Toyota Kata training sessions, we initially added examples from an IT context to illustrate the relationship between the Vision, Challenge and Target Condition levels, Toyota Kata Events and the difference between Outcome, Qualitative and Process metrics. However, the feedback from attendees was that they needed something simpler to understand the concept. Therefore, we added a Personal Health example to the training material.

It is not perfect, and you can argue that there are some minor problems with it from a physiological standpoint but if you read it with the mindset of understanding Toyota Kata, it can be very useful. It also provides us with a chance to introduce the elements of the Toyota Kata Improvement Board, which will be covered in more detail in Chapter 15. And do not worry – there will many IT-specific cases and examples later.

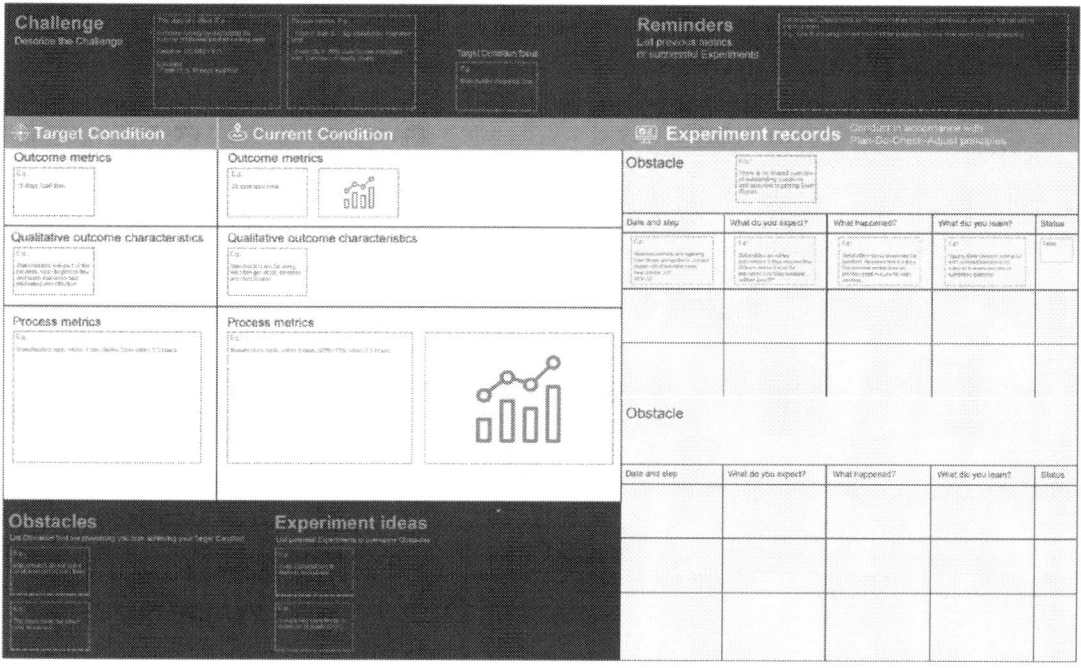

Figure 13: Improvement Board template

The example we used looks like this and deals with a guy named Adam who is trying to get into shape:

Personal Health Vision

Title: Healthy, fit and good-looking.

Outcome metrics (lagging):

- Weight: 75 kg.

- VO2max: 55

- Polar BodyAge: -15 years compared to actual age

Process metrics (leading):

- Daily Exercise (30 min.)

- HighIntensity Interval Training 2 times per week

- Calorie intake = Calorie burn

- Food 80% compliant with *www.sst.dk recommendations*

What Adam really wants are the results described in the Outcome metrics: a weight of 75 kg., a VO2max of 55 and a Polar BodyAge indicating that his body is 15 years younger than his birthdate suggests. In a Toyota Kata setting, however, that is NOT what he will focus on. In this case, he has a firm belief that he will get that result by installing the process of daily Exercise (30 minutes), high-intensity Interval training two times per week, eating the right food and not overeating. Thus, he will focus on trying to install that capability and use the Outcome metrics to judge whether he is truly moving in that direction. He might never get there but it represents the direction he is aiming for.

The vision is not visualized on the Improvement Board, as the board focuses only on the current Challenge and Target Condition. For the remainder of the example, all elements are represented on an example Improvement Board. To follow the logic and sequence, you must look at the board and the details within; you won't find all the information in the text alone.

Identifying the Current Condition and Setting the Challenge

The second step is to identify our Current Condition. Let's assume Adam's Current Condition looks like this:

Outcome metrics (lagging):

- Weight: 95 kg.

- VO2max: 30

- Polar BodyAge: 48 (actual age 39)

Process metrics (leading):

- Daily Exercise (0 min.)

- Calorie intake = 3800, Calorie burn = 2900

- Food 0% organic

- Food 20% compliant with *www.sst.dk* *recommendations*

Adam is quite far away from the Vision. He eats too much and the wrong things, and he does not exercise. This has resulted in both a fitness level and a weight far from his idea of his optimal levels. But from a Toyota Kata standpoint, that is neither good or bad; it is just the Current Condition. Because the Vision is often far away or even unobtainable, we do not want to spend time explaining why we are not there yet. Instead, we spend our energy on how we can take a step in the direction of the Vision. Fortunately, this is something the human brain is good at because we are much better at moving toward a desirable goal than away from a problem (Knight, 2010)

From this, Adam sets an ambitious and motivating Challenge three month into the future:

Title: Fit for wedding!

Date: October 10th (3 months ahead)

Outcome metrics:

- From 95 to 85 kg.

Process metrics:

- From 0 minutes to 30 minutes of exercise, 5 days per week
- From 4500 calories to 3000 calories, 6 days a week

His daily focus will be on establishing a capability in which he exercises and eats less. He hopes this will result in a weight loss from 95 to 85 kg. He will use that metric only infrequently to check on whether things are moving in the right direction (maybe bi-weekly). Also, notice that he is not addressing the entire vision but the subset that is most important and that he believes will generate the biggest effect.

Visualized on the Improvement Board, it looks like this:

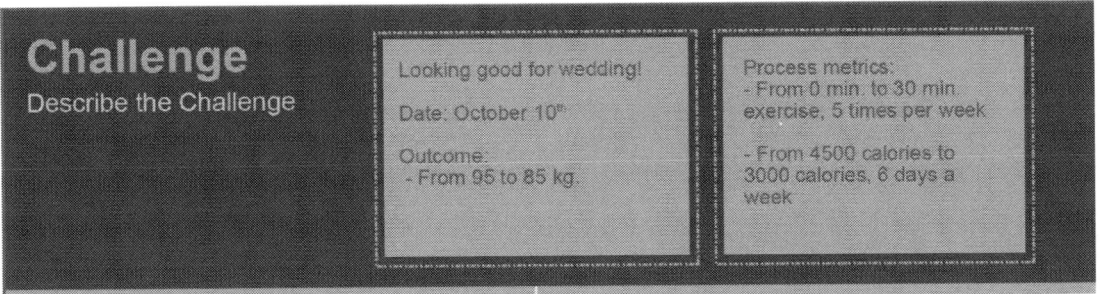

Figure 14: Challenge example

Establishing the Target and Current Condition

Once the Challenge is identified, it is time to set a specific four-week goal. That is what we call the Target Condition. The Target Condition is a subset of the Challenge. In this case, Adam will focus exclusively on exercise.

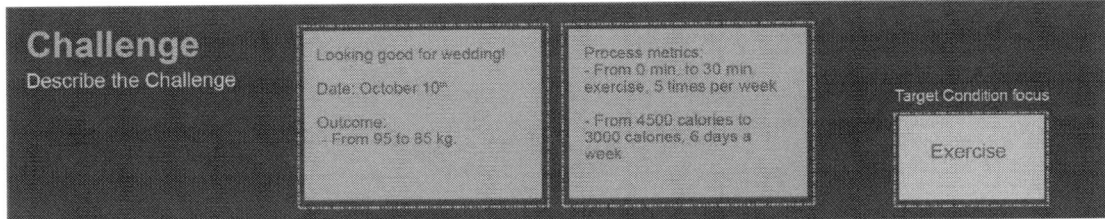

Figure 15: Target Condition Focus example

He will continue to eat too much, but not more than before. If he is nervous that his food intake might increase, he can set a constraint metric to ensure that it does not get worse. However, we do this only when the risk is real. He could also have chosen to focus on both lowering food intake and increasing exercise, but then he would probably have had to lower the goal to stay realistically ambitious.

When establishing the Target Condition, we start with the process metrics and strive to keep the symmetry between the Target and Current Conditions.

The Target Condition ends up looking like this:

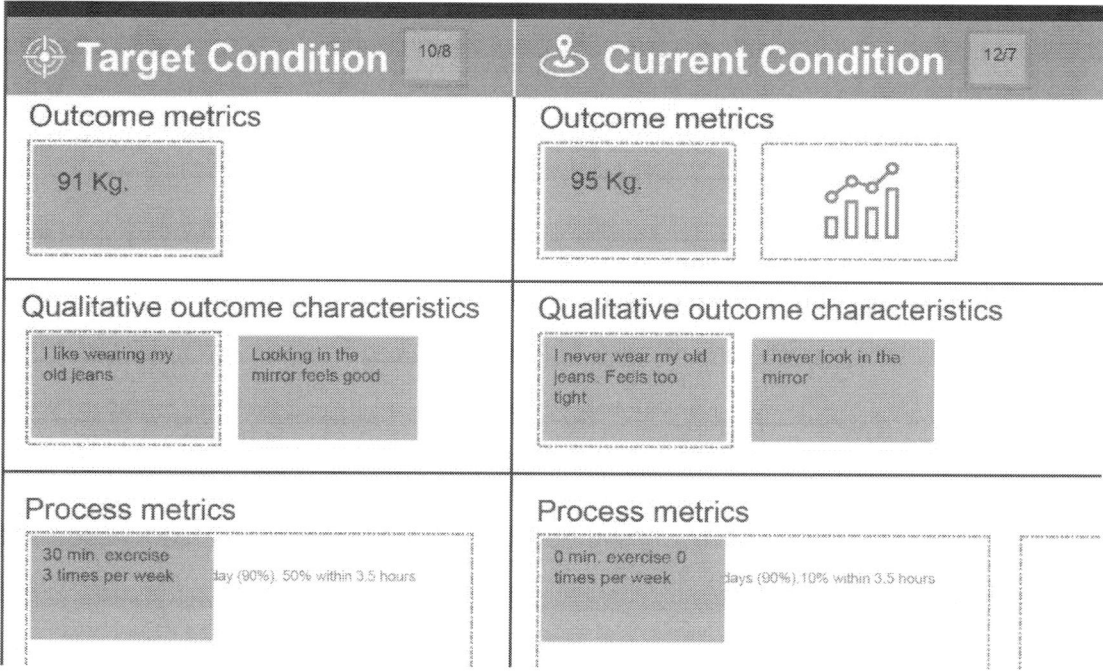

Figure 16: Target Condition and Current Condition example

We start with the process metrics and add qualitative characteristics and Outcome metrics afterward. But why add qualitative observations when they cannot be objectively measured? Qualitative characteristics help explain why we are doing it, what we want to observe when we reach our goal and what drives us toward this Target Condition. They also indicate that if we start gaming our Process metrics, we will not get what we are aiming for. Optimizing the numbers without changing anything for real does not make any sense. What drives Adam to reach his Target Condition is the prospect of feeling good when he looks in the mirror and being able to wear his old jeans.

Obstacles

Having set an ambitious Target Condition, you know your goal but not how to get there. We must iteratively navigate the unclear territory. We do this by identifying Obstacles and later experiments to remove them.

Obstacles should NOT be regarded as a Backlog that must be completed. We should neither strive to identify all Obstacles in the beginning nor expect all identified Obstacles to be solved. Obstacles are there only to give our experiments focus and direction toward reaching our Target. In this case, Adam identifies two main Obstacles:

1. It is unclear what exercise intensity is the best to start with.
2. There is a large discrepancy between the plans for exercise and the actual execution of those plans (33%).

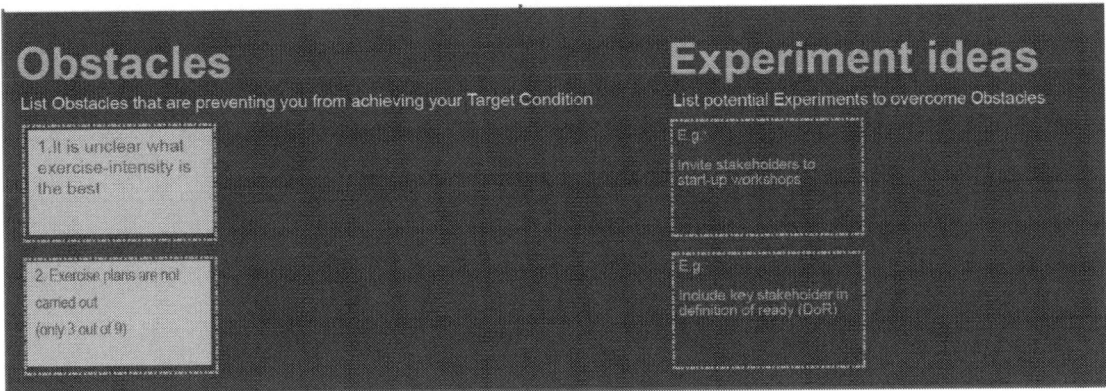

Figure 17: Obstacles example

We allow for a maximum of two Obstacles to be worked on simultaneously in the Experiment Record to minimize work in progress and make sure we can separate the effect of experiments. We work on only two Obstacles simultaneously if they are not closely related. In this case, we can easily see how one might affect the other. Adam chooses to work only on number two and it is moved to the Experiment Records.

Experiments

When Obstacles are placed in the Obstacle section of the board, they are essentially just options. You can choose to address them now, you can leave them for later or you can remove them altogether. You have the option to spend time on them or the option to throw them out. Once an Obstacle is moved to the Experiment Record, you have committed yourself to spending time on trying to remove it.

Adam selects the Obstacle: "2. Exercise plans are not carried out (only 3 out of 9)". He comes up with these possible experiments to solve the Obstacle:

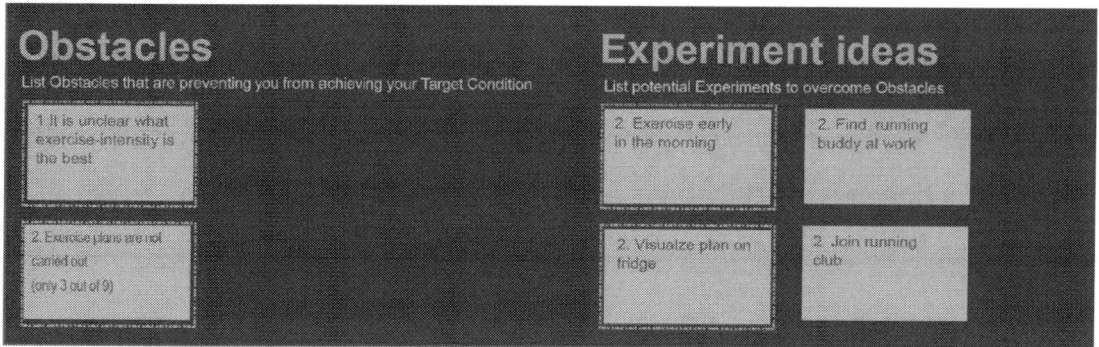

Figure 18: Ideas for experiments example

They are not moved to the Experiment Records section, so for now, they are still just Options that we can choose to execute, keep for later or throw out. We have prefixed them all with "2" to indicate that they are related to that Obstacle.

Adam concludes that his exercise plans fail because urgent things tend to come up that change his plans. Kids need to be picked up from an unscheduled play date, extra trips to the supermarket are necessary, he needs to go to the bicycle repair shop or the kids get sick. He opts to try the Experiment of exercising early in the morning, when unplanned events are less likely to happen.

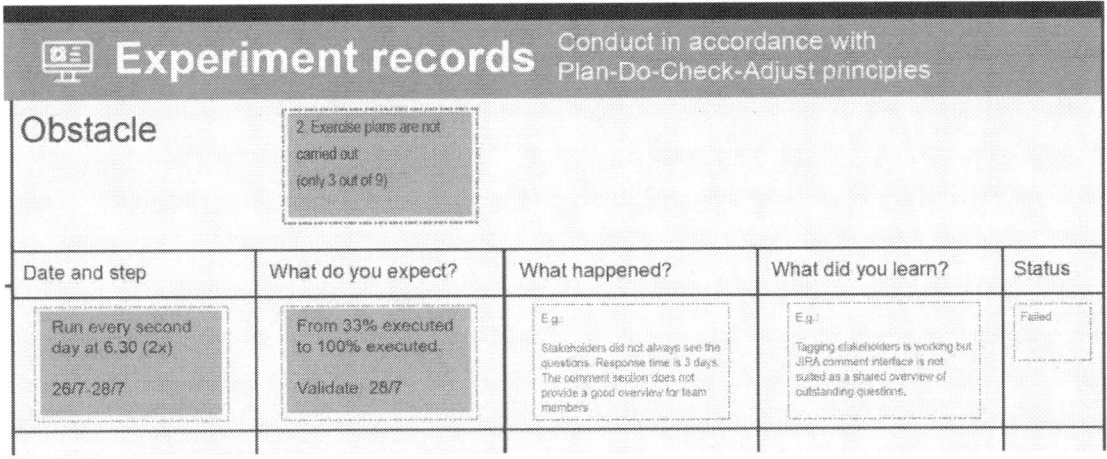

Figure 19: Experiment record, starting experiment cycle example

After carrying out the Experiment, Adam reflects on the result by completing "what happened" and "what did you learn". As you can tell in the figure below, Adam's experiment failed but he learned something. A failed Experiment in Toyota Kata is a chance to learn, reflect and prepare a new and more effective step. Learning is maximized when there is a 50/50 chance of failure (Reinertsen, 2009). After evaluating the result of his first experiment, Adam decides to see if joining a running club will provide the push and motivation to carry it out. As you can tell from the next figure, this was a much greater success.

Experiment records — Conduct in accordance with Plan-Do-Check-Adjust principles

Obstacle	2. Exercise plans are not carried out (only 3 out of 9)			
Date and step	What do you expect?	What happened?	What did you learn?	Status
Run every second day at 6.30 (2x) 26/7-28/7	From 33% executed to 100% executed. Validate: 28/7	Only happened once	I feel really bad if I exercise in the morning	
Trial practice at running-club (2x) 28/7-1/8	Plans carried out 33% -> 100%. Validate: 1/8	100% carried out! Lots of fun	Scheduled Exercise with others is much better.	Success

Figure 20: Experiment record, failed and successful experiment example

48

The fact that trial practice in the running club was an initial success does not necessarily prove that the Obstacle has been solved and that Adam should pay the fee for joining the running club. Often, we must repeat the same experiment several times with small alterations to make sure we have indeed found a sustainable way of addressing the Obstacle. Thus, Adam might choose to add another, very similar experiment to his Experiment Record and validate that before removing the Obstacle.

This concludes the introduction to the Improvement Board and the Improvement Kata. In the following chapters, we look at how Toyota Kata roles, events and concepts translate into the context of Agile organizations and IT.

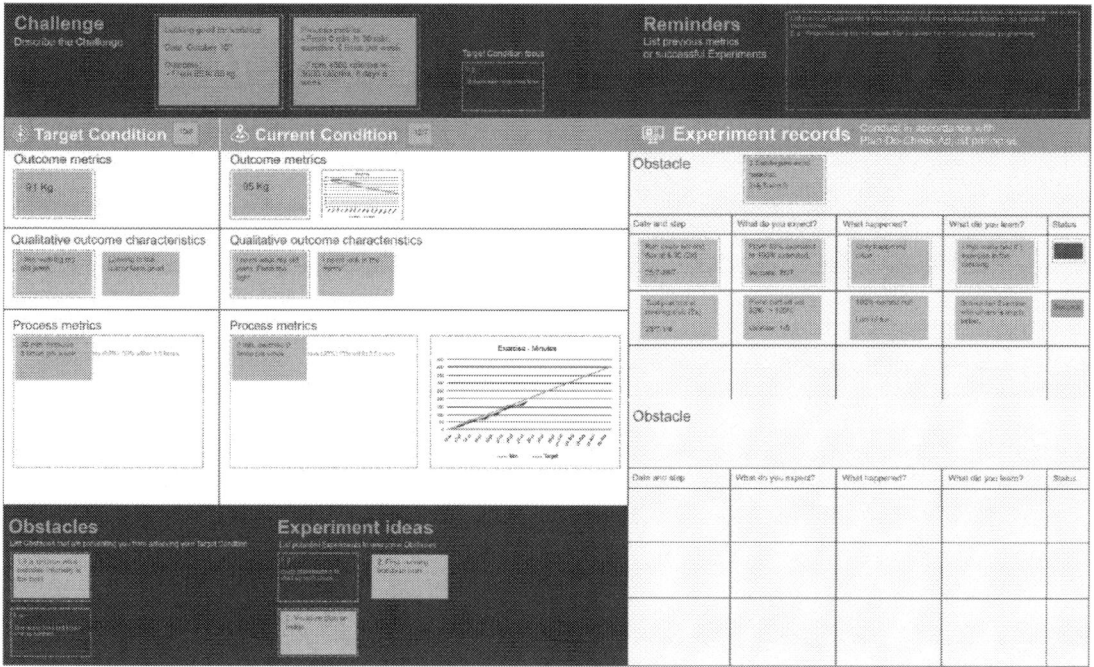

Figure 21: Complete Improvement Board example

Learning objectives and questions for real-life application of the Toyota Kata basics

The last three chapters introduced the overall Toyota Kata framework. Before we move on to all the specific details of applying it in an Agile context, it is time to reflect on the learning objectives so far. By now you should have realized that:

- The Toyota Kata framework includes two Kata: "The Improvement Kata" and "The Coaching Kata".
- Both Kata are "Starter Kata", meaning they are designed to teach you how to apply scientific thinking to improvement initiatives through practice. Once the basics are in place, you should adapt them to fit your own context.
- The cadences of Toyota Kata events must be adjusted to fit the Agile context but the patterns and focus remain the same.
- It is suggested that you officially allocate time for improvement work and communicate it throughout the organization. 10-20% of total capacity is often a good fit.
- Toyota Kata improvement efforts that focus on reaching a desirable Future State and problems are interesting only in relation to that goal.
- Toyota Kata has a process focus. We put things upside down and our daily focus is on establishing the process that will generate the outcome we really want.

Before you continue, write your answers to the following questions to the best of your ability:

- What is the purpose of the two Kata?
- What is the suggested duration of a Challenge?
- What are the suggested durations and cadences of Toyota Kata events (Coaching Kata, Improvement Kata Planning, Daily Kata)?

Part 2. The Starter Kata

Roles, Events and Concepts

Having introduced the overall framework, it is time to take a look at the details of making it work in an Agile setting. How do we interpret the different roles and how does an Improvement Kata Planning meeting work? We will also look at the concepts of the Vision, Challenge and Target Condition Level and the details of removing Obstacles through Experiments to reach our desired goals. Finally, we will take a closer look at the evolutionary development of the Improvement Board as well as the specific changes we had to make to get it to work.

You are encouraged to read the whole chapter to get a deeper understanding of all the included elements. You will probably return to this chapter once you start applying the principles in real life and find yourself struggling with some of the elements. It is a Starter Kata, and though I would encourage you to practice it by following it relatively strictly in the beginning, never forget to ask yourselves "why". Even in the beginning, it is extremely dangerous to follow a process without understanding why it makes sense, both overall and in terms of the individual elements.

The goal of the Starter Kata is not that you should stick to it forever but that you should get to a point where the following core Process improvement capabilities are deeply rooted in the entire organization:

- A shared Process Vision sets set an overall direction for Process improvement – a "True North" desirable Future State.
- At all levels of the organization, people are involved in taking measurable steps toward the Vision by setting and delivering on realistically ambitious improvement goals.
- Each step is validated using scientific thinking – taking an iterative and experimental approach toward Process improvement.
- Steps are short, and continuous improvement is a natural part of daily work.
- Coach and Learner relationships ensure that Process improvement capabilities are continuously improved at all levels of the organization.

7. Toyota Kata Roles

This chapter introduces the three primary roles in Toyota Kata: "the Process Lead", "the team" and "the manager". They might carry different names in your context; it is not a matter of changing the organizational structure but rather adjusting the existing responsibility and focus. As Toyota Kata is fractal, a single person will often have multiple Roles. We will cover the scaling of Toyota Kata across all layers of the organization in depth in Chapter 17. For now, the most important thing to understand is that Toyota Kata is built on the notion of a coach/Learner relationship between managers and their direct reports:

- Department Manager coaches Process Leads

- Area Manager coaches department managers

- Director coaches area managers

- CEO coaches Directors

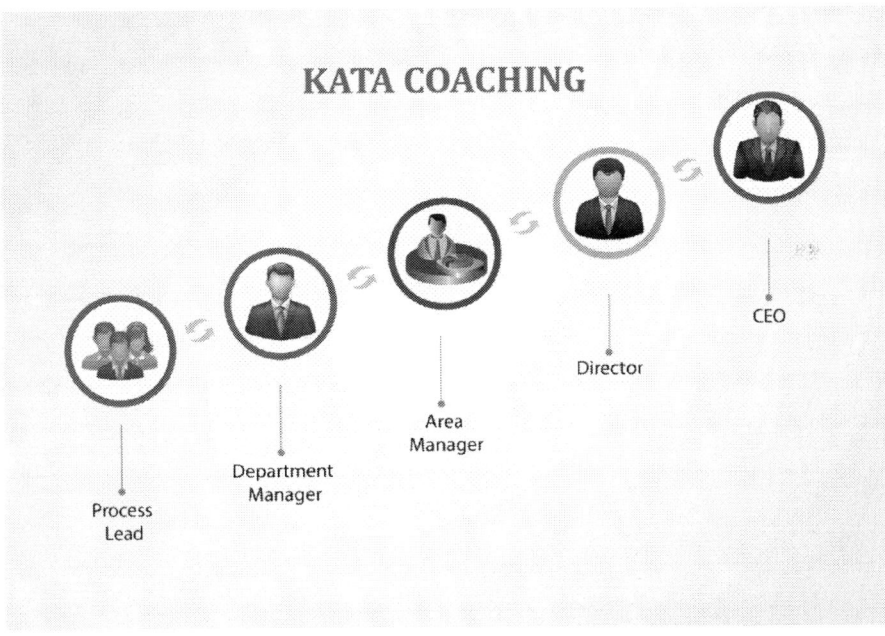

Figure 22: Kata Coaching relationships between organizational levels, adapted from the Toyota Kata Practice Guide (ROTHER, 2018)

Let us look at how these roles translate into an Agile organizational structure and how the setup can provide lots of input, reflection and success.

The Team-level Process Lead

Most Agile organizations are familiar with Scrum and the Scrum Master role: a role dedicated to creating the best possible environment for self-organization and to coach and guide the team and the organization in the adoption of Scrum, Lean and Agile. Because a team lead title might suggest that we are reintroducing an outdated management pattern and the Scrum Master role is heavily anchored in the world of Scrum, we chose to refer to this person as a Process Lead instead.

Strengthening the Scrum Master role

I apologize to those who do not find themselves in a Scrum-like context and who are not aiming to get there for having to dedicate so much of this chapter to explaining the Process Lead from the perspective of the Scrum Master. Because such a large part of Agile organizations is influenced by Scrum on the team level, however, it is necessary to avoid too many misunderstandings, as there is an overlap between the Scrum Master role and that of the Process Lead.

For years, Scrum Trainers and Coaches have been preaching the notion of the Scrum Master as a Servant Leader with the responsibility of coaching and guiding both the team and the organization in the adoption of Agile, Lean and Scrum. This person is responsible for creating the best possible environment for the team to succeed and for using their deep knowledge of Scrum, Agile and Lean to move the team and organization in that direction. There are more aspects to the Scrum Master but because this book is about Process improvement and not Scrum, these are the traits we will focus on in this section.

In almost all larger organizations I have worked with throughout the last 12+ years, I can only say that this does not always match reality "on the ground". Often, Scrum Masters lack the organizational mandate, knowledge, skills or personality to truly drive Process improvement. A large part of the problem is simply that organizations have not taken the role seriously and have neither made it clear what is expected nor provided the needed training, support and decision authority for people in this role. That is a shame, as we are leaving lots of untapped personal and organizational potential on the table. We are also not providing an interesting career path for people who could have become effective change agents.

The problem is that the "leading" part of the Servant Leader seems to be missing. This is true to the extent that some organizations reduce Scrum Masters to facilitators with only the ability to ask the question "What do you think?" when it comes to Process improvement and "leading" the team and organization in the adoption of Scrum, Lean and Agile.

A Scrum Master should be the team expert on Lean, Agile and Scrum, so they can challenge the team and organization to work as effectively as possible and create the right environment for doing so. If your main area of specialization (not the only one – Agile promotes T-profiles) is UX, frontend or backend, probably your main motivation and drive is to become great at that. It is totally fair that you spend time reading blogs and exploring new possibilities within that area of specialization and not on Lean, Agile or Scrum.

Team members might have a very narrow view of Process optimization, and if you do not have a strong and knowledgeable Scrum Master, sub-optimization might be right around the corner. Here are a couple of examples of dysfunctional strategies and retrospective SMART goals that I have seen at least a dozen times each:

- Include all possible design and solution details in the Definition of Ready (DoR) to avoid communication and uncertainty during the Sprint
- Re-order the Backlog to fit specialist skill sets in the team instead of value
- Split User stories into backend, frontend and test stories to make them smaller or to keep individual skill sets busy
- Extend Sprint length to reduce "overhead" in Scrum events (there can be other good reasons to do this but the overhead of events is not one of them – transaction costs are not static)
- Cancel the feedback loop with external parties to avoid rework or because the feedback is not valuable (feedback is mandatory – if it is not working, you should change the way it is done, not cancel it)
- Introduce "hardening Sprints" or "test Sprints" before a release
- Introduce several refinement Sprints at the beginning of a project
- Introduce new User Stories in the Sprint to keep the team busy when existing ones get blocked
- Split the team into a business team and a development team with separate Sprints and velocities

All these things can seem to make sense from a certain perspective and nobody did them to make things worse. If organizations are expecting Scrum Masters to be able to ask only "What do you think?", there is a good chance that both the team and the organization will move in the wrong direction.

The Scrum guide might be intentionally vague in terms of what is truly expected of the Scrum Master regarding Process improvement. But, as you will learn in the next section, that is not the case with the Toyota Kata Process Lead. The Scrumguide states that a Scrum Master should "guide", "lead", "help" and "coach" but a Toyota Kata Process Lead "drives" Process improvement in the right direction.

The responsibility of the Process Lead

Whether you are working in a Scrum context or not, each team must assign a person with the dedicated responsibility of driving directed Process improvement. We call this person the "Process Lead" and we expect that person to become the team's primary expert on Agile and Lean as well as help guide the team and the organization to achieve the most they can. We have found that comparing this role to the Agile Product Owner makes a lot of sense. If Agile product ownership is a foreign concept to you, I highly recommend using 15 minutes of your time watching Henrik Kniberg's excellent YouTube video, titled "Agile Product Ownership in a Nutshell", before you continue with this chapter.

As with the Product Owner, the Process Lead is responsible for driving the process of selecting the goals that will make the biggest difference, refining them to a state such that the team is able to plan it in detail at the Improvement Kata Planning meeting and provide metrics and feedback to ensure that they are getting the expected results. The only real difference is that the Process Lead is concerned only with the process and not with which specific User Stories or Products are being delivered. The opposite is true for the Product Owner.

The Process Lead can and should not do it alone. The development team and Product Owner are important stakeholders and should be involved in validating and setting the direction as well as iteratively working to reach the goal. A Process Lead who climbs into an ivory tower and believes that they know it all will get the buy-in and quality they deserve. But as with the Product Owner, it remains the Process Lead's responsibility to make the final call and decide when to turn the discussion from "where to go" to "how to get there".

To some Process Leads and Scrum Masters, this has proven more difficult than we originally thought. The prospect of having to take responsibility for actual decisions, coaching and guiding the team and for organizing and driving the process of optimization seems to be a scary and daunting task. That is not their fault but the result of the way in which the organization has hired and trained people to fulfill this important role. We found that existing Process Leads and Scrum Masters could roughly be divided into four groups:

- **The Servant Leader.** Real Servant Leaders have a deep knowledge of Lean and Agile, with great visions of how the team could work and a proven track record of success. They love Toyota Kata, as it simply provides a more effective and engaging framework for doing what they are already doing. A minor percentage of these are also among the biggest opponents, as they see Toyota Kata as an unwanted complexity in an already good improvement process. However, most are convinced over time when actual results start to show.

- **The aspiring Process Leader**. Scrum Masters or Process Leads have the will and potential to guide and coach but lack the deeper knowledge of Agile and Lean. With intensive coaching, they can become great Process Leaders, as their personalities and drive re already in place. They do need training and possibly an expert with them for a longer period to observe and provide feedback.

- **The facilitator.** Typically, this is a person who loves the idea of facilitation but is not very interested in Lean and Agile. "Facilitators" have proven to be the most difficult to work with, as they often resist the concept of responsibility. They typically lack a deeper knowledge of Lean and Agile and do not see any reason why they should strive to get it. "The team always knows best" and they purposely ignore or misinterpret the part of the Scrum Guide who asks them to coach and guide the team and the organization in the adoption of Scrum, Lean and Agile. Management intervention or other job opportunities might be necessary as a last resort.

- **The "nobody else wanted the role"**. By organizational decree, all teams need a Scrum Master and because this person was the last to say no, he/she got the badge. With this type of Scrum Master, it is necessary to have an honest and open discussion about what Process Leadership means in the context of Toyota Kata and what is expected of them. Most will not want to continue in the role, and the difficult task of finding a good replacement will need to be undertaken before going further with the Toyota Kata initiative. Some, however, have the opposite reaction and clearly state that they find the challenge and opportunity interesting and are prepared to invest the time and effort required to succeed in this role. They often become great Process Leads.

I want to stress that this is not a people problem but an organizational one. As an organization, we must take the Process Lead role much more seriously than we have done previously, and we must provide both clear expectations to management in terms of what the responsibility is and the support to grow talented people to become true improvement drivers. If the organization allowed people to be placed in that role because nobody else wanted to, were they told that they should act purely as a facilitator or not given the support to drive actual improvement? It is no surprise that we are not witnessing the behavior and potential laid out in both Toyota Kata and the Scrum Guide. However, once we realize that we can change that perspective and provide a clear future direction, some existing Process Leads will flourish instantly. Some will need additional training and coaching, and some will find that it is not really the job they were looking for. That is perfectly OK, too.

A story illustrating the role of the Process Lead

It is hard to underestimate the importance of having a great Process Lead on the team, as the effect is like having a good or bad Product Owner. It is not easy but that's why we should put so much effort into getting the right people in that position. The following story shows how hard it can be in real life:

When selecting the first Challenge, a lot of help and coaching were given as part of the training and workshop concept to introduce Toyota Kata. For this team, everything had gone well; they had successfully achieved their first Challenge and had done so faster than they thought possible. Lining themselves up for the second Challenge, the Process Lead had done most things correctly. He had gotten a deep and thorough understanding of the current process with the help of the rest of the team. He had identified the biggest improvement potential directed by the Process Vision and he had narrowed it down to two possible Challenges they could embark upon. He had presented these to the team, received feedback and chosen the one with the biggest potential.

One team member, however, had not been present at the last session and at the Improvement Kata Planning Meeting. When they were about to discuss the details, he strongly suggested that they choose the other Challenge instead. Within five minutes, half the team supported that suggestion. The Process Lead was left with a split team and the second Challenge option had not been refined to a state where it could be effectively included in the Improvement Kata Planning. The discussion went back and forth with both halves of the teams arguing passionately for either option. At the end of the 90 minutes, the Improvement Board was still empty.

I was surprised to get a call from this Process Lead, as everything had indicated that he was doing well. He explained the situation to me and asked for advice on what to do. To understand the situation better, I asked him to give me a brief explanation of the options involved. I then asked him what his own opinion was. He could see both sides of the argument but would still go for the original Challenge if he should choose. I asked him why. He had good arguments and showed a deep understanding of the Current Condition as well as the Challenge's relevance from a deeper Lean/Agile perspective. He also explained that he believed the argument for choosing the other Challenge was fueled more by a single individual's personal interest than by the belief that it would benefit the whole team.

I asked him who was responsible for choosing the right Challenge and he replied "the team" – almost on autopilot ☺. I reminded him of the similarities to the Product Owner role, which he understood well. "So I can choose the Challenge?" he asked. I said, "Yes. Like a Product Owner, you have input from all your stakeholders and you must decide. There is no guarantee it will be the right decision, but it is your responsibility to make the final call".

He booked another session for the Improvement Kata Planning meeting and asked me if I could join them. At the meeting, he was quite nervous but went on to explain that he had chosen the original option and that the next 90 minutes would be spent discussing the details of that Challenge and not whether the direction was right or wrong. The person who had previously voiced a strong opinion for choosing the other Challenge immediately spoke out. Yet instead of starting another argument, he simply said, "Next time, I think it would be a good idea if you made that call after 10 minutes. Last time, we spent 80 minutes going nowhere and we left the meeting drained of energy and motivation. You are responsible, and I will respect your decision, especially if you continue to show that you involve us and take our suggestions into account".

Don't be afraid to take on responsibility

Naturally, this type of reaction won't be the one you get from all teams and team members. But it very clearly shows a pattern. If Process Leads involve the team and make a good case for choosing a Challenge or Target Condition, they need not fear making a decision. In most cases, team members have not been opposed to the Process Lead taking on decision responsibility. Rather, they have been motivated by being able to spend most of the time discussing the details of the goal and how to get there. Our brain really likes looking toward a desirable goal, so it is not surprising that we get more energy and motivation doing this rather than discussing a wide range of problems. If you involve the rest of the team and recognize them as an important stakeholder, taking on decision responsibility will often feel like a breath of fresh air.

Another way of looking at it is from the perspective of marketing. As a Process Lead, you should be able to sell the "Challenge" and "Target Condition", as with any other marketing campaign that involves market analysis and close collaboration and feedback from end users and key stakeholders. You must have a great product and be able to explain why this product will make a difference. If the team is not buying, there could be a problem with the product you are trying to sell or maybe it is simply not backed by the necessary data or a good-enough sales pitch.

What are the main responsibilities of the Process Lead on the team level? We have stated most of them previously but here is a list of the key areas:

- Choose the Challenge (with help and input from the team, managers and other stakeholders)
- Choose the Target Condition (with help and input from the team and other stakeholders)
- Investigate and describe the Current Condition – including Workflow Mapping, etc. (with help and input from the team and other stakeholders)
- Participate in Coaching Kata

- Update the Improvement Board
- Visualize progress and trends in Current Condition metrics
- Book and facilitate Improvement Kata Planning meetings
- Book and facilitate Daily Kata
- Challenge the team and organization to set ambitious improvement goals

To some, the list might seem daunting, while to others it represents a chance to more effectively do what they've always wanted. After an initial introduction to the Toyota Kata framework, a Scrum Master approached me and said, "This is great – now I finally understand what it was the trainer was talking about when I did my Certified Scrum Master training five years ago. To be honest, I have probably just been facilitating Scrum events until now, but now I am beginning to understand what is expected of the Scrum Master role in terms of guiding and coaching the team and organization in the adoption of Agile, Scrum and Lean".

Who should be the Process Lead?

As I warned at the beginning, we have spent a large part of this section comparing the Process Leader to the role of the Scrum Master. If you find yourself in a Scrum-like setup. there is no doubt that I would expect the Scrum Master to act as the Toyota Kata Process Lead because Process Leadership is clearly part of that role. If you are not working with Scrum, there is no reason why two people could not share the Servant Leader responsibility. It might be that one person is great at driving change and is a deep expert on Agile and Lean while another is much better at taking on the other parts of the Servant Leader role: protecting the team from external interruptions, facilitating events, making sure that people are alright and so on.

In terms of recommended time allocation for being an effective Process Leader, the important thing is recognizing that it is the primary responsibility of that person. If the Process Leader is not able to effectively drive improvement, it should never be because time was spent on, e.g., analysis, development or test of specific work items. If a person can drive improvement effectively and if time is left to do other things, there is no reason why that person cannot and should not take on additional responsibilities, e.g., as a team member. In this sense, you will find it very similar to the recommendations regarding the Scrum Master in "The Official Scrum Guide" at www.scrumguides.org.

The team

Agile strives to create a structure in which cross-functional teams can deliver end-to-end value without the need to involve other teams or external experts. This can be very challenging in some situations but when successful it drastically reduces coordination overhead and makes it possible for the people involved to focus on the actual end-user value and not on intermediate handovers and results. That is why Agile favors cross-functional teams over component teams. Making sure that such a structure is in place is often a management responsibility and, thus, could be a great challenge on the manager level. This will be covered in detail in Chapter 17.

Don't despair if you do not find yourself in that ideal situation on the team level. Toyota Kata will still work in a component team, but it is naturally a more complex setup because each handover increases the chance of sub-optimization of the process.

Whether you find yourself on a functional component team or a real end-to-end cross-functional team, it is important that you learn to see yourself as a "service". The first step in doing that is asking the simple questions:

- What can people buy from us?
- What kind of needs do we support and through which products?
- Can you buy maintenance and operation of the product or only new features?
- How quickly do we respond to different kinds of defects to match customer needs?

Essentially, you are just like any other "shop". If you are a shop selling fish and people ask for a sausage, you should not try to create a sausage but, instead, politely turn them in the direction of the sausage shop and find a way to make sure they go there first the next time.

If you are a component team, your main customers are probably internal, but it is still essential that we can recognize what these customers can and cannot buy in our shop and how well our service is set up to deliver on those demands. If we can do this, we can optimize the flow, throughput, quality and predictability of our service.

If most teams are primarily servicing internal customers, it could be a sign that the organizational structure is not ideally set up to support an Agile workflow. From a team-level Toyota Kata perspective, they are just like any other customer, and our goal is to optimize our process to deliver the best possible service. Whether you are dealing with Internal or external customers, ALWAYS take an outside-in perspective!

The importance of a stable team

A key point of an Agile team is that it should remain relatively stable over time. That is important from an effectiveness perspective but has proven essential for the success of Toyota Kata. I first observed the importance of not constantly switching people around when I was helping a large Danish company. They did not recognize the importance of stable teams and were constantly moving people from one project to the other. While this had dire consequences in terms of meeting deadlines and creating useful products, it was catastrophic in the process of implementing Toyota Kata. When you think about it, this should not have come as a huge surprise because:

1. Nobody is motivated to build long-term process capabilities in a context that will not remain.
2. New people, new customers and new products will change the process anyway so why bother optimizing the existing one?

These experiences have led me to believe that if there is one prerequisite for successful application of Toyota Kata, it is the relative stability of the organizational structure around it. This does not mean that you cannot make changes to the structure, but that you do it with the goal of long-term results and not as a desperate attempt to reach a near-term deadline.

What about the Product Owner?

Let's assume that we are now looking at a stable, cross-functional Agile team with the ability to deliver recognized customer value to internal or external customers. In a Scrum context, you would expect to find Team members, a Product Owner and a Scrum Master in such a situation. From a Toyota Kata perspective, it is even simpler. The Product Owner is just a part of the team, as is any other Subject Matter Expert (SME), and only the Process Lead (Scrum Master) has a special role to play.

This means that the Scrum Product Owner is expected to take part in team-level optimization just as any other member of the team is. The Product Owner does not have any special decision authority and must use their skill sets to help the entire team improve. As with any other SME, the Product Owner will be involved in the actual improvement work depending on the Product Owner's specific skills and the nature of the Challenge. If the team is focusing on end-user feedback or how to regain decision authority on product changes, the Product Owner might play a very active role. If the focus is on test or deployment automation, the Product Owner might be less active. The same will be true for any other SME on the team, with people who count UX, Design, BA, Frontend, Backend or Test as their primary area of expertise also being more or less involved depending on the nature of the Challenge.

In an Agile context, it is especially important to draw on the creativity and execution power of the entire team to generate results. So, though it is the responsibility of the Process Lead to drive the continuous improvement process the entire team must participate in both planning and executing it.

How is the team involved in planning and executing Improvement Kata?

Let us look at how that works in real life. As with the refinement of User Stories for the Sprint Planning meeting, the Process Lead will need help from the rest of the team in preparing for the Improvement Kata planning meeting.

The work being done in an Agile team is simply too complex for any one person to fully understand the current process or qualify whether a Challenge or Target Condition is realistically ambitious. A Process Lead who does not involve the team will realize that they did not understand the Current Condition and, thus, failed to set the right level and direction for the Target Condition. As in Scrum, there is not a dedicated event for "refinement". That is because it varies a lot from Challenge to Challenge and depending on the context. It is the Process Lead's responsibility to ensure that it happens, but the rest of the team must be prepared to set time aside to help. My personal preference is to allow for this on a more on-demand basis in which the Process Lead can ask for help twice a day: after the morning meeting and after lunch. At these points in time, team members are "disturbed" anyway and, thus, we can avoid additional task-switching. Often it is as simple as the Process Lead asking questions like:

- "I am not fully aware of how our deployment process works right now. Can I get one or two of you to help me understand this?" or
- "Both regression test automation and end-user feedback are areas where we have huge improvement potential. Would some or all of you spend 15 minutes with me to listen to what I have listed as for and against selecting either one and give your opinion?"

The same is true once a Challenge and Target Condition is decided upon and the team turns its focus to how to reach it. Coming up with the best ideas for experiments is a creative exercise and teams benefit from combining the creativity of the entire team. Specialist skills are almost always had to execute experiments, which means that many team members must put real time and effort into getting results.

That is also why all team members can put up ideas for new Experiments at any time during the day. The Daily Kata provides a chance to introduce those new suggestions and take responsibility for executing them.

The Manager

As previously stated, managers have a central and very specific role in Toyota Kata. Much like the team-level Process Lead, they have their own Challenges and Target Conditions, but they are also acting as coaches to their direct reports, who can either be managers or team-level Process Leads depending on seniority. I have come across the argument that managers do not exist in true Agile organizations. I cannot find any evidence of this being true in any of the organizations I have worked with, nor can I find anything in the Agile manifesto or the 12 principles behind it. Though the manager role might become an outdated concept, I hope you agree that, for now, it makes sense to match the framework to the reality in which most organizations find themselves.

The fact that the work of a manager has changed drastically with the introduction of Agile is another matter, so while the title often remains the same, the job does not. Fortunately, that turns out to be a perfect fit with Toyota Kata, as we aim to replace the operational responsibility of the manager, found in traditional organizations, with the focus to drive improvement and provide the best possible chance for teams to succeed.

A new perspective on management

Having your own measurable department-level or area-level process goals and the responsibility of reaching them can be an alien concept for many Western managers, particularly in an Agile or IT context. As previously mentioned, however, this is an integrated part of the Toyota Kata framework, as Process improvement is regarded as the primary management responsibility. It is not an add-on, not something extra on the existing list of activities and responsibilities, but the primary reason the manager role exists.

Essentially, this means that if a manager does not prove the ability to systematically and continuously improve the environment and processes around their teams and employees, the manager has failed in their area of responsibility. At Toyota, this is made clear, and it is impossible to advance in the company without demonstrating improvement capabilities (Rother, 2009).

In an Agile context, a single team can often handle the entire Value Stream from vague needs to working software. This is great, as the Value Stream becomes simpler, the flow is faster and Process optimization does not include handoffs between teams and unnecessary interfaces. It does, however, mean that we must regard management-level responsibility for Process improvement in a slightly different light.

First, managers in an Agile organization are rarely operational experts. As with the Process Leads, we expect Subject Matter Experts (SME) at the process level to have a better understanding of what is going on within their areas of specialization than any manager above them. Some managers might previously have developed or tested software, but tools, practices and processes evolve so quickly that even if they were experts five years ago, their knowledge is now outdated.

So, does it even make sense for managers in an Agile organization to have their own Challenges and Target Conditions? or should they focus only on coaching team-level Process Leads? The short answer is, yes it makes sense and here are the reasons why:

1. Some team-level Challenges require budgets or changes to structures and processes that are beyond the team's control. If such a Challenge is tied to a department- or area-manager Challenge, there is a joint responsibility to reach it and the manager must use their influence and creativity to help achieve the joint goal.

2. Organization-wide improvement initiatives often end up on the desks of Managers with the responsibility of implementing them across their departments or areas. Sometimes, multiple initiates are launched at once and there is no process or systematic approach toward prioritizing them. Even worse, the goal is launched as the need to complete a series of workshops but without any focus on whether it creates any kind of lasting change. Using a framework like Toyota Kata, there is a clear framework for prioritizing and implementing lasting change and we can avoid both overburdening and ineffective implementation.

3. Managers often deliver a service that needs optimization. It could be anything from the process of hiring new people to budgeting processes or forecasting on the portfolio level.

How the different manager types fit into a Toyota Kata context

As with the team-level Process Leads, there is a difference in how individual Managers take to Toyota Kata in an Agile organization and how well their approach toward management aligns with the principles. Nobody was born thinking, 'I'm going to micro-manage every single detail,' but incentives, culture, blame games, habits and governance models have consciously or unconsciously driven people toward behaviors that are no longer "fit for purpose" in a modern organization. The good news is that with Toyota Kata, there is a clear expectation in terms of what to do and how to act, and we can make a deliberate choice to follow a new type of management paradigm. When embarking on this journey, there are naturally different starting points. We have seen at least four types from a Toyota Kata perspective:

1. **True Servant Leader**. For some managers, taking responsibility for Process optimization and growing the skills of their direct reports comes naturally. They have always worked to create an environment for teams and people to succeed and improve their own processes in parallel. Toyota Kata just adds a framework to do this more effectively. They are not afraid to challenge assumptions and to set a clear direction. They realize that they must develop the

skills of their direct reports so that they can delegate decision authority without the need to be involved in the daily operation.

2. **Micromanager.** For others, it is quite the contrary. They might still be struggling to let go of micro-management patterns and are deeply involved in the daily work of the teams. Responsibility for improvement goals is not aligned with their approach toward management, and with all the time spent firefighting on the team level, they cannot see how they can find the time. Their strong side is that they are not afraid to make decisions and take on responsibility. With Toyota Kata, we can channel that energy in the right direction instead of trying to coordinate the work of others. It is not unusual for this type of manager to become a great improvement driver. The main issue is to avoid the tendency to direct rather than coach Process Leads or other managers. These managers have typically struggled with the concept of Agile but will often welcome the chance to make a real difference. They will need intensive coaching to break old habits. In extreme cases, the old management pattern is so deeply rooted in the identity of the micromanager that it is necessary to find another job function or place to work.

3. **The Aim-to-Please Manager.** In many aspects, this is the opposite of the micromanager. They aim to please and, as such, are deeply concerned about the well-being of their employees. If people ask for budgets for training, new tools or additional team members, they listen and do the best they can to help. They are typically great at asking questions instead of providing answers and, as such, they are initially more successful at Coaching Kata sessions. What they lack is the ability to set direction and provide different perspectives on problems and solutions. They typically accept answers to Coaching Kata questions as facts and fail to challenge the underlying assumptions and truly explore the Learner's knowledge threshold. They are often popular as managers but team-level Process Leads also indicate that Coaching Kata sessions are getting less valuable. As with some Scrum Masters, they are missing the "Leading" part of being a Servant Leader, and we often see that the content of their Improvement Boards is just a summary of what is found at the team level. Aim-to-please managers often benefit from watching other managers in action and observing the content of their Improvement Boards. Getting a chance to watch their colleagues in Coaching Kata sessions and Improvement Kata Planning meetings can be very beneficial. When they observe how other managers probe, question and challenge, they often get the "aha" experience we are looking for. After that, they typically still need intensive attention from a second coach to provide feedback and reflections on their work and help set a direction for their own improvement goals.

4. **The Know-It-All Manager.** This manager feels that they must have the answers at all times. They rarely rely on the team to provide solutions through discovery but instead lead by edict.

This is different from a micromanager because they do not have to control all aspects of the team dynamic and process. Rather, they act like architects in a manager's role. This type of behavior can be just as toxic to team health, as it stifles innovation and often creates resentment and discontent. Toyota Kata can help correct this behavior by building a level of trust that the Team can provide answers and manage Process improvement on its own. In the case of the know-it-all manager, it is especially important to have a second coach in place who can give feedback and course correct when the manager stops listening and is concerned primarily with showing that they know the answer.

How is this different from the original Starter Kata?

In a manufacturing context in which the manager or team lead is also an operational expert, the coach/Learner relationship is straightforward. The coach has a deep understanding of the processes at the Learner's level of responsibility and understands the details of ongoing experiments. It is not the coach's job to find solutions in a manufacturing context but, with deeper technical knowledge, they have the ability to more accurately judge the Learner's grasp of the situation and determine how best to coach them.

In the context of Agile organizations and IT, this takes on a different form, as each level in the organization has its own specialized skill sets and might not understand in-depth what is going on below it. But that is also a benefit. If you do not know the details, it is easier to do actual coaching, as you are not already jumping to conclusions and trying to make the Learner adopt your specific solutions. (This also happens in an Agile context, though.)

In a manufacturing context, there is typically a team lead role with responsibility for part of the Value Stream. That also includes coordination activities, as the notion of a self-organizing team is not widely adopted in that context. In Agile organizations, the coordination responsibility is not placed on a single person because the entire team is responsible for both the success and how to plan and coordinate the work to achieve it. Often, this includes a move away from titles like "Team Lead" or "Project Manager". The need to involve team members in both setting the goal and coming up with great experiments is even greater than in a manufacturing context.

From the perspective of establishing a Challenge above the team level, it is quite easy to picture how such a responsibility might be delegated throughout the organization in a manufacturing context, as team-level processes are typically part of a larger process which is, again, part of the product Value Stream. A manager might then have the responsibility of optimizing the process of building one part of the product while their manager might be responsible for optimizing the entire Value Stream. This relationship is not as clear in an Agile context, in which, ideally, the entire Value Stream is present at the team level.

Learning objectives and questions for real-life application of Toyota Kata roles

Through the last four chapters, we have introduced the three roles that drive improvement in a Toyota Kata setting. Before we move on to the Toyota Kata events, it is time to reflect on the learning objectives so far. By now you should have realized that:

- The team-level Process Lead is responsible for driving improvement in the team. They need the help of the rest of the team and stakeholders but are accountable for making sure it happens and that the Improvement Board is updated and ready for the Coaching Kata session.
- In an Agile setting, it is essential for the team to help frame the direction, identify Obstacles, and identify, execute and validate Experiments. No single person has the perfect process overview in the context of complex adaptive organizations.
- The manager is responsible for coaching their direct reports and for working to reach the manager's own target condition. "If the learner did not learn, the teacher did not teach" is a central aspect of the coach/Learner relationship.

Before you continue, write your answers to the following questions to the best of your ability:

- Describe the responsibility of the Process Lead. Add details on:
  - Who would be the Process Lead in your organization?
  - How is the responsibility of the Process Lead similar to or different from that role?
  - What is the biggest Obstacle (if any)?
- Describe the responsibility of the team regarding Process improvement. Add details on:
  - Does the team already fulfill this responsibility in your current situation?
  - What is the biggest Obstacle (if any)?
- Describe the responsibility of the manager regarding Process improvement. Add details on:
  - How many levels of managers do you have in your organization?
  - Who would be coaching whom?
  - Do managers already recognize improvement as a key responsibility? If not, why and what would need to change for it to happen?
  - What is the biggest Obstacle (if any)?

8. Toyota Kata Events

We have already touched upon all Toyota Kata events but in this section, we will dive into the details of the Coaching Kata, the Daily Team Kata and the Improvement Kata. Because many organizations that are striving to become more Agile have an established cadence of retrospectives we will close the chapter by discussing how that fits within the Toyota Kata framework. Again, it is important to remember that the entire content of this book should be regarded as a Starter Kata for Agile organizations. This is a way to get started on applying Toyota Kata and scientific thinking and building a culture of directed continuous improvement. It is a start, and once you have mastered the basics you should expect it to develop and evolve to fit your specific context. This very much includes both the cadence and content of Toyota Kata events.

Coaching Kata

Because the Coaching Kata exists to grow the skills of the Learner, it is the Learner's responsibility to participate in and show up prepared for the Coaching Kata session. That means having updated data in place on the Target Condition Metrics as well as a good understanding of the Experiment Record. If most of the time allocated for the Coaching Kata is used in trying to find information about the basic Coaching Kata questions, there will be little time for the important part – namely, the coach's chance to evaluate the skills and maturity and use this information to Challenge the Learner to increase their improvement abilities.

The Coaching Kata should take place in the open space. Unless you are working in a distributed context, that means it should take place in the team room where everybody can follow the dialogue if they are present. There are several reasons for this:

- It is readily available for the Daily Kata. Moving the Improvement Board for each Coaching Kata session will take time and introduce unnecessary complexity.
- It supports the mindset of a blame-free and transparent process. There should be no reason to hide anything. All elements should be transparent and visible to everybody.
- Though the Process Lead is responsible, team members will often have a deeper knowledge of the Experiments on which they have worked. Being in the open offers them a chance to pitch in when the coach asks for additional details or clarification.
- When you are in the process of rolling out Toyota Kata in the organization, the Coaching Kata can serve as a great marketing tool to get interest and sell the concept. Being in the open drastically increases the chance that people will notice it and ask about what is going on.

The original Coaching Kata has five questions and we have added a sixth. They are as follows:

1) What is the Target Condition?

2) What is the Current Condition now?

3) Reflect on the last step.

- What was your experiment?

- What did you expect?

- What actually happened?

- What did you learn?

4) What Obstacles do you think are preventing you from reaching the Target Condition?

- Which "one" are you addressing now?

5) What is your next experiment?

- What do you expect will happen?

- When can we evaluate the result?

6) What did you learn from this Coaching Kata?

The Coaching Kata questions aim to cover the elements of the Improvement Board that are relevant to the current Target Condition. The most important thing to understand is that answering these questions is NOT the goal of the Coaching Kata. The answers simply provide the basis for the coach to evaluate the knowledge threshold of the Learner and to guide and challenge the Learner to increase their improvement skills by asking follow-up questions. The Coach does not know how to get to the Target Condition but is helping the Learner develop skills to navigate through the unclear territory and move beyond the current knowledge threshold.

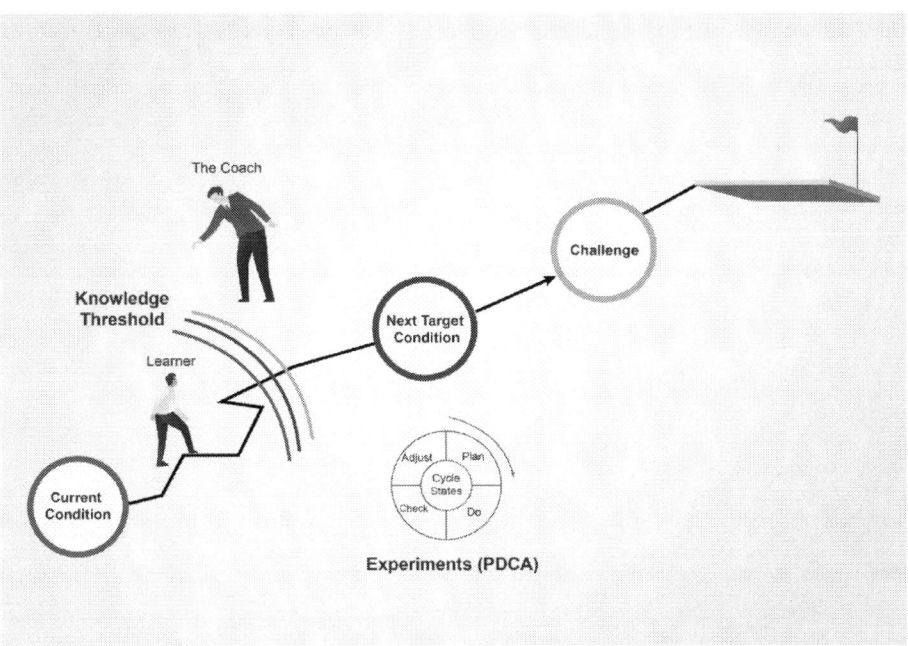

Figure 23: The Coach does not have the answer to the Coaching Kata questions but is helping develop the Learner's skills to navigate beyond the current knowledge threshold. Adapted from the Toyota Kata Practice Guide (ROTHER, 2018)

That is why we added the sixth question to indicate that if no learning has occurred, the main purpose of the Coaching Kata wasn't fulfilled. If you have simply defined a new Target Condition, it is not possible to answer question number 3, as no experiments have been completed yet.

It cannot be stated clearly enough that the Coaching Kata should take place in a blame-free environment. If Learners feel that they are being ridiculed or blamed for not doing a good enough job, they will start to hide information or even find excuses to not show up. The whole point of the Coaching Kata is to improve the Learner's abilities. If the learner did a "perfect" job already, it would be a waste of time. Any "problem" is an opportunity to improve. It is a success, as it provided the Learner with insights and reflections and the opportunity to do better next time.

When starting out, Coaching Kata might be mechanical and the answer to question number 6 might not be as clear as we had hoped. After four weeks, however, we should expect the focus to move from the ability to understand the status to actual coaching and learning. For some, this has been true from the very first Coaching Kata session, while others took a bit longer to get there.

In some situations, the Coach will judge that a specific step is needed to get to the next learning point. In these situations, it should not be a guessing game, in which the Coach directs the Learner toward the specific solution through a series of leading questions. It is much like a sports coach. The goal is to develop the player's ability to successfully navigate changing and challenging situations, though getting to that state involves both specific guidance and helping the player understand the context and come up with their own solutions.

As the Learner's skills improve, the Coaching Kata mostly take the form of pure coaching, as the Coach does not know the answers to the questions and is more concerned about increasing the Learner's knowledge and maturity than offering specific solutions. Instead of giving the Learner a fish, the Coach is teaching the Learner how to fish. If we believe that modern management is about gradually challenging direct reports to be able to take on more decision responsibility, Coaching Kata provide both the chance and framework to do this in a "safe-to-fail" manner.

We were initially surprised about the positive feedback we got from the Coaching Kata sessions. Most seemed very mechanical in the beginning and focused on answering the first five questions. They included very little relevant feedback and reflections for the Learner. However, we found that the fact that someone was showing actual interest was perceived as a very positive thing. The fact that Coaches took the time to show up for the meeting demonstrated commitment and the Learner was equally likely to show up prepared and ready.

As mentioned previously, the follow-up questions are the real benefit of the Coaching Kata, as they seek to explore the knowledge threshold of the Learner. To give Coaches a more specific idea about what such follow-up questions might be, we included the following examples in the training material:

Regarding Target and Current Condition:

- Is that actually an Outcome Metric (typically something your customers/users care about) or a Process metric (something that will get you there)? Can you tell me the difference?

- Where does your Current Condition data come from? Is it a guess, a qualified guess or do you have real data? Please show me.

    - If it is just a guess, is there a way to qualify it in a better way?

- Can you remind me of why this Target is important?

    - Do you have buy-in from the rest of the team and if not, why?

- What is the relationship between your Outcome and Process metrics?

    - How will your Process metrics help you deliver on the intended effect?

- How frequently can you measure progress on your Process metrics?

- Is it frequent enough to serve as a leading indicator and drive daily/weekly experiments?
- Is your process metric related to the flow of work?
  - If not, could you change it so that it would be?

Regarding Obstacles:

- Will you have reached your Target Condition when you have solved all the listed Obstacles (typically asked when more than two or three Obstacles are listed)?
  - What Obstacles are you observing right now?
  - Is it a goal to list all possible Obstacles in the beginning? If not, why?
  - Are they all still relevant?
- Is that Obstacle related to getting from your Current Condition to your Target Condition?
  - If yes, how are you observing this?
  - If no, please explain the reasoning behind selecting it.
- Is that a true Obstacle or just an experiment/action described as an Obstacle?
- How do you know it is a real Obstacle? Do you have any data?
- When the Obstacle is removed, would you be able to observe a change in your Target Condition metrics?
- Is the Obstacle you are addressing right now a symptom or a root cause?
  - Will removing it provide a long-term or short-term benefit?
- You have chosen to work on two Obstacles in parallel. Why?

Regarding Experiments:

- Why did you select that experiment and how will you determine whether it is a success? Please explain.
- It seems it will take several days to implement and validate the result.
  - Can you think of a way to take a smaller step so you can get feedback earlier?
- You seem to have more than one "ongoing" experiment per Obstacle.

- Is that a problem? Why?

- How is that experiment related to your chosen Obstacle?

- If the only requirement is that the next step should allow you to take a better step after that, how would you frame the Experiment?

- What is keeping you from doing it today?

It is both a strength and a weakness that managers do not have the knowledge to act as operational experts in an Agile context. Quite naturally, this situation reduces the manager's ability to challenge assumptions or to deeply understand a concept or situation. But it is not only bad. Several managers have told us that they found it easier to coach a team that was working on a topic about which they knew little. In that situation, they could more easily concentrate on coaching because their own ideas and solutions were not constantly popping up in their heads.

We received the same feedback from Learners who told us that a Coaching Kata with a stand-in had provided very relevant learning and reflections, in cases in which their Coach had been, e.g., sick or on vacation. This turned into a general recommendation to switch Coaches at a regular cadence and for the original Coach to observe the Coaching Kata with the stand-in. Remember that the questions, cadence and form of the Coaching Kata are simply elements of the Starter Kata; we expect it to evolve and improve as you adjust it to your context and organization. The goal is not to continue with the original recipe forever, and this was just one example of that.

Planning Coaching Cycles

While the Coaching Kata primarily focuses on the current Target Condition, it took us some time to realize the importance of including the element of upcoming Challenges and Target Conditions. This wasn't mentioned in Mike Rother's first book, and though I might have come across it in the additional material, it wasn't until we saw several teams struggling to be ready for their next Target Condition that we introduced the concept to both Coaches and Learners. Recognizing the importance of an effective "refinement" process for Agile teams, this should not have come as a great surprise.

The concept is quite simple. As we are closing in on the time for the next Improvement Kata Planning Meeting (typically two weeks beforehand if we suspect a need to initiate a new Challenge and one week beforehand if we are continuing with the same Challenge), the Coach will start adding questions to the Coaching Kata to evaluate whether the Learner is set up to facilitate it successfully.

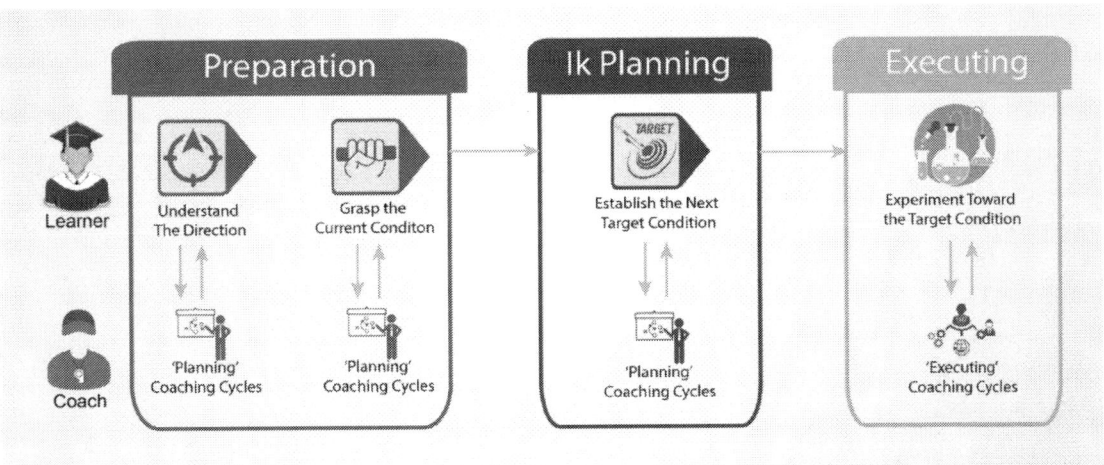

Figure 24: Planning vs executing Coaching Cycles, adapted from the Toyota Kata Practice Guide (ROTHER, 2018)

Because planning the next Challenge or Target condition depends much more on the individual, the context and the specific Challenge, we do not recommend following a rigid question guide in the "Planning Coaching Cycles" (not even in the beginning). Instead, Coaches are given the following cheat sheet in training for inspiration:

Planning Coaching Questions:

- What is your current Challenge?

- Will you continue with that Challenge?

    - Why? What does your data show? What will you achieve? Have you considered the 80/20 rule?

- If no, what should the next Challenge be?

    - Why? What will you achieve? How does it relate to the Vision and the current organizational focus? Where are you starting from? What is the Current Condition data? When can you show me? Do you have team buy-in/can you get it?

- If yes, what should the next Target be?

    - Why? What will be your focus process? What will you achieve? How does it relate to the Challenge? Do you have team buy-in?

This is also the chance for the Coach to influence the direction in case they want the team to focus on a specific topic relevant to their own Challenge – more on that in Chapter 17. The 80/20 rule refers to

74

the point that we want 80% of the payoff with 20% of the effort. One-hundred-percent goals leave very little room to be pragmatic and deal with unique cases and we can spend a long time trying to get the final 20% right. We will cover how the 80/20 rule applies to many aspects of Toyota Kata in Chapter 10.

Opportunity to "Go to the Gemba"

"Go to the Gemba" is a term used in Lean to state that managers should go to the place where the actual work is being done instead of sitting in an office. IT is largely invisible and, thus, it is difficult to get a real feeling of what is going on simply by walking around the team rooms. Toyota Kata makes it possible for the director to approach any team in the organization and get honest and valuable insights into what is going on, not from the perspective of controlling but to get a deeper understanding of possibilities and constraints. Instead of asking random questions, the director can simply use a short version of the first five questions of the Coaching Kata:

- What are you trying to achieve?
- Where are you now?
- What obstacle is in your way?
- What is your next step and what do you expect?
- When can you go and see what you have learned from taking that step?

Because everybody is focused on improvement, this should not feel like an intrusion but, rather, a chance to show off and share obstacles and constraints. If teams are not able to answer these questions, if they feel threatened or if they share excuses rather than information and data, the director will learn that they have not been able to create a transparent and blame-free environment and can work to improve it by coaching their direct reports. We do not recommend that directors do this every day but visiting each team once a month is usually a good fit. It does not have to be planned and should take no more than five to 10 minutes.

The Daily Team Kata (Daily Kata)

As mentioned, the Daily Kata is an event we introduced specifically for the Agile Context. It is necessary because the frequency of Coaching Kata is not high enough to ensure a daily focus on improvement and creating a true culture of real continuous improvement.

The Daily Kata focuses mainly on the Experiment Record (PDCA cycle) and aims to ensure that:

EVERY DAY team members prioritize and discuss possible new ideas for Process improvement experiments and challenge each other to take the smallest possible step! (Plan)

EVERY DAY team members hold each other accountable for executing Process improvement experiments! (Do)

EVERY DAY team members discuss whether they learned something from past experiments! (Check)

EVERY DAY team members reflect on what they learned and adjust accordingly! (Act/Adjust)

This PDCA cycle is at the heart of Scientific Thinking and is sometimes also referred to as the "Deming Loop". I personally always refer to the "A" as short for "Adjust" rather than the original "Act". This is because many people have a hard time distinguishing between "do" and "act", while it is clearer that "Adjust" applies if we consider whether the process change should result in actual adjustments to our current process.

Because experiments often last longer than a single day, the Daily Kata makes sure that we keep the pressure on fighting the Daily Whirlwind and that there are no delays because of a lack of focus or an inability to find other solutions.

As previously stated, the Daily Whirlwind of User Stories, defects and deadlines can be a hard competitor for attention. The point is that we are not competing for 100% of the capacity, but for the 10 to 20% that will ensure the long-term success of the company. As Steve Covey states in his management classic, "The 7 Habits of Highly Effective People" (Covey S. R., 2004) (P=Production, PC=Production Capability):

"To maintain the P/PC balance, the balance between the golden egg (production) and the health and welfare of the goose (production capability) is often a difficult judgment call. But I suggest it is the very essence of effectiveness."

The agenda of the Daily Kata does not follow an exact script like the Coaching Kata but often involves some or all of the following questions depending on the status of experiments:

1. What did we learn since yesterday, if anything (from experiments)?

     a.   What did we expect? What actually happened?

     b.   Did we take a step toward removing the Obstacle(s)?

     c.   Did we move the process metric(s) closer to the Target Condition?

2.   What is/will be our next experiment?

     a.   What Obstacle will we address and why?

     b.   How will that move us closer to the Target Condition?

     c.   Who is responsible?

     d.   Is it the smallest possible step?

     e.   What do we expect?

     f.   When can we execute it and when can we evaluate the result (date/time)?

The Daily Kata is also a chance for the Process Lead to challenge the team to explore new paths and change existing habits. During our coaching, we often find that a team naturally looks toward a specific team member for the execution of experiments within a certain domain. Even before discussing the nature and details of an experiment, it is already assumed that this cannot be done before next week because "Peter is away for the next three days". Situations like that are a great chance for the Process Lead to challenge the team to think outside the box by asking questions like "What would it take if we had to execute and validate the result of the Experiment tomorrow?" or "If we had unlimited power, how might we address that Obstacle?"

Figure 25: Thinking outside the box to challenge the status quo

In the beginning the Daily Kata will often take longer than the allocated five minutes. However, as the team matures and learns to focus, they are able to bring it down to the five-minute timeslot in most cases. As they learn to make experiments shorter, they are less nervous about experimenting. Failing a one- or two-day experiment does not seem as dangerous; thus, they spend less time discussing whether they dare try it. Another reason is that they get better at keeping their focus on the actual Target Condition. Immature teams will often end up discussing various Obstacles and

Experiments that will not really get them closer to their Target Condition. Thus, they spend a lot of time at the Daily Kata on aspects that are not moving them forward.

Learning to experiment – A real-life example

A team was working toward a Target Condition of being able to have more periods of focused work during which they were not disrupted by meetings or unplanned external requests (internal team "interruptions" were not included). They had found that during a normal day, only an average of one team member would have a single period of 2,5 hours of uninterrupted work out of a potential of 14 (7 team members and a maximum potential of 2 periods per day). They had set a Target of reaching 5 and had identified personal emails as the major cause of external interruptions – the "Obstacle".

They spent almost 30 minutes in the Daily Kata discussing whether they should do the Experiment of simply forwarding personal emails to the team email with a standard message to the external party (stating that it had now been forwarded to the right place) or whether they should instead call the person to explain it to them. They were nervous that an auto-email would offend the external party and that calling each person would consume too much time. They found arguments for both solutions and were getting no closer to an agreement when one team member asked the question "How quickly can we test this?" They found that:

- Setting up the auto-reply would take about five minutes.
- With the normal incoming flow, they would have the chance to try it out roughly five times before the end of the day.
- They could then call two of the senders and ask them how they had felt about the auto-forward and whether they were likely to use the right channel the next time.

As an afterthought, they reflected that they had spent 7 x 30 minutes discussing whether they should conduct an experiment that would take one person less than 30 minutes to perform and through which, instead of speculating about the outcome, they would have gained real information to support the hypothesis.

Improvement Kata Planning Meeting (Improvement Kata Planning)

As previously mentioned, the Improvement Kata Planning meeting is very similar to a Sprint planning meeting. If the Product Owner shows up with just a few rough headlines that have been neither seen nor validated by the team, it takes either an extremely mature team or a lot of luck to establish a clear and relevant Sprint Goal. Instead, it becomes a mentally draining exercise and people leave the meeting discouraged even after having exceeded the allotted time.

The same is true for the Improvement Kata Planning meeting. We have seen multiple attempts to "wing" them but having participated in hundreds of these meetings, we find it very evident that a successful Improvement Kata Planning Meeting requires preparation very similar to the "refinement" or "Backlog grooming" process found in many Scrum Teams. This means that we expect to spend the 90 minutes getting the details in place and not trying to define the overall direction.

Sometimes finding the necessary data to support the Current Condition takes some effort or calendar time. Getting this in place before the meeting allows us to focus on setting the Target Condition. Having a whole team present is also time-consuming. Because data gathering and investigation can often be done much more effectively in smaller groups or by a single person, we want to reserve this meeting for getting the entire team's buy-in to an ambitious and realistic Target Condition.

Sometimes the Process Lead will already have selected an overall topic or chosen to follow the direction set by a department or organizational initiative. Thus, the analysis of the Current Condition can focus more narrowly on that part of the process.

After getting a good picture of the Current Condition, the Process Lead should draw a rough sketch of a proposed Challenge. Sometimes this is done alone or with the help of a few team members. Once done, the proposal is validated during the Coaching Kata sessions and through feedback from the entire team. It is crucial that this take place BEFORE the Improvement Kata Planning meeting. Ninety minutes is enough to get the details in place, but we have seen almost no successful attempts to define the overall direction of a new Challenge and establish the Target Condition for the next four weeks during a ninety-minute meeting. Good preparation is key!

Often, the Coach is also present at the Improvement Kata Planning Meeting for three reasons:

- It is a chance to see how the Process Lead performs and what to focus on during the next Coaching Kata session. The Process Lead might, e.g., have improved considerably in terms of getting an informed picture of the Current Condition but still lack the ability to get full team buy-in. The ground rule in Toyota Kata is "If the learner didn't learn, the teacher didn't teach", so this is also a chance for the Coach to reflect on their own abilities.

- It is a chance to show support and dedication and to influence the ambition level. Often, the Coach will be able to provide knowledge and insights about external constraints like tool choice, budgets or collaboration with external stakeholders. Eliminating some of the uncertainty around these elements or promising the full support of management can help the team strive for a more ambitious goal.

- It is a great chance to "go to the Gemba" and observe the team at work. Software can be a difficult process to observe, and walking by the team room to have a chat does not necessarily provide great insights into how work is being done. The Improvement Kata Planning Meeting is a great chance to observe how the team members work together and the constraints and obstacles they face. It is difficult to underestimate the necessity of this. In many organizations, managers have been moved so far away from the actual work, they are essentially operating blindfolded. They remain in charge of hiring, firing, incentives, salary and people management but lack the insights to do this on an informed basis.

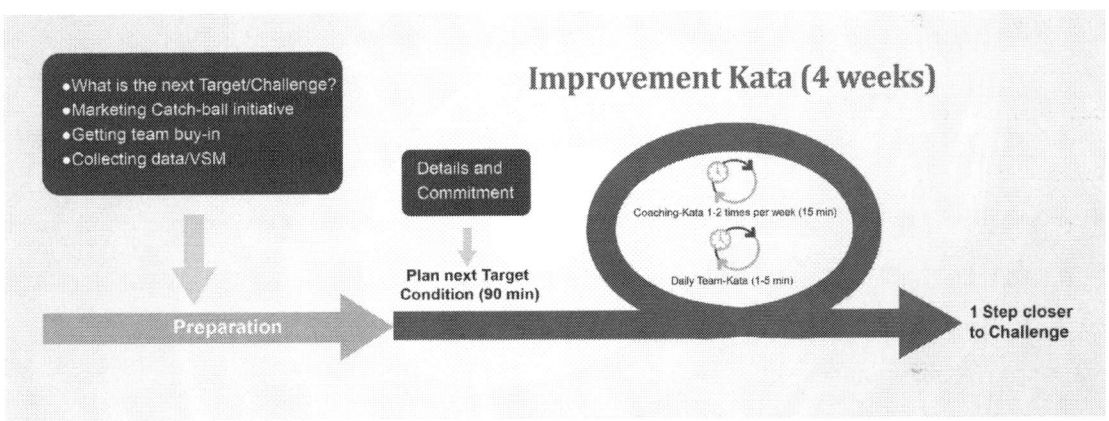

Figure 26: Improvement Kata preparation

If we are taking one more step toward an existing Challenge, the meeting is often very straightforward, as the team will look at the gap between their updated Current Condition and their Challenge and identify the next four-week goal. Mature teams will often be able to finish the meeting in considerably less time than the allocated 90 minutes.

If the team is starting a new Challenge, more work is needed. Even with great preparation, questions often arise in terms of how to interpret the direction of the Challenge, what it takes to gather and update metrics and what part of the Challenge should be part of the first Target Condition. With a new Challenge in play, teams often use the full 90 minutes at their disposal. You might also recall the figure from the previous chapter, showing the need for proactive preparation of a new Challenge:

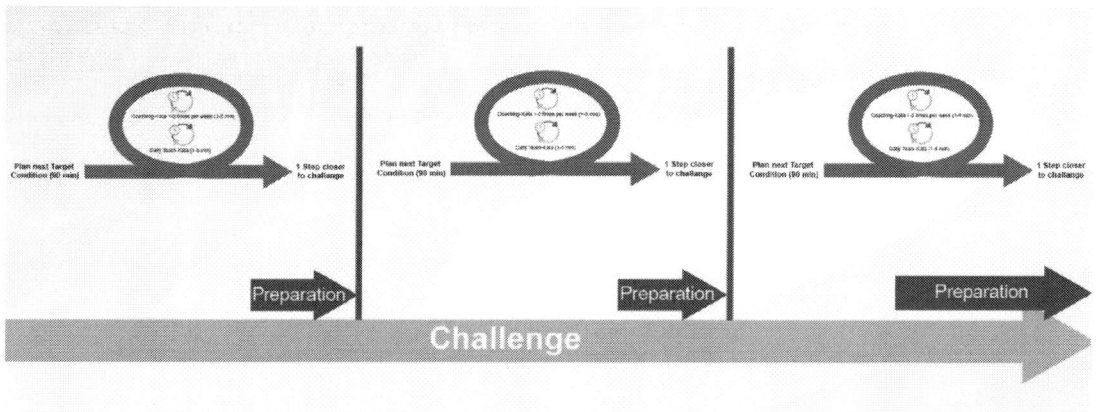

Figure 27: The right amount of preparation is key to setting a successful Target Condition

Improvement Kata Planning Pitfalls

It is the responsibility of the Process Leader to guide the team through the meeting. It is impossible to cover all potential pitfalls in this book but here are a couple of key patterns of which to be aware:

1. Once a Target Condition has been established, we move the conversation from what the goal is to how to get there. Not everybody will always agree, and they tend to reintroduce the question of the validity of the goal when discussing Obstacles and Experiments. It is important to stop this before it ends up consuming the entire 90 minutes.

2. Most people do not like uncertainty and will try to identify all currently observed Obstacles as well as those that could possibly occur during the next four weeks. This is not the goal, as we are navigating unclear territory. As a facilitator, you must turn the conversation back to discussing the most important Obstacles you are observing now and defer speculations about future issues. It is much like the bottleneck approach – solve the most important one first and the next real one will surface.

3. Not everybody gets the idea of "good-enough" metrics and will challenge the integrity of the available numbers. This can be healthy, but it is important to make sure that you do not spend 90 minutes challenging numbers that are good enough. Keep asking the question "Is this number good enough to give us a clear indication of our direction and Current Condition and to see whether we are closing the gap?" If the Target is to lower the response time from key stakeholders to three hours, there is probably not much to gain by discussing whether the Current Condition is 6.5 or 6.9 days. You might also simply ask yourself "Is it fit for purpose?"

4. We are aiming for optimization of the team's entire Value Stream. This sometimes means that an individual team member will not get everything the way they want it. It can be

81

anything from knowing that they will not be able to offer much help in reaching the Target Condition, having to spend time on knowledge sharing or participating in boring work they have previously managed to avoid. In this case, it is important to recognize the individual's point of view but also to remind them about what the overall goal is and why there is no "I" in team.

As a guideline, we created the following default Agenda for the Improvement Kata Planning Meeting. (We will cover Value Stream Mapping in detail in Chapter 21)

1) **Did we achieve our last Target Condition?**

   - **If not, why? What happened? What did we learn?**

2) **What is the Challenge?**

3) **What is our Current Condition?**

   - **Review the updated Value Stream Map.**

4) **What is/are the proposed focus area(s) for the next four weeks?**

5) **Agree on the next focus area.**

   - **Identify the Target and Current Condition for the chosen focus area (iterative).**

6) **Identify Obstacles.**

7) **Find Experiment ideas and choose the first Experiment.**

We will cover the details of a good Target Condition as well as how to identify Obstacles and Experiments in more detail in Chapter 11, 12 and 13. At the end of the Improvement Kata Planning meeting, the Improvement Board should be updated and both the Target and Current Condition, as well as the first Obstacle and Experiment, should be chosen and placed in the Experiment Record on the Improvement Board. This signals that the team is "ready" to proceed and that there are no "gaps" between Improvement Kata. Ideally, the next Experiment should begin on the same day as the Improvement Kata Planning meeting.

Toyota Kata and Retrospectives

Most Agile organizations are familiar with the concept of retrospectives. Through the implementation of Scrum, retrospectives have become the default approach toward Agile continuous improvement. But how does Toyota Kata fit with this concept? Should we integrate it into the existing retrospective events? Does it replace the need for retrospectives altogether? Should it run in parallel as an addition?

In my first attempts with Toyota Kata, we chose to integrate the framework into the existing retrospective events and cadence. At this point, I had not fully grasped the Toyota Kata framework and the first try was closer to just introducing a new practice in the meeting – much like fish-bone diagrams or stop-start-continue. Yet even at that point, it struck me that both the potential and effort went far beyond just the retrospective meeting. After numerous attempts to merely integrate Toyota Kata into the retrospective meeting, a series of problems had surfaced with this approach:

- Toyota Kata has a more long-term focus and though nothing forbids you from working with the same theme at more than one retrospective, the mapping of several Target Conditions toward an overall Challenge wasn't an easy fit.

- There is much more to Toyota Kata than simply the Improvement Kata Planning meeting. Retrospectives are not set up to handle the iterative nature of Toyota Kata and people continuously tried to plan all experiments at the meeting despite being told to take only the first step.

- The usual cadence of bi-weekly retrospectives wasn't a good fit. The feedback I received was that there was barely time to iterate toward the Target Condition before a new Target had to be set.

- The word "retrospective" implies "looking back". Though we work to understand our Current Condition, Toyota Kata is focused on reaching the desired Future State; we are "looking forward".

In the end, we had to conclude that Toyota Kata needed its own place and platform from which to evolve. The framework is not "just" something you adapt to an existing process but a fundamental change of mindset and approach toward Process improvement involving new roles, practices and events. Here is a short list of the biggest differences:

1. Instead of asking, "What problems can we fix?" (Problem-focused), we ask, "What does the ideal process look like?" (Goal-focused)

2. Instead of asking, "Do we have everything on our impediment Backlog?" (Assumes all problems should be fixed), we ask, "What is/are the obstacle(s) keeping us from our Target Condition?" (Assumes we must focus our limited capacity)

3. Instead of asking, "What are our SMART goals?" (Plan-driven – assumes success), we ask, "What experiment could effectively remove our Obstacle? What do we expect and how quickly can we validate our results?" (Iterative – assumes uncertainty)

4. Instead of asking, What should be fixed in the next two weeks?" (Short-term – two-week focus), we ask, "What should our process look like two to six month from now?" (Ambitious long-term goals)

5. Instead of asking, "What actions do we take in the next two weeks?" (Focus on execution), we ask, "How will our experiment move our metrics?" (Focus on effect)

6. Instead of asking, "How do you feel about our test process?" (Based on intuition), we ask, "What is our Current Condition? Do we have data? Show me!" (Based on data)

The next attempt was to run both processes in parallel, keeping retrospectives focusing on more short-term problem-solving and Toyota Kata working on the bigger long-term ambitions. Unfortunately, that also quickly presented some problems. Teams found that too many were competing for the same mental capacity and the overlap between retrospective actions and Toyota Kata experiments generated some very unproductive discussions of where things belonged. "It is a mess," as one team member stated.

The next experiment was to drop retrospectives altogether and use Toyota Kata as the one and only approach toward continuous improvement. Though initially far more successful than the parallel solution, it did not take many weeks before Agile Coaches, Process Leads and team members voiced the opinion that the softer parts and the go-fix-it stuff were missing. As one Scrum Master stated, "I know our Agile Coach is telling us not to wait for a retrospective to fix the small stuff, but the truth is that we are so focused on our work that it just does not happen during the Sprint. Go-fix-it issues like adding a label in Jira or moving our standups 15 minutes are not going to make the difference between success and failure but solving small problems increases motivation and just feels good". They missed the opportunity to fix the small stuff, simply complain about things not being perfect and talk about the softer issues like communication patterns or personal issues.

In the end, we came up with the solution to replace every other retrospective with the Improvement Kata Planning Meeting and to keep existing retrospectives to focus on the smaller, often problem-oriented "just-fix-it" issues and "people-over-process" areas. It is not a perfect solution but has been by far the most successful one. Because most teams run two-week Sprints, it also fits well with the four-week Target Condition Cadence. For teams using a three-week Sprint cadence, it has been a mix of running a six-week Improvement Kata Planning cadence or sticking to the four weeks and dropping the synchronization with Scrum events.

An interesting side note is that some of our most dedicated Toyota Kata promoters have insisted on including "people over process" in their Toyota Kata work. Though we advised them against it, they found observable and measurable patterns of trust and communication and defined metrics for both the Target and Current Condition. To our surprise, they had great success with this. Though I would not advise this as a general concept, it just shows what you can do with creativity and dedication. Some examples of the communication and trust metrics included:

- Percent of User Stories completed with only official reviews. (Team members did not trust each other's ability to write good code and the review process and, therefore, reviewed commits and made changes without telling the rest of the team. Even with a collective code-ownership philosophy, this felt like a huge breach of trust to the individual.) They wanted to go from 30% to 90%.

- Number of unnecessary repetitions per day. Everybody on the team felt the need to comment on every single point – explaining the same point in their own words. This was a cause of huge frustration because meetings and discussions ended up consuming too much time. They wanted to go from 30 to 5. We warned them that gathering Current Condition data might be a challenge, but they insisted and had great success with this goal.

Learning objectives and questions for real-life application of Toyota Kata events

If anything, I hope this in-depth introduction to Toyota Kata events made it clear that Toyota Kata is not just a small add-on to your existing process but a major continuous improvement driver in need of its own dedicated space. Before we move on, it is time to reflect on the learning objectives so far. By now you should have realized that:

- The Coaching Kata is not a status meeting but a chance for the Coach to explore the learning threshold of the Learner and help the Learner take the next step to become an even better continuous improvement driver. On the team level, 15 minutes is allocated for this. It is recommended to have two sessions per week.
- The Daily Team Kata is a five-minute daily meeting focusing primarily on the Experiment Record. This meeting ensures that Experiments are carried out and validated continuously and is, thus, an essential part of building a true continuous improvement culture and effectively battling the Daily Whirlwind.
- The Improvement Kata Planning Meeting is a 90-minute meeting during which the Target Condition for the next four weeks is defined. The meeting is about getting the details in place. For it to be carried out effectively, it is necessary to prepare the content accordingly.

Before you continue, write your answers to the following questions to the best of your ability:

- What is a Coaching Kata? Add details on:
    - What is the purpose of the Coaching Kata?
    - Who participates?
    - What are the six Coaching Kata questions?
    - Why are follow-up questions the most important part of the Coaching Kata and can you remember any examples?
    - When would the Coaching Kata meeting take place in your organization?
- What is a Daily Kata? Add details on:
    - How does the Daily Kata support the Plan-Do-Check-Adjust cycle?
    - Who participates in the Daily Kata?
    - What are sample questions asked during the Daily Kata meeting?
- What is an Improvement Kata Planning Meeting? Add details on:
    - What is the purpose of the Improvement Kata Planning Meeting?
    - Who participates?
    - Why is it important to prepare for the meeting and who is responsible?
    - What is the recommended cadence of Improvement Kata Planning meetings and how would you align it with existing events in your organization?

9. The vision

As you might recall, "Understanding the direction" is the first step toward the successful application of Toyota Kata. If understood and communicated broadly, a "True North" can help channel energy in a common direction and avoid short-term sub-optimization. We may introduce Toyota Kata events, roles and Improvement Boards but if we do not "understand the direction", we are at risk of sub-optimizing, as we do not share a common vision of where we want to go. As Russel Ackoff (a friend of Dr. Deming) stated in his 1994 talk on systems thinking (Ackoff, 1994):

"When you get rid of something you do not want, you do not necessarily get what you do want. Finding deficiencies and getting rid of them is not a way of improving the performance of the system … An improvement program must be directed at what you want and not what you do not want … If you do not know what you would do if you could do whatever you wanted to, how in the world can you know what you can do under constraints?"

To me, this very nicely captures the essence of the difference between directed improvement and reactive problem-solving. At Toyota, all Process improvement is guided by the True North "One-by-one flow at the lowest cost to the customer". Understanding the purpose of the Vision as well as how we might choose to frame it in an Agile setting is the content of this chapter. Directed improvement starts with the Vision and I suggest you give it the attention it deserves.

What is a Process Vision?

A Process Vision states the ultimate capabilities of the organization. Thus, 100% more throughput is not a Process Vision because it does not tell us anything about what capabilities we want as an organization, but only the Outcome. The ability to distinguish between Outcome and Process has turned out to be crucial for the successful application of Toyota Kata but remains one of the most difficult aspects both on the Vision, Challenge and Target Condition levels. Not everybody has a clear understanding of the term "Process"; some find it easier to think of the "capabilities" the organization must establish to deliver at its optimum. We will deal with this in depth under the theme of "Challenge" in the next chapter.

Because this book deals primarily with the application of Toyota Kata in an Agile setting, we will spend most of this chapter discussing the Vision from an Agile perspective.

A recent 2018 study published in Harvard Business Review (Cappelli & Tavis, 2018) showed that 86% of companies in Western Europe are adopting Agile methods and organizational structures and 42% are also doing it outside IT. This indicates that not only is Agile booming but it has moved far beyond IT development and is now influencing the entire organizational structure and the related processes. It is, therefore, not only relevant but crucial to establish and align the perception of what Agile means to be able to pull organizations in the same direction.

But is clear Vision, then, a prerequisite for starting with Toyota Kata? No. As we will discuss in Chapter 18, a Vision is not needed at first but can be developed in parallel with the first local Challenges.

Framing the capabilities of an Agile organization

Looking at the Agile Manifesto, many of the elements are highly influenced by the notion of "one-by-one flow" but the Agile True North also includes elements like delegation of authority, organizational structure and communication patterns. Some might argue that all Agile principles will naturally follow from a focus on one-by-one flow over time, but my own experience is that it is purely a theoretical perspective. Agile and Lean share many principles and values but they are not the same. If you discuss Agile purely from the perspective of one-by-one flow, you will find that while people might agree on the surface, they do not share the same mental model behind the words they are using. Try asking five people in a company what Agile means and I guarantee you will get very different but also mutually exclusive statements. That is because everyone is assigning their existing mental models to words like "Adaptive", "Iterative" and "High Performance".

If your existing mental model is not challenged by a clear direction, we won't recognize that we are not moving in a shared direction. I am sure that some Toyota Kata practitioners will find some of the included elements of the proposed Agile Vision to be at a too detailed level, but personally I have found a clear and rather specific discussion about which Agile capabilities are a very valuable exercise.

The Vision should represent the long term or even an unattainable description of the organization working at its absolute best. The vision should be tool-, role- and practice-free, allowing for local solutions to be developed to fit the individual context. The Agile vision we will use in this book includes the following elements:

- Strategic alignment
    - Highly aligned, loosely coupled. At all organizational levels, people can identify how their "service" is contributing to the overall success and how it is aligned with the strategic direction. Without a strategic direction, iterative development can become a buckshot approach.
    - Funding is transparent, dynamic, outcome-focused and based on unbiased financial modeling.

- Empowered, self-organizing teams
  - Self-organization is the only way to effectively handle the complexity involved in innovative work across skill sets. Trying to coordinate the work of others results in information bottlenecks and uninformed decisions.
  - Empowerment makes it easy to respond to process and product feedback. Once a high-level strategy is decided, the empowerment to make all necessary Product and Process changes to deliver on that strategy belongs to the team. That includes empowerment to both identify user needs and decide how to implement them.
- Stable end-to-end teams with 100% allocation
  - Bring the work to people – not people to the work. It takes time for people to learn how to coordinate and collaborate effectively. Average team churn is measured and kept below an officially communicated threshold (e.g., 25% per year). Zero-percent churn is not a good goal, as it implies a static structure that is unable to adapt and attract new talent.
  - There is no need for external experts or help from other teams to turn vague user needs into working functionality. End-to-end teams reduce coordination overhead because the entire Value Stream is found within a single team.
  - Bringing work to people and having stable teams makes sense only if people are not allocated to several teams. 100% allocation of team members is key to long-term effectiveness and fast flow.
- Always releasable – all code, any time, fully automated on demand
  - It is never a technical decision to release. All code is continuously committed and always releasable, avoiding any kind of technical batching.
  - Test and deployment is a fully automated process – no exceptions. Only with zero transaction costs of test, deployment and release can we fully get the benefits of small batches and one-by-one flow.
- Small batches (MVP, MVF), always outside-in approach
  - New enhancements, features and products represent the smallest possible vertical slice and are deployed all the way to production within 1 day (enhancements), 3 days (features) and 1 months (new products) to reduce cycle time and risk and to get early feedback.
  - All estimated, tracked and visualized work is relevant and prioritized from an end-user perspective and the flow of those items is the only real measure of progress. Only work items representing end-user value count and each work item includes a hypothesis of the actual monetary value!

- Visual management – full transparency
    - Full visual transparency in terms of system health and the status and progress of all ongoing work. Available to all interested stakeholders – nothing is hidden.
- Continuous qualitative and quantitative customer and end-user feedback
    - Customer feedback is sought and incorporated into the design of our products. New products and features are validated by performing user research from the beginning of the process lifecycle. Qualitative studies are performed and real-time data on quality and usage against new deployments to real users are collected. Developers have access to real users and user data, to enable flow and feedback.
- One-by-one flow (Limit WIP)
    - The ability to effectively finish one feature before starting a new one and limiting the number of features in progress to a maximum of one per workflow step – harvesting the full potential of all the other elements of the Vision.

As you can tell, the Agile vision includes more than one-by-one flow. I hope I made the point earlier in terms of why this is necessary to provide a real direction for your improvement efforts in an Agile context, but it does present one problem that we must address. One-by-one flow is an unachievable but desirable Future State. You might be able to establish one-piece flow at a single process but across an organization, it is simply not possible, as no buffers would be available to deal with even the slightest amount of variation in flow and quality. The same is not necessarily true for all the elements in the proposed Agile Vision.

I have tried to create a basic overview in the following figure to align expectations in terms of when we are reaching for the unattainable and what is within our reach. None are easy, so I am using a four-point scale (Challenging, Difficult, Very Difficult, Almost Impossible) and differentiating between being able to do it across the entire organization and being able to do it in a single team:

Capability	Organizational level	Single team
Strategic alignment	Difficult	Challenging
Empowered, self-organizing teams	Difficult	Challenging
Stable end-to-end teams with 100% allocation	Almost Impossible	Challenging
Always releasable – all code, anytime, fully automated on demand	Very Difficult	Difficult
Small batches (MVP, MVF) always outside-in approach	Almost Impossible	Very Difficult
Visual management	Almost Impossible	Very Difficult
Continuous qualitative and quantitative feedback	Almost Impossible	Difficult
One-by-one flow (Limit WIP)	Almost Impossible	Very Difficult

Figure 28: Achieving organizational capabilities

Adding and adjusting elements of the Vision to fit the context

For one organization, better forecasting was an essential motivation behind their Agile transition. Recognizing that most of the above elements would help them deliver on better predictability as an Outcome, they still felt the need to add the following to their specific vision.

- All forecasting is probabilistic and based on available and updated throughput, WIP and cycle time data.

It might sound counterintuitive that an Agile initiative would drive higher predictability, but it is not so farfetched. Being done with specification, design or implementation in a Waterfall context provides very little insight into the completeness of actual customer value because nothing is truly tested, validated and live with real users. In an Agile world, we show real progress by implementing and validating vertical slices, and despite the ability to embrace change and adapt to feedback, we are often able to do much better forecasting when we must. Also, notice that they wrote "probabilistic", which clearly indicates that they work from the Agile mindset of handling uncertainty instead of trying to eliminate it.

We have found a clear and concise Vision to be incredibly useful. If we use vague terms like "High-Performance Teams", "Learning Organization", "iterative and adaptive", "leadership" and "Trust", nobody will disagree. That is because everybody can place the vague terms within their existing mindset. A good vision challenges assumptions and starts a discussion, and some will disagree on individual elements or concepts. If everybody just nods and smiles, it is probably too vague and abstract.

In one company we put "stable teams" in the Vision. Coming from a project-oriented organization, this sparked a heated discussion among senior management. They believed the ability to constantly shift people around to match the workload and specialist needs of the individual projects was the key to success. I also remember when, ultimately, they decided to remove it from the Vision and how it ended up affecting the success of their Agile transition. On the positive side, we were at least aligned. Three years later, they finally concluded that the root cause of their problem was, in fact, the lack of organizational stability and it was reintroduced as a key element.

Using the Vision as a "True North"

Once established, the Vision should serve as the guiding light. Discussions should no longer focus on whether the Vision is correct but on how to get closer to it. You can use Scrum, XP, SAFe, Nexus, Less, Lean UX or Proto-Kanban roles or practices to help you get there but not as the end goal.

If you are already using the Kanban Method to its full potential, you might not need Toyota Kata at all, but because the vast majority of Kanban implementations are Proto-Kanban (using Kanban as a delivery method rather than a Process optimization method), my experience is that you are much more likely to release the full potential of Kanban by adding Toyota Kata. We will discuss that in further detail in Chapter 22

A good vision will Challenge the organization to look beyond current capabilities and strive for excellence. In Toyota Kata training, I always include the "Poking Life" video interview on YouTube with Steve Jobs. Though he is talking about life in general, his points are very useful in a Toyota Kata setting. If we dare not rethink or redesign our processes and every Process improvement is limited by existing rules, guidelines or policies, our ability to truly improve and "Poke Life" will be seriously limited. All we can do is problem-solve our existing dysfunctional processes. In the interview, Steve Jobs states:

"...once you discover one simple fact. That is that everything around you that you call life was made up by people that were no smarter than you. And you can change it, you can influence it."

Later he adds:

"I think that is very important and however you learn that, once you learn it, you'll want to change life and make it better, cause it's kind of messed up, in a lot of ways."

As with life, many of the rules, processes and policies in organizations are "messed up, in a lot of ways". It might seem a daunting task to change but being able to point to a clear Process Vision True North really is a game changer. Though it might take months, years or an eternity to deliver on the Vision. We constantly strive to get closer to it and perceive any obstacle in the way as something we can and should remove.

It is also important to understand that capabilities are closely related to culture. You cannot tell people to trust each other, show leadership or take larger risks. You cannot make a more experimental approach mandatory or tell people to stop blame games. Culture changes when you change the actual things people do every day, the very specific actions from moving a ticket on a whiteboard to talking to an end user (Kahneman, 2013). Or to quote Jerry Sternin, "It's easier to act your way into a new way of thinking, than think your way into a new way of acting" (Pascale, Sternin, & Sternin, 2010)

So instead of telling people to, e.g., "trust each other" or "experiment", we should focus on building the capabilities that enable those virtues. If you build the capability to deploy automatically to any environment and if each deploy is tested automatically, if any serious error is caught before reaching production or after being exposed to only a small subset of users, a culture of thrust and experimentation will have a much greater chance of evolving. If you invest in team-building sessions, trust workshops and the importance of close customer collaboration, but if your technical environments are fragile, if deployment takes weeks and if you are not set up to actively gather feedback, chances are that all that money spent will generate more frustration than actual benefit.

Nor can you ask people to "be transparent and trustworthy" but you can build the capability to consistently visualize the status of all ongoing work as well as system performance and functional health and make it available to all key stakeholders. This might seem like a go-do aspect and not something to include in a Vision, but end-to-end Visualization can truly be a difficult thing to strive for in many organizations. So, when we set up our company Process Vision, we are really asking ourselves the question: "What process capabilities does our company possess when we are working at our absolute best?"

Based on experience, I recommend that you keep your Process Vision limited to a maximum of seven to nine capabilities. We can always add more detail as we get to the Challenge and Target Condition level, but the Vision should be clear and concise. We can then focus 100% of our energy on taking steps that will bring us closer to it. This is a subtle but very important point that Mike Rother stresses multiple times in his books.

Setting an overall direction can be a challenging and mentally draining exercise. Once done, it is time to release all our energy in moving toward it. If for every step, we want to stop and discuss whether the direction is valid, we lose focus and motivation. You will find that this model repeats for every step by finding the Challenge and Target Condition. Toyota's operational vision has remained unchanged for over 60 years and it is still working every day to take small steps in the direction of one-by-one flow.

Identifying the Current Condition based on the Vision

I have seen many attempts to rate individual teams, managers, departments or entire organizations on their Agile maturity and I have taken part in developing a few scoring systems myself. A lot of time and resources are put into framing the overall content and individual questions and the idea is that it can generate valuable insights in terms of specific retrospective actions on the team level as well as organizational insights into the status of Agile and potential actions.

However, it is rare that an organization uses this rating systematically beyond the first weeks or month on both the team and organizational level. From my own experience, it is primarily due to three factors:

- Systematic improvement is not part of the culture and, thus, nobody is responsible. A central department might develop the maturity rating, but it is then handed over to be used and followed up locally.
- Questions are at too low a level of abstraction and are too simple. It could be statements like "We are always using the User Story format to describe work items" or "Our Sprint lengths are always the same". If people feel that they are deviating for good reasons, it becomes a case of explaining why they are not following the official process rather than trying to improve.
- Questions are subjective and not actionable. Statements like "In our team, we trust each other and have a blame-free environment" or "We have an honest and open dialogue with customers" might reveal that something is wrong but do not set a direction for actions.

Yet that does not mean it does not make sense. Aligning the rating with the Vision provides a level of abstraction that is high enough to allow for solution-specific details while low enough to provide actionable direction for improvement. Naturally, you would need to adapt it to your own specific version but having done that, I would strongly encourage you to get a deeper look into the organizational Current Condition by using questions like the ones found below and establishing an organizational cadence for updating it (e.g., every second month). Some questions are inspired by the results of the DevOps survey populated in the excellent book "Accelerate" (Forsgren, Humble, &

Kim, 2018). We will cover the use of it to develop Agile organizations in more detail in Chapter 19, but already you should realize how actionable a Vision can be in driving improvement efforts at all levels.

On a scale from 1 to 5 (1=Strongly Disagree, 2=Disagree, 3=Neither Agree Nor Disagree, 4=Agree, 5=Strongly Agree), how would you rate the current capabilities of your team?

- Strategic alignment
  - There is a clear strategic direction providing the alignment and guardrails for local decision-making on the tactical and operational level.
  - Remaining dependencies between teams, departments and external parties are handled proactively without unnecessary complexity, interfaces and delays.
  - Funding is transparent and continuously evaluated based on unbiased financial models recognizing outcome as a primary risk dimension (instead of hidden, based on yearly budgets, decision committees, highest paid person's opinion (HIPPO) and a cost focus).
- Empowered, self-organizing teams
  - Given a strategic direction, we have the product decision authority as a team to iteratively scope, prioritize and deliver WHAT we find is needed to maximize business value.
  - We have the technical decision authority as a team to decide HOW we want to develop features (including Design, UX and code) and what tools to use.
  - It is a shared team responsibility to coordinate work to maximize outcome. No single person coordinates the work of the team.
- Stable end-to-end teams with 100% allocation
  - Our team is stable, allowing us to optimize for the long term.
  - Our team is cross-functional and has the internal capabilities to deliver work items end-to-end to real end users, without requiring help from external parties.
  - Team members are 100% allocated to the team.
  - We implement, validate, deploy and release our application independently with no technical constraints or dependencies to other teams or technical environments.
- Always releasable – all code, any time, fully automated on demand
  - We have fewer than three active branches in our code with very short lifetimes (less than two days) before being merged into trunk/master. We do not experience "code lock" periods when no one can check in code or do pull requests due to merging conflicts, code freezes or stabilization phase.

- Deployments are fully automated and do not require manual intervention. This still leaves room for manual approvals but once approved, all changes are applied automatically.
- We can provision our environments and build, test and deploy our software in a fully automated fashion from information stored in version control.
- All code is checked in at least daily, and each check-in triggers a set of quick tests to discover serious regressions, which developers fix immediately.
- Tests run automatically and continuously throughout the development process. Tests find real failures and only pass releasable code and unit and acceptance tests are run against every commit.

- Small batches (MVP, MVF), always outside-in approach
  - We slice new product initiatives into Minimum Viable Products (MVP) with just enough features to validate the business model against real users and to be completed in one month or less.
  - We slice work items into Minimum Viable Features (MVF) that deliver end-user value – just enough to get early feedback and can be completed in three days or less.
  - Work items are always written and prioritized from an outside-in, end-user perspective and include a clear statement of the customer/end-user value hypothesis expressed as a monetary value.
- Visual Management – full transparency
  - We visualize the flow of work from business needs all the way through our Value Stream to customers and end users to coordinate and manage work effectively in a single place
  - We create and maintain visual displays showing key quality and system health metrics and make them available to team members, leaders and customers. We use threshold warnings to enable us to proactively detect and mitigate problems.
  - We visualize and use cycle time, WIP, defects and throughput data to improve the flow and predictability of customer value through our Value Stream.
- Continuous qualitative and quantitative customer and end-user feedback
  - Work items are framed as measurable experiments. Real-time data on their quality and usage is collected from real users and product changes are made based on this feedback.

- o We have direct access to real users and customers and perform qualitative user research from the beginning of the product lifecycle. Product changes are made based on this feedback.
- One-by-one flow (Limit WIP)
  - o Teams and team members focus on finishing started work and are not interrupted by changing priorities, expedites or meetings. The priority of not-started-work can be changed and adapted continuously without causing stress, demotivation or task-switching.
  - o The active use of setting and lowering WIP limits makes obstacles and constraints to higher flow visible and drives Process improvement through the entire Value Stream.
  - o We work systematically to remove bottlenecks, blockers, variance and wait time to create a smooth and level flow from our commitment point to work items validated in production. We avoid stress and overtime and optimize for a highly effective but sustainable pace.

Learning objectives and questions for real-life application of the Vision

I hope that through the previous chapter, you have realized the importance of a clear direction that describes a long-term desirable future process state. Before we move on, it is time to reflect on the learning objectives so far. By now you should have realized that:

- A Process Vision defines the process capabilities the organization can master at all levels when it is operating at its absolute top performance.
- Moving beyond vague terms like "high-performance teams" and "a learning organization" helps us align improvement initiatives across the entire organization and organizational levels and pull in a shared direction.
- The Vision describes an idealistic Future State and, thus, serves as a True North that might never be possible to reach.
- You can start your Toyota Kata journey without a Vision in place but should strive to work on defining it along with the first pilots.

Before you continue, write your answers to the following questions to the best of your ability:

- Why is a Vision important?
- What is the difference between a Process Vision and an outcome goal?
- Which of the listed example Agile capabilities would you include in your Vision?
- Whom would you include in the work to define your organization's overall Process Vision?
- Why is it important to get high-level buy-in from senior management in the organization?
- What do you think would be the result if we chose to focus only on one-by-one flow, our True North?
  - What would be the benefits and drawbacks compared to the Vision presented in this chapter?
- What would happen if you chose to focus exclusively on extremely low cycle time (e.g., minutes) as the True North?
  - What would be the benefits and drawbacks compared to the Vision presented in this chapter?
  - How would that differ from a focus on one-by-one flow?

10. The Challenge

Setting the Challenge is arguably one of the most important aspects of successful Process improvement with Toyota Kata, as it sets the direction for the focus, energy and effect you will set yourself up to achieve in the next period (Rother, 2018). For this reason, you will find this chapter rather extensive and divided into several sub-sections to deal with the many different aspects of setting a good Challenge in an Agile context.

In Mike Rother's first Toyota Kata book, the aspect of the "Challenge" was only briefly mentioned. It took some time going through Mike's additional material and experimenting with the concept in practice before we realized the importance (this was before the Toyota Kata practice guide was published).

A Challenge represents a step toward the Vision and should represent a desirable future state that you cannot reach with your current structure and processes (Rother, 2009). In Mike's books, a Challenge might reach two years into the future, but we have found that shorter periods of two to six months are often a better fit in an Agile setting. The whole idea of a Challenge is to dare reach for at least a subset of the stars and pressure yourself to build new capabilities. From experience, we have learned that Challenges that are shorter than two months tend to set the bar too low to drive creativity and motivation. On the other hand, Challenges that are longer than six months do not feel close enough to create the urgency, drive and motivation required to achieve superior results and the world around us changes too quickly for the Challenge to remain stable over longer periods of time. So, while the two- to six-month focus is not a hard rule, our experience is that most successful Challenges fall within this timeframe.

A Challenge represents a desirable Future State – NOT a problem

The important thing to notice is that a Challenge represents a desirable Future State and NOT a specific problem. This is a very important aspect which has proved difficult for some people to understand and something with which the Lean community has struggled for years. Let us look at bit closer at what to do and what not to do.

The use of Value Stream Mapping (VSM) is a common practice in both Lean and Agile approaches. An example might look something like this:

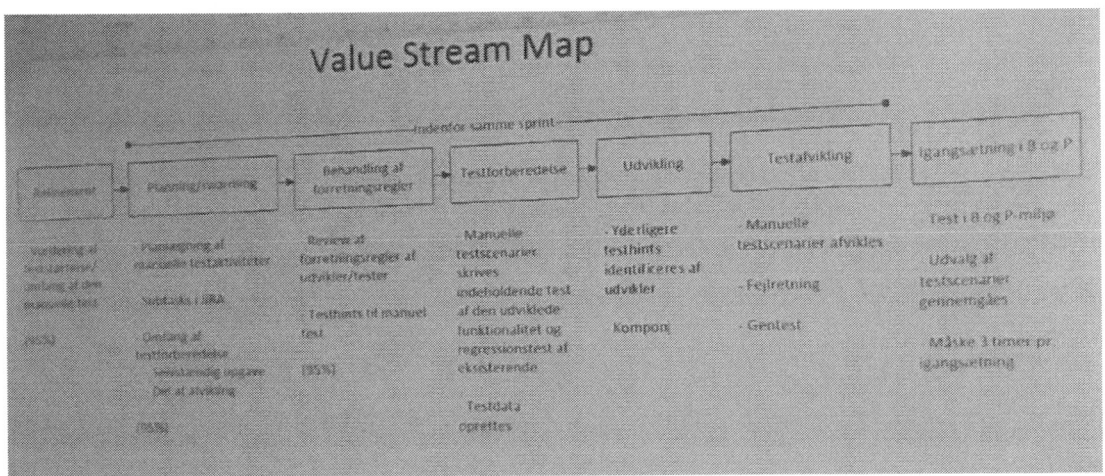

Figure 29: Value Stream Map example

We cover the basics of VSMs and WMs in Chapter 21, but as you can tell from the picture, it involves a rough overview of the primary workflow steps through the production cycle as well as details and numbers associated with each step.

Traditionally, many Agile coaches and Lean consultants have looked at the VSM, identified a specific problem and then used SMART goals or Kaizen events to fix that problem. That is the WRONG way to do it. Being problem-focused will keep you anchored in your current process. Numerous psychology studies have also shown that humans are much better at working toward a goal than away from problems (Kahneman, 2013).

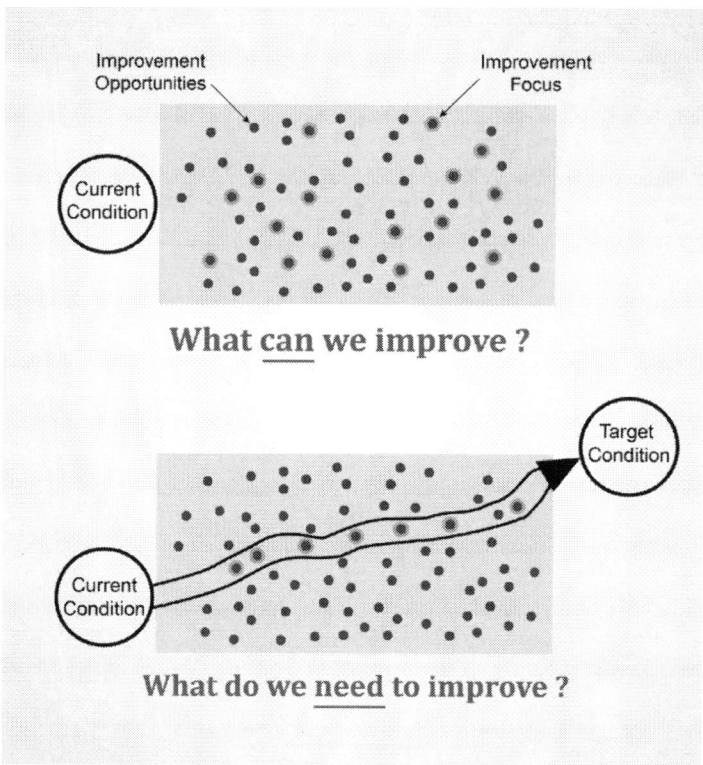

Figure 30: Traditional vs. focused improvement, adapted from the Toyota Kata Practice Guide (ROTHER, 2018)

In Mike's latest book, The Toyota Kata Practice Guide (Rother, 2018), he encourages us to ask the more interesting question, "Wouldn't it be great if we could...?". Looking at our Agile process vision, we might continue that sentence with statements like:

- "... release individual User Stories to production as soon as they were ready, on all existing products, and our customers would like us to do so?"
- "... work in end-to-end teams, with each team releasing without dependencies on others?"
- "... always be in a releasable state and it never being a technical decision if we should deploy to production?"
- "... describe all work-items from an outside-in perspective and make progress visible across the value stream in one single place?"
- "... make funding continuous and validate the success of new features and products based on quantitative outcome data?"
- "... integrate quantitative and qualitative end-user feedback throughout the development process to validate assumptions early?"

- "... visualize forecast probabilistically based on available data with no need for manual work and subjective opinions?"
- "... prove the hypothesis of new products with an average investment of only $50,000?"
- "... deploy products automatically to production without any manual procedures?"

From those answers, we can make our Challenges even more clear and measurable. However, the key thing is to start thinking in terms of what we want instead of what we want to move away from.

An example illustrating the difference

A team looks at its VSM and concludes that the actual feedback loop is missing. Features are built, tested and deployed but rarely validated against end users or engagement analytics during development or test or after being deployed. The team looks at their Scrum Process and concludes that they must fix the problem that they are not getting enough value out of their review meetings because the right people are not present. They also conclude that the Product Owner is responsible for securing an effective feedback loop and plan actions to fix the problem.

On the surface, this looks like a logical and effective approach but let's take a closer look at what is happening and why this approach is problematic.

- First, the team is quickly diverting from the actual goal of getting feedback to focusing on a specific event. Already, that means they are ignoring all the other possible ways of getting feedback which could be a much better and cheaper fit in their situation. The team is so focused on their current process that they cannot break the chains of habits and their entire discussion will remain anchored in the current situation.
- The second problem is that the ambition level is already low from the beginning and the bigger potential of continuous feedback including both qualitative and quantitative (e.g., analytics) will likely not even enter the discussion.
- The third problem is that they are already narrowing their solution space to a specific event and a specific person. Seven people's resources and creativity are disregarded, and a single person is given the responsibility to succeed or fail.

Instead, we want the team to look at the Process Vision and come up with a clear statement of what the feedback process should look like, e.g., two or three months from now. What would "Continuous qualitative and quantitative feedback from real end users throughout the development process" look like and how would you observe it? We typically start with vague terms and then refine them until they represent a clear and measurable direction. So what might a challenge that focuses on feedback look like? (Outcome metrics are left out because we will deal separately with that topic later.)

Title: Continuous feedback from real users!

Date (should be achieved by): October 16th

Process metrics:

- From 0% to 60% quantitative engagement analytics on deployed features
- From 0% to 40% qualitative validation of features with end users during implementation
- From 15% to 50% qualitative validation with early adopters after deployment

We have borrowed the "from X to Y <content>" wording from the book "4 Disciplines of Execution" (4DX) as it clearly states that we know both our Current Condition and the desirable Future State. X and Y should always be numbers. This also avoids the problem of people using wording like "increase feedback by 20%", which is just another way of saying, "I want to do more of it, but I have no idea about our current situation". ☺

As you can tell by the example above, we have purposely left all implementation details and solutions out of the Challenge. We want to stay open to all creative solutions but chase the core capability of integrating better feedback loops in our process.

Yet will we not eventually be looking at problems to fix? In some cases, that will be a correct assumption. If we are aiming for 100% automated deployment, naturally our Challenge will focus on eliminating the problem of manual deployment steps. So, it is not that we cannot include problem statements in our Challenge, but often we tend to go there too quickly and limit our possible solution space when defining the Challenge. Here is an example:

Instead of:

- "From 20% to 50% of User Stories compliant with Definition of Ready (DoR)"

Consider:

- "From 55% to 80% of User Stories completed without blockers"

Why?:

- The real goal is to achieve flow. One reason for work being blocked could very well be a failure to be compliant with the definition of ready, but as we dig deeper, we might find that there are other and equally important Obstacles. Focusing on DoR compliancy might be OK on the Target Condition level but is probably too specific and problem-oriented to be included in the Challenge.

Current Condition data in an Agile Context

An objective and measurable Challenge has proven key to the successful application of Toyota Kata. But if we want to set challenging goals, we must know where we are starting from – the Current Condition. If the data in our Value Stream Maps is pure guesswork, we risk setting Challenges we have already achieved or that are overly ambitious. If we do not know our Current Condition, we might also fail to truly understand where we are coming from and not be able to identify the real Obstacles that are keeping us from reaching the Target Condition.

We also risk identifying the wrong Experiments or misinterpreting the results of our improvement effort. The real "state of the nation" is often a surprise to managers, teams and Process Leads and often it is not in a positive way. I have seen cases in which:

- Defect rates were many times higher than people believed.
- Actual cycle time was over double the initial guess.
- Compliance with DoR and DoD was 0%.
- The actual engagement of deployed features was less than 1% of what people expected.

In a manufacturing context, processes are visible and flow and cycle time is often counted in seconds or minutes. You are usually able to visually observe a process to get the necessary data. In an Agile context, we cannot do that in the same way. The actual process is not visible, and only by representing our work with Post-its on a whiteboard or cards on a board in an electronic system are we able to follow the actual flow of value. Once we start to observe work, we find that it may take days or even weeks for work to move from one end of the board to the "Done" column. If we need a valid sample of data, it could take weeks or months for us to gather enough information to find our Current Condition. Because variability is high in development work, a small sample size might give us a very wrong picture of what is truly going on.

If we must spend weeks or months on data gathering before identifying a Challenge, that would mean we should start planning far ahead into the future, which is not exactly very Agile/Adaptive. Another problem is that it is almost impossible to observe a process without changing it in an Agile setting. If you count the number of reoccurring defects, your brain will consciously or unconsciously start to improve it. The same will happen if you focus on deployment time, test coverage or T-profiles.

It took some time and frustration for us to figure out what to do instead but the combination of two principles finally solved the problem in most cases, using the 80/20 rule and historical data. The same principles apply at the Target Condition level.

The good thing about historic data is that it is relatively unbiased. Work has already been completed so any chance to influence the result should be in the past. The bad thing about historic data is that there might be missing details and that our memory sometimes fails us. This is where the 80/20 rule applies – if we can get 80% of the accuracy of data with 20% of the effort collecting it, it is good enough in almost all cases. If we want to go from having 5% of our User Stories covered by automated tests to 50%, it matters little if the actual starting point was 4% or 8%. "Perfect" is the enemy of "good enough"! This might scare Lean consultants who are used to aiming for decimal precision. However, in a development context, we are creating something new all the time and variability will be high anyway. Whether we change our process or not, our metrics today will not be the same in a week.

It is important to look at historical data from an objective perspective. If we use samples, we must choose them randomly. If we count, we must not do it with the aim of making the number look bigger or smaller. We can do this only if we have managed to create a blame-free environment around Toyota Kata. If a team is punished for visualizing that their current deployment involves 12 manual steps and takes five man-days to complete, it becomes difficult to define a true Current Condition.

An example

Let us look at a specific example of how to use historic data and the 80/20 rule. Defects are a natural part of development, as we do not want to perfect things too much in an Agile context before getting feedback on the actual value. If we have gold plated what nobody wants to use, we have wasted time and money. Seeing the same type of defect occur again and again is, however, not an efficient use of our time and money because that is a clear sign that we are not fixing the root cause of our problems. In this example, a team was looking at the Vision of "zero reoccurring defects" and the high amount of failure demand draining their development capacity and wanted to investigate their Current Condition to judge the potential of this as their next challenge.

Guided by the principle of using historical data, they chose to look at the last four weeks of reported defects, which amounted to 77 in total. They decided to go through the list and evaluate whether defects were new or re-occurring (the same defect being reported before). The first two defects took a total of 10 minutes to cover, discussing them in detail and even opening a code editor to see where it occurred in the code. Some quick math revealed that continuing with this level of detail would result in seven people spending an additional 375 minutes or six-and-a-half hours going through the list. Remembering the 80/20 rule, they decided to accept a level of uncertainty but trusting that the law of large numbers would keep it at an acceptable range.

For the remaining 75 defects, they did a majority vote from just reading the headline and only in the few cases in which they did not understand what it was about did they dive deeper. It took a total of 23 minutes to cover the remaining 75 and they arrived at 50 out of the 77 being reoccurring defects –

65%. Of those that had been solved, only 5% had received any kind of root cause analysis. Their Challenge included going from 65% to 30% reoccurring defects and 5% to 50% root cause analysis.

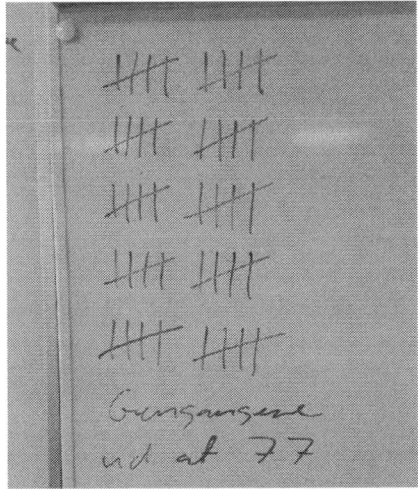

Figure 31: Current Condition data using the 80/20 principle example

Green, yellow and red Challenges

To find a Challenge that is both realistic and ambitious, we found the notion of green, yellow and red helpful.

Green Challenge

A green Challenge is too easy – typically something you can achieve by planning a few workshops or something in which you already know the steps ahead and there is limited uncertainty involved. This is what 4DX calls stroke-of-the-pen initiatives. Green-zone goals might still be relevant but can typically be planned and executed by simply agreeing to do it and placing the needed work on the Backlog.

It is, however, a valid point that habits can be hard to change. Developing T-profiles to balance a cross-functional team might, e.g., seem like a green-zone Challenge on the surface. We have, however, had countless teams talking and planning to do this for months or years without achieving any success. Only when we set up a measurable Challenge and allowed creativity and iterative improvement to try to move the numbers did they break the deadlock. So, whenever you are discussing a Challenge that involves changing human behavior, habits or thought patterns, ask yourself whether it is truly as easy as you think. There is a reason why countless change management books have been dedicated to that topic. ☺

Red Challenge

A red Challenge is too difficult. If you are in the red zone, people do not believe it is possible to reach the goal. Worst case, they give up before even getting started. It is, however, important to realize that some organizations have not previously been ideally set up for employees to get the decision space and trust to change things. In those cases, Challenges that might be in the yellow or even green zone can seem impossible. This is where leadership and management play an essential role. We will cover this in much more detail later, but I have seen acts of leadership and great managers who have been able to bring a red-zone Challenge well within the yellow-zone space.

This can be done by providing examples of what other teams and organizations have achieved in similar situations or ensuring authority, support and budget to make the necessary changes. Sometimes it has simply been a matter of reminding a team that the organization is not in the same place as it was five years ago and, thus, they should not limit their potential to follow an outdated structure. It is, however, also important to acknowledge when something is truly in the red zone. Often, this is a signal that the Challenge must be initiated at a higher level in the organization.

Yellow Challenge

A Challenge in the yellow zone is ambitious enough to push the team, department or organization out of its comfort zone and achieve results that could not be realized with the current process. It sets a goal that is both realistic and ambitious. The road to the goal cannot and should not be known at this point, as the whole point of iterative Process improvement is to navigate the unclear territory ahead.

Not all parts of a Challenge are always in the same zone

It is important to realize that Challenges might include aspects of both green, yellow and almost red. Some parts are almost too difficult to achieve while others include limited uncertainty and creativity. When setting up a Challenge, we judge the Challenge as a whole, and that is what we should find within the yellow zone.

We have also learned that uncertainty is often reduced over time as we work through the Obstacles and learn more about the context. The "Cone of Uncertainty" applies to many different contexts and simply visualizes that when embarking on a new project or initiative, uncertainty is highest in the beginning. As we work on the new project or initiative, knowledge gradually increases and uncertainty is reduced, which gives us a nice cone-shaped picture:

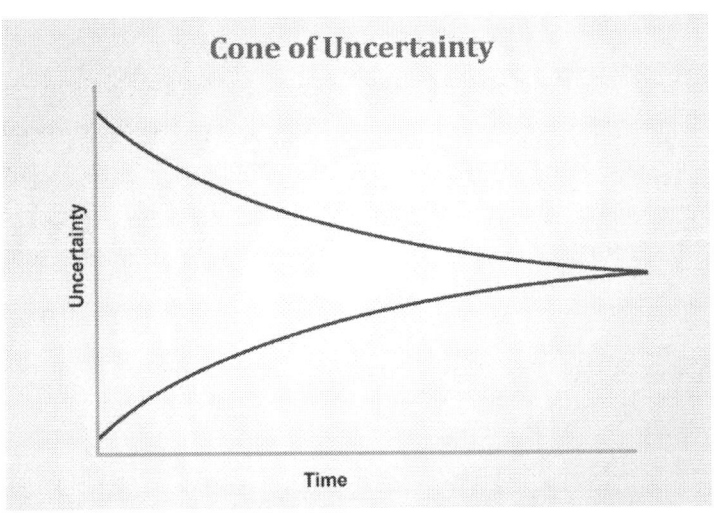

Figure 32: Cone of Uncertainty

Thus, the first part of the Challenge might be closer to red, while achieving the final part of the Challenge can sometimes feel like it is almost in the green space. That is perfectly fine. Finding themselves in the green zone for the last step in the Challenge (e.g., the fourth Target Condition), some teams decided to skip Toyota Kata and just place the needed work on their Backlog and continue with a new Challenge. For a long period of time, we thought this was fine. They made a good point that Toyota Kata was better suited to the more uncertain work of navigating unclear territory. The cone of uncertainty was now so narrow that they believed the last part was a straight road from A to B. We now strongly advise against this for several reasons:

- Though the last pull to reach the Challenge might be a straighter road, it will often require the same capacity and effort. That capacity is now competing with the capacity needed to work on the next Challenge and the mere fact that we are now working on two things can jeopardize the result. And remember, low uncertainty does not equal small effect.

- The road was often more winding than predicted, and as with traditional retrospective SMART goals, the planned sequence of work had difficulty dealing with the iterative nature. That meant that effectiveness dropped and the goal wasn't achieved.

- You lose the feeling of success with Toyota Kata if you are almost there and the topic is then replaced by something else on the Improvement Board. Toyota Kata simply does not get the credit it deserves internally or externally.

- We do not normally recommend listing "lack of time" as an Obstacle because it is more an ever-present condition within the world of IT. Toyota Kata has proven incredibly effective at creating actual room for improvement work. Once the last part of the Challenge is removed

108

from the Improvement Board and placed on a Product or Sprint Backlog, the Daily Whirlwind can battle it at full strength. We have countless examples of the Daily Whirlwind winning this battle on the Backlog and teams ending up frustrated because they did not reach the final and most important part of their Challenge.

The importance of a measurable Challenge and metric update frequency

We will cover measurable daily improvements and the relation to scientific thinking in more detail in the next chapter on Target Conditions. However, having clear metrics on the Challenge level is very important.

I must admit I had my reservations when reading both the first Toyota Kata book by Mike Rother and the book "The 4 Disciplines of Execution" (Covey S. , 2015). In Rother's book, measurable improvements seemed to be taken for granted as part of the scientific approach of testing and validating hypotheses, while 4DX spent a large chunk of the book explaining the importance of being able to assign numbers to your Process improvement goals. After seeing the effect of putting metrics on improvements, I am, however, convinced that not only is this important, it is crucial! You cannot imagine how big a difference there is between vague intentions and putting concrete metrics on your goals. It is like playing a sports game in which, after a warm up, you start keeping track of the score and playing to win. The whole game changes and the energy, motivation and creativity you put into reaching the goals simply become a different game.

In a manufacturing context in which tact time is measured in seconds or minutes, you do not have to pay too much attention to metric frequency when choosing your leading process metrics for the Challenge and Target Condition level. No matter what you focus on, there is a good chance that you can continuously measure your ability to achieve it.

In an IT development context, it is different, as we often work with iteration lengths of one, two, three or even four weeks. If we can observe changes to our process metrics only on a bi-weekly basis, it naturally becomes difficult to do short experiments and validate them against our goals. To make it fit, we must do two things:

- Find metrics that can be observed often enough to generate a culture of true continuous improvement.
- Adapt Toyota Kata events and cadences to fit the IT context which we covered in the previous chapter.

The first bit of advice is to choose metrics that are closely related to the flow of User Stories, Backlog Items or Defects (or whatever you call your value-adding work items). This has three major benefits:

1. You keep focussing on the flow of value delivery, which is what you are ultimately aiming to improve. That way, you keep focussing on the end goal and not the solution-specific details.

2. Most Agile teams plan, start or finish at least a handful of work items per week. If metrics are tied to those, you are guaranteed the possibility of an update on your metrics weekly.

3. Your metrics will be relatively objective, as they are tied to the actual work flowing through the system.

Once you go a level deeper and start focusing on specific events, tools or artifacts, you are already one step away from the core process capabilities and looking directly at solutions.

The second bit of advice is to define a simple and measurable PROCESS Future State. How would you observe the process when it is working realistically and ambitiously better than it is right now? Besides being an essential part of Toyota Kata, focusing on process has the following benefits from a metric-frequency perspective:

1. Let's say that you fix 10 defects per week and that the ideal process involves three workflow steps, from identifying the problem to validating the fix in production. Then you have 10x3 = 30 points on which to measure every week. That is more than enough to provide you with daily feedback on the success of your experiments. Remember that Kata is about working to reach a process Future State, so the fact that 0% of your defects follow the new process just shows room for improvement.

2. Process metrics are typically much cheaper to collect, as you are already "moving" something. Asking people to put a mark on a board or sheet when a step is finished is a cheap way of gaining insights and a high frequency of measurements.

3. While your Challenge might include an ideal state including five workflow steps, you can choose to focus on the one or two most important at the Target Condition level.

But what about subjective metrics like:

- The quality of the Backlog on a scale from 1-5. Simple vote.
- Internal team communication 1-5, 1 being terrible, 5 being perfect. Simple vote.
- User Story quality 1-10. Simple vote.

And I am sure you can find many other examples of using a vote to judge the maturity of a part of the process. Sometimes it is unavoidable and even our most creative suggestions fail to come up with something objective and useful. In those cases, we can use more subjective metrics as a last resort and set up a simple cadence of how often we will "measure". Though they can be cheap to gather, and we get to decide the cadence, we generally use it only as a last resort for the following reasons:

- Subjective scales can be interpreted very differently from person to person. This is, of course, a minor problem if the same people rate the Current Condition.
- Subjective scales can be influenced by many things other than the process: bad weather, time of day, poor food in the canteen at lunch, mood, unpopular/popular organizational changes
- You never really know whether you reached your goal or whether you were unconsciously tempted to rate it higher to make sure you got there. Thus, the feeling of having achieved a great success is often not as clear as it is with more objective measures.

Mentioning time of day as a subjective factor might sound disturbing to some people but a scientific study showed just how little it takes to influence the minds of humans. You would think that judges are trained to be factual, impartial and rational but a study of more than 1,000 parole decisions researchers found that the most influential factor was simply how long judges had been working since their last break. Thus, 65% would be granted parole in the morning and right after lunch, while this dropped to almost 0% for those appearing in front of the judge in late afternoon or just before lunch (Kahneman, 2013).

Be careful of aiming for 100%

Once the theme of a Challenge or Target Condition and associated metrics have been decided, you must agree on the actual numbers. Again, we use the notion of realistically ambitious Challenges and Target Conditions. The default response is often 100%, e.g.:

- 100% code coverage
- 100% root cause analysis on defects
- 100% root cause fixes on defects
- 100% of User Stories should be done with more than one team member involved
- 100% of User Stories should get qualitative feedback from real end users
- 100% of work should be able to be completed by more than one person on the team
- 100% of work should be visualized
- The team has decision authority over 100% of User Stories

On the surface, they might look good but they leave very little room for pragmatic maneuverability, e.g.:

- Anyone who has tried aiming for 100% test code coverage has experienced the pain of updating and maintaining a huge suite of tests that never reveal any real issues with the code.
- Insisting on structured root cause analysis and fix for all defects will likely result in a mentally draining exercise of little value because a small defect on just-released functionality will need to undergo the same treatment as everything else.

- 100% visualized work would mean that a 30-second phone -call or a 2 min. discussion with a colleague who dropped by your desk to ask a question would need to be created as a ticket or Post-it and moved to "done".

- Insisting that all team members should be able to help implement all User Stories would mean that you would have to cross-train the entire team to handle even a type of non-urgent User Story that happens only once a year.

So be careful about setting 100% goals. Often, the 80/20 principle applies and aiming for 80% is often a good balance (though in the case of code coverage, I would personally consider aiming for 80% code coverage to be quite extreme).

Use absolute measures over relative

I use percent in many of the examples. That is because the number of work items we process often changes from week to week. Stating a goal of going from 5 to 10 work items compliant with our Definition of Done (DoD) simply does not make any sense if we completed 12 the previous week and only 8 this week. So, whenever there is variability in the number of items associated with our metrics, we must use percent. There are, however, exceptions and whenever it is possible to use exact numbers, we do that. Here are a couple of examples:

- From 12 to 7 WIP limit on "development"
- From 1 to 2 average people having worked on User Stories
- From 12 to 7 manual deployment steps
- From 5 minutes to 30 seconds CI build time
- From 0 to 8 automated regression tests

The last bullet might seem strange but it is a good example of the principle of starting with quantity over quality. We often apply this at the Target Condition level to get the machine "running" (in this case the ability to write automated tests) and later worry about the quality of those tests and whether we can keep doing it for all future incoming work.

What we should always avoid is using terms like "reduce", "increase", "lower", "minimize", "more" and "add". We do NOT want to see Challenges or Target Conditions Process and Outcome metrics framed like this in a Toyota Kata setting:

- Lower deployment time by 50%
- Automate 30% of manual procedures
- Increase DoR compliance by 50%
- Lower defect rate by 20%
- Increase code coverage by 30%

- Increase velocity by 20%

What these statements are telling us is that we do not know our Current Condition and are trying to get around that fact. They often also lack the details of how we will measure it because it is, e.g., not clear whether velocity is measured in story points or number of completed User Stories and what timespan it includes. Instead, we must find out where we are starting from so we can set a real target. Once we have done that, we can frame the same goals much better:

- From 20 to 10 hours deployment time
- From 10 to 7 manual steps in gathering data for the daily report
- From 40% to 60% of User Stories on the Sprint Backlog compliant with DoR
- From 80 to 64 defects per week
- From 40% to 52% code coverage
- From 20 to 24 completed story points per week

Let's look at a real-life example of what to do and what not to do:

Balanced Team Example

Team A decides to focus on the capability to solve User Stories in order of business priority and not individual skill sets. They investigate and find that of 10 User Stories finished in a Sprint, only 3 were the highest business priority. They formulate the following Challenge:

Title: Delivering work items in order of business priority

- "From 30% to 80% finished User Stories in Sprint is the highest business priority."

This might look great on the surface. They have investigated their Current Condition and found a realistic and ambitious target. Had they written "30% more User Stories are completed according to business priority", they would be in trouble, but this looks about right. Metric frequency is however low. It can be measured only at the end of each Sprint and is poorly suited for iterative experimentation and improvement.

We can improve this quite easily with a simple change. Instead of measuring it across an entire Sprint, we can update the metric each time a User Story is finished.

- "From 30% to 80% finished User Stories is the highest business priority."

But if we assume that WIP is stable and started work will finish earlier than not started work we can get information even earlier.

- From 30% to 60% of started User Stories is the highest priority

Outcome (lagging) and Process (leading) metrics

A Challenge consists of both Outcome and Process metrics. Learning to tell the difference has proven to be an important but difficult skill to master. A large part of the 4DX book is dedicated to this subject and does an excellent job of explaining the difference. I highly recommend it as additional reading should you find the need for a deeper explanation than that provided in this section. The reason it is so difficult for us is two-fold. First, we need our brains to grasp the concept that we spend our daily work chasing something different from what we truly want and second, there is a grey zone which can be hard to identify.

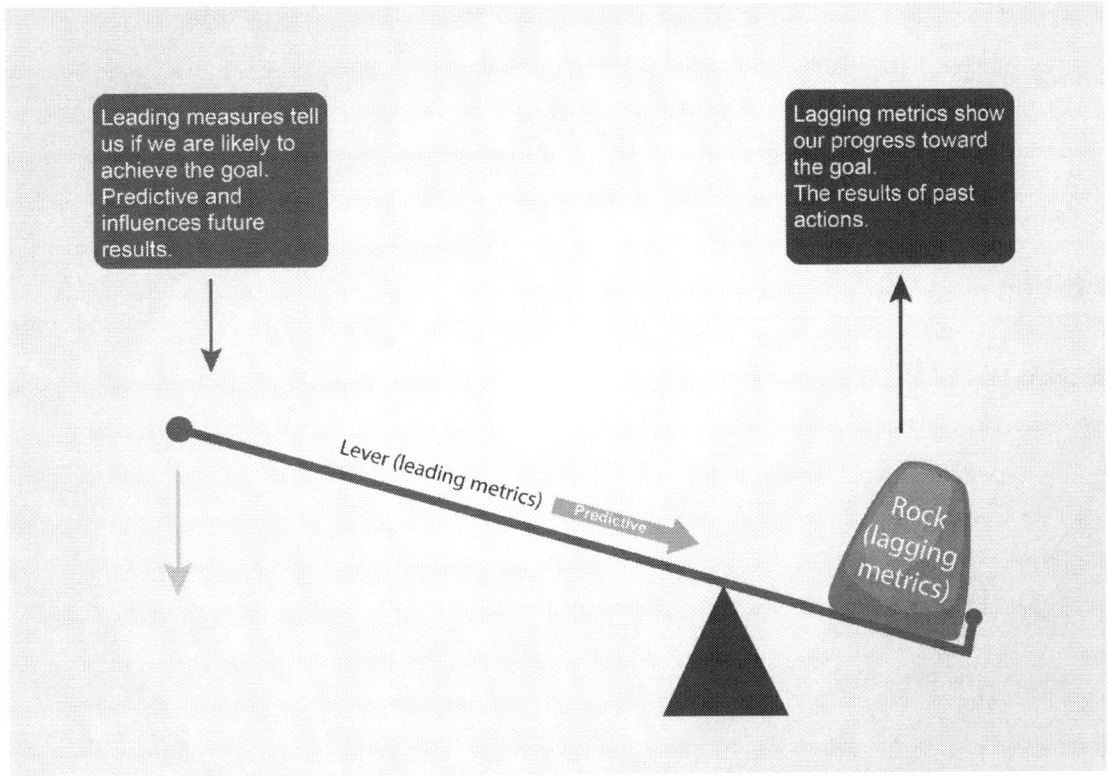

Figure 33: Leading vs. Lagging indicators

As you might recall from the first part of this chapter that we established a Challenge which included only the leading Process metrics:

Title: Continuous feedback

Date: October 16th

Process metrics:

- From 0% to 60% quantitative engagement analytics on deployed features
- From 0% to 40% qualitative validation of features with end users during implementation
- From 15% to 50% qualitative validation with early adopters after deployment

But we did not yet ask the question "As a customer, end user or sponsor of your service, how will I notice a difference when you have successfully reached your Challenge?" Yet there is a reason why we are first and foremost looking at the Process metrics.

You might say that working with Toyota Kata, we put things upside down. No customer ever asked for "one-by-one flow" but still, that is what Toyota has been chasing for 60+ years. The Vision does not say anything about increased profit, shareholder value, throughput, higher Net Promoter Score (NPS) or better quality. That is because the Vision deals with the Process and not the Outcome of that process. Similarly, customers are not interested in "quantitative engagement analytics" unless they actually own the product and are responsible for, e.g., updating content.

Working with Toyota Kata is a process focus. The firm belief is that if we take one step in the direction of our Process Vision, the side effect will be that we get higher throughput, better quality, etc. That is why they call Process metrics for leading indicators in 4DX.

But why not focus on Outcome metrics like quality, throughput or profit? On the surface, it seems logical to focus on the end result and not the process behind it. There are many reasons, but the four main ones are:

- **1. They are lagging indicators**. This means that if we do something today, it is going to take weeks or even months before those metrics will change. If you start automating your test suite today, you will probably not see either quality or throughput metrics improve in the near future and you might see throughput drop while you invest time and effort into writing the tests. The 2018 State of DevOps Report (Mann, Stahnke, Brown, & Kersten, 2018) reveals that in fact throughput will be lower and the rate of manual testing will increase as you navigate through the initial phases of automation. If we want Process improvement to be motivating and engaging, we must work with dials we can move. If we want to be able to perform experiments and validate the results, we cannot wait weeks before validating whether it was a good or bad idea or give in to panic arising from the previously mentioned J-curve of successful change (see Chapter 2).
- **2. They are easy to game**. In my experience, it is unlikely that people will consciously try to "game" Outcome metrics unless actual monetary incentives are tied to achieving them. But the unconscious part of our brains can easily play tricks on us, from registering a defect as an

enhancement to lower the defect rate, to estimating a feature slightly higher to increase throughput. We might not even think about it but the old saying "You get what you measure" can trigger some strange behaviors. In the unlikely event that a company should get the very bad idea to tie actual monetary incentives to achieving an Outcome goal, both conscious and unconscious creativity in pretty-printing that metric has no bounds, as most Outcome metrics can be very easily gamed.

- **3. They may tempt you to do short-term sub-optimization**. Most Outcome metrics can be improved by short term sub-optimization. You might, e.g., push to finish more work at the expense of the pipeline of new work. You might sacrifice throughput to increase quality (or the other way around). Or you might delay writing off expenses to make profit look bigger. Shareholder value is a great example of this. Companies that focus on shareholder value are less likely to get it over the long term than companies not focusing on it as a goal (Stout, 2012).

- **4. Variability.** Even with four-week cycles, we might not get a valid picture, as lagging indicators are influenced by both a degree of variability and chance/luck. Because chance does play a role in defect numbers, throughput (velocity), cycle time, value and predictability, they all suffer from the problem known as "regression toward the mean". That means if you have had two Sprint velocities far below normal, you are statistically much more likely to do better next time, without changing a thing, in the same way that a golf player who had a poor first round is more likely to do better and the golf player who played a brilliant first round is likely to get a lower score in the second. So, if you initiate a Toyota Kata Challenge based on two Sprints with low velocity, you are almost guaranteed improvements no matter what you do (at least in the short term).

But that does not mean that Outcome metrics are not useful. The last thing we want is to create Process for Process's sake. But instead of making Outcome metrics our only goal, we use them to check on whether our Process optimizations are generating the expected results. In this way, we use Outcome metrics as a sanity check on the validity of our Process goals. Being a lagging indicator, it is typically not something we can check every day but maybe bi-weekly or once a month. In that way, we can keep our focus on improving our leading Process metrics in our daily work and use Outcome metrics to check the validity of those goals on a more infrequent basis.

An important thing to understand is that there are first- and second-level Outcome metrics.

The first level deals with the overall success of the company. They typically include elements like:

- Revenue
- Gross Margin

- Sales Growth

- ....

They are typically influenced by both our internal capabilities as well as the market in general. Essentially, we can do everything right but if the overall economy is failing, we might still experience a decline in sales. The second level Outcome metrics are still lagging Outcome metrics but more directly related to the Process capabilities. We often separate these into objective and subjective:

Objective second level:

- Throughput – you get more/cheaper
- Cycle/Lead Time – you get it faster
- Quality/Defect Rate – you get it at a better quality
- Predictability – you get a more predictable service
- Value Delivered (can be difficult to measure) – you get something better suited to your needs
- Mean Time to Recovery – you get a more stable service
- Deployment Frequency – you get it more often

Subjective second level:

- Net Promoter Score (NPS) – you get more promoters/you get more customers
- Employee Net Promoter Score (eNPS) – you can keep and attract qualified employees
- Product Reviews – people like your products

It is important to recognize that these Outcome metrics are from the perspective of "IT as a service", meaning that our customers are requesting the actual features and defect fixes we are making. It might be an employee in a bank who experiences fewer errors in the software, a lawyer who was able to gather relevant information for a case with a new AI feature or the insurance company that managed to stay compliant with recent legal regulations because features were finished on time.

A customer using your online shop probably cares less about the throughput or cycle time of new features but might care a lot about being able to complete the purchase without system errors. Conversion rate or customer engagement is, thus, e.g., a subcategory of "Value delivered" as it is a way of measuring our ability to deliver features that provide more business value. David Anderson uses the term "Customer fitness criteria" to describe second-level Outcome metrics that can serve as real Key Performance Indicators (KPIs). They are the ones that make customers choose your service over the competitor's and we expect any change in those to be reflected in the first-level Outcome metrics and, thus, in the bottom line.

The key thing to understand is that though we really want to see these metrics improve, it is only considered a side effect in the context of Toyota Kata. Improvements registered in these metrics are the result of building the process capabilities which are the focus of our daily work.

Looking at the content of the Process Vision example in the previous chapter, all elements represent capabilities that are not very relevant from a customer perspective but that we believe will make our organization work at its top performance. Though we might imagine that our customers are interested in our automated test and deployment frameworks or our ability to get continuous feedback, they are often much more interested in the end result. In fact, customers would probably choose not to be involved in giving feedback at all if we could deliver a perfect product to them without any kind of interaction. That is why we call the following elements leading Process metrics and why we choose to strive for those capabilities because we have a validated hypothesis that they will ultimately optimize the Outcome metrics we really want. Examples of specific leading Process metrics include:

- Test coverage –> faster regression testing –> shorter lead time
- Feedback response time –> building the right thing (Value)
- Defect root cause fixes –> fewer future defects
- Work In Progress –> connected to lead time
- DoR and DoD compliance –> fewer defects, value
- Blocked items and time –> shorter lead time, higher throughput
- Manual deployment steps –> higher deployment frequency, higher throughput
- Static code health metrics –> shorter lead time, better quality
- Speed of CI build –> faster feedback –> better quality, higher throughput
- Process-step cycle time –> shorter lead time
- Open incidents older than one day –> higher quality, lower cycle time
- ….

An interesting observation is that most organizations seek to establish control using metrics but simply fail to choose metrics that are aligned with their goal of long-term performance. In many cases, metrics are chosen that are counterproductive and that make performance worse. The most obvious one is the utilization of individuals within their area of expertise. Though it might generate a short-term success through an increased number of billable hours, the long-term results are unstable teams, increased coordination overhead, high churn, and lower quality and throughput. You will find many examples of metrics in Chapter 24, where we present an inspiration catalog of Challenges and Target Conditions, including the associated process metrics.

Cycle time – the "grey area"

As if the topic of lagging and leading indicators and Outcome and Process metrics wasn't difficult enough to grasp, a grey area exists where the same metric might be placed in both the Outcome and the Process category depending on the context. In a context in which work items are flowing through the system in a matter of hours or days "cycle time" can be used as a process metric to drive improvement because it is a powerful indicator of flow. We might, therefore, establish a Target Condition to reduce the average cycle time of User Stories from six to four days. It is, however, also an Outcome metric because it demonstrates our ability to respond rapidly to customer demands. If, however, cycle time is measured in weeks or months, it would be a poor leading indicator, as it would probably take weeks before we could validate the result. In this case. it could still make sense to focus on the cycle time of an individual process step (e.g., test) and set a Target Condition to bring that down. Cycle time remains one of the most effective metrics to focus on both the Outcome and Process levels, as a decrease in cycle time is highly valuable at both the Outcome and Process levels. However, it is important to get a good picture of the Current Condition to be able to use it correctly.

The problem of measuring "building the right thing" (Value)

In the "Continuous feedback" example, finding a good and objective Outcome metric can be quite difficult. If we strengthen the feedback loop, we must assume that we can use that feedback to build better features or to enhance existing ones. If we get both qualitative and quantitative insights on our end users, we can get away from speculating about their needs and toward validating hypotheses and assumptions. From increased knowledge of user engagement and usage patterns we can optimize the user experience and reduce support calls. But of all the possible Outcome metrics mentioned, "Value" is by far the most difficult one to measure and isolate. If we get more customers, is it then the result of the general Process improvement or "just" the latest deployed feature? Are we seeing an improvement in the Net Promoter Score (NPS) because we are getting better at matching end-user needs or simply because we chose to lower the cost of our service? Are the number of support calls lower because we got quantitative feedback on usage patterns and made key adjustments or because we launched a new FAQ?

Only the most mature organizations have the data and tools available to answer questions like that and even a small amount of batching can make it very difficult to isolate the effect. Often, when we find ourselves in situations in which the expected Outcome of our Process improvement work is "Value", we might choose to leave Outcome metrics out of the Challenge definition and write a "Theme" only, which could, e.g., be "Value". With all the focus on objective metrics, this might come off as a weak statement. Had the expected Outcome been related to throughput, quality, cycle time or predictability, it would have been easy to find objective metrics, as none of those are difficult to measure. But because the problem of assigning metrics to Value is a real-life scenario that we encounter in some cases, I used this example to demonstrate what we might do in those situations. It is not ideal, but neither is assigning a metric that we cannot isolate or trust.

Research does exist on how to isolate the effect of specific changes. The best book on the subject is "How to Measure Anything" by Douglas W. Hubbard. It presents a series of strategies to measure anything from the value of Brand awareness to releasing a specific product. It includes matching changes to expected outcomes and measuring the relationship. If, e.g., you expect increased user engagement from our Continuous Feedback Challenge, your ability to do that in real life should follow the progress of that metric. But, as stated previously, it takes a high level of organizational maturity to do this in real life at an acceptable cost. The truth is that being able to measure and isolate the Outcome metric "better value" is a Challenge topic of its own.

Specific solution design or desirable capability? Getting the level of abstraction for the Challenge right

The effect of establishing Agile process capabilities has been proven many times over and there is a reason that companies across the world are using Agile to release themselves from traditional command-and-control patterns and enable innovation, reduce cycle time and increase the joy of work.

Recent research has even tied specific Agile and Lean capabilities to organizational performance. Though there is always an element of confirmation bias, I recommend reading the 2018 book "Accelerate" (Forsgren, Humble, & Kim, 2018) to get deeper insight into the specific capabilities. Fortunately, almost all the listed capabilities in the book tie nicely with the Agile Vision presented previously and, being at an even more detailed level, they serve as an excellent inspiration for choosing the actual Challenges.

Yet that comes with a word of warning. There is a reason why we apply Outcome metrics at the Challenge level. Though the concepts of automation, feedback, visualization and limiting WIP are all well-proven, there is no guarantee that we implement them in a sensible way. There will always be an element of solution design built into a Challenge or Target Condition as we strive to be specific and concrete. I have, e.g., seen teams optimizing for code coverage ending up with thousands of tests that took hours to run but rarely helped identify any real problems with the code. One of the toughest parts of coaching Toyota Kata is that you cannot make a rulebook or checklist that will clearly show you when you are at the right level of abstraction.

There is just one way to go – practice, practice, practice and with time you will get a feeling for getting it right. Hopefully, the examples in this book will help speed up that learning process. We now know that a large catalog of specific examples is a great help. That is why all of Chapter 24 is dedicated to that. The essence is that you want a Challenge that is aligned with the Vision and that is high-level enough to allow implementation details to emerge, but that is also specific and measurable so that it sets a direction and you can determine whether you are achieving it or not.

Learning objectives and questions for real-life application of the Challenge

I hope that through this rather long chapter, you have realized the importance of setting a realistically ambitious Challenge. Before we move on, it is time to reflect on the learning objectives so far. By now you should have realized that:

- A Challenge represents one step in the direction of the Vision.

- A Challenge should include both Outcome (lagging) and Process (leading) metrics.

- A Challenge should be realistically ambitious – daring you to move outside the box while being something you believe you can achieve.

- Included Process metrics should be as objective as possible, and you should be able to observe changes at least one or two times per week.

Before you continue, write your answers to the following questions to the best of your ability:

- What is the purpose of establishing a Challenge?

- What is the recommended duration of a Challenge in an Agile setting?

- What is the difference between Process and Outcome metrics?

- How can we gather Current Condition data effectively?

- Write down an example of a Challenge that would be relevant in your context. Take a guess at the actual numbers. It is not important that you select the most important topic. It is just an exercise to practice working with the concept. Make sure to include:
    - Date
    - Process metrics (use "from x to y" format)
    - Outcome metrics (use "from x to y" format)

- Looking at the Vision from the previous chapter, what Challenge topic do you think would have the greatest effect? Once you have established that, write:
    - How would you support that hypothesis?
    - How would you gather data about your Current Condition?
    - How would you create buy-in from the rest of the team/organization?

11. Target and Current Condition

The Target Condition should represent one step toward the identified Challenge, but you can add details and be more specific than the Challenge statement. Therefore, you will find that almost all the elements discussed at the Challenge level also apply on the level of the Target Condition. However, instead of using a simple "From x to y <details>", we use the Improvement Board to visualize the content in more detail.

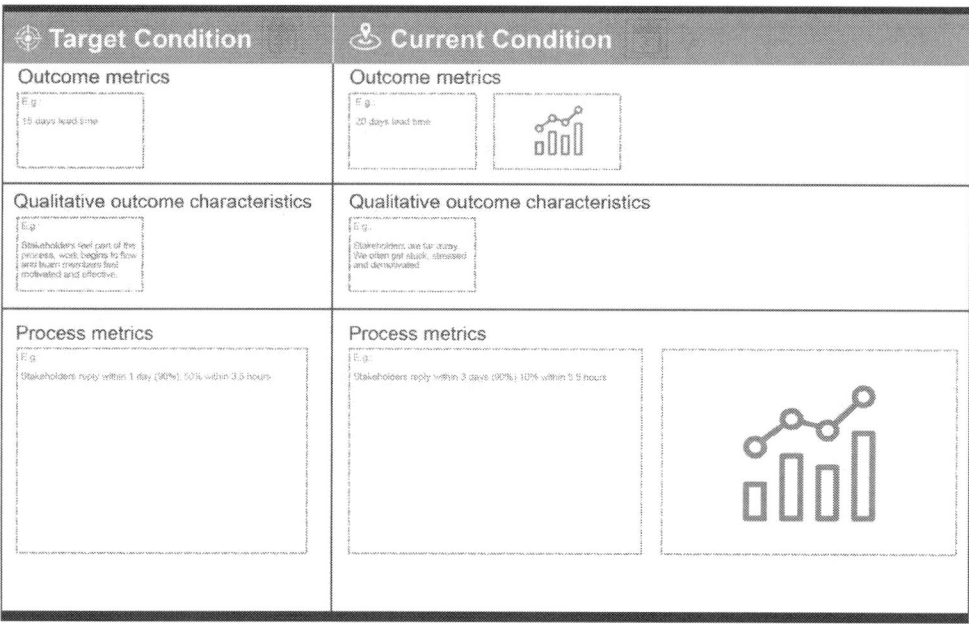

Figure 34: Current Condition and Target Condition divided in 3 sections

The next Target Condition is established at the Improvement Kata Planning meeting. The first part of setting the next Target Condition involves agreeing on the "Target Condition Focus", which is a specific field on the Improvement Board (shown in the figure below). It signals that for the next period, we will work only on that specific part of the Challenge. Remember that Toyota Kata is about focus, so we take the liberty of focusing our energy where it matters most and ignoring the remaining part of the Challenge for the duration of the Improvement Kata.

If we look at the Challenge example from the previous chapter, we can see that three elements are included at the Process level:

- From 0% to 60% quantitative engagement analytics on deployed features
- From 0% to 40% qualitative validation of features with end users during implementation
- From 15% to 50% qualitative validation with early adopters after deployment

We can choose a Target Condition focus that involves working on all three aspects of our Challenge, but often it makes more sense to focus on an individual aspect of the Challenge. Working on one aspect might also improve other parts of the Challenge, but it will be recognized only as a nice side effect and not as part of our chosen focus.

Let's assume that we choose to focus on "quantitative engagement analytics" for the first Target Condition on our new Challenge. In that case, we will simply write "quantitative engagement analytics" in the "Target Condition Focus" field on the Improvement Board. We do not include metrics and numbers because that is reserved for the Target and Current Condition fields on the board.

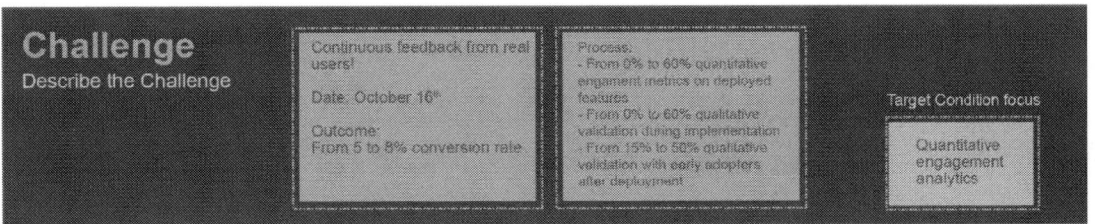

Figure 35: Continuous feedback Challenge example

Filling out the Target and Current Condition areas of the board starts with the easiest part – the dates. Because we work in four-week cycles, the Target Condition Date should be a simple matter of checking the Calendar. The Current Condition date indicates when our Current Condition data was last updated.

Once done with the simple matter of updating the dates, we move on to the more difficult part of setting a realistically ambitious Target Condition.

Looking at the Improvement Board, we start from the bottom, focusing on the Process metrics first. Our Target Condition should represent one step toward the Challenge but that does not mean we cannot add details or narrow the focus. Starting with the Target Condition first, it is an iterative exercise in which we switch back and forth between Target and Current. The result might look something like this:

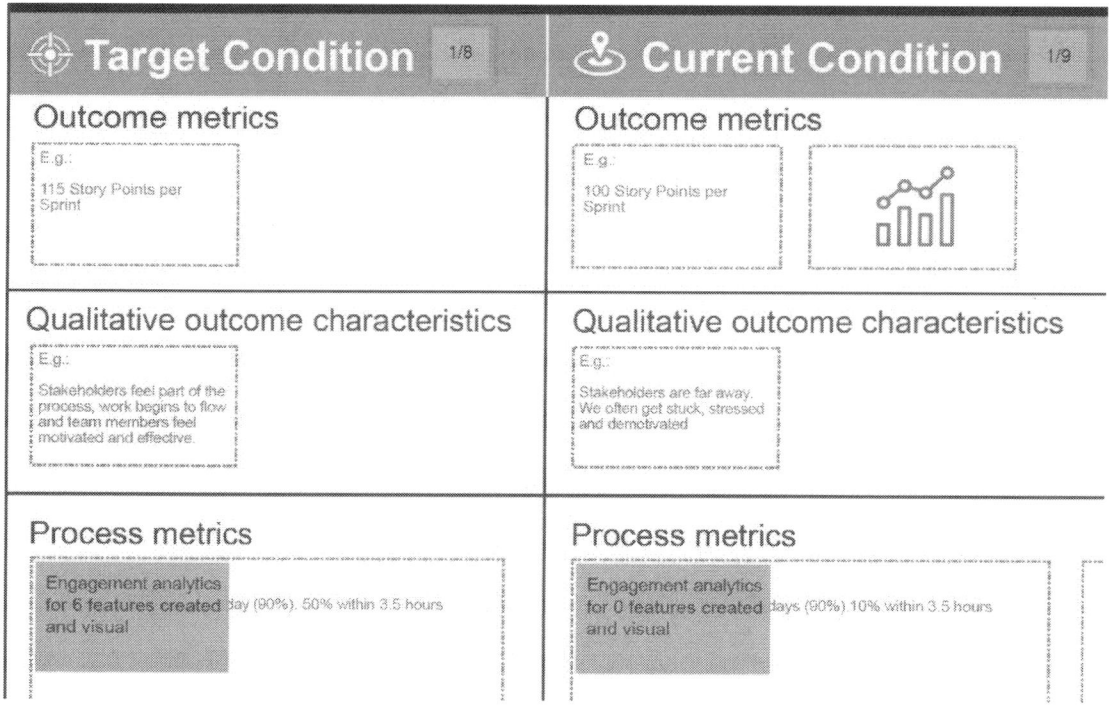

Figure 36: Continuous feedback Process metric example

But why not choose a percentage of new features? That is, after all, the true capability that we want to develop and the direction of the Challenge. Remember that the Target Condition is the most effective step toward the Challenge – not the only step. In this case, the team does not have the capability to create or visualize engagement analytics at all. To take the first step in that direction, it does not matter if they are doing it on already-deployed features or new ones. This way, they have the flexibility to choose the best path. In general, we have found that it is often better to initially focus on quantity rather than quality for the first Target Condition.

Another point is that they have purposely left out all implementation details. The Target Condition does not state where the metrics are visualized, which elements of engagement analysis should be included and so on. They consider it realistically ambitious if, at the end of the four weeks, they have analytics running for six features and the result is visual to the team.

We then move on to the qualitative part. This is where we ask questions like:

- What drives you toward this goal? What feeling do you get when you reach it?
- What do you hope to observe besides the metrics?
- Why is this important to you?

Being qualitative, we are not asking for metrics and objective statements but are instead allowing ourselves to discuss more subjective behaviors and feelings. The result could look something like this:

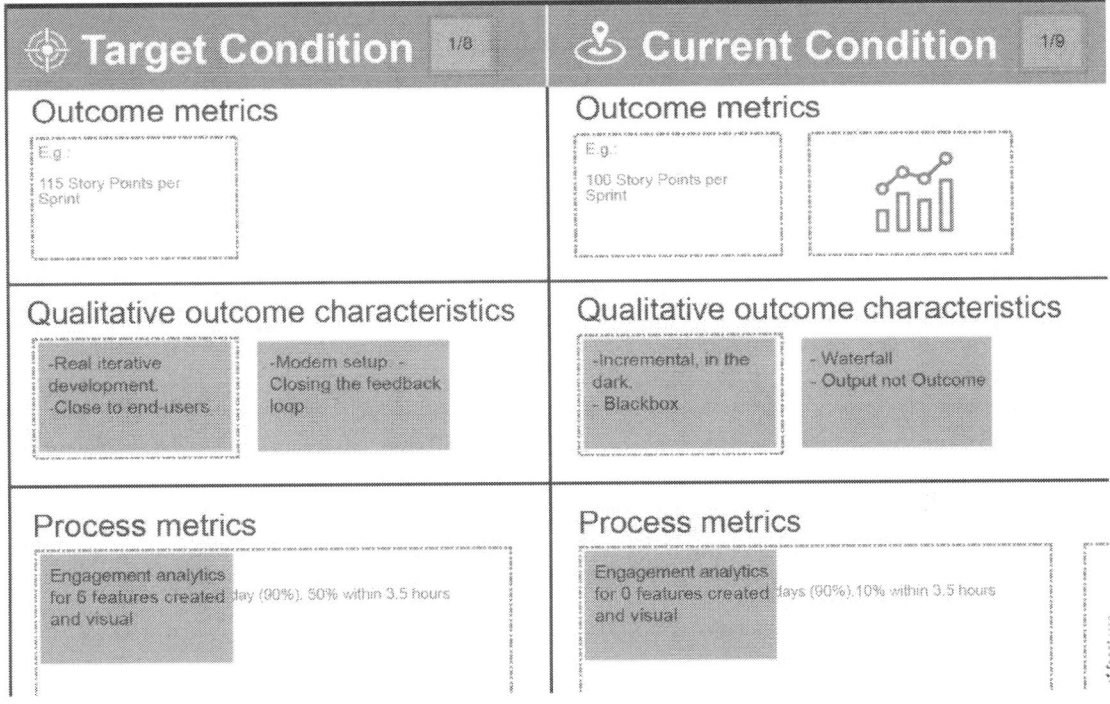

Figure 37: Continuous feedback qualitative characteristics example

Ideally, we should now move on to the aspect of Outcome metrics, but as we discovered earlier, that can be a very tricky thing when "better Value" is the expected goal. Had we expected higher throughput (velocity in Scrum), better quality, increased predictability, lower variance or shorter cycle/lead time, we would have had an easier time doing it. As mentioned previously, in cases in which we are not at a maturity level where it is possible to identify an objective Outcome metric, we have found the best alternative to clearly visualize this problem by writing only the theme and placing it between Target and Current. This way, we are clearly stating that we expect a specific Outcome but that we are not yet able to measure it. Not only is this a very honest way of doing it, but it is also clearly shows where we need to mature our process improvement skills – a great topic for the next Coaching Kata!

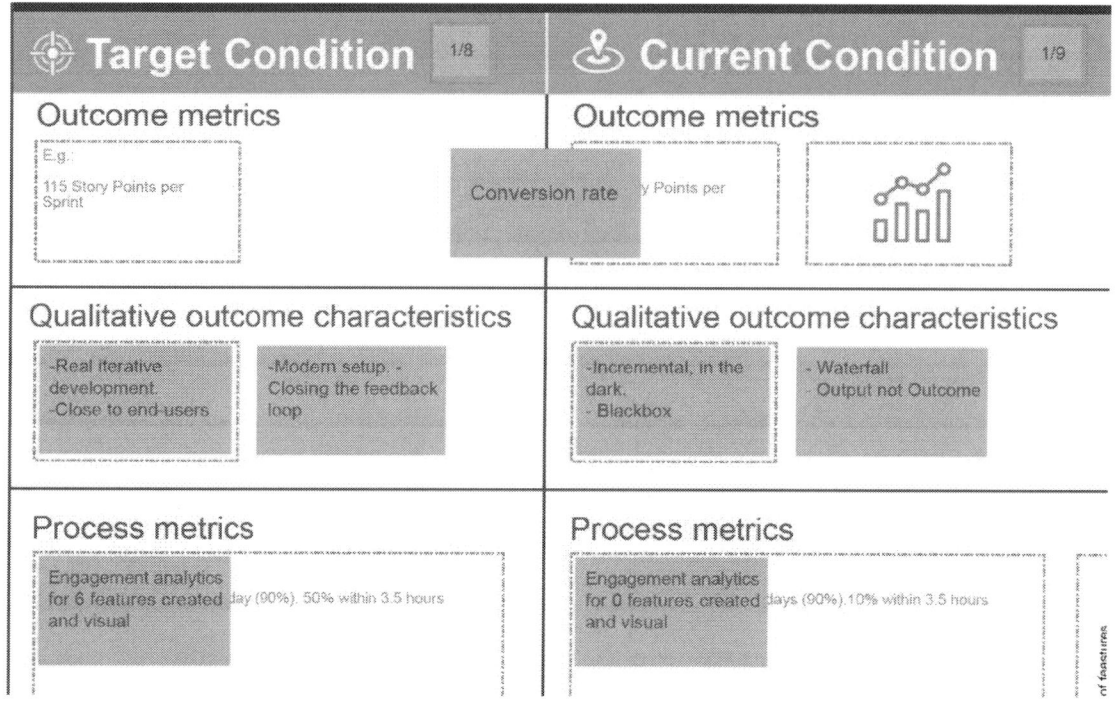

Figure 38: Continuous feedback unknown Outcome metric example

The Target Condition is a chance to dig deeper

In the previous chapter a team set the challenge:

- From 30% to 60% of started User Stories is the highest priority

As they start qualifying the first Target Condition, they investigate their Current Condition in more detail guided by the Process Vision elements of a perfectly balanced cross-functional team, with a minimum of work in progress. They find that:

- The Backlog consists of 10% type Y-work, 50% type X-work and 40% type Z-work.
- X-work waits an average of 4 weeks in "Sprint ready", compared to 1 week for Y and Z.
- X-work selected for the Sprint Backlog has a 50% chance of being finished within the Sprint, compared to 80% for Z-work and 95% for Y-work.

This might sound like a lot of work but using historical data and aiming for 80% accuracy in the numbers, they are not difficult to find. An analysis like the one above should be possible to complete in an hour or less with the right people available.

Looking specifically at the Vision elements of a perfectly balanced team with low WIP and the Current Condition they think about the process they would like to observe in 4 weeks and set themselves the following Target (We still include only the Process metrics to simplify things.)

Process metrics:

- From ? to ? User Stories in progress (includes: development, test, review)
- From 4 weeks to 1 week X-work wait time in "Sprint Ready"
- From 30% to 45% of started User Stories is the highest priority

They have included WIP limit and wait-time goals, which eliminates the risk of starting work without finishing it. Through the details in the Current Condition, the team also recognized that the main target is related to X-work and that the fact that it is often prioritized initially, but then waits in the "Ready" queue for extended periods.

It is OK to include elements in your Target Condition where information is missing. The team does not know its current average WIP and, thus, puts a question mark in that aspect. They know they must establish the capability of lowering WIP, but without available data, they cannot do that yet. Question marks in the Target Conditions and Challenges will later become an Obstacle on the Improvement Board because they must find the data to be able to set a valid Challenge and Target Condition. Ideally, this data should have been gathered during the "refinement" leading up to the Improvement Kata Planning meeting, but the real world is not perfect. In a Toyota Kata setting, it is better to acknowledge that we do not know than to come up with a wild guess.

Another important element is that they looked at the Vision and the desirable Future State first and then matched it to their Current Condition. Had they done it the other way around, they might have opted to try to solve all Current Condition problems instead. When you draw a Value Stream Map, you will find many problematic aspects of the process for even the most mature teams. The standard reaction is to want to fix them all. Going through the individual workflow steps, people will remember all the small problems that occurred during the past weeks: a failed deploy, an unfinished User Story, a bug that should not have made it to production, a false red build, an angry stakeholder or a disagreement about an implementation detail.

Our brains are programmed to extrapolate patterns from those tiny details, even when they are not there, and we are quick to identify both the cause and the fix. "What you see is all there is" is a famous quote from the book "Thinking Fast and Thinking Slow" (Kahneman, 2013). But we must resist that temptation and try to gain a more objective view of the situation. One outlier is not necessarily a pattern and though our Vision states that we should always be releasable, a single failed deploy due to a rare coincidence might not deserve four weeks of our attention. That is why we put so much effort into understanding the actual Current Condition and how work in general is flowing through our system. In a development setting, we will always experience outliers or chance events beyond our control, but in terms of Process improvement we are aiming for establishing capabilities that we can use again and again and that will make a real difference.

You can also tell from the example that they have chosen lead indicators that they believe will create a balanced flow. It is something they can influence directly and measure the changes with a high frequency. They have not stated how they will get to the operating pattern above but only the desirable Future State.

Current condition is "real time"

The value of visualizing actual trends and progress toward the target was something we underestimated in the beginning. Most teams would just update their Current condition and a previous "5" was now a "7". The problem is that we quickly forget where we came from. If we started from "5" and our goal is "25", by the time we have reached "15", we do not recognize how far we have come.

To harvest the drive, engagement and motivation generated by progress, it became a central principle to visualize the trends and not just a single number in the Current Condition. It does not really matter if you do it as a nice-looking printout from Excel or simply by hand on a piece of paper. The important thing is that everybody can easily see the progress.

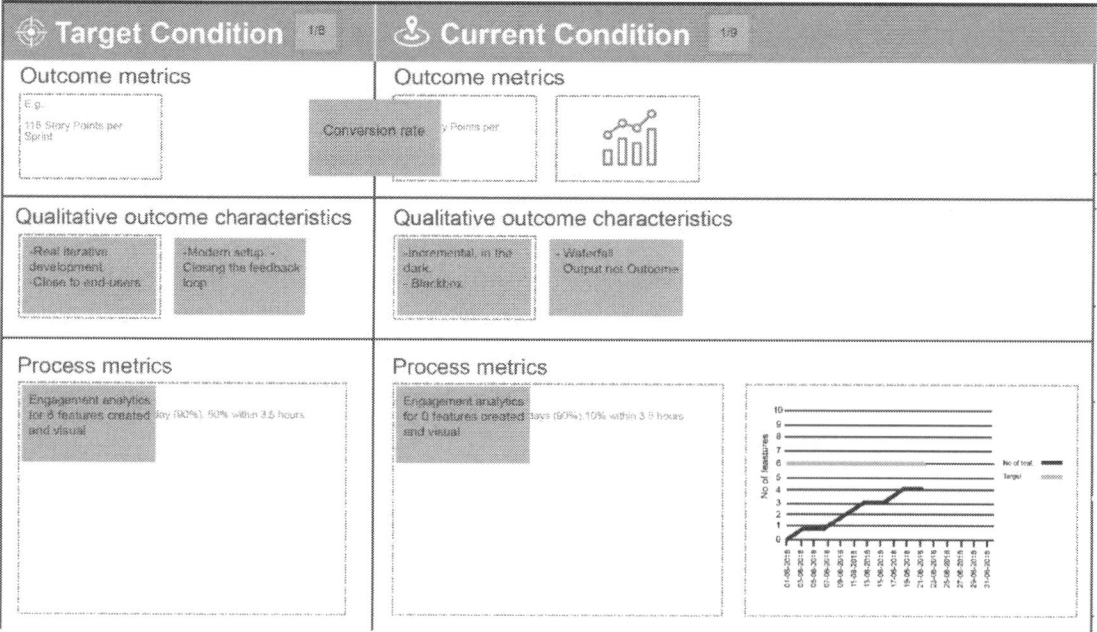

Figure 39: Continuous feedback Process metric graph example

Current Condition data accuracy

If you want to update the Current Condition continuously, naturally you need updated data. In some cases, the updated numbers are readily available from your chosen process tool (Jira, Target Process, LeanKit, TFS, etc.) but often they are collected manually through simple checkmarks on paper or a whiteboard. Again, we use the 80/20 principle, as we want 80% of the benefit of collecting metrics but with 20% of the effort.

One team was working with deployment and chose to gather metrics on the individual time spent on each deployment step. They added an additional seven items in their time-registration system and spent several hours trying to automate the update of an Excel graph based on that data. This took a long time and having to register time on seven different items felt like a strain on the team. When asked what they really aimed for ("good enough"), we found that we could get 80% of the insight by simply putting a checkmark on a piece of paper. So, be careful aiming for precision that you do not truly need. Naturally, this should already be taken into consideration when choosing the actual Target Condition metrics.

Here are some examples of data which can be collected on a whiteboard or piece of paper very easily without any need for tooling or complex registration beyond a field where you are able to write the number or checkmark with a pencil or whiteboard marker:

- Number of focused periods of two-and-a-half hours a day without meetings or external interruptions
- Current number of manual deployment steps
- Number of User Stories compliant with DoR or DoD
- Process/cycle time
- Number of User Stories with automated tests
- Broken WIP limits
- Root cause analyses or fixes
- Operation/maintenance tasks handled without help
- Support calls per day
- Number of "team" emails in personal inbox
- Response time from stakeholders

In general, I have found that you should explore simple manually collected metrics first. If you find that it is not doable because of the complexity of the domain, the frequency of updates or other factors, look to tooling or automation. We have found teams and managers drowning themselves in complexity when a simple and manual setup would have been enough. Remember that Challenge and Target Condition metrics are usually not there forever. They are used for a period to indicate whether you are moving closer to your goal.

Reaching the Target early or not at all

As stated previously, we have made adjustments to the teaching of the Toyota Kata framework to make the Improvement Kata resemble the well-known concept of a Scrum Sprint. As with a Scrum Sprint, there is no guarantee that our improvement capacity matches the Target Condition. This section deals with what to do in those cases. If you are familiar with Scrum, I trust that you will recognize many of the same aspects, though they have been adapted to the concept of Toyota Kata and Process improvement.

It can be very hard to judge what a truly realistic and ambitious Target Condition is when we are navigating unclear territory. I am sure that even a hardcore Toyota Sensei must sometimes face the fact that uncertainty is involved, as well as that the hard rule of "never changing but only adding to a Target Condition" must sometimes be bent to fit the real world.

Yet that does not mean that we expect failure. To quote Yoda from Star Wars: *"No! Try not! Do or DO NOT, There is no try."*

Once a Target Condition is set, we do everything we possibly can to reach it. That mindset is needed to tackle the Obstacles we will face. If we give up at the first sign of trouble, we will never push ourselves to think outside the box and release our creativity.

We might, e.g., find that the tool we had to measure code coverage on a legacy platform could be bought only through an expensive company license, which could take weeks or even months to get approval for, if ever. We could argue that it wasn't our fault that we missed the Target and then sit down and wait for the decision to be made while we work on something else instead. That would typically not be the behavior we expect in a Toyota Kata setting. Instead, we would expect suggestions like these to pop up:

- If we limit the functionality to the absolute essentials, could we code it ourselves?
- What if we called the supplier? They must be interested in selling company licenses. What better way to give a single team a chance to try it out?
- Are there other tools that might not be perfect but good enough – maybe an Open Source solution?
- There must be at least 15 other teams facing the same problem. Could we contact them and find out what they have done?

When the Target Condition proves over-ambitious

But even with the best efforts, we will sometimes discover that we cannot reach our Target. In those cases, we simply bring it up as a topic at the Daily Kata. Typically, the discussion will center on the topic of how to still reach a valid result but leaving out some details. Once an agreement is made, we officially Change the Target Condition and make a formal agreement to do everything in our power to reach the new one.

In cases in which the Target Condition is simply not valid anymore, we are left with two choices:

- If we realize this at a late point in time, we might simply pause our Improvement Kata work for the last few days and wait for the next Improvement Kata Planning.
- If we realize this at an early point, we might schedule a new Improvement Kata Planning Meeting.

Because an invalid Target Condition will often indicate a serious problem on the Challenge level, the Process Lead should expect to set aside considerable extra time to get the process back on track, especially if it includes setting a new Challenge.

When the Target Condition proves under-ambitious

Teams and Managers are often surprised when they realize their actual improvement capacity. They might have discussed and/or worked on an improvement for months or even years without really getting anywhere. They then set themselves a measurable Target Condition and work systematically to reach it with short experiments and daily evaluation. Within weeks, they have gone much further than they imagined. First, we want them to celebrate that instead of telling them that they did a poor job of planning their Target Condition and they should be more ambitious the next time. We tell them to open a bottle of champagne, buy some cake or do whatever they prefer to celebrate a job well done. Once they are done celebrating, we ask them to look at their Challenge and consider what they might realistically ambitiously add to their Target Condition with the time left until the next Improvement Kata Planning meeting.

That is the great thing about moving toward an even more ambitious longer-term Challenge goal: We can simply add from that pool of options.

Learning vs. Improvement

There is no doubt that in terms of motivation and engagement, Target Conditions that generate an actual improvement have proven much more effective. People like to see the effect of what they are doing and, though Process geeks like me can get a huge kick out of getting a deeper perspective on the Current Condition, most teams and managers are driven by seeing actual results. That is why we recommend that we strive to create Target Conditions that move the Challenge metrics and represent a clear step in that direction.

It is, however, important to acknowledge that we do not always find ourselves in that perfect situation. As previously mentioned we sometimes lack the data to qualify the Challenge, and getting that data in place becomes the first Obstacle to deal with. Or we might not understand the flow of value clearly enough. We always try to address these issues as part of the preparation for the Improvement Kata planning but not always with 100% success. In those cases, it is preferable to move ahead with a learning Target instead of postponing the Improvement Kata Planning meeting. We might, e.g., set a Target Condition to be able to:

- Visualize a workflow/Value stream map of the integrated test process, including numbers on cycle time, defect rate and completion rate
- Identify the main sources of defects
- Identify the main sources of interruptions to started work
- Identify deployment frequency, steps, the cycle time of each step and the failure rate
- Map the end-to-end Value Stream of the program across 10 teams

If most of your Target Conditions end up representing "just" learning, some warning bells should start to ring, as it equals the well-known analysis-paralysis we so often experience in product development. If it happens occasionally and is often limited to the first Target Condition, you should not consider it a problem. Learning can be a great step toward improvement but at some point, we must turn learning into actual results.

Learning objectives and questions for real-life application of Target and Current Condition

By now I hope you have a picture of how Toyota Kata might be applied to your situation, from establishing a Vision to working with the specific Target and Current Condition. From this chapter, I hope you gathered that:

- Target and Current Condition are symmetric and include both Outcome and Process metrics as well as qualitative observations.
- Qualitative observations are important because they state what is driving us toward our goal. This makes it unattractive to try to "game" the metrics, as we will not get what we want.
- Target Conditions should represent a real improvement in most cases.
- By reaching the Target Condition early, you can add to your goal by pulling in more aspects of the Challenge.
- Current Conditions is updated continuously and should display the actual trends and not just the latest number.

Before you continue, write your answers to the following questions to the best of your ability:

- What is the purpose of establishing a Target and Current Condition?
- What is the difference between a Challenge and a Target Condition?
- Why do we not include specific solutions in our Target Condition?
- What is the purpose of Visualizing Current Condition trends and not just the current number?
- Using your sample Challenge from the previous chapter, define the Target and Current Condition for a sample four-week goal (again, take a guess at the actual numbers). You are honing your ability to work with the format, so getting the exact numbers right is not important. Remember to include:
    o Date
    o Process metrics
    o Qualitative observations
    o Outcome metrics

12. Obstacles

Picture yourself navigating the unclear territory and discovering a river, mountain, swamp or waterfall that you must find a way to navigate. We have identified an Obstacle in our way, but we have not decided whether we want to build a boat, navigate around it, jump, swim, climb or fly. Obstacles are not solutions framed in a negative way; therefore, these statements would not qualify as Obstacles:

- "Story Point" is missing in our Definition of Ready.
- Stand-Up is held too early at 8:00.
- One refinement meeting per Sprint is not enough.
- There is no cake at retrospective.

They are all clearly solutions formulated as Obstacles. There are obviously Obstacles behind them, which could be:

- "Story Point" is missing in our Definition of Ready.
    - o Real Obstacle: We do not know our true workload capacity.
- Stand-Up is held too early at 8:00.
    - o Real Obstacle: We are not coordinated and work in different directions.
- One refinement meeting per Sprint is not enough.
    - o Real Obstacle: We experience idle time because work is not ready.
- There is no cake at retrospective.
    - o Real Obstacle: Process improvement is not done because people fall asleep (we can try cake at retrospectives but maybe they need Toyota Kata instead).

The real Obstacles can be overcome in various ways. Therefore, we should not limit ourselves to one possible solution when describing the Obstacle in front of us.

Often, we find that when we solve one Obstacle, many of the others we had identified are no longer relevant. That is because Obstacles are closely related and we tend to drastically overestimate the number of problems that stand in the way of our goals (Kahneman, 2013). You will, therefore, find that you are perfectly able to reach your Target Conditions without fixing all the Obstacles you observe or imagine. It is not unlikely for a team to identify six Obstacles but address only one or two of those and still reach the Target Condition.

Structured problem-solving or not?

Should we do 5-why or more structured problem-solving to get to the root cause of our Obstacles? This is a very relevant question and it started a heated debate among participants at the Kata-Con Europe Conference in Amsterdam in April 2018. It is possible to side with both arguments as there are two competing goals and perspectives at play which are both right and wrong depending on the actual context:

1. I agree with those against 5-why and structured problem-solving on the Obstacle level who say that because we are navigating unclear territory, we should be very careful treating this as a known path on which we can get our answers simply by digging deep enough. We must experiment to learn more. Thus, a very strict approach to, e.g., 5-why rarely makes sense. We can simply learn quicker and cheaper by testing and validating our hypotheses.

2. If we always stay on the surface and never try to dig deeper before starting our experiments, we risk treating symptoms and coming up with short-term solutions that won't generate a long-lasting effect. In one case, a team listed the Obstacle "The Product Owner is never present to answer our questions" in relationship to a Target Condition focusing on optimizing flow efficiency. They were about to launch experiments to address it when one team member politely asked, "Aren't we treating a symptom here?" After asking "why" a few times, they arrived at the deeper Obstacle that the Product Owner had become an information bottleneck. Not only did this inspire a much broader view of possible experiments, but it also avoided experiments that might have exacerbated an existing problem.

So, if you are relatively sure you are addressing an important and real Obstacle, do not force yourself to dig deeper and do 5-why or other problem-solving analyses. If, however, you find yourself in doubt, spend a few minutes discussing the roots of the problem and maybe even draw a 5-why analysis on the whiteboard, even if you stop after one or two "whys".

Cynefin and Obstacles – "How unclear is the territory?"

In Mike Rother's books, the Coach will often ask the Learner to find more data when faced with an Obstacle to better understand the Current Condition. This is also true in an Agile Context, where we tend to jump to conclusions, as we saw in the previous example. But we should be careful to not overdo it and to keep to the 80/20 rule of "good enough". In a product development context, we are not dealing with manufacturing machines but knowledge work. Therefore, Obstacles are often "softer" and where the context of manufacturing might encourage you to gather more data, we are sometimes better off trying things out to test the response.

This is because we are in the context of "complex adaptive systems". When humans interact, changing the system often has consequences that we could not identify beforehand. Using Dave Snowden's Cynefin framework, we are given a model to understand what type of approach is beneficial in which context (Snowden):

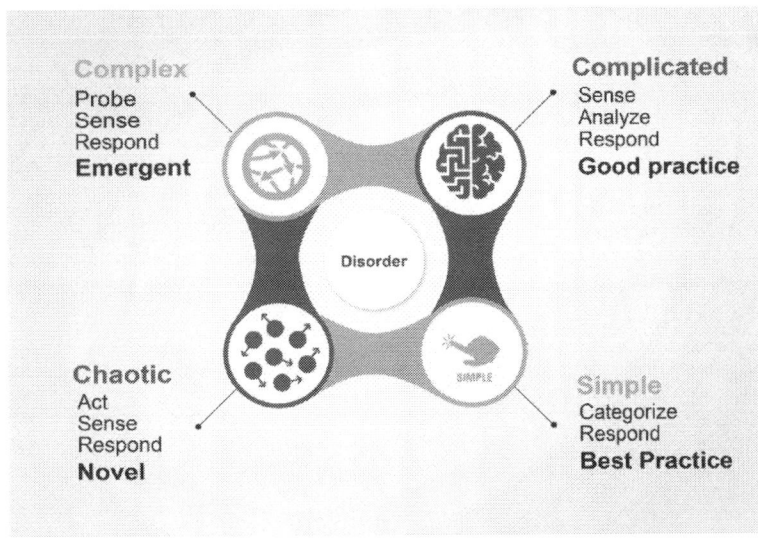

Figure 40: Cynefin, concept by Dave Snowden, adapted from
https://en.wikipedia.org/wiki/File:Cynefin.png

We often find ourselves going back and forth between a "Complicated Context" where more expert analysis will provide additional and valuable insights and the "Complex Context" where knowledge can be bought much cheaper by "probing" the system. You might even find yourself in the "Simple Context", in which you can plan your way forward by copying existing solutions. You will often recognize the "Simple Context" as the place in time when the only Obstacle affecting the Target Condition is "Time". Because we do not recommend including Time (which is essentially The Daily Whirlwind) as an Obstacle, you might choose to move directly on to experiments and leave the Obstacle part of the Experiment Records (PDCA) blank.

We might also venture into such unclear territory that it does not even make sense to discuss Obstacles, as the best thing we can do is jump right to very creative Experiments. In the "Chaotic Context", even probing is difficult, as we must make direct Changes to the system to better understand our context and navigate the unclear territory. In the "Chaotic Context", identifying and analyzing Obstacles will not provide much insight, as the unclear territory is so unknown that we do not know which Obstacles we face until we try something out. Teams insisting on using Obstacles in the Chaotic Context usually use phrases like "We do not know X" when describing what their

138

Experiments are targeting. That is also fine and can be a good solution to provide some element of focus.

Cynefin is a sense-making framework, and acknowledging that we can find ourselves in all four situations is very valuable. I have observed teams that were in the "Simple Context" but insisted on trying out wildly creative experiments. It wasn't until I asked them to look at their situation from the perspective of Cynefin that they realized what was truly going on. But the opposite has also occurred, in which a team was venturing into an unknown collaboration setup with their stakeholders and insisted on a deeper analysis to break the constraint. That did not happen because they were just anchoring themselves deeper and deeper in the Current Condition. Only when they took a leap of faith and dared try a new "visualization of decisions" did they move toward their target.

Most of the time, we find ourselves in the "Complex" or "Complicated Context" in which the use of Obstacles and varying degrees of analysis of those Obstacles makes good sense. If you are unable to identify an Obstacle try doing exactly what is written in your Target Condition. If you have set yourself and ambitious Target you should quickly realize that it is impossible and the reason why – that is your first Obstacle!

Looking at the example from earlier on the Challenge of "Continuous feedback from real users" and the Target Condition "Collecting engagement analytics on 6 features", we might list the following Obstacles:

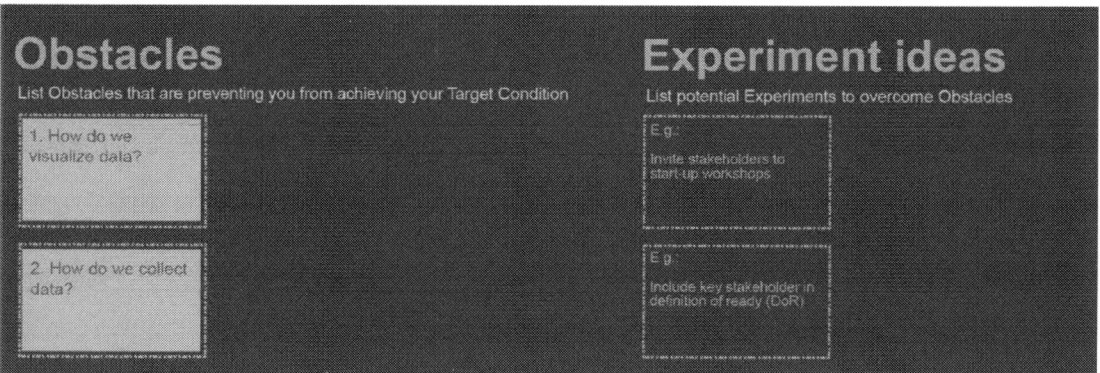

Figure 41: Moving Obstacle to Experiment Record

We have given each Obstacle an ID, as they were put on the board to identify which Experiments belong to which Obstacle. We have chosen to look at only one Obstacle because they are tightly coupled. By looking at how to collect data we might, e.g., very well also find the answer to the visualization part.

13. Experiments and Experiment Record (PDCA)

Once an Obstacle has been selected and moved to the Experiment Record, we start looking for Experiments to navigate around or through that Obstacle. In the case of a "Simple Context" or "Chaotic Context", you can choose to leave the Obstacle section blank and look directly at the Target Condition.

Remember that Obstacles and Experiments exist only to help focus our energy toward reaching our Target Condition. Therefore, we always keep our Target Condition in mind when selecting appropriate Experiments to make sure we do not divert from our goal. When coaching, we tend to ask these questions again and again in the beginning:

1. How will removing this Obstacle move you closer to your Target Condition?
2. If this experiment is a success, how will it move you closer to your Target Condition?

Quite often, Learners do not have a clear answer, as they have started to move down an alternative path that will not really help achieve the Target. They might have encountered an interesting problem and without realizing it started to solve it even though it is not related to the current Target Condition. That is good, as it provides a learning opportunity and proves the validity of having Coaching Kata.

We prefix each experiment with the ID of the Obstacle so that we can identify where they belong. In our previous example, this is not a problem, as we have selected only one Obstacle, but as we move through several Obstacles or simultaneously work on two, it is nice to indicate the relationship. The following example shows that we decided to focus on Obstacle "2. How do we collect data" and a brainstorm of possible Experiments generated the following output:

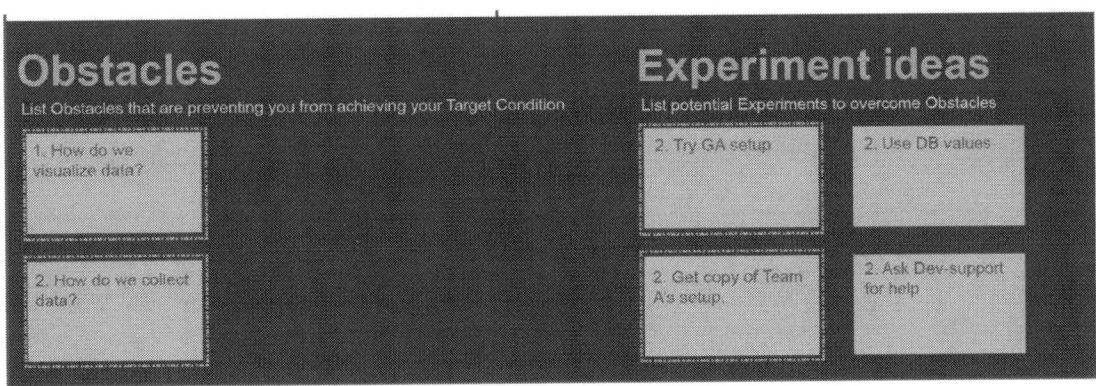

Figure 42: Generating ideas for experiments

If Experiments are in the "Ideas for experiments" section of the Improvement Board, they are still considered options. They are typically only a headline indicating the rough scope of the idea. When we select the Experiment with the highest potential, we move it to the Experiment Record. Once an Experiment is moved to the Experiment Record, it is no longer an option and details are added to define both the time and expected result. We are now committed to trying it out and validating the effect. Testing a hypothesis is the very core of scientific thinking but we can do this only if our hypothesis is described concretely enough to be validated.

When starting a new Experiment Record, we use one Post-it to define what we will do, when it will happen and who is responsible (if we are working in a team). We use the second Post-it to write what we expect to observe if the Experiment is a success and when we can validate the result. Including specific details on what, when and responsible person might sound overly detailed but research shows that were are 3 times more likely to carry out the change when we make a detailed plan compared to vague statements and good intentions (Münster, 2018). As with the Target Condition, we try to avoid vague statements like "more", "less", "increased" and "minimized" because we want to avoid the temptation to prettify the results by unconsciously lowering the bar for success.

It might look something like this:

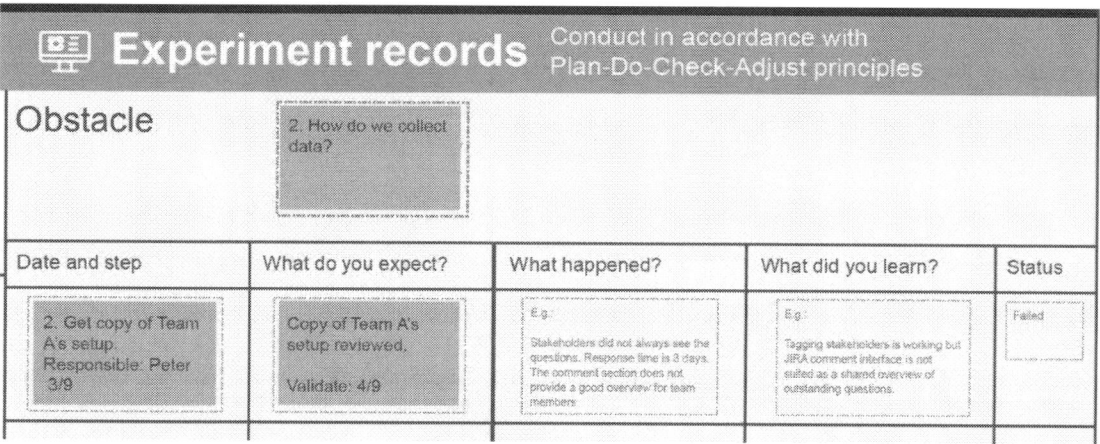

Figure 43: Starting Experiment

As you can see, the team plans only as far as the next learning point. Had they included the entire installation of Team A's setup on their own server, in the first experiment, it might have taken days to validate the result. This way, they can plan the first step and, from there, plan a better next step with the knowledge they have obtained. A bonus of the short feedback loop is that Continuous Improvement becomes a Daily Cycle and, thus, much more likely to be integrated as a natural part of the daily work.

141

When the Experiment has been carried out, we fill in the right side of the Experiment Record with the actual results and match them against our expectations. Part of the Toyota Kata mindset is building resistance to failure and accepting uncertainty and learning as a natural part of daily life. If we fail once every month, we tend to see it as a catastrophic event that should be avoided at all costs. If we fail every week, we teach our brains to acknowledge it as a natural thing and we can focus on learning from the outcome.

In our example, the first experiment "failed" to deliver on the expected outcome but was very successful from a learning perspective:

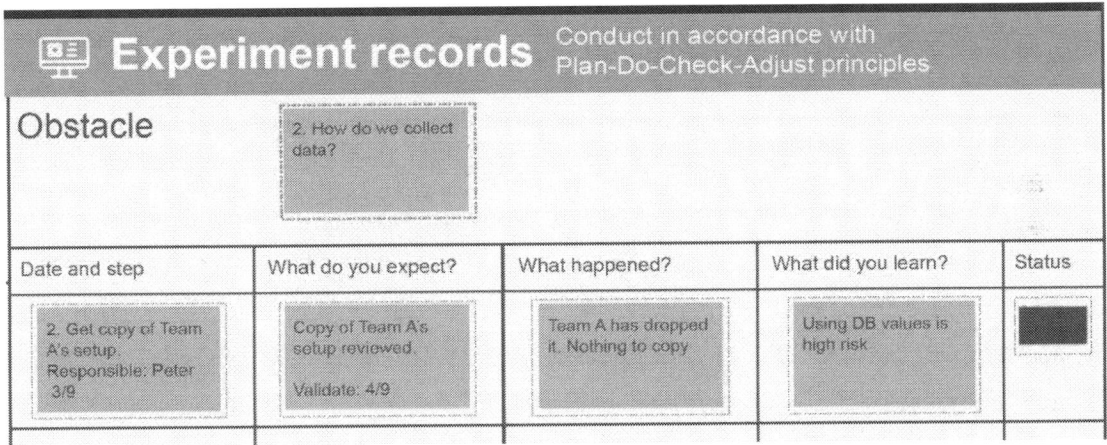

Figure 44: Evaluating the result of Experiment

The result shows the value of not planning beyond the first learning point. Already from asking about the code from Team A, they learned enough to take a better next step. It turned out that while Team A's solution was initially an easy and quick way to get some insights, it had proven way too difficult to update, expand and maintain in the long run. We bought a lot of information with very little effort!

This is a very important point. There is a reason they are called "Experiments" and sometimes it is much better to try something out than to spend hours discussing whether we should choose one Experiment or another. You are navigating unclear territory and that means you cannot and should not expect to get everything right in the first shot. As a ground rule, there should never be more than one ongoing Experiment per Obstacle. Multiple Experiments will make it next to impossible to separate the results and find out what is working and what is not. As with many other things in life, you can find situations in which it makes sense to break this rule, but out of the hundreds of Obstacles and Experiments I have witnessed, I can think of only a handful of situations in which it made good sense. In those cases:

142

- The experiments were typically low on effort but high on calendar time.
- The results could be clearly separated.
- Two options with high uncertainty and low cost seemed equally valid, the results could be separated and trying out both would buy information faster (much like set-based development).

This leads us to another important point that it took us a long time to find a way to communicate effectively. Looking back to the Personal Health Example, the fact that trial practice in the running club was an initial success does not necessarily prove that the Obstacle has been solved and that Adam should pay the fee for joining the running club. Often, we must repeat the same experiment several times with small alterations to make sure we have indeed found a sustainable way of addressing the Obstacle. Here are a few examples of such cases:

- We might have experienced success with Pair Programming for knowledge sharing but need to try it with a wider range of team members before declaring it a success.
- We might have found that the new test tool could run sample tests 10 times faster but need to include different variants of test.
- We failed the Experiment of getting feedback from an early adopter during development but need to try it with another person to determine whether it was just a special case.
- Pair refinement worked well in the first try but is it also a success with the more complex part of the domain?

Some teams have hurried on to the next Obstacle and the next Experiment as soon as they saw initial signs of success. This generated so many unstable process changes that they could hardly keep up with them and most were never established as part of the routine.

Here are a couple of good recommendations for successful Experiments:

1. Make them as short as possible. Don't plan further than the next learning point that will enable you to take a better next step than you can right now. You can add the next step later when you know more.
2. An Experiment does not have to solve the Obstacle but should simply be a step in that direction. You are navigating unclear territory, so we expect to learn as we proceed.
3. Always keep the Target Condition in mind. It is easy to get sidetracked and start working on Obstacles and Experiment that will not move you toward your Target Condition.
4. Build resistance to failure by daring to Experiment and learn. If we can test and validate an assumption today, maybe go ahead and skip a 20-minute discussion with seven people present to judge whether it is a good idea or not.

5. Remember Cynefin! If you are at the narrow end of the Cone of Uncertainty and find yourself in the "Simple Context", it is OK to have predictable Experiments with a high chance of success. Instead, celebrate the fact that you are moving quickly toward your Target Condition. The opposite is true when you are closer to the Chaotic Context.

6. Be very specific in terms of what you will do and what you expect as a result. Ideally, a successful Experiment should improve the chosen metrics in your Target Condition, but often we do get immediate validation in a knowledge work context. But still we should always ask ourselves the questions "If this is a success, how can I see it?" and "What has changed? What do I get?"

7. Focus on results, not the people involved. Remember that there is no "I" in team. If the team benefits, it matters less who was involved in executing the Experiment. We are aiming to make the team more effective, and sometimes the best way to do that is to have a few people focusing on the improvement or to sacrifice individual productivity to share knowledge or balance the workload. It is not the goal of Toyota Kata to have the entire team involved at all times.

In most Agile organizations, there is a tendency for people to fall into the trap of thinking of everything in iterations of two or three weeks. It seems that Scrum and other methods with a fixed iteration cadence have programmed people to the extent that it is difficult to break out of this shell. If we are to apply Toyota Kata successfully we must break this habit. If one experiment takes two weeks to execute and validate, we can do between only two and four in the four weeks we are trying to reach our Target Condition (given that we work on one or two Obstacles at the same time). We found that the following guideline was a good enabler for planning short Experiments that focused on reaching the next learning point:

Expected experiment duration (execution + validation) in workdays:

- At least 1 in 10 experiments should take 1 day or less
- At least 5 in 10 experiments should take 3 days or less
- At least 19 in 20 experiments should take 5 days or less
- No experiments should take longer than 10 days.

This means that we expect a maximum of one in 20 experiments to last more than a workweek and that more than half should be executed and validated within three workdays. The advice given above will help do that, but slicing experiments is a skill that can be perfected only through daily practice. In that way, it is much like User Stories. In the beginning, it seems almost impossible to develop a useful feature within a Scrum Sprint but with time and practice, a majority of teams are able to slice most down to a few days of work. Some will argue that it cannot be done, and experiments will often be longer at the beginning, but it is essential to keep striving for shorter cycles, as this is a key prerequisite for establishing a culture of true continuous improvement and navigating through the unclear territory.

Here are a couple of examples of taking smaller steps:

- Carl won't be here tomorrow; can Henrik do it instead?
- Do we need to try pair refinement for a week, or will we have learned something from doing it just once or twice? Is anything keeping us from trying it out today?
- If we need a session with all five people, it will not be until 10 days from now. Can we learn anything from doing it with three people in two days instead?
- Ideally, we would test the suggestion for a new review process on both major defects, and User Stories from all three product segments, but would we learn anything from just doing it on a defect and the next User Story?
- What is keeping us all from trying out Pair Programming for two hours tomorrow morning? Would we learn anything from that?
- Can we call them now and ask instead of writing an email later?
- Do we need to install the tool to reach the first learning point, or could we simply check on whether somebody has ever used it on our legacy platform?
- Maybe the first experiment is to see if people will actually "accept" the meeting. If nobody accepts, we will need to take a different next step anyway.

When we face an Obstacle like "We do not know 'x'" we often refer to the related experiment as a "go-and-see" Experiment, since we aim to find out more but are not making any changes to the process. Experiments like doing exactly what is written in the Target Condition are called "exploratory" as we are simply probing the context to identify the first Obstacle (Rother, 2018). Most experiments fall into the category of "hypothesis" as we aim to validate it against our system.

Should the Experiments also be on the Kanban or Scrum Board?

In the latest version of the Scrum Guide, it has been made an explicit policy that at least one improvement should be on the Sprint Backlog. Also, many teams find it useful to have one place where all ongoing work is visualized. So, should we duplicate the Experiments from the Toyota Kata Improvement Board, so they are also visible on the board where User Stories and Defects are visualized (the Scrum Board, Kanban Board, Sprint Board…)?

The answer to this question is very simple. Do what makes sense in your context. If you do not mind the double bookkeeping of having the same item in two different places, go ahead. If, on the other hand, you find that it is advantageous to separate things clearly and to represent the Daily Whirlwind in one place and Improvements in another, that also works. The only thing we do not want to see is trying to plan and prioritize Experiments on the Sprint Backlog in the Sprint Planning meeting. That goes against the very nature of Toyota Kata, as that would imply that your Target Condition can be reached by carefully planning the road from A to B.

Using Success Cards to celebrate success and make changes "stick"

Many teams and organizations are not always good at remembering to celebrate success. We make an excellent process change that made a huge difference and two weeks later we have all but forgotten what our process used to be like. Or we learn a lot from a failed experiment which enables us to take a much better step and soon after we are discussing the value of short experiment cycles. One team went from finishing 50% to 95% of work without blockers and doubled their throughput; one month later, they were doubting the effect of improvement work. To more easily get the motivation and enjoyment from celebrating success as well as make changes "stick", Adam Light and Kathy Iberle introduced the concept of "Success Cards" which I find a great addition to working with experiments in a Toyota Kata setting (or maybe just in general).

What is a Success Card?

Success Cards help Coaches, Learners and teams recognize and celebrate progress. For each successful process change, a Success Card is created on a four-by-six-inch or five-by-eight-inch card and posted under the Improvement Board. Because change happens in such small increments, a physical record makes the steady progress more visible. The Success Card format requires the Learner to explain what they learned and how that led to process change.

SAMPLE SUCCESS CARDS:

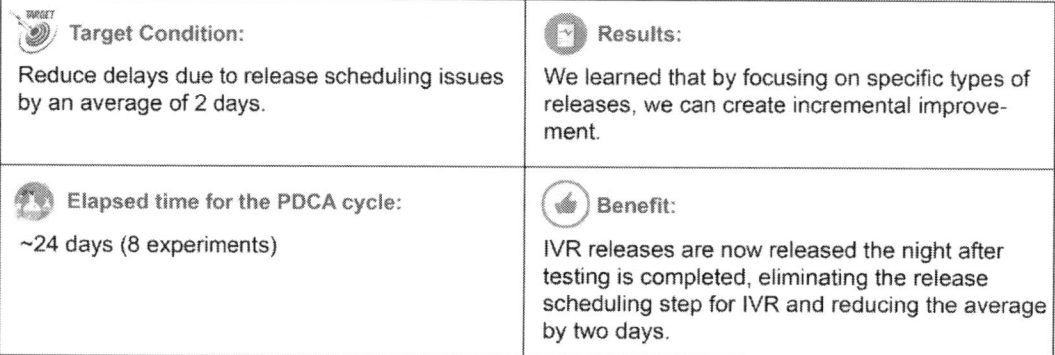

🎯 Target Condition:	☑ Results:
Reduce delays due to release scheduling issues by an average of 2 days.	We learned that by focusing on specific types of releases, we can create incremental improvement.
♻ Elapsed time for the PDCA cycle:	👍 Benefit:
~24 days (8 experiments)	IVR releases are now released the night after testing is completed, eliminating the release scheduling step for IVR and reducing the average by two days.

Figure 45: Success Card example 1

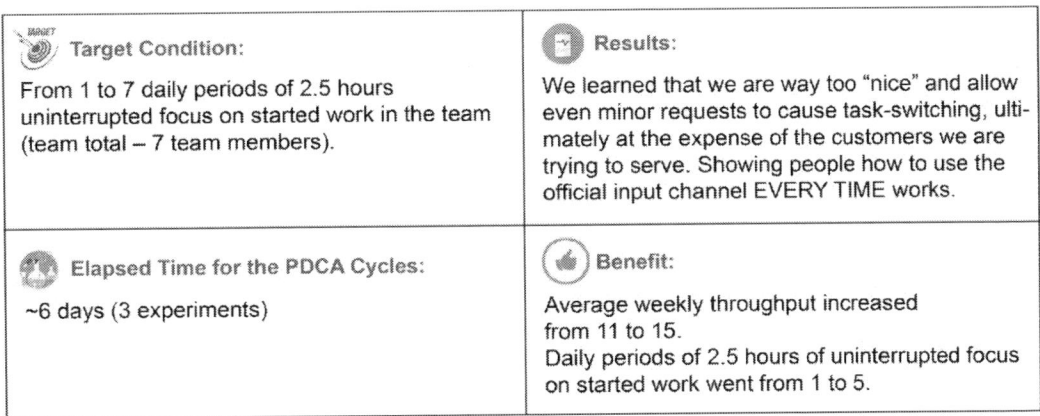

Target Condition: From 1 to 7 daily periods of 2.5 hours uninterrupted focus on started work in the team (team total – 7 team members).	Results: We learned that we are way too "nice" and allow even minor requests to cause task-switching, ultimately at the expense of the customers we are trying to serve. Showing people how to use the official input channel EVERY TIME works.
Elapsed Time for the PDCA Cycles: ~6 days (3 experiments)	Benefit: Average weekly throughput increased from 11 to 15. Daily periods of 2.5 hours of uninterrupted focus on started work went from 1 to 5.

Figure 46: Success Card example 2

Basically, you capture the result of a successful PDCA cycle on a single card. Each PDCA cycle might have contained several experiments; if you have learned a lot from a failed experiment, it is OK to include that in the result section, too. You should keep a Success Card visible until it is no longer getting any attention.

Remember that Success Cards are not only for you. It is also a great way for others to get a quick overview of the implemented changes. Thus, it might inspire other people or teams to follow a similar path.

Key points of Success Cards:

- Success Cards make progress more visible.
- Success Cards demonstrate how learning leads to successful process changes.
- There is one Success Card for each successful process change.
- Success Cards are an easy and cheap way to share information with others

The power of short Experiments

It is hard to overestimate the power of well-framed Experiments in a Toyota Kata setting. It is the very engine that pushes us toward our desired Future State and where actual change happens. It is how our culture changes from a slow cadence of good intentions and risk-avoidance to short, focused initiatives driven by actual results and high risk tolerance. Without daily experiments, we easily fall back on old habits and plan-driven improvement. That is why we stress again and again that we must learn to make them short and effective. It is much like Agile in general – if we do not learn to slice products and features in small vertical slices, it affects the entire setup. As we cannot claim Agility if our work items take weeks to complete, we cannot get a culture of continuous improvement if our experiments take weeks to validate.

It is also important to understand that Process improvement is a stress factor to your brain (good stress), but not a natural state. Research has shown that our brains will often choose to avoid coping rather than dealing with something that takes us outside our comfort zones. Only by making it a natural part of our daily work can we teach our brains to treat Process improvement "stress" as a natural state and not something to be avoided. That is the essence of "Muscle memory" and the recent understanding of the brain as a constantly changing structure, also known as neuroplasticity (Doidge, 2007).

Learning objectives and questions for real-life application of Obstacles and Experiments

Working with Obstacles and Experiments is where we turn goals into real-life results. They are the engine in Toyota Kata driving us forward to achieve our ambitious goals. From this chapter, I hope that you gathered that:

- Obstacles are not a Backlog of problems to be solved. We should not strive to identify all possible Obstacles upfront but focus on the few we are observing now that are keeping us from reaching the Target Condition.
- We can work on two Obstacles at the same time but only if they are not closely related.
- Obstacles should be real obstacles and should not include the solution.
- Cynefin can help us understand the nature of our "unclear territory" and how much structured problem analysis will make sense in the given situation.
- Both Obstacles and Experiment Ideas should be regarded as options before they are moved to the Experiment Record.
- Learning to take small steps through short Experiments is as important to the success of Toyota Kata as small vertical slices are to the success of Agile.
- For each Experiment, we should be able to frame a hypothesis of what will happen.
- Success Cards can help us capture the result of successful process changes and make them "stick".

Before you continue, write your answers to the following questions to the best of your ability:

- When do we move Obstacles and Experiments to the Experiment Record on the Improvement Board?
- What is the recommended maximum number of Obstacles being worked on at the same time and why?
- What is the difference between an Obstacle and an Experiment?
- What information do we capture before we start an Experiment and what do we capture after it is finished?
- How can Cynefin help us better understand the nature of our Obstacles and Experiments?
- What is the recommended distribution of maximum Experiment duration?
- Write two examples of Obstacles and their related Experiments. (Use the Target Condition you previously established as inspiration.)
- What is the difference between a "go-and-see", "exploratory" and "hypothesis" experiment?

14. Final notes on the Starter Kata in an Agile context – is it just Scrum for Process improvement?

If after reading this chapter you find yourself thinking, 'This sounds a lot like using Scrum for Process improvement', I won't blame you. If we look at the Scrum Master as the responsible person for the Process improvement Backlog ("Process" instead of "Product" Owner), we can match a lot of the terminology by simply looking at it from a Process rather than a Product Development perspective

Toyota Kata	Scrum
Process Vision	Product Vision
Challenge	Release goal
Improvement Kata (4 weeks)	Sprint (1-4 weeks)
Process Lead	Product Owner
Target Condition	Sprint Goal
Process Metrics	PBI's
Outcome Metrics	Business Value
Experiments	Tasks
Challenge/Target preparation	Backlog Refinement
Improvement Board	Scrum Board (though only implicitly part of Scrum)
Improvement Kata Planning Meeting	Sprint Planning Meeting
Daily Kata	Daily Scrum

Figure 47: Toyota Kata vs. Scrum

As mentioned previously, this is both the consequence of deliberately changing the way specific elements of the Starter Kata are framed and taught (not the actual) to make it easier for those familiar with Scrum to understand as well as actual similarities.

Regardless of the reason, it is a benefit and not a problem! To most people, Toyota Kata introduces so many new aspects to effective Process improvement that any recognizable concepts or artifacts will make it easier to understand. The trick is naturally to be able to separate them. We do not want, e.g., experiment options to be thought of as a product Backlog. Toyota Kata is not Scrum and Scrum is not Toyota Kata, but we have found that being able to frame concepts from the perspective of something you are already familiar with can be a great help.

15. The naming and layout of the "Improvement Board"

This chapter introduces the details of the Improvement Board, which has proven to be an important element of making Toyota Kata work in real life. I will cover the design iterations we went through as well as why we ended up adding and removing some elements compared to the original layout. Through this chapter, I hope you will get a deeper understanding of the specific elements of the board and why they might be a good idea to include in your Starter Kata.

The board found in Mike Rother's books looks something like the one below and is typically referred to as the "Learner's Storyboard" or just "Storyboard". While keeping most elements of the original layout, we have made some changes and adjustments to better fit the Agile Context.

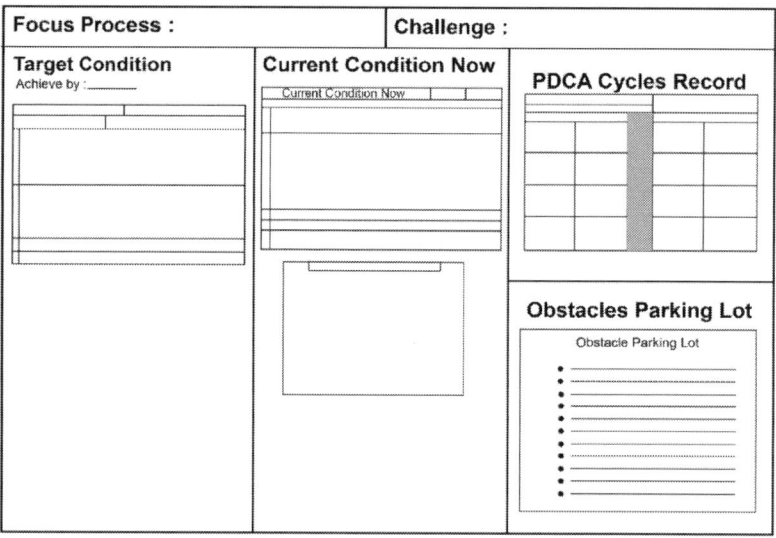

Figure 48: Standard Toyota Kata "Improvement Board" (Learner's Storyboard)

One of the most obvious changes is the naming. In Agile, work items are often called User Stories and the word "Storyboard" might, therefore, already refer to either the board where the flow of work is visualized (also called a Kanban or Scrum Board) or the board where User Stories are planned and prioritized (also called the Story Map or Story Mapping Board). So, in Agile, we already have at least two popular boards in play and both could be referred to as a Storyboard, though they contain something entirely different from the board used in a Toyota Kata setting.

What sets the Toyota Kata board apart in an Agile setting is that it very specifically focuses on Improvement and not the Daily Whirlwind of deadlines, defects and User Stories to be completed. Though nobody can remember when and how it specifically happened, people just started referring to the Kata board as the Improvement Board. The name was born and integrated into workshops, coaching and training material.

Besides the name, we also made some changes to the layout of the board, which we will cover in the following sections.

Though we will focus on the latest version, we went through at least four major redesigns along the way. We started with a very simple version but gradually discovered the need to include more elements from the original board and even added a few details on the way. You learn a lot from failing, even in something as basic as board design. In retrospect, it is difficult to judge whether you must go through those failures to truly appreciate and understand the "end result" (which is not the end result but simply the latest version), or you can jump directly to the latest version and evolve from there. There is no doubt that we have found the latest layout to be a huge improvement over earlier versions but there is no guarantee that you will share that experience.

Here are a couple of examples of the different Improvement Boards we tried as well as their drawbacks and benefits.

The flipchart

The first version was drawn on a simple flipchart with four fields (Forhindringer = Obstacles):

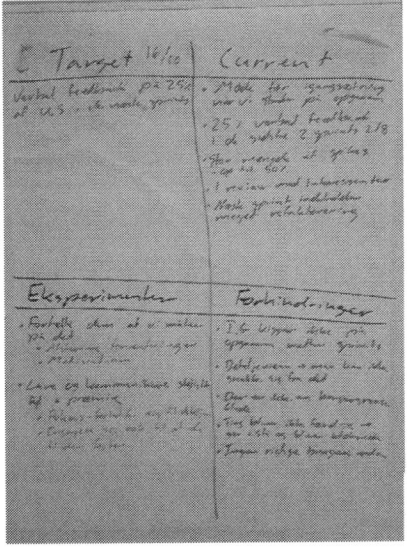

Figure 49: Improvement Board version 1

Benefits:

- Simple
- Cheap
- Easy to get going

Drawbacks:

- Not enough room for a real Experiment/PDCA Record
- No room for Challenge
- Difficult to make corrections
- No guidance, high risk of diverting from essential Toyota Kata principles

OneNote

The second version was a digital board in OneNote to try to facilitate easier adjustments and add more content. Unfortunately, I failed to take a picture of this, but it was very close to the flipchart version, with a few minor changes to allow for, e.g., a better Experiment/PDCA Record.

Benefits:

- Easy to access older boards (history)
- Easier to do distributed Coaching Katas

Drawbacks:

- Had to start OneNote
- Quickly got messy – everything jumped around and fields overlapped
- No guidance
- Not visual in the team room; failed to create team engagement

First poster

"Don't cross the stream to get to water" is an old Danish saying, but apparently that is what we had to do. After several attempts at a simpler version, we ended up designing the next using the original Toyota Kata Storyboard as an outset. We did that because the feedback we received from teams and managers clearly indicated that we needed:

- To include the Challenge
- A clear separation of Target Current and the Experiment Record

- A board design matching the sequence of the Coaching Kata questions

Additional feedback included:

- The need to include a field for Experiment ideas (uncommitted options)
- The need to include reminders of previously achieved improvements that were considered unstable
- Separation of Outcome, Qualitative and Process metrics
- The possibility of using Post-its instead of writing on the actual Board, so it would be easier to make adjustments and corrections
- BIGGER – much more room to get a better overview and not have to use handwriting in an XXS font size

The result was a 1.7-meter wide and 1.06-meter tall poster in thick glossy paper that would withstand the use of Post-its coming on and off.

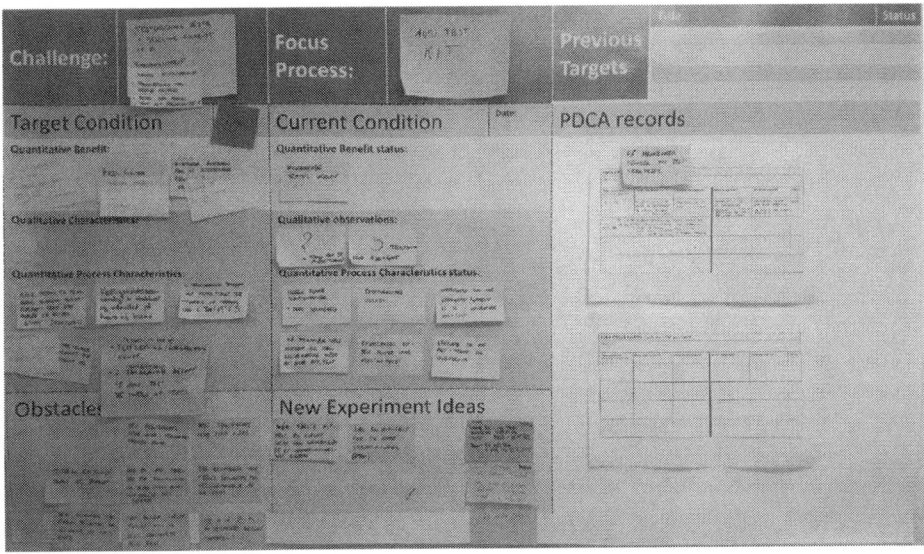

Figure 50: Improvement Board version 3

It delivered on most of our needs but with the following requests for additional changes:

- Nicer design matching Bankdata's design template (minor)
- PDCA record using Post-its instead of A3's
- Guidance/examples
- Simpler wording (don't use nerdy language like "PDCA")
- Room for two big Post-its in Challenge definition

- More room in "Current condition" to visualize trends

Latest version

The latest version looks like this. Guidance is implemented through examples and help text, and wording has been simplified (at least to some extent).

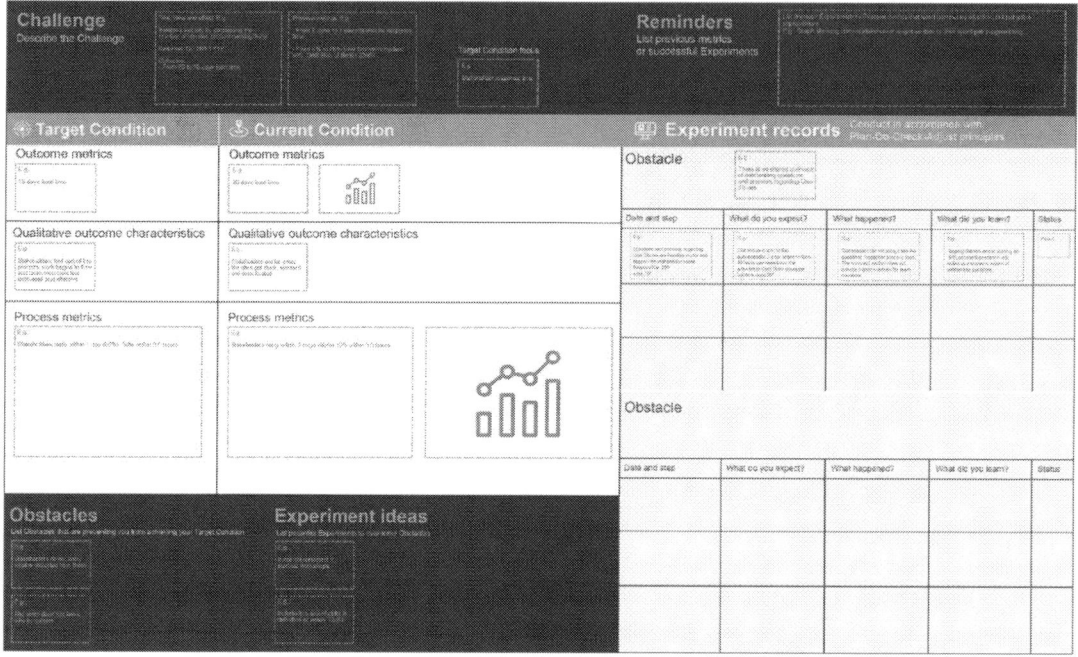

Figure 51: Improvement Board version 4

Naturally, it always gets a bit messier once you start using it in real life:

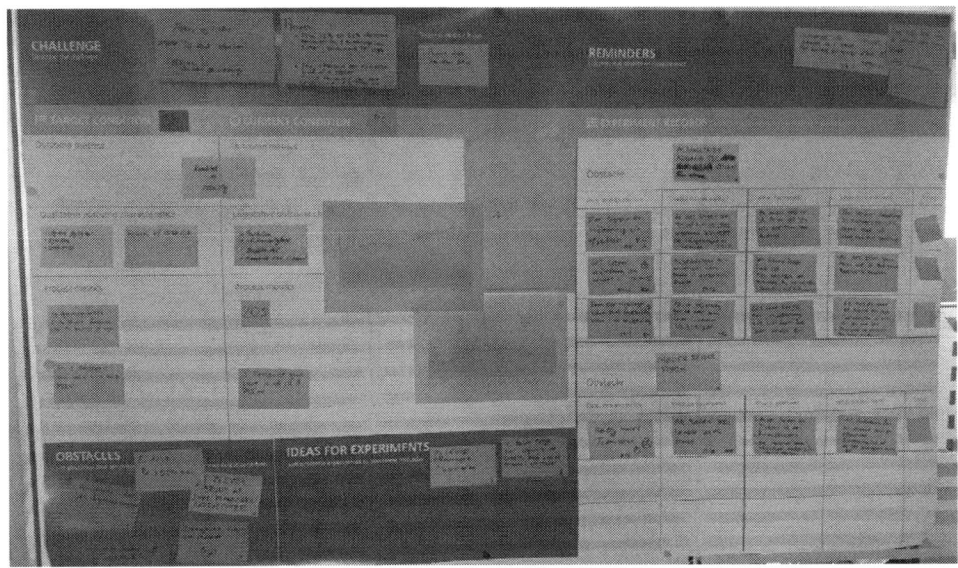

Figure 52: Improvement Board, real life example

Let's look at some of the adjustments we made to make it fit the Agile Context in more detail.

Dividing Target and Current Condition in three sections:

In the beginning, we opted for a simple version of framing the Target and Current Condition, but gradually we found that a stricter format was necessary to avoid mixing Outcome metrics, Process metrics and qualitative observations. Getting this right is arguably one of the most important factors in an Agile Setup, as you can easily end up targeting metrics that you cannot directly influence, put Targets in places that you cannot validate objectively and unconsciously sub-optimize toward a short-term Outcome goal.

From a coaching perspective, Qualitative Characteristics also serve a very specific purpose. People who have not worked with metrics before are very likely to place Qualitative observations under Process metrics. They might, for example, write "less stress", "better Backlog" or "clear communication". With this field on the board, we can explain that those are not incorrect statements – they simply belong in a different part of the board. This is typically followed up by the question "How would you measure/observe that this is, in fact, happening?"

The same goes for Outcome metrics. It is not bad or wrong to want throughput to go from 100 to 120 story points per Sprint in the next four weeks. It is simply not a Process capability and, thus, belongs under Outcome metrics. Having that dialogue and being able to place it in the right section of the board has proven invaluable to obtaining a good understanding of leading, lagging, qualitative and quantitative.

158

Therefore, we ended up with the following:

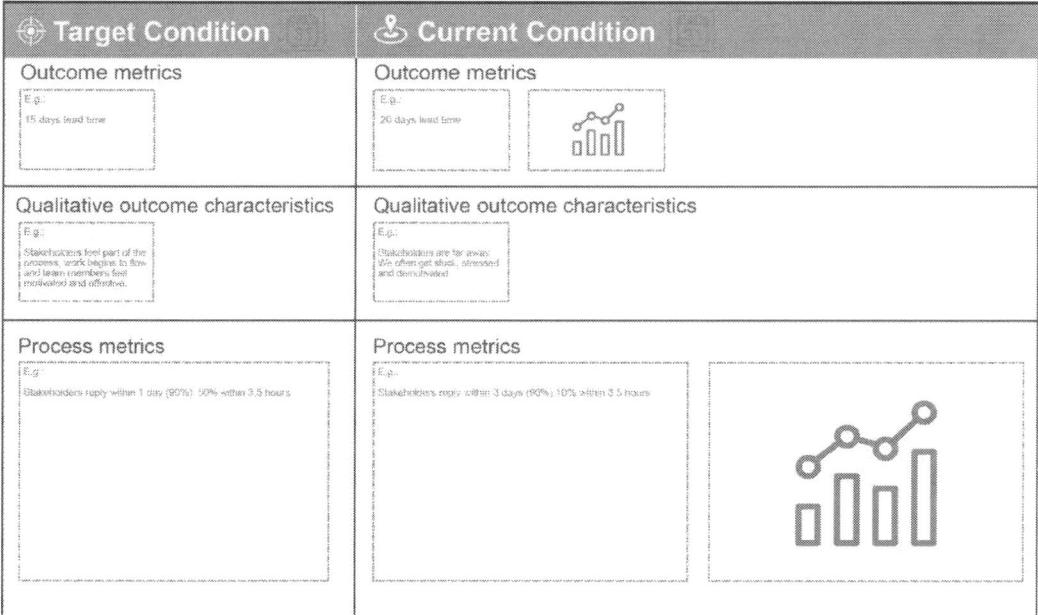

Figure 53: Improvement board Target and Current Condition

Why a place for uncommitted Experiment ideas?

One of the main Agile concepts is the cross-functional Agile team with shared responsibility for success. This means that no team member is individually responsible for a subprocess or part of the Value Stream. It is all a team effort, and everyone is free to present creative solutions and ideas outside their main area of expertise. In a Toyota Kata setting, those great ideas might pop up at any time of day or during dedicated brainstorm sessions. Changing habits and processes involving humans is often not a clear causal effect and it may take many tries to get the result we want. This field gives us a chance to collect and visualize those options whenever they occur and to use them as an inspiration catalog for taking the next step. Because they are uncommitted options, we keep them at a level of abstraction where they can be described in a simple one-line format. This section of the board is also an indicator of the options available to the team. If it is empty, it might be a sign to initiate a shared brainstorm or another activity to generate more options.

It has been very interesting to see the difference from team to team in this aspect. For some teams, we struggle with the fact that they generate so many Experiment Ideas that we lose the overview. Here, we must coach in the aspect of selecting the ones with the biggest potential and cleaning up the rest.

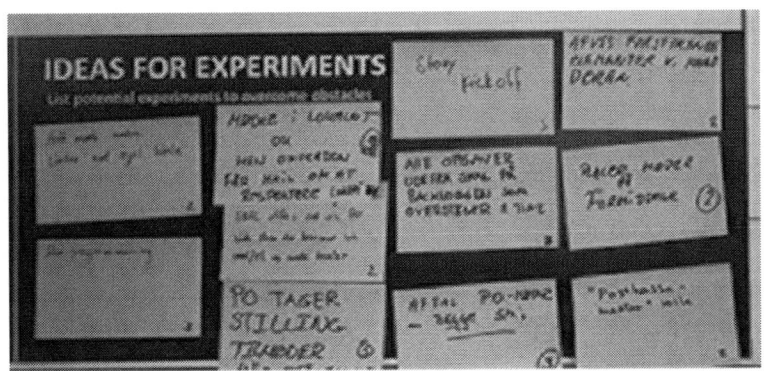

Figure 54: Ideas for experiments, real life example

Other teams have the opposite problem; we must coach them in how to think outside the box and find creative solutions. It could involve questions like "What would you do if you were the CEO or Superman?", "What would you do if you had to make absolutely sure that this Obstacle remained in place forever?" or "How is this situation similar to that of a hospital, manufacturing plant or nursing home and what would they do?" If you find the context of hospitals and nursing rooms too alienating, you can substitute examples that you are more familiar with. The only point is that it should be far from the world of IT. ☺

The "reminder" section

We also ended up including a "reminder" section. When changing human behavior and habits, it is sometimes hard to stick to a successful improvement in the long term. We might, e.g., have discovered that Pair Programming was an excellent capability or that policies surrounding effective knowledge sharing were a great success when finishing each User Story. However, though successful, we sometimes forget and believe that those process changes are deeply rooted while they are actually still fragile.

The problem is that though they might be fragile and new, the team has already proven the value of these changes through their Toyota Kata Experiments and validated the benefits. They have also proven the ability to successfully follow these new policies in the short term so there is no longer any uncertainty involved. Therefore, it makes little sense to try to "artificially" place these in the "Experiment Record" section on the board, as the Target Condition has already been reached.

But what do we do, then, if we know that there is still a real risk that we might "forget" these improvements? If they are left unattended and we simply move on to the next process change? Will we then leave a trail of short-term improvements behind and never fully realize the benefits of Toyota

Kata? In a manufacturing context, the answer to those questions might be easier, as flow is quicker and you can more easily validate your ability to follow "standard work" procedures. But when teams and managers would ask those questions in the Agile Context, we did not have a good answer for them until one team came up with the idea of adding a "reminder" section to the board.

The important point is not to place the results of all successful process changes or all previous Target Condition metrics in that section. Some changes are technical and, once installed, it takes a deliberate effort to make them not function; also, some Target Conditions metrics are considered fully integrated immediately after they are reached. We use the reminder section only to illustrate the changes and process metrics that we consider successful but fragile. Often, we simply continue measuring our ability to follow the process change and, once it has proven stable and integrated into our team culture, we remove it from the reminder section. Reminders can include the ability to deliver on actual Target Condition metrics as well as following specific process changes implemented through successful Experiments. Here are a couple of examples of what were considered fragile:

- Time spent Pair Programming
- Ability to follow WIP limits
- Division of operation and maintenance tasks in the team
- Failed build recovery time
- Early end-user feedback on User Stories in Sprints
- Percentage of root cause analysis on defects
- Number of "Ready" items (minimum WIP limit)

Experiment Record adding a "Status" field but leaving out "Process Metric"

We changed the name from PDCA Record to Experiment Record due to the simple fact that teams and managers found the term "PDCA" somewhat alienating and also because most had already started to refer to it as Experiment Record even with "PDCA" written on the board. This was a minor change but another example of simply adapting to the context and feedback.

Another simple but valuable change was to actually preprint the layout of the Experiment Record to allow for Post-its to be used instead of writing directly on an A3.

A3 paper:

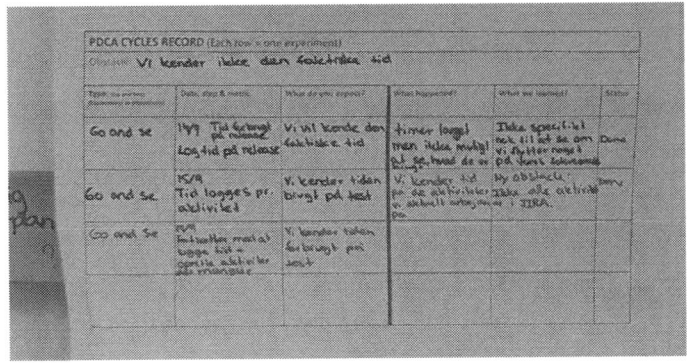

Figure 55: Experiment record (PDCA record) A3 paper example

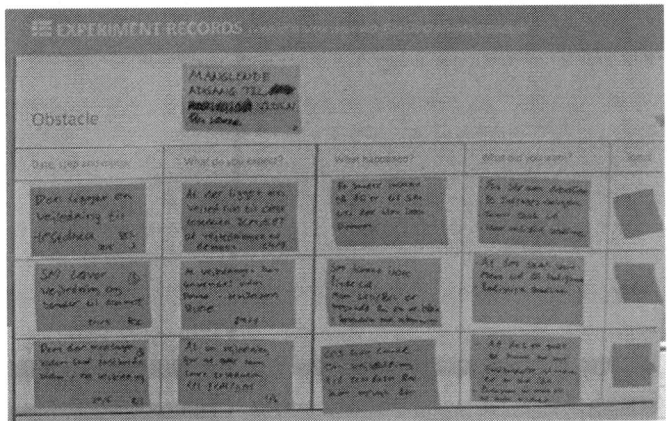

Figure 56: Experiment record, preprinted with Post-its

It might seem like an irrelevant minor change but the possibility of moving the actual Obstacles and Experiments to the Experiment Record, the added flexibility of adding, removing and making corrections, and the ability to write in letters big enough for the team to see when standing in front of the board made a real difference.

Preprinting the Experiment Record on the actual board also made it possible to communicate even more clearly that we expect teams and managers to work on a maximum of two Obstacles at any one point in time (a very physical Work in Progress limit). The only drawback is, naturally, that you will need to clear one Experiment Record once you have fixed more than two Obstacles within a Target Condition. However, because our Experiments often have longer cycle times, this not a problem in real life; we have rarely experienced that the recent Experiment Record history has not been available for the Coaching Kata sessions.

162

It does, however, limit our ability to review our Experiment Record over longer periods of time and look for patterns in terms of how many experiment cycles are spent on the same Obstacle or the fact that it took four Experiments simply to understand the Target Condition metric. A picture of the Experiment Record before it is removed solves this problem in a simple way. Just remember to use standard naming (including date) and upload it to a designated place. Otherwise, it will quickly become a mess.

Adding a "status" column

Though it is probably not an issue that is specific to the Agile Context, we also found that "failing" is a huge problem for most. As previously mentioned, we tend to avoid failure to the extent that it becomes challenging to think outside the box and try something new. Part of that problem is likely related to the usual cadence of retrospectives in which you plan and evaluate Process improvement only once every two to four weeks. If your iteration length is long, you naturally push to eliminate uncertainty and the risk of failure. The irony is that this fact is one of the core reasons for choosing Agile over more traditional waterfall methods.

To make it very clear that we expect some Experiments to fail and that this should be part of the natural learning cycle, we added the "Status" field to the Experiment Record (see Figure 56: Experiment record, preprinted with Post-its). That way, we could clearly teach resistance to failure by ensuring that it was a clear and visual element of both daily life and the training material. This had a surprisingly positive effect. When we started implementing the Toyota Kata framework, people had a hard time accepting that not everything was a great success. However, with adapted coaching, training material and board layout, more people are now proudly writing "failure" in big letters on a pink Post-it to signify that they are, in fact, experimenting, learning and taking chances.

Removing the Process field from the Experiment Record

There are multiple examples of Toyota Kata Boards that do not include Process as an explicit element, so it seems that this is not a unique concept in the Agile space. However, most of them that I found looked like this:

PDCA CYCLES RECORD (Each Row=One Experiment)			
Obstacle:		Process:	
		Learner:	Coach:
	What do you expect ?	What Happened	What we learned
Date,Step & Metric			

It is valuable to discuss why we ultimately chose to remove it to prevent others from making the same mistakes we did. When applying Lean in general to development and innovation work, we must be very clear that while many principles make sense, it is often dangerous to blindly copy specific practices. We need people to believe in the concepts and find value in the application of those principles without feeling that they are being forced into a box that does not make sense in their context.

The entire area containing Process, Learner and Coach turned out to be exactly that. Through there might be times when substitute Coaches and even Learners would be present, it added no value to register them on the board. The same turned out to be true for "Process", in which the argument was that writing "development", "test" or "review" did not provide any additional insights and that it was downright annoying when an Obstacle turned out to include more than a single process. So, based on very clear feedback from the first teams that were exposed to the more detailed version, we decided to remove it.

This is really something to be very aware of in general. As a coach and trainer, you must be able to clearly and convincingly explain the value of every element you ask people to use. It is not enough to state "because that is what they do at Toyota or Company X". Once you go down that road, people will start doubting the value and integrity of the whole concept. That is the same when introducing Scrum or other Agile methods. We have probably all seen coaches and Scrum Masters hiding behind the explanation "because you are only just starting to learn (shu level/beginner); just do it by the book and do not ask why". That is never good advice, especially not when half the people you are talking to have a master's degree or Ph.D.

Though I absolutely agree that you must practice by the book at first (that is the whole idea behind the Starter Kata), you should train people to ask why, why and why again from the very beginning. This will give you a chance to build teams and organizations that show real acts of leadership instead of blindly following directions. Even on the first day after introducing Toyota Kata, Scrum or Kanban, I will ask people why they are at a specific meeting or using a specific tool or practice. Their response to that question is often more valuable than simply rating their ability to follow the guideline.

Why does Target Condition come before Current Condition on the board?

Though not an adjustment because we are following the outline of the "typical" board, one of the questions we have had to answer during initial training is the one above. The point was: "We read from left to right in the Western world, and not from right to left like in Japan at Toyota, so Current (now) should come before Target (future)".

First, modern Japanese is written horizontally left to right just like English and has been for over a century. (Before that, it was vertical but never right-to-left). So, if this were the reason, the Japanese would be equally confused about the sequence. The real reason is that Toyota Kata is driven by the desire to reach a Future State. That is why the first Coaching Kata question focuses on the Target Condition and the same reason that Target Condition is the first element on the board (if you read left to right, top to bottom).

At one point, we got so tired of hearing people complaining about the sequence that we made a version in which the two columns had changed place. We thought it a minor issue and a chance to show the organization that feedback was welcomed. We did not realize how wrong it was until we saw it in action. When you spend several slides in the training material focusing on the desirable Future State, when you repeat the message of working toward a goal and not away from problems and when the Coaching Kata questions naturally start with the question of the Target Condition, the small change of moving those two columns seems to work against the very core of the Toyota Kata framework. Even teams that had never seen the previous design voiced a strong opinion on this subject and we quickly reverted back to the original setup.

Improvement board for distributed teams

Most companies are starting to realize the future is global, which typically means an increased number of people working together across time zones and geographical distances. In a Toyota Kata setting, that usually calls for an electronic version of the Improvement Board. Because the structure of the board is quite simple, this is not a big problem; teams and managers have successfully used PowerPoint templates, Google Docs and Confluence. However, using an electronic tool while retaining the constraints of a physical board does seem silly, so people soon start experimenting with direct links to graphs in Excel and similar solutions to avoid copy-pasting. Though some solutions work initially, they often require maintenance and easily break down when new boards are set up or links are changed.

As more people started requesting a dedicated electronic tool, I decided to build one together with some former colleagues. It is called Teeka (guess why?) and can be found at https://teeka.io. As of the time of this writing, it is open only to early adopters. If you want to become an early adopter, send an email to agileupgrade@gmail.com with a short description of who you are and why you wish to become an early adopter. Right now, the tool makes it very easy to start Experiment Records and display/update progress on Process metrics. However, future versions will include Challenge and metric inspiration catalogues, team and organizational maturity ratings, and the ability to handle catch-balls.

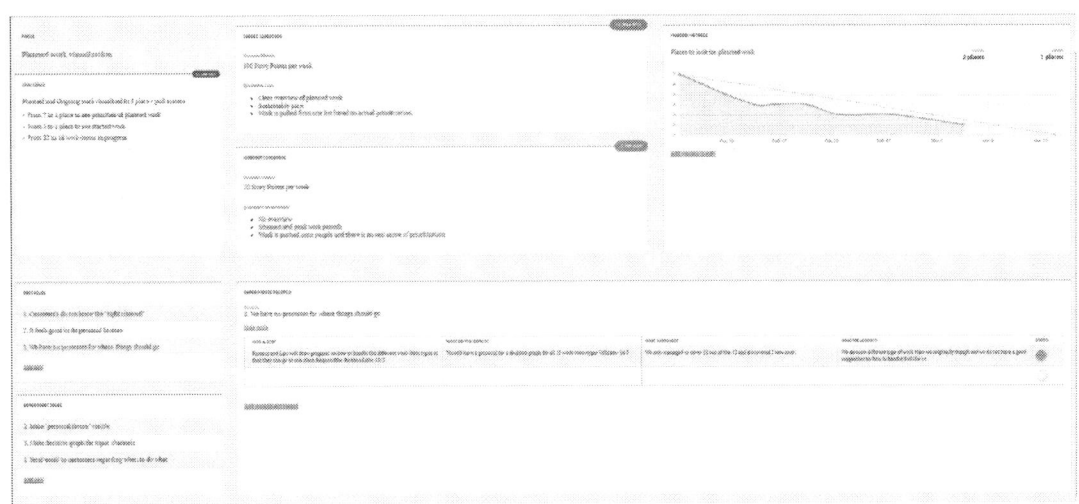

Figure 58: Teeka board example

166

Learning objectives and questions for real-life application of the Improvement Board

The Improvement Board represents Toyota Kata's own example of the principle of Visual Management. Besides getting some insights into the design iterations of the board, I hope you managed to grasp the following learning objectives:

- The Improvement Board helps frame the Challenge and the Improvement Kata.
- The Improvement Board should always be updated visualizing the latest experiments and the trends toward the Target Condition.
- An updated Improvement Board provides the foundation for a successful Coaching Kata session.
- For a team, the Improvement Board is also a collaboration tool clearly displaying the direction and who is responsible for carrying out the individual experiments.
- The Improvement Board is an effective and transparent tool for battling the Daily Whirlwind and creating room for improvement work.

Before you continue, write your answers to the following questions to the best of your ability:

- Why is the Target Condition placed before the Current Condition on the board (reading left to right)?
- What is the purpose of the "reminder section"?
- Why did we find the need to add a section for Experiment ideas?
- What is the difference between Obstacles and Experiments found in the left-most part of the board and those that are part of the "Experiment Record"?

Part 3. Toyota Kata in the Wider Organization

Until now, we have only touched briefly upon the use of Toyota Kata in the wider organization as part of covering the basic aspects of Toyota Kata. In this part, we take a step deeper in that direction as we cover the Coach/Learner relationship, the roll-out of Toyota Kata across organizational levels and Catch-balls and the Challenges and Target Condition above the team level. Finally, we will investigate the use of Toyota Kata as an alternative to driving an Agile transformation as well as scaling Agile principles across multiple teams working on a shared product.

16. The Coach, Learner and second coach relationship

We have already touched upon the Coach and Learner relationship in previous chapters when discussing both the Coaching Kata and the role of the manager in a Toyota Kata setting. The coaching relationship is, however, of such importance that it deserves a section of its own. This short chapter introduces more details about the Coach, Learner and second coach relationship as well as suggestions for specific applications.

As mentioned, a Manager will often act as a coach to their direct reports in a Toyota Kata setting. This means that the director will coach their area managers, the area managers will coach their department managers and the department managers will coach the Process Leads in the teams. We do this to make it possible for the entire organization to pull in the same direction and for knowledge about constraints and possibilities to have a natural way of being shared across organizational layers.

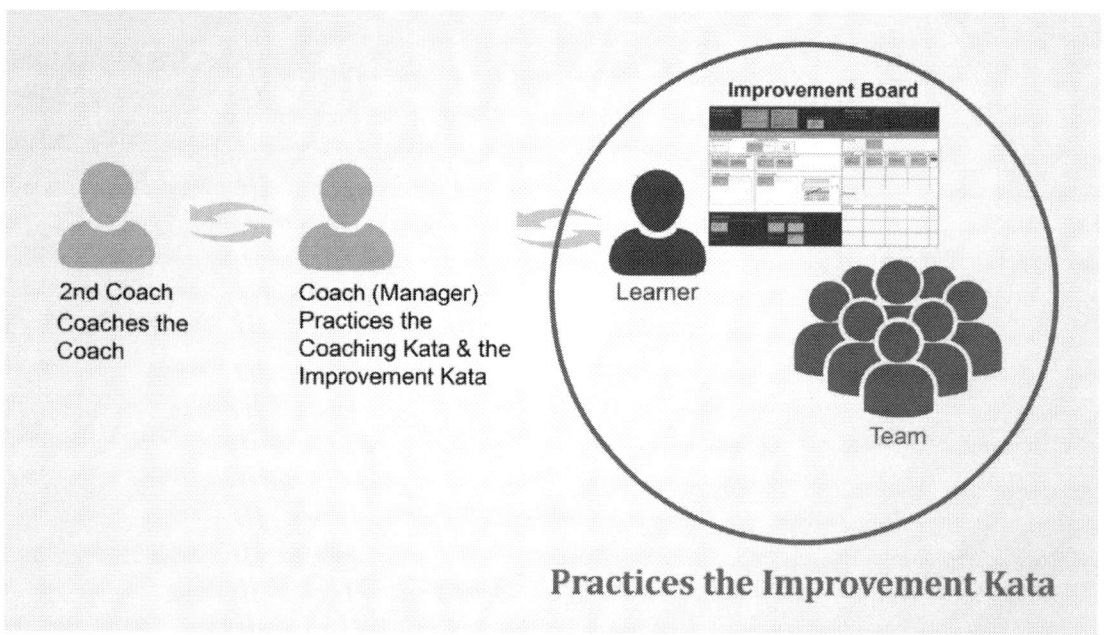

Figure 59: Second Coach, Coach and Learner relationship, adapted from the Toyota Kata Practice Guide (ROTHER, 2018)

You may, however, choose the Coach/Learner setup that fits your organizational structure. There are no strict rules in terms of how you should implement the Coach/Learner relationship.

A key element of Toyota Kata is "If the learner did not learn, the teacher did not teach". Therefore, if Learners are struggling to drive improvement effectively, this fact reflects on their Coach. They are bound together in a mutually dependent relationship in which one cannot succeed without the other. Because most are both Coaches and Learners, this means that there are two aspects to being successful: working effectively with your own improvement targets through the Improvement Kata and developing the skills of your direct reports through the Coaching Kata. It is not enough to be successful in just one of the two.

There is no doubt that talking about this is much easier than doing it in real life. It is not uncommon for Coaches to give directions when they should be coaching, or even to coach when they should be clearly suggesting a specific next step. However, because only Toyota has an organization in which both Toyota Kata and the Coach/Learner relationship is in the very DNA of the organization, we must be even more aware of providing a blame-free learning space. To do this, we use the principle of the second coach.

The second coach

The second coach is responsible for giving the Coach feedback on their coaching sessions with the Learner. Anybody can act as a second coach and, as previously mentioned, it has proven useful for, e.g., department and area managers to observe and give each other feedback. Not only is this valuable from the perspective of the Coach but the second coach also gets a chance to watch and learn by seeing other people in action.

We have also found it valuable to build a team of internal Toyota Kata coaches. This team regularly visits Coaching Kata, Daily Kata and Improvement Kata meetings to provide feedback and share experiences from other teams and sessions. They are also able to act as stand-ins when people get sick, are fired or quit their jobs. In this way, the second coaches provide a service to the organization that enables it to continue in challenging situations as well as engage in knowledge sharing across teams and departments.

Figure 60: Second Coach and Coach focus, adapted from the Toyota Kata Practice Guide (ROTHER, 2018)

Toyota Kata coaches are not born with 10 years of experience. We cover this in more detail in the next chapter, on rolling out Toyota Kata in the organization. However, it naturally involves quite a lot of on-the-job-training as well as simply acknowledging that "perfect" is the enemy of "good enough".

You might be excused for thinking, 'Does this never end? If there is a Coach and a second coach, what is next? Do we also need a third coach to coach the second coach and a fourth coach to coach the third coach? If everybody is busy coaching, will there be any budget left to do real work?' To be honest, I have acted as a third coach in the beginning, when the learning curve is steep for Learners, Coaches and second coaches, but rest assured that this is simply a temporary measure and not a part the future setup. You should be prepared for some smiles and comments when half the people in the room are there to coach each other.

As you have probably already realized, there is not a big difference between the Agile setting and a typical manufacturing context regarding the role of Coaches and second coaches. The pattern of establishing a team of internal second coaches, as well as having coaches provide feedback to each other, is well-known and we have applied it successfully without the need for adjustments.

17. Catch-balls, Challenges and Target Conditions at the manager level

At this point, I hope that you have a good picture of how Toyota Kata works, and the events, practices and principles involved in the Starter Kata for Agile organizations. In this chapter, we will look at Toyota Kata from the perspective of what goes on above the team level. If you find yourself in one of the few organizations without the traditional hierarchies of, e.g., directors and area- and department-level managers, you might need a bit of imagination to translate the content of this chapter into your context. However, I would encourage you to read along anyway.

We have previously established that a key capability of an Agile organization is the ability to create small end-to-end teams that can successfully identify, deliver and validate real end-user value. But in organizations where that is not yet the case or where large programs make it necessary for multiple teams to work together, there is no way around looking at it from a systems thinking perspective, as striving to optimize a single part (team) of a system without looking at the system as a whole is "doomed to failure". Organizational theorist and pioneer on systems thinking Russell Ackoff shares this insight (Ackoff, 1994):

"Until managers take into account the systemic nature of their organizations, most of their efforts to improve performance are doomed to failure."

As we discussed at the beginning of this book, continuous improvement with Toyota Kata is fractal and, thus, something that happens at all levels of the organization all the time. This means that we expect to find Improvement Boards, Improvement Kata and Coaching Kata at all organizational levels. Though fractal, there are a few things to be aware of once we move up the levels in the organization. I will try to outline these things in this chapter.

Looking back over the last few years, there is no doubt that the higher you get in the organization, the harder it is to maintain the focus on continuous improvement. It seems that leaders and managers, in general, are very fond of the idea but are struggling to make it a natural part of their daily lives. It is not because they do not want to do so; most recognize the importance and potential of making improvement a key aspect of modern management. We have observed at least a couple of factors that seem to work against it:

- Many managers are used to a work calendar governed by firefighting and meetings, with few elements of fixed routines. Therefore, they struggle when they are asked to set aside time for Coaching Kata and Improvement Kata Planning meetings and prioritizing their own experiments.

- The long-term perspective is threatened by a never-ending stream of urgent ad-hoc requests that seem more important to get through the day.
- A fully booked calendar weeks in advance does not lend itself well to the notion of "navigating unclear territory" where we cannot plan to set aside time for Obstacles and Experiments we have not yet identified.

But despite the difficulty, it is crucial to find a way around this Obstacle. It is not enough that the director likes the idea of the area managers doing it, that the area manager likes the idea of the department managers doing it and that the department manager considers it a success if the teams are doing it. All leaders and managers must act as role models in driving continuous improvement. That is why we came up with this general statement:

"As a manager, you have the potential to make it a great success or to really screw up. Every time you cancel a Coaching Kata or fail to prioritize time for your own Improvement goals, you are telling your direct reports that it is OK for them to do the same. Nothing is more important than being a good role model!"

That is also why we put as much effort into measuring the adoption of the Starter Kata at the management levels as we do on the team level.

Adjusting cadences to fit organizational levels

As we move up from the team level, it is not surprising to find that it takes longer to execute and validate experiments. This is due to several aspects:

- We are often indirectly influencing processes and, thus, we must convince people to participate.
- Challenges may include the need for change in the organizational structure, which is often slow as it involves not only people but also physical constraints like office space.
- The delivery cadence is often slower the higher you get.

This is not always the case, and managers who have chosen to optimize some of their own processes with a high delivery cadence have opted to match the Toyota Kata cadences found at the team level. In most cases, however, we found the need to adjust to match the context. We ended up with this general recommendation for the cadences at the different levels of the organization:

Department level:

- Challenge: 2-6 months
- Target Condition: 6 weeks

- Coaching Kata: 1 per week (30 min.)
- Experiment Duration: 1 week or less (at least 50% of experiments)

Areal level:

- Challenge: 3-9 month
- Target Condition: 12 weeks
- Coaching Kata: 2 times per month (30 min.)
- Experiment duration: 2 weeks or less (at least 70% of experiments)

Director level:

- Challenge: 3-9 month
- Target Condition: 12 weeks
- Coaching Kata: 2 times per month (30 min.)
- Experiment duration: 1 month or less (at least 90% of experiments)

To be honest, at first we aimed for considerably shorter cadences on both meetings and experiment duration for the area and director levels, but we had to face the fact that this wasn't working as intended. It is not impossible that it was due to the nature of the chosen Challenges or other unique factors. As you will learn in the following sections, however, it is also a matter of cadences slowing down once you reach the higher levels of the organization, as we are moving further from hands-on development work and Challenges typically involve multiple teams, departments or areas.

Catch-balls

When more than one organizational level is involved in a shared Challenge, we call it a "Catch-ball". At some point, most people have played a simple game of "catch". The objective is cooperative. Attending closely to one another, players throw the ball back and forth. They attempt to keep the ball in play as they build skills together and expand their repertoire of moves. Both players learn from the game. "Catch-ball" refers to a chain of Coaching Kata relationships where, e.g., the director coaches the area manager who coaches the next level in turn toward a shared goal. Because each relationship is a game of catch, skills and information pass up and down the chain over time. Catch-balls, thus, align improvement objectives across organizational levels.

Working with Catch-balls in an Agile setting

Though a Catch-ball is typically initiated top-down, it does not have to be. The Catch-ball can also begin at the team level and gradually expand to higher levels in the organization as Obstacles are identified or new opportunities arise. Finding early opportunities for senior managers to practice and learn coaching skills is, however, key to enabling the power of alignment.

Using Catch-balls is arguably where we found that the Agile organization differs most from more traditional setups and where examples from other contexts turned out to be less useful. It is important to recognize this difference; I hope that with a deeper understanding, I can save you from some of the mistakes we have made.

Let me illustrate the difference with a simplified example. In traditional organizations, value often passes through several functional teams or departments before reaching the end user or customer. Agile mechanics might have been implemented in these teams and departments but without changing the organizational structure. For simplicity, let us say that there are four teams in this setup:

- A business team responsible for identifying market trends and customer engagement and for deciding which feature or product should be built next, as well as their acceptance criteria.
- A development team responsible for designing and implementing the feature or product so that it looks good, is easy to use and is in compliance with the acceptance criteria.
- A test team responsible for making sure that the feature or product works on all platforms and that all alternative flows of data have been thoroughly tested; this team is also responsible for more explorative testing
- A deployment and operation teams responsible for deploying the feature or product on the right servers and monitoring the application to report any quality issues

Each team is part of a larger department focusing on that specific area of expertise, so the test team is, e.g., sitting together with three other test teams and sharing both a department manager as well as the physical workspace. Any product or project striving to create an actual delivery must then coordinate deliveries from all four teams.

Analyzing our Current Condition Value Stream, we find that:

- There are huge queues/inventories of work among each of our four teams in this example (a total of 250 work items).
- Each team has started an average of 5 work items per person (a total of 7 people x 4 teams x 5 items = 140 work items)
- It takes an average of 10 workdays for each team to respond to change requests from the other teams when something must be fixed or changed due to failing tests, changes in requirements or quality problems in production.

This is the kind of case that is often presented in examples of using Toyota Kata. Let us imagine looking at this situation from the perspective of Agile and a traditional setup and how that would influence the chosen Challenge.

From the traditional perspective

In a traditional organization, functional departments or teams are not seen as a problem and, therefore, there is no Vision of establishing cross-functional end-to-end teams. Nothing keeps us from forming end-to-end teams to minimize WIP and increase flow, but neither does anything point us in that specific direction. Thus, the typical Challenge in the more traditional setting will focus on optimizing for one-by-one flow within the existing structure. It might look like this:

Organizational Challenge example:

- Outcome metrics:
    - From 150 to 70 workdays average lead time for product changes
- Process metrics:
    - From 1000 to 250 queued between teams
    - From 2300 to 1100 work items in progress in teams

Areal-level Challenge example:

- Outcome metrics:
    - From 127 to 60 workdays average lead time for product changes
- Process metrics
    - From 250 to 100 work items queued between teams

Department-level Challenge example (test department – 3 teams):

- Outcome metrics:
    - From 20 to 12 workdays cycle time for new tests
    - From 10 to 1 day cycle time for re-test
- Process metrics
    - From 140 to 40 work items in progress
    - From 50% to 10% unscheduled work per day

Team-level Challenge example (test team):

- Outcome metrics:
    - From 16 to 9 workdays cycle time for new tests
    - From 8.5 to 1 day cycle time for re-test
- Process metrics
    - From 140 to 40 work items in progress
    - From 10 to 2 expedites per day

There is a direct correlation between each level's ability to deliver on both Outcome and Process metrics and reaching the overall organizational goal.

In a typical Agile organization, this situation would not exist, as value would not flow through four teams but one or more cross-functional teams with the ability to deliver end-to-end. Reviewers of this book did, however, remark that though many organizations consider themselves "Agile", they still have a more traditional organizational structure with functional departments and teams.

Let us look at the same situation from the perspective of an organization striving to become more Agile but still without the basics in place. How might a Catch-ball look in this setting?:

Organizational Challenge example:

- Outcome metrics:
  o From 150 to 70 workdays average lead time for product changes
- Process metrics:
  o From 90 to 40 handovers between teams

Areal-level Challenge example:

- Outcome metrics:
  o From 127 to 60 workdays average lead time for product changes
- Process metrics:
  o From 18 to 8 handovers between teams
  o From 250 to 100 items queued between teams

As you can tell, this Catch-ball will initially not go beyond the area level in the organization striving to become Agile. We cannot yet frame a Catch-ball on either the department level or the team level, as we are navigating unclear territory with the defined goal of reducing handovers as well as queued items. From the area management perspective, this might include changes in the allocation of product responsibility as well as structural changes. It is very possible that at one point, the area manager will need to try to make both department managers and teams focus on this Challenge as part of their Improvement Kata, though the area manager cannot yet do that, as the very structure and responsibility might change first.

I am not saying that it is easy to do end-to-end Process optimization in a more traditional setup. From a Catch-ball perspective, however, there is no doubt that it is easier to picture how the different levels might work toward a common goal, as they are part of the same Value Stream.

But what do we do when we are already within an Agile organizational structure?

In the example above, there was a connection between the overall goal of reducing lead time to the actions on the different levels of the organization. But what does it look like when an Agile organizational structure has already been established and we are essentially dealing with the entire Value Stream found at the team level? What might Challenges and Target Conditions look like at the area and department level when there is no area or department Value Stream, but instead areas supporting multiple products through dedicated teams?

First of all, it is important to ask "Why?" Why are you considering a shared improvement theme across the organization, area or department and what do you hope to achieve by it? What makes you believe that a broad and shared focus will have a bigger effect than a local improvement topic created closer to the actual customers and Value Streams? One of the purposes of Agile is to delegate decision authority to the place where the actual customer value is produced, so a Catch-ball should be initiated only when there is the real benefit of a more "global focus". Valid reasons for initiating a Catch-ball might include:

- Many areas, departments or teams face the same constraints in terms of delivering on the Vision.
- To succeed, improvement initiatives require budget and commitment beyond a single department or team.
- Improvement potential is related to organizational structure and involves reorganizing people across areas, departments or teams.
- Program/Scaled Agile initiatives in which many teams work toward a shared goal and with shared parts of the Value Stream.
- Leveraging the potential of the energy, motivation and drive when uniting the organization, area or department toward a common purpose (making employees feel part of something bigger than their team).

The last point might seem to stand out as less motivated by actual improvement potential and more of a social initiative. That is correct to some extent, but it is something we heard again and again when speaking to department managers and teams. This typically happened not at the beginning, when people were busy learning the Toyota Kata framework, but once they were past the first successful Challenge, when people were asking for the chance to be part of a bigger and more global improvement initiative. I suspect that the need to be part of something bigger increases with an Agile organization structure. When you find yourself in a cross-functional team focusing on a single or small portfolio of products and working together with the same team members every day, you are more likely to feel like an "island".

The question of "why" is important but, to be honest, we probably forgot to ask this question enough during our struggles to establish initiatives across organizational levels. We fell into the trap of focusing too much on the ability to use Catch-balls rather than on the more important question of

"Why do we want to?" But asking "why" also revealed another important aspect of Catch-balls – namely, that they must be a real Challenge for Toyota Kata to be a good fit. If the organizational goals are not Challenging but more the stroke-of-the-pen type of initiatives mentioned earlier, Toyota Kata might be an overhead rather than an effective implementation engine. The beauty of a Toyota Kata Catch-ball Challenge is that it makes it possible for information to flow easily across organizational levels and for everybody to work toward a common goal with a shared commitment. If your initiative is not in need of such a structure, there are better ways of doing it.

Two examples of failed Catch-balls come to mind in this area: "forecasting template" and "process revision compliance".

Forecasting template

At one point, Bankdata was reacting to a broad customer need for a standardized interface for forecasting of future deliveries. A template was created with input from Agile Coaches, teams and managers and the actual implementation and continuous updating of the forecasts using the template was thought of as a great chance for an organization-wide Toyota Kata Challenge.

This did not work very well:

- The speed of actual adoption was so fast that we could not establish a Current Condition before it was already outdated.
- The template was easy and simple to use and, thus, involved little experimentation in getting it to work.
- Basically, it was a matter of introducing it through a workshop and booking the time to update it at the requested interval.

It was clearly a stroke-of-the-pen initiative and not a Challenging capability to build across the organization.

Process revision compliance

Having transitioned to Agile, Bankdata's traditional product delivery model was now outdated and replaced with less formal process compliance, frequent deliveries and adaptive planning: a great situation if not for the fact that you cannot pass an audit in the financial sector without demonstrating a product delivery model and the capability to use it. Rather than implementing a less heavy version of a traditional phased delivery model, Bankdata took a different approach and chose to define a set of capabilities that each team should evaluate their ability to follow, including things like "security by design" and "traceability of deliveries".

To pass the audit, you do not actually have to follow the model but demonstrate the ability to reflect on all aspects of the model and make a conscious choice to follow it or not. As an additional bonus, the new delivery model was made available online and each team had to move the different capabilities to "done" once they had reflected and adapted their process accordingly. This meant that Current Condition data was readily available and the trend toward the goal of using it could be followed continuously: on the surface, a great Catch-ball but, alas, we were disappointed again. This is what happened:

- The Areas that chose to formulate what they thought of as an ambitious Challenge were overtaken by those that simply went ahead and did it. Though not as simple as the forecasting template, it still did not require navigating unclear territory.
- The fact that it required creativity, experimentation and cleverness to design a different approach that auditors would approve is not the same as its being difficult to use once in place.

In retrospect, there is no doubt that both these Catch-balls were too simple and were "stroke-of-the-pen initiatives". I won't take any offense if you consider it surprising that we did not see this beforehand. But nevertheless, they taught us a very valuable lesson: Don't go around searching for something you can turn into an organizational Catch-ball. If (as we did) you go around searching for Catch-balls among existing initiatives, chances are that your light will shine on something interesting and, despite obvious problems, you will find a way to explain why it makes perfect sense.

Examples of successful Catch-ball Challenge topics include:

- Aligning 10 teams in a Scaled Agile setup toward a shared goal and end-to-end visualization of the shared Value Stream
- Shared focus on failure demand through visualization of defect root causes across products and technical platforms
- Stakeholder and end-user feedback and involvement
- Dedicated team members with 100% allocation
- Team Churn

Looking at a Catch-ball as a marketing initiative

But what do we do if a team or department is already busy working on a local improvement initiative and the wider organization wants to launch a Catch-ball with a different topic, or if a local initiative simply seems more important?

In general, we adopted the principle of Catch-balls as marketing initiatives. Basically, this means that if, as a manager or leader, you want to launch a Catch-ball, you must sell it to the rest of the organization. That means you must build a convincing case and provide arguments, data and material to support it. If areas, departments or teams are not buying it but are convinced that a local improvement initiative will yield a higher return on investment, obviously the topic or the marketing of the topic wasn't good enough.

Managers who are used to a more command-and-control leadership style might find the concept of having to "sell" a Catch-ball rather than simply telling their direct reports to "do it" a strange concept. There are, however, at least two very good reasons for adopting this principle:

- If people are not buying, they are not committed. If they are not committed to reaching the goal, then the energy, creativity and willingness to take risks and experiment are much lower and you will not get the effectiveness you are looking for.

- Using a command-and-control by telling rather than asking might be counterproductive in a situation in which you are trying to teach the organization the values of Agile. Nothing ruins an otherwise great change initiative than the supposed role models acting against the very basic principles we are trying to implement.

Mostly, teams and department managers are more than willing to grab a Catch-ball if it is marketed well and if they believe that the proposed result can be achieved. Similarly, in cases in which a Catch-ball has been rejected by a team or department, it is often done on solid grounds and with mutual agreement.

Though I must admit that I have never seen it used in real life, we officially adopted the principle from 4DX that a leader or manager can veto but not direct. If, e.g., a team or department should choose a Challenge that conflicts with the overall Vision, their manager has the right to veto that decision but the manager cannot tell them what to do instead – only suggest and ask.

Catch-balls and Outcome metrics

We have found that the higher you get in the organization, the greater the tendency to focus on Outcome over Process metrics. This is quite natural, as the higher you get the more distant you are from the operational level processes and the more responsibility you have for overall organizational performance – the bottom line.

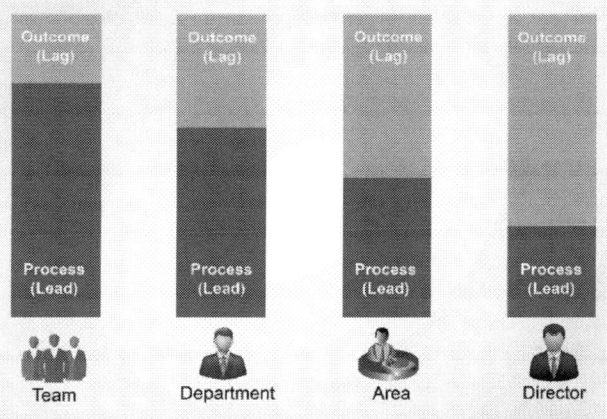

Figure 61: Focus on Outcome and Process depending on organizational levels

In terms of Toyota Kata, we have found that this has both good and problematic implications.

The good news:

- As we move up in the organization, our leading indicators become less leading as we move further from the operational processes and the cycle time of experiments increases. Outcome metrics, however, often remain the same. This means that the update frequency of process metrics and outcome metrics come closer to each other. Focusing on Outcome metrics becomes less of a problem because there is no longer a delay in seeing the effect compared to the "leading" Process metrics.

- When the update frequency of lagging and leading indicator move closer to each other, there is a higher chance that we focus on both. Ultimately, we do want to see our lagging Outcome metrics move in the right direction!

The bad news:

- It is a well-known organizational anti-pattern that senior leaders start an Agile or Lean initiative but fail to grasp what it truly means besides what they hope to see reflected in the eventual Outcome metrics. Not taking the time to fully understand the process capabilities they are striving to build in the organization makes directors highly vulnerable to short-term optimization, unknowingly making decisions that conflict with that direction or diverting from the goal when pressured by a temporary problem.

- Ultimately, senior leaders might try to delegate the responsibility of finding the Process Vision to others in the organization and present it to the group of directors only for approval. This seems attractive, as it makes it possible for them to focus on Outcome while leaving the details of how to get there to the specialist. While I recommend using both internal and external specialist in helping frame the Process Vision, it is crucial for directors to be directly involved, as it is the ground on which all Process improvement will be made.

So, though we can benefit from having senior management take an active part in making sure we are also delivering on Outcome metrics, we must ensure that they also invest time and effort defining Process targets. It is not one or the other but both!

A Catch-ball does not have to influence the team level

Another important lesson we learned was that a Catch-ball must reach the team level directly to be effective. Reading books about, and examples of, the application of Toyota Kata Catch-balls, we had not even contemplated this option, as all the examples we found had always included the operational level of the organization directly. When end-to-end teams cover the entire Value Stream, Catch-ball Challenges often focus on structural rather than specific workflow processes.

We might, e.g., set an area and department Challenge to increase the number of feature teams (reduce the number of functional/component teams). Though it will influence how teams are structured and/or what products they deliver, we do not expect such a Challenge to ever appear on the Improvement Boards at the team level. It might also be the case that there is value in reducing the number of decision "gates" that teams must use to allow for faster experimentation cycles; while teams might celebrate the result, they are not part of changing that part of the IT governance.

So, when launching a Catch-ball, you should not first think about how you can INVOLVE the entire organization but instead about what process capabilities would BENEFIT the entire organization. It could be that you must market the Catch-ball through all the organizational layers but sometimes it will appear only on Improvement Boards at the director or area-manager level.

When is a Catch-ball a stroke-of-the-pen or an ambitious Challenge?

As with Challenges in general, it is unfortunately not possible to use a standard formula to judge whether a Catch-ball is a stroke-of-the-pen initiative or an ambitious Challenge that requires you to navigate unclear territory. Instead, we have found it useful to apply the concept of green-, yellow- and red-zone Challenges at the organizational level. We simply ask ourselves, "Given that we can convince the different organizational levels to adopt this Challenge and deliver on the intended process capabilities, who will find themselves in the red, green or yellow zone?" We might conclude that only area and department managers are in the yellow zone while, on the team level, it is a simple matter of getting it prioritized on their "Backlog" – and that is fine! There is no reason to try to convince a team to drop their existing Challenge if all they must do is simply free up 10% of the capacity on their "Backlog" to work with a well-defined set of instructions. In that case, part of the department-level Obstacle and experiments will be about convincing teams to free up that capacity.

You learn from mistakes and though I personally think I learn as much from success, you should prepare to be wrong! It is more difficult than we originally thought to judge whether a Catch-ball is truly in the yellow, red or green zone and which layers of the organization it includes. You must make your own mistakes, and though I do not recommend that you assume you will be wrong, you can benefit from initially asking the question, "What do I expect to observe when I am right?" A bit Meta-Kata, I know.

Non-Catch-ball Challenges at the manager level

Challenges above the team level do not necessarily have to be Catch-balls. In many organizations, multiple processes going on at these levels need optimization, and an area manager might, e.g., set a personal Challenge to free up available time for Gemba-walks or unscheduled requests from teams and department managers. The area manager will still be coaching department managers through the Coaching Kata but the department-level Challenges might focus on very different topics.

Given the extensive focus on Catch-balls in the Toyota Kata cases and literature, it was surprising for us to discover how often managers at all levels found it valuable to work with local Challenges instead. I do not know if this is specific to the Agile organizational structure. I suspect that when most of the delivery responsibility is delegated to the team level, managers will focus more on their own service to the organization rather than how they can be part of lower-level processes and decision-making.

The great thing about this is that once managers start looking at themselves as a service, they often find that, like on the team level, service is not always "fit for purpose" from a customer perspective. Looking at the Vision, we might ask questions like:

- If my main purpose is not to make product decisions and be involved at the operational decision level, why is my calendar still packed with meetings that look like it is?
- If my main purpose is to create the best possible environment for teams to flourish, why do I not have any time available for that?
- Why have I attended only half the Coaching Kata with my managers or teams?
- Why is my work not prioritized and visual?
- Why do I have 25 things in progress and seven items that were started over four months ago?
- Why am I not making Minimum Viable "Features" and validating my assumptions when I am asking teams to do so?

- Who are my customers? Why am I here? What service do I deliver?
- Why do I spend seven hours a week manually filling out spreadsheets when such a process could be automated?
- Why does it take two hours to get the data I need for the budget?
- Why is current area data like allocation, money spent, budget and open positions not gathered automatically and visualized in a shared place?
- How do my customers evaluate my service and how will I find out?

It has been surprising to see how many of the Process Vision elements also apply to the management level. We focus so much on the team level that we forget that processes are in place at all levels of the organization. Process optimization is not reserved for teams developing new features. I am sure you can already picture most of the Challenges resulting from the questions asked above but, if not, here are just a few examples:

- From 0% to 70% visualization of work
- From 5% to 49% unscheduled time in the calendar
- From 2 hours to 1 minute finding budget data
- From 35 to 20 work items in progress
- From 0 to 5 "customers" who are continuously evaluating my service

Learning objectives and questions for real-life application of Catch-balls, Challenges and Target Conditions above the team level

In this chapter, we discussed the application of Toyota Kata above the team level. I hope it made you realize that to drive improvement effectively, we must involve the entire organization and move beyond the notion of continuous improvement as something that goes on only at the team level. Key learning objectives of this chapter include:

- As we move up in the organization, we must adjust the cadences of Toyota Kata events accordingly.
- Catch-balls can be an effective way of aligning continuous improvement toward a shared direction.
- Think of Catch-balls as initiatives that you must sell to the rest of the organization. They should adopt it because they believe in the importance and not simply because they are told to do so.
- Challenges and Catch-balls at the manager levels do not necessarily have to end up as a topic on the team-level Improvement Board.
- As we move up in the organization, the update frequencies of Outcome and Process metrics move closer to each other.
- We must separate stroke-of-the-pen initiatives from real Challenges, as Toyota Kata is not always an effective way of delivering on the former.
- Managers deliver a service as well. Optimizing that service can be an excellent candidate for a Challenge focus. Don't assume that Challenges at the manager level always involve the wider organization.

Before you continue, write your answers to the following questions to the best of your ability:

- Look at the Process Vision and try to come up with two or three topics that you think would be relevant to focus on as a Challenge on the manger level. Once completed, consider:
  - Is it a Catch-ball?
  - Whom would it involve?
  - How would you frame the Challenge using the format introduced earlier?
- Can you think of upcoming or previous stroke-of-the-pen improvement initiatives in your organization that would not lend themselves well to Toyota Kata?
- Looking at it from the perspective of a senior manager, how would you "sell" a Catch-ball in your organization? What marketing concepts would you use to convince managers and teams to adopt the Catch-ball?

18. Roll-out of Kata in the organization

This chapter will focus mainly on experiences with rolling out the Toyota Kata framework across Bankdata, from the initial pilots to deciding to do it as an organization-wide initiative. To better understand the context, I will start with an overview of the time sequence and later discuss individual concepts and the roll-out strategy we ended up with, in more detail. You will find that much could have been done better and some mistakes and problems were entirely avoidable. I do, however, find it more useful to provide an adequate account of what happened instead of the pretty-printed version.

All organizations have constraints, and even the most important change initiatives are limited by time, budget and available skills. There is no doubt that the roll-out at Bankdata would have been much easier if, from the beginning, we'd had a team of 10 Toyota Kata coaches with 10 years of experience implementing the framework in the context of knowledge work, product development and Agile organizations. It would have been even easier if internal managers were already experienced coaches with a deep knowledge of Agile and Lean and if team-level Scrum Masters and Process Leads had years of experience. In retrospect, there were points where we scaled too quickly or were too slow to act on the available feedback. But that is the whole point of Toyota Kata: to set an ambitious direction and then learn to gradually become better at iteratively navigating the unclear territory that organizational change always is.

It is beyond the scope of this book to cover the hundreds of small and large adjustments we made to the training material, workshops and roll-out strategy. Instead, I will provide an overview of the major phases we went through and later explain how a Meta-Kata was used to navigate the unclear territory.

The first pilot (August 2016 – December 2016)

The first Toyota Kata pilot involved a single area, four departments and only six of the 18 teams. The pilot was initiated by Flemming Krath Engedal, who was at that time director of the area. Flemming had recently joined Bankdata and, though impressed by the scale and commitment to Bankdata's recently deployed Agile initiative, found that he needed an even stronger improvement engine to move his area, departments and teams in a Lean and Agile direction. By chance, Flemming and I ended up discussing continuous improvement after a meeting and he immediately recognized the potential of Toyota Kata. Because Flemming is not the type of leader prone to sitting back and waiting, we quickly got into discussing how we might launch a Toyota Kata pilot in his part of the organization.

One of the things that had struck Flemming in his first period at Bankdata was that though he saw many Scrum artifacts and events in play, he did not find the focus on customer value and feedback that he had expected. Flemming had the hypothesis that it was mainly because of three reasons:

- The delivered Backlog Items represented mostly technical activities rather than end-user value and, thus, the stakeholders present would need a technical background to appreciate the results.
- Stakeholders did not seem very interested in the finished items that did provide end-user value because the matter wasn't relevant to them personally.
- The stakeholders present did not know what was expected of them

Inspired by the notion of aligning the organization toward a common goal, we introduced Toyota Kata through a shared area initiative focusing on getting verbal feedback from stakeholders and end users. We believed that this would be a great leading indicator of Flemming's area's ability to move beyond Scrum mechanics and start interacting and iterating with the real world. If no stakeholders had verbally expressed their opinion on a finished Backlog item, it would count against the goal. We required it to be a real opinion; thus, "It looks great" would not count. We acknowledge that the definition allowed some room for subjective interpretation but trusted that clearly explaining the goal of feedback and collaboration would avoid the temptation to game the metric.

The initiative covered all four departments, so all department managers were involved but only six of the 18 teams were involved, to limit the blast radius and avoid overloading the department managers. To find the Current Condition, each team was asked to look at their finished Backlog Items during the previous two or three Sprints and identify finished items that had received real verbal feedback from an end user or stakeholder. As expected, the number was quite low, with less than 10% fulfilling that criteria.

This pilot took place before Toyota Kata became my primary responsibility in the organization, so most of the time I was busy introducing Agile/Lean principles, structures and processes in a large program. This was quite a change compared to my previous experience with Toyota Kata, but it gave me my first experience introducing Toyota Kata in a setting where I would not have the chance to follow the individual teams and managers closely myself.

From a metrics perspective, the initial pilot was a great success. Initially, only around 9% of all finished Backlog Items got valuable feedback from stakeholders but by the end of the first two-and-a-half months with Toyota Kata, that number was closer to 50% and continued to rise. The pilot had successfully engaged both teams and managers in achieving the result. Experiments had been creative and included anything from engaging with early adopters during the Sprint, getting the right stakeholder and slicing User Stories vertically to proactive communication around the Sprint content.

As you can tell by the graph below, there was a temporary decline around the beginning of December. This was because one of the teams chose to dedicate an entire Sprint to refactoring work and went from 70% to 0%.

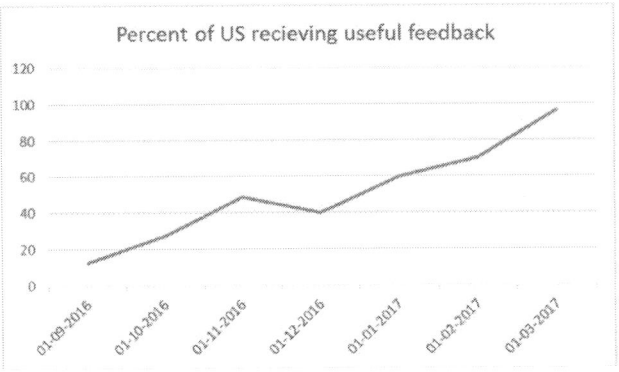

Figure 62: Feedback graph

Because it is hard to claim any kind of Agility without a functioning feedback loop, it should have been an undeniable success. Alas, that wasn't the whole truth. From the perspective of learning, the pilot was a great success, as it made it possible for us to do much better when introducing it to the wider organization. But from the perspective of the managers and teams involved, it wasn't an undeniable success. The key points we learned were:

- Though our first Challenge was a success from a metrics perspective, teams had been very frustrated about having to learn a new concept while working on something that had been decided top-down. They had been confused at multiple levels at once, and even though they agreed that it had been a success, they did not feel they really understood what had happened and could repeat it for the next Challenge. Teams unanimously encouraged us to let the next teams start with a local Challenge and introduce shared initiatives once they were familiar with the process.

- A similar point was made that many teams already had aspiring, ongoing and sometimes failing improvement initiatives. Demonstrating how Toyota Kata would enable them to think differently and execute more effectively on these would be a great marketing tool for further and deeper adoption.

- Much more intensive training and coaching were needed at the beginning for team members, Process Leads and managers. A single experienced coach with half a day available per week wasn't nearly enough (and, yes, we knew that beforehand).

- Even mature Agile coaches with extensive knowledge of Lean and Agile and coaching experience had difficulty grasping the key elements. We trusted too soon that they were able to act as a second coach. It was by no means their fault but simply that I had forgotten how much time and effort it takes to learn a new skill to the extent that one is able to coach others. This was a valuable experience for me personally, as it made me realize how much I had learned during the past four years.

We were fully aware, even from the beginning, that we did not have enough capacity to provide the needed support. We also knew that the only alternative was to drop the initiative. Thus, we went ahead and explored how far we could go with our limited capacity. Introducing a new framework through a one-and-a-half hour introduction and with limited capacity to provide follow-up coaching is guaranteed to fail in some aspects. The goal was to learn quickly and to move forward with the initiative on a more serious scale. From that perspective, we succeeded. When we asked the Process Leads, team members and managers who were part of the first pilot what they thought about the way Toyota Kata had been introduced, the response was: "You threw us all into the deep water without any kind of flotation device to help us and it turned out that not all of us could swim".

The second "wave" (January 2017 – May 2017)

The second "wave" included five more teams as well as extensive lobbying by Flemming and me to get buy-in for spreading Toyota Kata to the wider organization. At this point in time, I was able to double my capacity to use one day a week on the Toyota Kata initiative. It was still not nearly enough to provide the support we wanted but, fortunately, the internal coaches now had more experience.

In the second wave, we came up with the notion of the top-down, bottom-up approach. Managers would get priority in terms of initial training and coaching to enable them to start coaching teams from the very beginning, while teams would be the first to start with actual improvement targets. Instead of a top-down Challenge, their initial Challenge would be decided locally – an approach Mike Rother also recommends (Rother, 2018).

From this, we also learned a lot:

- A more structured roll-out concept was needed. Expectation management in terms of what help would be offered and when it was in high demand.

- If moving from a traditional functional structure with a waterfall process equaled 100 in change, our initial belief was that introducing Toyota Kata was around 30 to 40. We were now starting to realize that it was probably closer to 70 to 80 as the Toyota Kata onion started revealing more layers.

- Simple practices, tools and examples make adoption easier. A Starter Kata starter kit with preprinted boards, guides and examples was requested.

The third "wave" – Implementing Toyota Kata in new areas (May 2017 – December 2017)

Sometimes luck also plays a part and lobbying to make Toyota Kata a companywide initiative wasn't made more difficult by Flemming's promotion to CIO. But still, we had to convince the directors as well as get the budget approved. By this time, we had realized that leading the initiative wasn't a part-time job.

In late spring of 2017, we finally got the approval and I left the role of lead Agile coach of the large program to focus exclusively on Toyota Kata. We chose to use a pull-driven, marketing approach toward finding the next areas to start with and created a small internal marketing campaign to encourage areas to sign up to be next in line. We had anticipated that it would be difficult, but our marketing efforts were highly successful. I ended up doing interviews with the most eager directors to judge who would be the best to start next.

In parallel, we were formalizing the new roll-out concept to offer a package that would make it easier for the next in line to adopt Toyota Kata. Because not all the initial teams and managers had a successful first experience, we chose to test it on them to get some early response. The initial responses to the new concept were very positive and we were quite surprised at how much better it seemed to work. The roll-out concept looked like this:

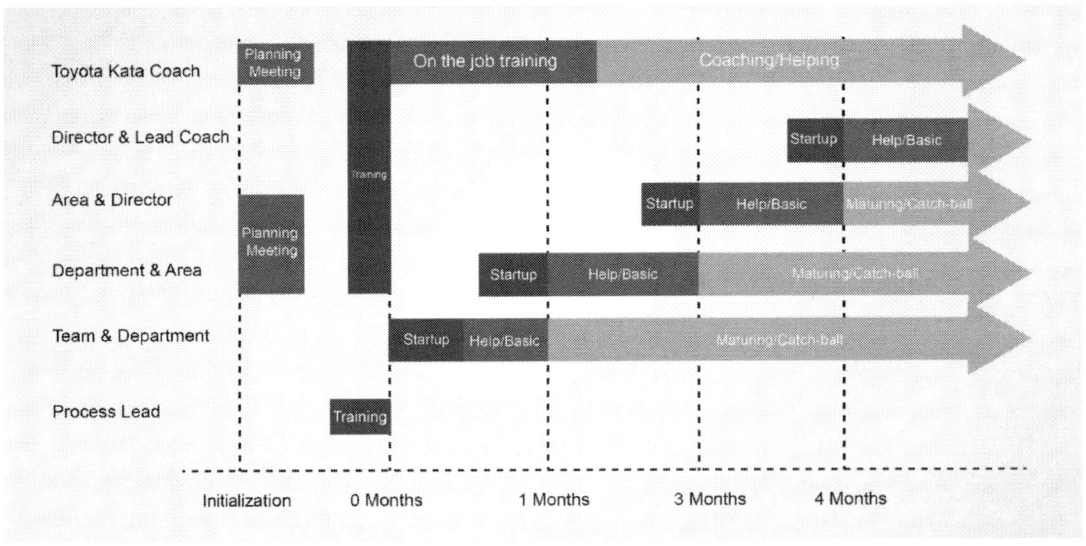

Figure 63: Roll-out overview

The naming in the rows, e.g., "Team & Department", refer to when the Coach/Learner relationship is initiated between the different levels. It is not entirely consistent, as it also communicates who will be

191

involved in which activities. Thus, department managers, areas managers, directors and Toyota Kata coaches all participate in the initial planning meeting.

The flow reads like this:

- **Step 1**: At an initial planning meeting, the roll-out concept is introduced, and it is decided which departments and teams will be part of the roll-out and in what sequence. Before the meeting, department managers and Toyota Kata coaches are given the job of discussing with the individual teams how well they are set up to handle being introduced to Toyota Kata at this point.

- **Step 2**: A one-day Toyota Kata workshop is held for Process Leads, department managers, area managers, directors and Toyota Kata Coaches. They are given a basic introduction to Toyota Kata as well as information about what is expected of them in their individual roles. They also get the chance to work with cases to go beyond a theoretical introduction and discover how hard it is to turn theory into practice.

- **Step 3** (not shown in the diagram): Process Leads from each team meet with the Toyota Kata coach and department manager to frame the topic of the first Challenge. Before the meeting, the Process Lead has facilitated a session with the team to decide on potential topics for the Challenge.

- **Step 4**: Teams are given a one-day introduction with the department managers and Toyota Kata coaches present. A Toyota Kata coach is assigned to each team and will follow them and their related managers to provide feedback and guidance. The last part of the day is a workshop with the goal of filling out the Improvement Board to be ready to get started with Toyota Kata the next day.

- **Step 5**: Toyota Kata Coaches facilitate the first Improvement Kata Planning meeting as well as the first Coaching Kata and Daily Kata. Toyota Kata Coaches participate in the following events and provide feedback to managers and Process Leads after each event.

- **Step 6**: A preparation meeting is held with the department manager to help frame the first department-level Challenge.

- **Step 7**: A five-hour startup workshop is held for department managers going deeper into the content of Coaching Kata, Catch-balls and Coaching Planning cycles. The last part of the workshop is used to fill out the department-level Improvement Board.

- **Step 8**: Repeat steps 6 and 7 for the levels above (area and director level).

Throughout the implementation, Toyota Kata coaches are doing on-the-job training and I participate and provide feedback to them as often as possible.

Naturally, the real roll-out is not as static as the figure above suggests. Not all teams, e.g., begin on the same date, but this shows a rough overview of the roll-out process.

We learned a lot from this exercise:

Scaling too quickly really hurts!

The initial pull to adopt Toyota Kata in more areas was so strong that despite our initial WIP limit of one area at a time, we agreed to do two in parallel. The problem was that reintroducing Toyota Kata with the new roll-out concept had generated "false positives". At this point, we did not realize how much the teams, managers and Toyota Kata coaches had learned during the initial pilot. Thus, we assumed that the new concept was working much better than it truly was. Therefore, we became overconfident and agreed to take on more than we could support. It is easy to see how we got caught in the enthusiasm and the joy of having such a strong pull for our "service".

It did, however, have quite serious consequences, as both teams, managers and Toyota Kata coaches in the new areas did not get the needed support. We discovered too late that the new roll-out concept required several important adjustments. The problem was made even worse because it almost turned into a "weapons race" between the two new areas in terms of who could scale the fastest. We were over one month into the roll-out in the new areas before I realized that all teams were being onboarded and we were facing 25 teams across 10 departments at the same time. Not only did we break our WIP limit on the organizational level but the same happened on the team level.

If you look at it from a change management perspective, we were communicating this step as an Early Adopter phase of the roll-out; we officially declared that major changes to the concept were expected and that we would need the help of teams, managers and Toyota Kata coaches to adjust and improve both the elements of the Starter Kata and the roll-out concept. However, though we repeated that message many times, we were scaling at a speed such that we simply could not inspect and adapt quickly enough to keep up with the feedback.

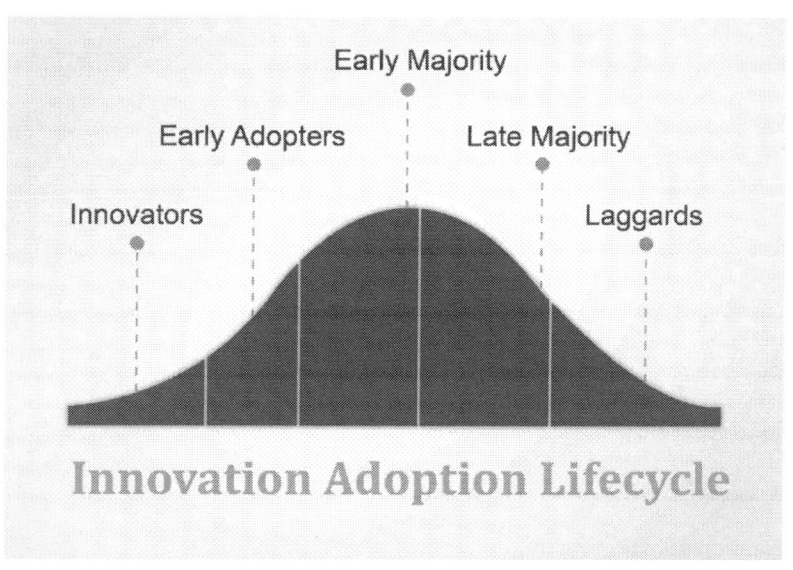

Figure 64: Innovation Adoption Lifecycle, Roger's Bell curve. Adapted from
https://en.wikipedia.org/wiki/Everett_Rogers

We did get a lot of success stories from this phase, as clever and enthusiastic people are often able to navigate a less-than-ideal situation, and we learned a lot in terms of framing both the Starter Kata and the roll-out concept. But we also experienced some serious problems that took a long time to "damage control" and from which some teams and managers have still never truly recovered. Examples included:

- Toyota Kata coaches who found themselves coaching before they truly understood the framework and with no experienced coach available to offer them feedback (again).
- Managers rightfully getting frustrated with the lack of support and success and starting to question whether Toyota Kata was the right way to drive continuous improvement or if it would be better to revert to traditional retrospectives.
- Teams starting without having framed a meaningful Challenge and Target Condition and without the ability to measure progress or validate the results of experiments.

Not everybody is ready

The "weapons race" mentioned above also clearly illustrated a well-known point but one we had not taken seriously enough – namely, timing. At this point, we were still realizing the true depth and many layers of Toyota Kata, and the change in mindset had to reap the benefits. We had, therefore, not been able to communicate the J-curve aspect strongly enough; it would take real time and effort in the beginning. We had also assumed a higher level of general Agile maturity and were, thus, surprised that people were still struggling with the basics and felt that it was simply too soon to introduce "another change". We ended up with a short list of things to look for. Most elements should not be surprising and some of them should not even exist in an Agile context. But if everything was already perfect, why would we need Toyota Kata?

- If a major deadline is coming up and people have been working toward it for months, a J-curve that will reduce their capacity in the short term is not an ideal fit.

- Teams or departments that have simply been reorganized require some weeks to land on their feet. Process improvement works best if there is already some kind of existing process.

- If a recent change is still top-of-mind, people do not yet feel they have the mental capacity to learn new frameworks and principles. From a rational standpoint, Toyota Kata might seem like the perfect engine to get the recent change to work but if people's change capacity is already loaded at 100%, it still does not work very well.

- Dysfunctional relationships become very transparent in a Toyota Kata setting. Having a team align on a Challenge and work together to achieve a shared goal in such a context is close to impossible. We realized that you must fix those interpersonal problems before starting any kind of Toyota Kata initiative (or any kind of initiative, for that matter).

Some department managers are part of department teams

Many Agile organizations strive to expand the concept of teams to include the management levels. The idea is that as a shared service, a team of, e.g., department managers can offer more expertise and can leverage the power of everybody to pull in the same direction when needed. The problem is that despite good intentions, it often sticks for only a period until the Daily Whirlwind and old habits manage to pull these manager teams apart to the extent that they are again working on a more individual basis.

Though that is also true for part of Bankdata, we found that within some areas, department managers have indeed managed to work as a joint team. Officially, they are still individually responsible for specific teams and people, but they share many tasks across and start each morning with a joint coordination meeting.

From a Toyota Kata perspective, this made things less complex, as we could simply copy-paste the setup from the team level. Being a team, the department managers worked on a shared Challenge. They selected a Process Lead and that person would be the one responsible for driving the Toyota Kata process in the team, as well as having Coaching Kata with the area managers. This also made it simpler from the area manager's perspective, as the area manager would have a single Coaching Kata instead of one per department manager.

You need more coaching and time to prepare the first Challenge

Getting the first Challenge right has proven to be a major factor in learning the Starter Kata. At this point, we had to realize that we simply could not do that on a consistent basis with the current roll-out concept. Teams and managers were complaining that more preparation was needed and that teams needed an introduction to the theory before helping prepare the topic of the Challenge.

We solved this by splitting the initial team workshop in two and placing the Challenge preparation meeting in between. The sequence came to look like this:

- Half a day: Two to four teams get an introduction to the theory and apply it using a domino exercise. At the end of the session, each team is assigned the homework of choosing a topic for their first Challenge. They are encouraged to seek inspiration in the Process Vision and related material but are free to choose any topic they want.
- Ninety minutes: Challenge preparation meeting with the assigned Toyota Kata coach and the department manager. It is up to the individual team as to whether they all participate or whether only part of the team participates. This meeting includes helping them draw a Workflow Map of their process and identifying the potential Challenge topics. Typically, we find that Current Condition data is missing, which becomes the homework for the next session.
- Half a day: Challenge and Target and Current Condition workshop. Only one team is present. Each part of the Improvement Board is introduced through a deeper dive into the related theory. It is then applied in real life before moving on to the next element. At the end of the workshop, the Improvement Board is filled out and they are ready to start using it the same day or the day after.

This small change made a huge difference; after it, we were able to start teams on a much more consistently successful basis.

You can scale team training but not workshops

Related to the topic above, we found that while we could scale the basic introduction to Toyota Kata (theory and the domino game), there were no benefits in having several teams present when filling out the Improvement Board for the first time. The original idea had been to do it as a shared workshop during which teams would share and learn from each other but at this point, they were 100% focused on their own board and found the scaled training to be confusing and unfocused. It also meant that they had to rely more on the recently appointed Toyota Kata coaches, as I could assist only one team at the time.

Ignore Outcome metrics for the first Challenge

We acknowledged from the beginning that creating measurable Outcome improvements required a deeper level of knowledge and experience. Still, we encouraged teams to try to achieve it from the beginning. We had had reasonable success with this in the first teams but, once scaling the concept to a broader audience, we found that despite our efforts to make them focus on Process metrics, they would continuously end up spending a lot of time during the workshop on Outcome metrics. Here are some examples of the Outcome metric discussion topics that ended up consuming such a large part of the workshops that we were unable to get the teams ready for their first Improvement Kata:

1. We are just about to launch a brand-new product area. How can we compare current defect rates to previous ones in such a situation?

2. Our throughput variation is +/- 40%. We will need at least two to three months to collect enough data points to see if we have made a difference beyond simply pure "chance". That will make it so lagging that it is essentially useless.

3. We will start working on a new part of the platform next week. How can we compare cycle time data when the work we are doing has changed drastically?

4. We can't trust the current throughput dataset from our process tool, as we have changed both the way we create work items as well as how estimates are assigned in the last month. Getting enough "new" data to form a Current Condition will take months.

5. Cycle time variation is so high, we will be unable to separate any improvement in the average score from pure chance.

6. Upcoming iterations will focus more on refactoring than previous iterations. How can we then compare the scores?

7. It will take hours simply to be able to register lead and cycle time correctly with our process tool. Why should we waste time on that simply to prove a point?

8. We lost a senior team member last week, as she found a new place to work. While trying to keep the boat afloat, we will be onboarding a new team member in the next month. How can we compare any Outcome metrics in such a situation?

That was just a small sample; teams that included members with PhDs in statistics could go into much deeper arguments than I am able to convey here without embarrassing myself. The point is that many of these (not all) are valid arguments, as it would require either a large effort or a long time to form a reasonably correct baseline. Essentially, the Outcome metric could be so lagging, it could take months from the time we reached our Process Metric target until the time we would be able to evaluate whether our Outcome metrics had changed. Yet even doing that would require that we had kept our process stable from that point in time, which would not be very attractive from a Process improvement perspective.

Outcome effects are surely more difficult, as you cannot influence them directly and teams would spend a long time discussing how to get it right. Though some were valid and insightful discussions, we really wanted them to focus on the leading Process metrics, as they would be the center of attention during their Improvement Kata and would take us one step closer to the Vision. Adopting a new framework and improvement culture is not done in PowerPoint slides but through daily actions.

Acknowledging our failure to turn our focus to leading metrics, we decided to change our approach in both training and workshops. We now recommend stating a theme for the Outcome metrics only in the first Challenge and focusing entirely on leading process metrics instead. Once the ability to focus on and move the leading indicators is established, we would then start discussing how to set up and measure Outcome metrics and targets.

Though on the surface this seemed like a small change, it had a very big effect on getting successfully started with the framework. Having worked with leading process metrics for a while, it was much easier to later discuss the issue of Outcome metrics and how the effect of their improvement initiatives could be validated. It also meant that people were less likely to mix them up. Having practiced with Process metrics, teams were more likely to accept metrics that were "good enough" without being perfect.

Same Process Lead, same organization, very different results

One thing you do not notice when you are dealing with a few teams is how different people react to the exact same concept. In one case, a Scrum Master was part of two teams. Both teams were given the same introduction, they started at the same time, they were part of the same department and they had the same Toyota Kata coach. One of the teams was among the quickest and most successful from the very beginning while the other team had a really difficult time getting just the basics in place. We often tend to forget one of the most important parts of the Agile manifesto ("Individuals and interactions over processes and tools") because so much of what we do is process-related.

In this case, it became very evident that we could standardize the roll-out concept only to a certain degree and that we should be careful in validating a new approach or change based on the experience of a single team. Though I do not usually recommend shared Scrum Masters as a general solution, the Scrum Master in question provided a valuable insight with the comment, "Had I just been part of one of the two teams, I would not have appreciated either the potential of Toyota Kata or how deeply it influences the culture of a team and how difficult those habits can be to change".

The fourth "wave" – Exposing new bottlenecks and finetuning the concept (January 2018 – present)

With the input and adjustments from the third "wave", we were starting to experience a much smoother introduction of Toyota Kata. When starting new areas, it was done more gradually; departments or teams that were not ready were postponed. We now also had the chance for new Toyota Kata coaches to train in existing areas and get feedback and advice from more experienced coaches. The new roll-out concept gave us the chance to be much more proactive in helping teams get started with the right Challenge, while removing the focus on using Outcome metrics made it much easier to practice the art of moving process metrics in the right direction through daily experiments. Yet, as with many things, once you have solved one bottleneck, a new one is exposed. This was also the case in this situation:

The problem of the second Challenge

Having received extensive help getting started, teams and department managers were now off to a flying start. We thought this was great and we celebrated the new roll-out concept as a success and a huge improvement over previous attempts. What we did not realize at first was that the startup was now so smooth, people did not appreciate the actual depths of what it had taken to get them there. Despite our best efforts to remind them of the importance of proactively planning the next Challenge, people assumed that because it had gone so smoothly the first time, it could be done in a day or two or even at the Improvement Kata Planning meeting for the next Challenge.

When you have not suffered the pain of a poorly framed Challenge and the dysfunctions of trying to apply Toyota Kata on a bad starting point, you cannot relate to the importance. Again, "What you see is all there is" applies. This meant we were now seeing previously successful teams and department managers grinding to a halt and being incredibly frustrated that what had seemed so easy was now the cause of frustration and missing results. On a lot of occasions, we had to help restart the Challenge from scratch, as they had simply not set themselves up for success.

In our eagerness to get them off to a good start, we had given them lots of fish but failed to teach them how to use a fishing pole.

This made it very apparent that the support of the Toyota Kata coach had to be intensified, as the time for the new Challenge was approaching. Also, it should focus purely on guiding them in the right direction and not stretch to the extent that we were providing the actual advice and solutions.

The problem of a bottom-up approach toward the roll-out

Another issue that revealed itself during this period was that, in a few cases, teams had problems identifying relevant Challenges. Looking at the Process Vision, they were still very far from the ideal Future State, yet no matter what "gap" they were looking at, they felt it was outside their circle of influence and would require the commitment of the larger organization to achieve, or it simply wasn't worth pursuing.

- Some would look at their legacy platform and quickly conclude that removing the manual steps associated with deployment would involve new tooling at a price that was not even remotely within their budget.

- Some would look at the possibility of test automation and conclude that it did not make sense to do it before it was offered on the centralized platform as a standard tool.

- Some would look at end-user feedback and conclude that they did not decide on the stakeholder representatives present at the Sprint review meeting.

- Some would look at refinement Sprints that failed to deliver any real value and conclude that the need for that had been decided in other places in the organization.

- Some would look at their process and conclude that because they delivered working functionality after most Sprints and because their stakeholders were happy, there wasn't much to improve at all.

Some of those were valid concerns but most could be traced to the root cause of the teams lacking the support and buy-in from the organization around them. Even in cases in which teams are deploying 10 times a day to production with the lead time of new features counted in hours rather than days, we can always improve. However, instead of seeing potential, teams were finding all the reasons why it could not work. The funny thing was that other teams in almost identical situations had found a way through or around those Obstacles with the support of their managers.

From this, we concluded that bottom-up works well in most cases and a local first Challenge is a good place to start. But in cases in which we could not find a good local Challenge to practice the basics of Toyota Kata, we would need a backup plan and, subsequently, the possibility of introducing department-level goals earlier. It also demonstrated the previously mentioned differences between department managers. Even though they did not yet have their own Improvement Board and Challenge, some managers were quick to show the support necessary to help bring a perceived "red" Challenge well within the "yellow" zone. Meanwhile, others were doing almost the opposite, showing a reluctance to provide assistance and even going on to discourage teams from adopting a Challenge they thought was too ambitious.

The Meta-Kata – Using Toyota Kata to implement Toyota Kata

So, how did we know how successful we were in the Toyota Kata adoption across the company? Taking your own medicine can be hard at times. It is often easier to tell other people what to do and then find good excuses for why it does not apply in your own context. But nevertheless, that is what we decided to do when we started on the organization-wide initiative of implementing Toyota Kata in Bankdata at the beginning of the "third wave". Though we had tried working with the Meta-Kata concept during the initial pilots, this was the first time we challenged ourselves to find real leading Process metrics and to work systematically to improve them.

We coined it the Meta-Kata. Essentially, we tried to follow most of the Toyota Kata principles. That included:

- Setting a Vision of what the successful application of Toyota Kata would look like
- Finding objective metrics to indicate whether we were successfully taking steps in that direction
- Setting short-term goals and identifying both Obstacles and Experiments for those goals
- Visualizing trends so the entire organization could follow the success and failures along the way

Being a Meta-Kata, a few adaptations were made but, in general, we tried to stick quite close to the Toyota Kata framework. The vision became a high-level description of the behaviors we would want to observe when Toyota Kata culture was established in all parts of the organization. It looked like this:

Toyota Kata vision

- Toyota Kata is implemented across all layers of the organization, and at all levels, people are working iteratively toward a shared Process Vision using measurable Targets and scientific thinking.

It might seem a bit abstract but there are quite a few very clear aspects of the direction:

- The goal is to involve the entire organization: all layers and all functions.
- There is a shared overall direction for the entire company.
- People work with measurable Targets.
- Scientific thinking is used to validate hypotheses and experiments.
- It is iterative. We set an ambitious goal but expect to learn and adapt along the way, navigating unclear territory.

What the Vision did not state was how to achieve this.

Introducing a Toyota Kata maturity score

At the Challenge level, we identified the behaviors we would expect to observe when the Starter Kata had been successfully implemented. We did that by having each team and manager update a series of yes/no questions every week to follow the success of the Starter Kata. Though it is called the Starter Kata, remember that it takes effort and time to learn the basics of directed improvement and scientific thinking. Therefore, you should expect months to pass before the core aspects of the Starter Kata are in place. We mapped the specific behaviors to a Starter Kata maturity model to make it easier to set goals and identify overall success. Our Starter Kata rating looked like this (team-level example, slight adjustments were made for department- and area-level managers):

Basecamp - Started				
Participated in Toyota Kata Training	Improvement Kata Planning and Coaching Kata sessions booked in calendar	First Experiment In progress/initiated	First Coaching Kata session held	Visual and updated Improvement Board
Yes	Yes	Yes	Yes	Yes
Camp 1 - Mechanics Working				
At least 1 Coaching Kata session per week (last 3 weeks. Holiday periods excluded)	Current Target Condition is engaging/motivating	Experiments are targeting specific Obstacles (75%)	1-5 min.Team Kata after Stand-up (at least 60% - last 2 weeks. Holiday periods excluded)	Improvement Kata Planning session carried out during the last 4(6) weeks (Holiday periods excluded)
Yes	Yes	Yes	Yes	Yes
Camp 2 - Mature Process and Positive ROI				
Quantitative!! Process metrics in current Target Condition on improvement Board	Process metrics show a positive trend on Improvement Board (History visualized)	Experiment duration less than 5 workdays (at least 7 out of the last 10 or 70%)	Realistically ambitions Target Condition (achievable but requires creative/focused experiments to reach it)	Avg. ROTI>3 for Toyota Kata work in the team (Team ROTI score Friday after Daily Kata)
Yes	Yes	Yes	Yes	Yes
Camp 3 - Measurable Effect and Improved ROI				
Quantitative!! Effect metrics show a positive trend on Improvement Board (History visualized)	3 out of 4 coaching Katas provide a learning opportunity	Experiment duration less than 3 workdays (at least 5 out of the last 10 or 50%)	Avg. ROTI >=4 for Toyota Kata work in the team (Team ROTI score Friday after Daily Kata)	
Yes	Yes	Yes	Yes	
Summit - Muscle Memory				
Kata is part of daily routine - feels natural	Ability to drive continuous improvement is the primary measure of the Process Lead's performance	Current Vision,Challenge and Target Condition are connected	Avg. ROTI>4.5 for Toyota Kata work in the team (Team ROTI score Friday after Daily Kata)	
Yes	Yes	Yes	No	

Figure 65: Meta Kata team-rating example

As you can see, we have mapped only the core aspects of the Starter Kata:

- **Basecamp** is rather easy, as most is included in the workshop and training concept. But still, it does test whether the first experiment has really been started, events are booked in the calendar and so on. It is also meant to be an easy "success", as it should not be difficult to reach.

203

- **Camp 1** aims to validate whether the basic mechanics are in place. Are Coaching Kata/Daily Kata held? Have they found a Challenge worth achieving? Are Improvement Kata Planning meetings carried out?

- **Camp 2** is the first time we start evaluating the quality and effect of what is being done. Are Process metrics quantitative? Are trends positive and visualized? Have they managed to create short experiments that can be quickly validated? Do they find the current focus in the yellow zone?

- **Camp 3** includes the ability to define and validate the result based on Outcome metrics and even shorter experiments. This is also where we expect Coaching Kata to provide actual reflections and learning beyond the mechanics of asking the six questions. This is not easy, and it is expected to take months rather than weeks to reach this level, though a few teams and managers were quicker. There is a reason why these maturity traits are not expected in the beginning.

- **Summit** is the final step of the Starter Kata. From here, we expect areas, departments and teams to adjust and find their own way of applying Toyota Kata even more effectively. Questions at the "Summit" are also more qualitative and subjective, as we expect that the basics are now in place and that it is time to validate how the process "feels". While we expect Camp 3 to be reached before major adjustments are made, it is not necessarily the case that a team or manager will ever answer "yes" to all questions at the summit level.

While we expect teams and managers to demonstrate the ability to get to Camp 3 before making a large adaption to the framework, there is still a lot of leverage to adapt the Starter Kata to the individual context. That includes:

- Changing the content and the layout of the Improvement Board
- Changing the sequence and content of Daily Kata and Coaching Kata questions
- Changing the content and Agenda for Improvement Kata Planning meetings

ROTI simply means Return on Time Invested. It is one of the only subjective elements and seeks to provide an indication of the perceived benefit of using Toyota Kata for Improvement work. If the score is below a 3, it is a negative investment, as the time used does not provide enough value to justify the investment. Above 3 indicates a positive return. To be honest, we have had such big problems communicating the ROTI scale that I would consider another option the next time. Even teams and managers giving a 3 (neutral) would state that the Kata was working well but because they could still improve, they did not use the 4 or 5. Even with numerous examples, we kept getting false negatives, so that is probably a sign that the scale is not very "fit for purpose".

The benefit of using a simple spreadsheet was that teams and managers had to change the responses only to the questions that had improved (or degraded). When we tried a similar initiative at another company, we sent out a survey every week. People did not respond positively to having to answer the same +20 questions from scratch again and again.

With the rating of our Starter Kata maturity, we could follow the success and failures of our implementation strategy and training and coaching experiments as well as the individual elements that people were struggling with.

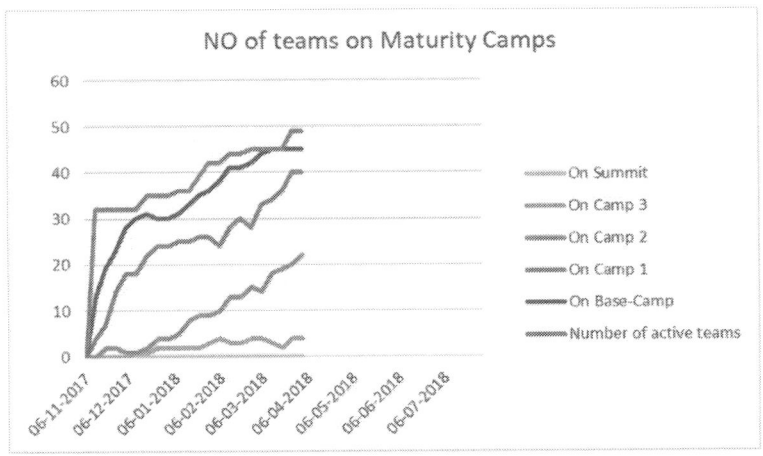

Figure 66: Toyota Kata maturity graph

Change in Complex Adaptive Systems is not simple

This gets us to another, very valuable point, which we will also get back to in the next section on using Toyota Kata to develop Agile organizations. On the surface, any change looks simple: Do some training, add some coaching and people will follow the principles and practices you have introduced and be happier and more productive. Looking at the Starter Kata questions in the rating above, it does not sound overly difficult; it is something you might expect to achieve in a few weeks for most teams and managers.

But learning new habits is difficult and, as you can see, it took time before we even got the number of teams on Camp 2 to increase. Had we not had a relative objective rating of the Starter Kata, we would probably have celebrated victory much too early. This is the same thing happening in Agile transitions, where success is celebrated when all teams have been through Scrum training and a standardized sequence of coaching sessions. But when you look closer, you will, e.g., find that many of those teams are working on Backlogs of activities rather than end-user value and that they are optimizing to keep people busy rather than finish started work.

No dataset is entirely valid when you ask people to judge their own capabilities or use any kind of scoring mechanism to validate the maturity or knowledge threshold of participants. Though we tried to keep the yes/no questions as objective as possible, we knew that they would be subject to interpretation. Despite our best efforts, we could not avoid false positives and negatives. Using the trends as guidelines, it remained important to "Go to the Gemba" to find out what was truly happening. Meta-Kata data and trends can show you where to look and what to focus on, but they will never provide any solutions if you do not get a deeper understanding of what is really going on.

What about the teams and managers who are failing?

It would be so much easier if people were not individuals or if teams and departments were roughly in the same circumstances and reacted in the same way to training and coaching. But organizations are complex, adaptive systems and it is impossible to judge the exact effect of any experiment or change that involves humans and their interactions. Fortunately, that is also what makes change management interesting. As with any other change initiative, you will discover that despite your best efforts to provide the needed training and coaching, not everybody will succeed. The reasons can be many, and we have already touched upon some of them. There is not a one-size-fits-all answer to what you should do in situations like that but there are a few things you can consider in those situations:

- First and foremost, you should never start a blame game. Even if you feel that people are purposely trying to create a failure, you must always think of it from a system's perspective. The system caused a team or a person to react in a certain way, so how can we change the system to enable success? Offer additional help, talk to them and try to understand the situation in more detail to get to the root of the problem. Sometimes it is simply a matter of correcting a small misconception. Admit to your own mistakes in not providing them with a better chance to succeed and use that as leverage to have an open and honest dialogue about future options.

- Acknowledge that sometimes it was simply bad timing. It might be a better option to put it on hold now when there is still a chance to get it on track later once the situation has changed. If people are about to be split into new teams or if they will be working on something totally different for the next six weeks, maybe a longer-term optimization focus does not make sense right now.

- Use the 80/20 rule. Your change management capacity is limited, so you want to invest it where it has the greatest effect. If two of 10 departments prove incredibly difficult to work with, you might not want to spend 80% of your capacity on them at the expense of the rest. It is tempting to focus all your energy on the teams and managers who are having the most problems, but it may not be where the return on investment is biggest.

- If you decide to put things on hold, agree on a specific date when you will meet and re-evaluate the situation. We often agree to "talk about it when it fits" or "discuss it after summer", but in a world where the Daily Whirlwind is ever present, "after summer" might become sometime in December for no apparent reason.

- Make sure you do not forget management buy-in. If managers or teams are reluctant to invest time, effort and energy, it can sometimes be a sign that their manager is not committed. The root cause could very well be that direct reports do not feel that it is considered important. If Coaching Kata are frequently canceled or a team or manager is asked to focus on the Daily Whirlwind instead of improvement, all your training and coaching efforts will most likely fail. If you expect this to be the case, ask for a meeting and for them to be honest and open about the reasons why. You might also find that they are 100% committed and the real problem is something different.

Meta-Kata as the first department-level Challenge

From the third wave, we experimented with using the Meta-Kata as the first department-level Challenge. We simply asked department managers to set a measurable Challenge for increasing the maturity of their teams in using the Toyota Kata framework. Though not without difficulties, this strategy had some obvious advantages:

- As we were already scoring all teams weekly, Current Condition data was available at 0 cost.
- They would be able to see weekly changes in scores and easily update trends.
- Focusing on Toyota Kata as a goal provided an excellent chance to dive deeper into the concepts of the Starter Kata and truly understand what it was about.

Several teams remarked, "What have you done to them? Why are they suddenly twice as engaged?" after they had started their Meta-Kata Challenge, while others remarked, "We have not had a canceled Coaching Kata session in weeks now and even if they get sick, they make sure that a substitute shows up". Because teams are rated on several aspects that can be directly influenced by department managers (e.g., the number of completed Coaching Kata), there were ample opportunities to work with specific Obstacles and see the results.

Though it was a success, there were also some problems:

- Some felt that it was too "Meta" and preferred something a bit closer to actual processes.
- After getting the initial things in place that could be directly influenced, some felt that it would be better to have a topic they could influence more directly and not "just" through Coaching.

- Several department managers voiced the opinion that though a Meta-Kata focus was valuable, they had other things that were even more valuable to address.
- Three months seemed to be the limit people could spend on the Meta-Kata; after that, engagement and motivation dried out.

The conclusion was that, for most, it made good sense to start with a Meta-Kata focus on the department level for the first three months, but that instead of mandating it, we would present it as a recommendation.

Can you coach others in something you have not done yourself?

I am sure that a lot of experienced Toyota Kata practitioners would answer this question with a definitive "no". But the problem is that most organizations like Bankdata that are seeking a better and more effective way to improve and stay competitive do not have 20 years to build the capability from scratch. As many Agile transitions have also proven, it is important to start building a team of internal coaches early to help maintain focus on driving the initiative forward, as well as spreading knowledge and sharing stories across teams, departments and other organizational boundaries.

Nobody would disagree that it would be a far superior situation if all Toyota Kata coaches had the ability to practice these capabilities and learn from experienced practitioners for years before helping others, but Toyota is probably the only company in the world in which that is an option. You might then argue that, instead, you should hire these externally for a period, but even if those people with experience in applying Toyota Kata in an Agile context were available (which is highly unlikely), the budget might not be there to support it.

So, really, it is about finding the best solution in a less-than-ideal context. In the case of Bankdata, we proved that it was possible to provide enough on-the-job training for the internal Toyota Kata coaches to offer deep feedback for both Process Leads and Managers. In some cases, it took longer than expected but I was consistently surprised by the level of depth to which some were able to coach during the last part of my engagement with Bankdata.

The same was true on the management level. It was a steep learning curve for many, as we were initially asking them to provide coaching in a framework they did not understand and had not experienced hands-on. Some picked it up very quickly, while others remained at the more mechanical level of coaching for longer. Fortunately, most got to the point where they were able to effectively challenge the knowledge threshold of the Learner and provide valuable reflections. One of the reasons is that through Coaching Kata, managers get a much broader experience with applying the Toyota Kata framework. This is especially the case with department managers, as they typically have the chance to see how three or four teams work, as well as have their own Challenges and Target

Conditions. In this way, they act like bees flitting from one context (flower) to another and bringing with them new ideas and inspiration (pollen).

Toyota Kata "guild"

Guilds are essentially communities of practice, but with the introduction of the "Spotify model", we all learned new and much cooler names for existing structures. After all, who would like to be on a team if you could be part of a "Squad" – and being in a "Tribe" sounds about 100 times better than being in a department. Don't underestimate names – they do affect culture! Because there were already numerous guilds in Bankdata (Scrum Master, UX, Product Owner, Test, etc.), we were nervous about introducing yet another one. The notion was that there were already lots of chances to share knowledge within the individual department and area where people would already meet and discuss the most present issues.

However, by the third "wave", the pull for establishing a Toyota Kata guild across the organization was so big that we started meeting once a month to share successes and failures. The agenda varied from time to time but often we would start with a short dive into the metrics of the Meta-Kata to explore interesting trends in terms of who seemed to be succeeding and failing and why. It also gave us a chance to discuss the individual concepts that teams and managers seemed to be struggling with the most and how we might design experiments to counter them. Cases were also on the agenda at most meetings and allowed us to dive into the details of the Improvement Kata and discuss how we might frame it differently. Getting the chance to discuss Toyota Kata at a very specific level instead of abstract general principles often revealed differences of opinion and ways we might align communication around specific topics.

The devil is often in the details. One participant at a guild was going through a specific case and explained how they used specific problems to frame both the Challenge and Target Condition but had the issue of choosing goals that were too easy to reach. Other participants at the guild quickly remarked that this was probably because they had forgotten to look at the direction and desirable Future State first; thus, all their goals became heavily anchored in their Current Condition. This started a heated discussion that went on for a long time and generated lots of insights that we would never have had if we had stayed at the abstract level.

In the beginning, it was mainly Toyota Kata coaches who participated in the guild but later we expanded it to include Process Leads and managers.

What Obstacles do we still face with the roll-out strategy?

When Flemming and I went to Amsterdam to present the Bankdata case at the first ever Kata-Con Europe Conference, we had the chance to meet with lots of other Toyota Kata practitioners and share experiences both inside and outside the Agile and IT-development setting. We left the conference with the notion that we had come very far and found strategies and tactics for dealing with many of the Obstacles others were still facing. We did, however, realize that there was room for improvement in our own setup in two very specific areas:

- From the examples and cases presented at the conference, it was clear that the quality of the coaching provided could be improved. Though many of the department and area managers had moved beyond simply asking the six Coaching Kata questions, many were not at the level we heard reported from other companies. Lots of excuses popped into our heads, including the time they had been practicing and the difficulty of doing it in an Agile setup, but we also acknowledged that to reach the full potential of Toyota Kata in Bankdata, this would need to be addressed more systematically than what we were presently doing.
- It also became apparent that we had not yet realized the full potential of focusing on shared Challenges across organizational levels. We were inspired by the reported use of organization-wide improvement metrics and the simplicity of visualizing it across the different levels.

That is the great thing about conferences; you get inspired to set the bar higher, even in situations in which you are doing well.

General recommendations for roll-out strategy

From the previous sections, I hope you got an idea of what we learned from the roll-out of Toyota Kata. No two organizations are alike but, hopefully, the story will make it possible for you to avoid some of the mistakes we made. To make it easier for you to get started, this section will provide a summary of the points above in a recommended roll-out strategy. Do not let the information below discourage you from experimenting with Toyota Kata in a single department or team; however, to do that you do not need a strategy and you will not face many of the constraints involved in a larger scale initiative. Do not over-complicate. Remember Agile principle number 10: "Simplicity – the art of maximizing the amount of work not done – is essential".

Step 1 – The pilot

Identify an area in which it would make sense to apply Toyota Kata. Include two to four departments and four to six teams. Choose teams and department managers who are "change-ready". The main points to remember for the pilot include:

- You need an experienced internal or external Toyota Kata coach to help you get started.
- Provide a starter kit with a pre-printed Improvement Board, example metrics and cases. Use those from this book until you have your own.
- Hold a startup training and workshop for teams. The recommended first Challenge should be local and last no longer than two to three months.
- Develop an area-level Process Vision in parallel with the first Challenge. Use the one from this book as a starting point
- After one month, hold a startup workshop for department-level managers.
- Start developing internal Toyota Kata coaches who can become future second coaches.
- After two to three months, hold a startup workshop for area managers (consider the Catch-ball initiative).
- After three to four months, hold a startup workshop for the director level.
- A high frequency of Coaching Kata should be a priority.
- Make Coaches observe each other and provide feedback.
- Make Coaches switch Learners and provide feedback.
- Document experiences – write case studies.

You will learn a lot from the pilot, so make sure you get input from all the levels involved and adjust accordingly.

Step two – Second area

Once you have established success in one area, you must get buy-in from the CEO and director level to spread the initiative to the wider organization. This requires using the documented cases as well as lobbying efforts. Once approved, use a pull-driven approach toward marketing the initiative and onboard the next area. Again, include two to four departments and four to six teams; choose teams and department managers who are "change-ready". The main points for the second area include:

- Use internal communication channels, meetings, blogs etc. to let the rest of the organization know what is going on. People will be talking, so you might as well be proactive and steer the communication in a positive direction.

- Establish a Meta-Kata Challenge – use the maturity score in this book as inspiration for collecting metrics.

- Use the same approach as in the pilot in terms of the startup of teams, department managers, area managers and directors.

- Start developing additional internal Toyota Kata Coaches who can become future second coaches.

- Establish a Toyota Kata coaching guild for second coaches, managers and Process Leads, e.g., once per month.

- Involve the director team and key specialists in developing an organizational Process Vision.

The second area is likely where you find out that some of the things you learned from the pilot were specific to the first area and that you must make more adjustments than you thought.

Step three – Wider organization

While working with the second area, you might have avoided a detailed discussion about the extent of the roll-out, when individual areas and teams should expect to be included and so on. Now that you are starting to include more teams in the existing areas and including new areas, you will face the fact that many people will be asking "When is it our turn?" I would not recommend that you create a complete Gantt chart in which you try to pinpoint when each individual area, department or team will be onboarded. However, you need a high-level strategy indicating the pace and the process for onboarding the rest. The main points include:

- Continue with a pull-driven approach – use a marketing approach to make people want to be on-boarded.

- Communicate the high-level onboarding strategy.

- Make visible posters explaining key Toyota Kata principles and the Process Vision and post them in common areas, hallways etc.
- Don't scale too quickly – you still have a lot to learn and adjust!
- Use the team of internal Coaches to help spread the initiative.
- If you have used an external Coach, it is time for that Coach to take a step back and gradually hand over the responsibility to internal drivers.
- Consider marketing an organization-wide Catch-ball if it makes sense to do so.
- Involving managers from the beginning gives them the confidence to be Coaches and teachers. It is more effective to bring them along and give them useful, concrete skills than to teach them vague knowledge about being Servant Leaders.
- Continue with Meta-Kata at all levels.

The last point is arguably the most important. Using Toyota Kata to implement Toyota Kata makes sure that there is a constant source of energy fueling the initiative and makes it possible for you to overcome all the Obstacles you are bound to face. And do not forget – once the Starter Kata has served its purpose, it is time to set it aside and focus on the core elements of Toyota Kata, as well as to replace Starter Kata practices with context-specific solutions. We are striving for the following core principles of continuous improvement – not how they are implemented:

- A shared Process Vision sets set an overall direction for Process improvement – a "True North" desirable Future State.
- At all levels of the organization, people are involved in taking measurable steps toward the Vision by setting and delivering on realistically ambitious improvement goals.
- Each step is validated using scientific thinking – taking an iterative and experimental approach toward Process improvement.
- Steps are short, and continuous improvement is a natural part of daily work.
- Coach and Learner relationships ensure that Process improvement capabilities are continuously improved at all levels of the organization.

Roll-out pitfalls

We have already touched upon many of the pitfalls you may encounter when you roll out Toyota Kata in the organization. Some are specific to Toyota Kata and some apply to any organizational change initiative. From the previous sections, you have been introduced to the pitfalls of Scaling too quickly and not taking the readiness of the individual team or department into consideration. Each context is different, but from personal experience, you should pay attention to the following additional pitfalls:

Don't forget the "why"

You can do a lot of things right but if you fail to clearly communicate the purpose of Toyota Kata, you are setting yourself up for failure. This message should be consistent across all levels and comply with the "elevator speech". We often take it for granted that people have understood the "why" but experience shows that we must keep repeating the same message many times over to avoid a purely mechanical focus.

The importance of communicating "why" is not related just to the high-level purpose of implementing Toyota Kata. It is also about the individual elements of the Starter Kata: the roles, events and artifacts. At no point should anyone be blindly following mechanics, so asking "why" is a key responsibility of, especially, trainers and second coaches.

Lack of buy-in

You can easily experiment with local pilot initiatives at the area or department level. You might even consider a single team but you should be aware that there is a chance that you will experience both false positives and false negatives. Being able to clearly communicate that there is buy-in from the top level of the organization will ensure that it is not a question of "if" but "how". Top-level buy-in is also a great chance to align the organizational direction.

Lack of shared Vision and Catch-balls

This might sound strange to experienced Agile Coaches, but once teams and managers have had the chance to practice Toyota Kata on local Challenges and Target Conditions, they will be requesting the chance to work toward a common goal. If no such goals are in place, people will start questioning the true buy-in at the organizational level. Also, managers in a hierarchy can easily sub-optimize as they work within their assigned span of control and focus on their own responsibilities.

Once you start introducing Toyota Kata, it is, therefore, important that you start working to frame the organizational Vision and investigate the Current Condition. From this, you should be able to communicate a shared Vision by the time the first team and managers have finished work on their first local Challenges. If it makes sense, the first Catch-ball could also be initiated at this time. It will provide needed practice in aligning the different layers of the organization and showing how much more can be done when it is a shared focus.

Focus on the team level

Teams are such a big part of the typical Agile organization that introducing them to Toyota Kata can easily end up consuming most coaching and training capacity. I have been guilty of this myself, and the pull to address team-level issues can become so strong that I now strongly encourage you to take proactive action before this happens. That includes specific planning of second coach attendance at manager-level Coaching Kata and Improvement Kata Planning meetings.

If you lose the drive and engagement at the manager level, this will quickly influence the commitment in other parts of the organization. You will not have the support to navigate difficult times when a Challenge is not ideally framed or external dependencies make it difficult to deliver on a Target Condition. Managers are acting as Coaches, and if they have not bought the concept of Toyota Kata themselves, they will not be able to coach teams or other managers in navigating this difficult situation.

Missing internal communication

Whether you are a big fan of ADKAR (Hiatt, 2006) or prefer a different model, it is important to recognize that once word gets out, people are going to have a lot of questions. If internal communication is not handled proactively, you can find yourself in a situation in which rumors and misinformation take hold. You then need to do a lot of damage control, explaining what the purpose and concept of Toyota Kata really are. When failing to do this, I have personally had to, e.g., deal with rumors that the Toyota Kata initiative:

- Is an attempt to abandon Agile and revert to command and control.
- Would mean that Scrum was no longer allowed.
- Dictated that everybody would be working on the same improvement with no local decision authority.
- Meant that only Scrum Masters would do improvement.
- Would be implemented as if it were a manufacturing plant, without any consideration of the context of IT and innovation.

I am in no way an expert in internal communication but regardless of the type of transition, I have found that failing to deliver on the bare minimum of the following can have drastic negative consequences.

- Getting the CEO to mention the initiative in the internal news feed or at a company meeting.

215

- Writing an internal news article with a brief explanation of what it is, why it is needed and how and when it will be introduced in the organization.

- Publishing a blog on the details of what it is, with links to external material. It might be months before everybody is given formal training or coaching, and people will want a rough idea about what they can expect.

- Having area- and department-level managers introduce the initiative at local meetings assisted by a Toyota Kata coach.

Really, it is simply about being proactive. A little time spent telling people what Toyota Kata is and what will happen can drastically reduce the anxiety and misinformation that is a natural part of any transition.

Rigid interpretation of principles and practices

Especially when you are dealing with early and late majority people will be asking for specific rules and explicit guidance. What is right and what is wrong? If we are not careful, this will quickly turn into an inflexible approach that is unable to deal with real-life situations. The Starter Kata is meant to provide a safe training platform for learning Toyota Kata, and we recommend following it until the concept is well-understood. But we can and should not take a religious approach, as that invalidates the whole concept. That includes:

- Insisting on an objective metric that is difficult to gather when a subjective score is good enough to get started.

- Insisting that it should always be the "right" Coach present at the Coaching Kata if, due to sickness, change of jobs or similar, it is not possible.

- Insisting that the Scrum Master should get the title of Process Lead if another team member is much more suited to take on the responsibility and an agreement on the division of responsibility can be found.

- Insisting that teams should use the official version of the Improvement Board even if they can practice all elements of the Starter Kata with their own version.

- Insisting on the recommended cadence of Improvement Kata Planning meetings every four weeks if two or six weeks is a better solution in the individual context.

Learning objectives and questions for real-life application of the roll-out of Toyota Kata in the organization

No context or organization is the same and though I hope the details of rolling out Toyota Kata at Bankdata will provide you with inspiration in terms of how you might approach it in your organization, it is important to look at it from the right level of abstraction. Therefore, I hope you grasped the following high-level points:

- Toyota Kata is not a small add-on to your existing process.
- You can get valuable insights from running a pilot in one area of the organization but make sure you are not just including the team level.
- Start developing a team of internal Toyota Kata coaches early who can become second coaches and help bring the initiative out into the wider organization.
- Establish a Meta-Kata. It is both a great chance to practice Toyota Kata at an organizational level and a way to get key insights into how specific experiments are helping drive the adoption of the Starter Kata.
- Starting with a focus on local Challenges and, in parallel, establish an organizational Process Vision that can align the future direction.
- The application of both the Coaching Kata and the Improvement Kata will likely be mechanical in the beginning but the important part is that it is continuously maturing and that you keep insisting that people be able to explain "why".
- Consider allowing teams and managers to focus on clear and objective Process metrics (leading) in the beginning and include Outcome metrics (lagging) only when they have demonstrated the ability to move those effectively.
- Pay attention to whether the timing is right in terms of introducing Toyota Kata in individual teams, departments and areas – are they ready for change?

Before you continue, write your answers to the following questions to the best of your ability:

- What would be the best place to start applying Toyota Kata in your organization?
- How would you get directors involved from the beginning, and especially in developing the Process Vision?
- Do you have any suggestions for good candidates who can serve as second coaches and help bring Toyota Kata to the wider organization?
- Who would oversee leading the initiative, and is ownership placed at the right level?

19. The true potential of Toyota Kata – Developing Agile organizations

So far, we have discussed how we can make Kata work in an Agile organization, including how events, cadences and boards can be adapted to fit the context of cross-functional teams, empowerment and iterative development. Throughout the previous sections, we took for granted that an Agile organizational structure and process were already in place. We assumed that though the organization might still be a mix of Agile and old-fashioned command and control paradigms, functional teams and stage-gate models that were an attempt to become Agile had previously been carried out. From this starting point, we discussed that Toyota Kata could help teams and the organization deliver on the full potential of Agile by going back to the roots and focusing on the core Lean and Agile capabilities.

But what if none of the factors are yet in place? What if the organization is delivering products or IT in a more traditional setup with functional departments, stage-gate models, project managers and top-down command and control and are now just discovering that their competitors are using something called Agile? You might be excused for thinking that it would be a waste of time to apply the previously mentioned principles and practices in such a situation and that you should start with a standard Agile transition of the company before even thinking about applying Toyota Kata. However, through this chapter, I hope to convince you that this is the kind of situation in which the full potential of Toyota Kata truly reveals itself.

As I mentioned in the beginning, many Agile transitions have ended up with lots of Agile tools and practices but little actual Agility. From my experience, a large part of the reason can be found in the way Agile transitions are handled, which roughly follows this format. (There are many versions, but this is the most common, though branded differently depending on the consultancy firm handling it.)

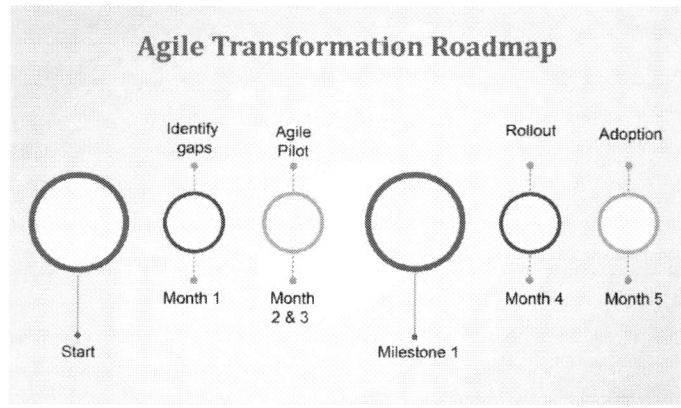

Though presented as Agile, the result of the gap analysis is almost always given beforehand and a Scrum-like structure is recommended at the team level while the consultancy's preferred scaling model (SAFe, Less, Nexus, etc.) for larger products is brought in when a few teams are not enough to deliver a shared result. In the worst cases, a scaling framework is used to drive the actual Agile transition because the consultant firm misunderstood the concept and thought that "scaling" meant organizational scaling. The firm missed the point that you should introduce the overhead of a scaling framework only if multiple teams are working on the same product.

Anyway, under time pressure, a Pilot is run with a couple of selected teams, rarely with enough time or span to truly validate the approach as a general concept in the organization above the team level. Even worse, the pilots may have included the parts of the organization that were most likely to be successful and, thus, have not had to deal with the real problems in the organization. The rest of the organization is then trained, and a team of internal Agile coaches is launched to help support the initiative when the consultants leave. The result is often that many Agile tools and practices are implemented at the team level but with only pockets of real Agility.

Again, Russ Ackoff's presentation on systems thinking gives us a clue to what might be wrong. He uses the analogy of an architect designing a new house based on the client's requests (Ackoff, 1994):

"What does the architect do? He has a set of properties that the client wants. Does he sit down and start to design the kitchen, then the living room, then the bedroom, and then the garage, is that what he does? Of course not! What he does is produce an overall design of the house. Now he produces the design of the rooms to fit into the design of the house. But he discovers in the process that he can modify the house in such a way to improve the quality of the rooms. He will never modify the house to improve the quality of the rooms unless the quality of the house is simultaneously improved."

But despite this fact, Agile adoption in large organizations often becomes a "bottom-up" affair. Managers frequently receive fewer hours of training and coaching than teams receive, and the training and coaching for managers is often less concrete. Immediately after training, team members begin working in Sprints and have little choice but to practice new skills every day. Meanwhile, managers can remain absorbed in business as usual. When the teams have begun reaching the limits of their new skills and all the low-hanging fruit of improvement opportunities is picked, impediments escalate. Suddenly all the teams come at the managers with sticky problems!

Picture our organization as the house and the existing functional departments, teams and governance structures as the rooms. What often happens is that we are so busy trying to optimize the "rooms", we fail to recognize that they shouldn't be there at all, that they should be joined or moved to a different place. That is why you cannot successfully implement Agile and Lean principles purely bottom-up. The successful application requires you to look at the end-to-end goal and not simply individual teams or processes. As we discussed earlier in Chapter 17, you also need to involve all layers of management in reaching that goal or you will often be stuck with "team-level" improvements.

A different approach

I propose that, like the Lean manufacturing consultants trying to copy tools and practices from the Toyota Production System, we also got it wrong. When we should be considering the process capabilities we want to achieve, we are already jumping to conclusions and in a hurry to implement specific roles, events, tools and other solutions. I am not saying that Scrum, XP, ProtoKanban, SAFe, Less, Nexus, Lean UX or other frameworks are wrong, but maybe we should bring them in to support what we really want instead of making the solutions they offer the actual goal.

It is very easy to see why this happens. When Agile is introduced through a series of vague statements, organizations will want to replace them with something more tangible. Research has proven that both early and late majority, as well as laggards, will expect concrete advice and not abstract principles. When we cannot offer this concrete advice, people will look for it somewhere else. Because these groups constitute close to 85%, we must give them something instead. That is why we must make a Process Vision clear enough to provide that direction.

I think that might be the most important point I gathered from reading Mike Rother's first Toyota Kata book from 2009. Specific tools and methods like Scrum, XP or SAFe can and should never be the goal. They are a means to an end but not the end itself. Therefore, we should bring them or parts of them in to support our deeper vision.

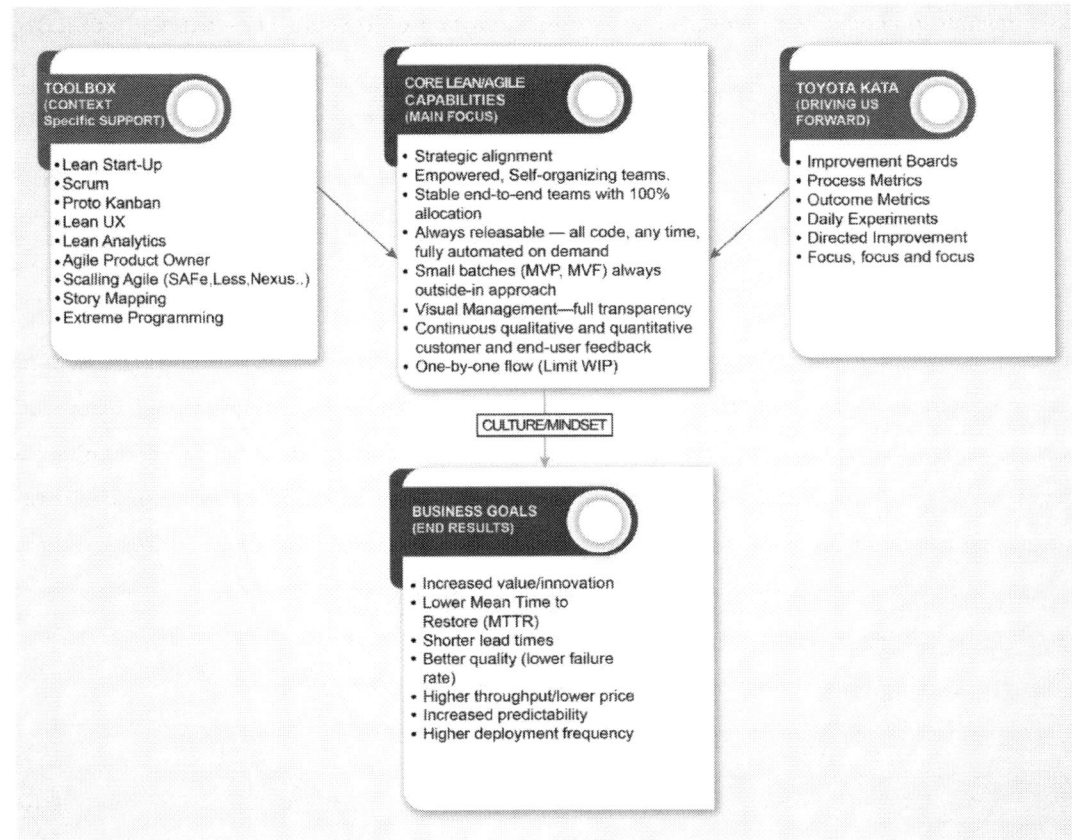

Figure 68: Agile Transition overview

As you can see in the picture above, we focus on establishing the process capabilities, but we have a toolbox of practices and methods that can help us achieve this (left-most box in the figure). Each time we consider using parts of, e.g., Scrum, we ask ourselves, "How does this get us one step closer to our vision?" A Product Owner role might be implemented to make sure actual product decision authority is placed at the team level or the notion of a "Sprint increment" is used to support Small Batches of actual value.

Anyone having witnessed a typical Agile transition should understand the difference in this approach, especially when you consider the number of Product Owners with little decision authority and the "Sprint increments" that provide very little actual end-user value. Toyota Kata (the right-most box in the figure above) ensures that constant attention is given to driving teams, managers and the organization toward the shared Agile goal – providing a constant and unrelenting source of energy. Ultimately, we see the effect in the Business goals represented at the bottom of the figure but because these are all "lagging indicators", we cannot use them to steer our Agile transition.

This brings us to another very powerful and surprising aspect of Toyota Kata – namely, that it helps us understand what we are already doing much better. In the beginning, I thought it was only a few lucky and unique hits but over time it kept repeating itself. Teams, Agile Coaches, Managers and Process Leads would continuously state things like, "Now I understand what Agile is all about", "Now I get the Product Owner role", "That is why we should not write 'as a Product Owner' or 'as a team member' in User Stories" or "Ah, so that is how you can actually use velocity". Through a deeper understanding of the Process Vision, the chosen solutions suddenly started making sense.

Another interesting fact we discovered was that, surprisingly, few managers, Scrum Masters and Process Leads had a good understanding of what end-to-end Process optimization is. It seemed that the narrow focus on the "Sprint" had brought many to the point where they had trouble looking for process-optimization beyond the Sprint boundaries. It was, therefore, a great surprise to some when we showed them that, e.g.:

- Only a small percentage of deployed features had been validated.
- Many "finished" User Stories had never reached production.
- Their Backlog represented four years of work at current velocity.
- Only 15% of started work was compliant with the Definition of Ready (DoR).
- The average cycle time from starting refinement to delivering a User Story to production was 47 days despite running two-week Sprints.
- No member of the development team had ever spoken to real users.
- The measured velocity made it impossible for them to forecast beyond the next Sprint.

The value of a simple Value Stream Mapping session in understanding the Current Condition was so great that a half-day training course was quickly established to offer it to the entire organization. We will cover the use of Value Stream and Workflow Maps in detail in Chapter 21.

So that is what Toyota Kata does. It forces us to look deeply at the capabilities we want to build in the organization and why, as well as our Current Condition. We can then use methods and tools like Scrum or SAFe to support that direction. Not only will that result in a better implementation of Scrum and SAFe, but it will also make sure that we do it for the right reasons and not the least increase motivation because we understand "why".

What are the downsides? There are at least a couple of points that we must acknowledge:

- Toyota Kata represents a mindset shift in the way we drive continuous improvement. Organizations that are embarking on a journey toward becoming more Agile will be faced with the fact that they must simultaneously adopt an improvement engine as well as a new organizational mindset. Therefore, you must carefully adapt the speed of change in both the process direction and the use of the Toyota Kata improvement engine to match the organization.

- When you are adopting tools and practices, people can often keep their traditional mindset for a longer period without facing the fact that they might be working against the very core of Agile and Lean. In a Toyota Kata setting, you must establish a clear Vision and that will cause problems to surface early. As we have stated before, this has some benefits but facing problems early also comes with the promise of early resistance. To counter this, it is even more important that senior management be 100% behind the Vision when it is communicated to the rest of the organization. Naturally, they must agree first, and that often presents the first chance for differences of opinion to surface early.

- Many people have built careers from knowing the details of specific tools and practices. Teaching them that their preferred tool is no longer the end goal but a potential way to support the Process Vision will not always be welcomed. To some, it will surface that they did not truly understand the purpose of the method, tool or practice. Others might feel that achieving Agility in a different way weakens their position and the value of their expertise. These people will not resist because they are against the Process Vision but because of the perspective of their individual status. It is crucial to get these people on board early, as they can become both the biggest drivers and the biggest resistors. We typically do that by repeating the message that applying Toyota Kata is about growing beyond, rather than obviating, e.g., the Scrum Master certification.

But does that mean we can't start with Scrum?

You are free to use individual elements of Scrum or the entire framework. You can use it in a single team or as a broader initiative. You can choose to not include a single element of Scrum or you can look at Scrum as a Starter Kata that enables the first steps toward Agility. But unless you decide to include Scrum in your Process Vision, Scrum or parts of Scrum would be an experiment and not the end goal. Therefore, you would need to measure whether Scrum or parts of Scrum drive you closer to your Process Vision. If not, you would need to inspect and adapt.

You might even declare that Scrum is the official "Agile Starter" in the organization and train every single team, manager and director. The overall Process Vision would still serve as the True North and any team, department or manager would have the freedom to experiment with all elements of their process as long as it gets them closer to the Vision.

To some Scrum trainers and Coaches, that might seem a frightening scenario and I have heard comments like:

- But then people might take the "easy" road and simply change Scrum instead of confronting their inabilities to follow Scrum.
- Then we would have 100 different processes in the organization and moving people around will be difficult.
- If we are no longer using the same framework, people will not be able to knowledge-share because they will have different roles and events and not be able to discuss them with each other.
- Customers would not experience the same service depending on the team they are interacting with.
- New people joining the company would not be able to get up to speed so quickly if we are not following a standard method.

And the list goes on.

First, most of those points make sense only if the goal is Scrum. But if the goal is Agile, as outlined in the Process Vision, it is not an issue if people find a different road. From a Toyota Kata perspective, success is defined by the ability to move one step closer to the Vision and not by the ability to follow a specific framework.

Second, it is the role of the coach to help people see when they have enough information to run a new experiment. Are they taking a step away from Scrum practices based on a mature understanding of flow and feedback or because it was simply easier to ignore an important aspect?

Third, if we aim for stable teams, moving people around is not something we aim to optimize for, as that would go directly against our Vision. If people change teams, it is my experience that we vastly overestimate the problems of learning the process of the new team. Even teams following standard Scrum work in different ways and it is often just a matter of days before people have gotten the hang of the basics. What does take time is learning to collaborate with other people on the team.

Fourth, some will argue that a two-week Sprint provides the ideal standardized interface to the organizations for customers and that this way they will not be confused when they are working with several teams. In real life, it is rarely the case that a single customer interfaces with several teams. If they do, the real issue is getting used to the close feedback loop and not whether it happens on Tuesday every other week or on a more continuous basis.

So, from a Toyota Kata perspective, Scrum is neither good nor bad, rigid nor flexible, effective nor dysfunctional. If Scrum or parts of Scrum move you closer to the Vision, great! If not, you may try a different approach toward implementing Scrum or find another path altogether. There are situations in which Scrum is a perfect "Starter Kata" to learn the basics of Agile and other situations in which it would be closer to an Obstacle. But unless it is included in the Process Vision, it can never be the end goal in a Toyota Kata setting.

Measurable insights on organizational maturity

I am sure that some Agile coaches despise the thought of measuring Agile maturity – "It is a mindset, not a measurable artifact". But we can and we should! Remember that we are measuring the process capabilities that will enable an Agile mindset, the behaviors that are the foundation for trust, experimentation, courage, close collaboration and the other "softer" aspects that are not actionable.

But we shouldn't measure our Agile maturity to judge people or to tie monetary incentives to the Current Condition. We should measure maturity to make sure we provide help where it is needed the most and to validate the result of organizational experiments. After all, how can we judge whether Scrum is truly moving us closer to the Process Vision if we do not have any metrics in place? But be careful – as soon as you start to punish teams or managers for not delivering on the direction or use incentives to try to make people improve quicker, there is a good chance that any objectivity found in the results will quickly be lost.

But how do you measure maturity when the Process Vision is "just" a direction? As you might recall from Chapter 9 on the Vision, we identified several questions related to each Vision element and came up with the following survey questions:

On a scale from 1 to 5 with 5 being in total agreement, how would you rate the current capabilities of your team?

- Strategic alignment
    - There is a clear strategic direction providing the alignment and guardrails for local decision-making on the tactical and operational levels.
    - Remaining dependencies between teams, departments and external parties are handled proactively without unnecessary complexity, interfaces and delays.
    - Funding is transparent and continuously evaluated based on unbiased financial models recognizing outcome as a primary risk dimension (instead of hidden, based on yearly budgets, decision committees, highest paid person's opinion (HIPPO) and a cost focus).
- Empowered, self-organizing teams
    - Given a strategic direction, we have the product decision authority as a team to iteratively scope, prioritize and deliver WHAT we find is needed to maximize business value.

- o We have the technical decision authority as a team to decide HOW we want to develop features (including Design, UX and code) and what tools to use.
- o It is a shared team responsibility to coordinate work to maximize outcome. No single person coordinates the work of the team.
- Stable end-to-end teams with 100% allocation
  - o Our team is stable, allowing us to optimize for the long term.
  - o Our team is cross-functional and has the internal capabilities to deliver work items end-to-end to real end users, without requiring help from external parties.
  - o Team members are 100% allocated to the team.
  - o We implement, validate, deploy and release our application independently with no technical constraints or dependencies to other teams or technical environments.
- Always releasable – all code, any time, fully automated on demand
  - o We have fewer than three active branches in our code with very short lifetimes (less than two days) before being merged into trunk/master. We do not experience "code lock" periods when no one can check in code or do pull requests due to merging conflicts, code freezes, or a stabilization phase.
  - o Deployments are fully automated and do not require manual intervention. This still leaves room for manual approvals but, once approved, all changes are applied automatically.
  - o We can provision our environments and build, test and deploy our software in a fully automated fashion from information stored in version control.
  - o All code is checked in at least daily, and each check-in triggers a set of quick tests to discover serious regressions, which developers fix immediately.
  - o Tests run automatically and continuously throughout the development process. Tests find real failures and only pass releasable code and unit and acceptance tests are run against every commit.
- Small batches (MVP, MVF), always outside-in approach
  - o We slice new product initiatives into Minimum Viable Products (MVP) with just enough features to validate the business model against real users and to be completed in one month or less.
  - o We slice work items into Minimum Viable Features (MVF) that deliver end-user value – just enough to get early feedback and to be completed in three days or less.
  - o Work items are always written and prioritized from an outside-in, end-user perspective and include a clear statement of the customer/end-user value hypothesis expressed as a monetary value.

- Visual Management – full transparency
  - We visualize the flow of work from business needs all the way through our Value Stream to customers and end users to coordinate and manage work effectively in a single place.
  - We create and maintain visual displays showing key quality and system health metrics and make them available to team members, leaders and customers. We use threshold warnings to enable us to proactively detect and mitigate problems.
  - We visualize and use cycle time, WIP, defects and throughput data to improve the flow and predictability of customer value through our Value Stream.
- Continuous qualitative and quantitative customer and end-user feedback
  - Work items are framed as measurable experiments and we collect real-time data on their quality, usage and test results against real users.
  - We have direct access to real users and customers and perform qualitative user research frequently, from the very beginning of the product lifecycle.
- One-by-one flow (Limit WIP)
  - Teams and team members focus on finishing started work and are not interrupted by changing priorities, expedites or meetings. The priority of not-started-work can be changed and adapted continuously without causing stress, demotivation or task-switching.
  - The active use of setting and lowering WIP limits makes obstacles and constraints to higher flow visible and drives Process improvement through the entire Value Stream.
  - We work systematically to remove bottlenecks, blockers, variance and wait time to create a smooth and level flow from our commitment point to work items validated in production. We avoid stress and overtime and optimize for a highly effective but sustainable pace.

No survey is perfect and quantitative data is never entirely objective. We have tried to ask questions that are as objective as possible but to truly understand the Current Condition of your transition, you must "Go to the Gemba" and talk to people. But we can use data to support the decision of where to go, whom to talk to and what to ask:

- Who seems to be struggling?
- What are the process capabilities that are the most difficult to establish?
- Why is a previously successful area declining?

- Why are these specific areas, departments or teams more successful?

- Why are we not seeing the expected effect of the extra attention given to this specific team or department?

Used in the right way, huge benefits are to be gained from having a continuous organizational overview of the Current Condition. The Agile community has a long history of navigating blindly through transitions, relying on a series of workshops and coaching sessions to navigate the unclear territory. Often it is not a positive surprise to discover the actual level of maturity. If we measure just the amount of implemented practices or the number of teams that have been trained in Scrum, there is a risk that we won't get an accurate picture of our Current Condition. The survey is very light and should take less than five minutes to update; as with the Meta-Kata, we have found that updating the score is better than sending out a new survey to be filled out from scratch.

But is Toyota Kata not just a set of practices like you find in Scrum or SAFe?

It seems there is somewhat of a paradox in play. I have spent most of this chapter and a considerable part of the book arguing that you should focus on building core Lean/Agile capabilities in your organization and pull in specific methods or practices to support that direction but not as the end goal. Yet, when we discussed the roll-out of Toyota Kata in the previous chapter, we introduced a rating of teams and managers on their ability to establish very specific Toyota Kata practices as part of implementing the Starter Kata for Agile organizations. We even set up a standard Improvement Board design for all teams and managers to use. Is Toyota Kata not itself an example of the same idea as introducing, e.g., Scrum or SAFe through a focus on mechanics, tools and practices?

Though this is a valid point, there are a few key aspects to consider in this regard:

- As stressed several times already, it is called a "Starter" Kata for a reason. We put the Starter Kata in place to teach the core principles of directed continuous improvement and scientific thinking but once this is in place, we expect people to adjust the framework to fit their specific needs.

- If you look at the questions from the Toyota Kata maturity score presented in Chapter 18, you should recognize that only the first camps include mechanical aspects of the Starter Kata. From Camp 2 and up, capabilities focus exclusively on aspects at a level of abstraction like those found in the Agile vision.

- I have not presented the argument that you cannot start with Scrum, but only that it should not be the end goal. The same is true for the Starter Kata. We use the Starter Kata to deliberately practice the core aspects of directed continuous improvement.

You might recall from the introduction to Part 2 that the real goal of the Starter Kata is for your organization to build the capabilities listed below. If they are deeply rooted in your organization, it matters little who the Coach is, whether Challenges are two to six months and whether Target Conditions, Coaching Kata and Experiment Records are part of your chosen setup.

- A shared Process Visions sets an overall direction for Process improvement – a "True North" desirable Future State.
- At all levels of the organization, people are involved in taking measurable steps toward the Vision by setting and delivering on realistically ambitious improvement goals.
- Each step is validated using scientific thinking – taking an iterative and experimental approach toward Process improvement.
- Steps are short, and continuous improvement is a natural part of daily work.
- Coach and Learner relationships ensure that Process improvement capabilities are continuously improved at all levels of the organization.

Learning objectives and questions for real-life application of developing Agile organizations with Toyota Kata

In this chapter, we discussed the aspect of using Toyota Kata to develop Agile organizations and how that can be a powerful alternative to more traditional approaches that often deliver heavily on mechanics but fail to create the process and culture we are truly looking for. It is not easy, but Toyota Kata provides the constant source of energy needed for an organization to keep striving to build the true capabilities of an Agile organization. Key learning objectives of this chapter include:

- Focus on core Agile/Lean capabilities instead of specific methods, practices and tools.
- You can use Scrum or other methods as a "Starter" but this is not recommended as the end goal.
- Any kind of transition is not a straight road from a to b, and you must navigate unclear territory.
- To navigate effectively through unclear territory, you need a continuously updated Current Condition at the organizational level focusing on the Process Capabilities stated in the Vision.
- A bonus of an organizational rating aligned with the Process Vision is that it keeps the attention on the organizational goal and, thus, becomes a clear inspiration for the Challenges and Targets Conditions that are chosen in the individual areas, departments and teams.
- Each Challenge and Target Condition should be aligned with the Vision. Thus, we expect to see local results reflected in increased organizational maturity.

Before you continue, write your answers to the following questions to the best of your ability:

- Why is it not recommended to include method-specific tools and practices like Scrum Roles and Scrum Events in the Vision?
- How can Toyota Kata help drive an Agile transition?
- Why is it recommended to provide a way of measuring organizational maturity?
- What would you include in your toolbox that could help support the Vision/direction?

20. Scaling Agile with Toyota Kata – A different approach

Scaling Agile has been a hot topic for the past few years and Agile scaling frameworks like SAFe, Nexus and LeSS are getting more attention. This chapter introduces an alternative perspective on the topic of scaling and how we might avoid unnecessary overhead by focusing even harder on delivering on the core Lean/Agile principles before looking to the specific scaling tools and practices. It is not a chapter against the notion of scaling or scaling frameworks but, rather, that we might get increased value from what they have to offer by looking at it from the right perspective.

When more than a few teams are truly needed to deliver a large product, we must put coordination and alignment mechanisms in place. I have nothing against the 300 so individual practices in SAFe and I am not against either release trains or PI planning meetings. I have successfully used many of the elements of the frameworks in my own coaching engagements and have felt both the adrenaline kick and the success of facilitating a PI-planning-like event.

But it is problematic when the framework becomes the goal and people are no longer focused on the value of practices but are using them blindly to follow the rulebook. The irony is that the rulebook is often made-up, as there are few actual mandatory practices. Another ironic point is that Less and Nexus include almost no practices at all beyond a few roles and rules. So, the "rulebook" is really optional practices, just like User Stories, Story Points, Burn-down Charts, Sprint commitments and Definition of Ready are not part of Scrum but seem to find their way into the Scrum "rulebook" in many organizations.

The intention behind scaling frameworks might be entirely valid. But instead of using them as an inspiration catalog of roles, events and tools, those practices become the end goal. Handling a large program is not easy and, therefore, it is extremely tempting to avoid the need to truly understand the context and possible solutions and substitute a one-size-fits-all approach. When I read the book on SAFe, I must admit that I was also drawn by the picture of all these practices coming together in a well-oiled machine, providing one answer for almost every question you might have and a practice for every eventuality. If anything goes wrong, you can always point to the inability to follow the practices correctly.

Though Scaling frameworks can provide much-needed inspiration to coordinate and align programs effectively, they can also be a crippling giant. At their worst, they remove independent thought and replace it with 100 practices, roles, events and tools offering a single answer to all your context-specific challenges. Any person responsible for a SAFe, Nexus or Less initiative will tell you that this is not how it should be done, and each practice should be selected and tailored to the context.

Experienced SAFe coaches will tell you that the only core practice of SAFe is the PI Planning, but many other SAFe consultants come up with a surprisingly long list when they are asked what you cannot leave out. The result is often that actual empowerment, feedback and end-to-end delivery have been replaced by functional teams working with "enablers". It is the application of those frameworks that are to blame and not the frameworks themselves.

That is why I suggest a different approach that I find to be much easier and to have a much bigger chance of success. It is also more aligned with the original intention of SAFe, Nexus Less and other scaling frameworks. When looking at a large product, do not think of scaling first. Look at your Agile Process Vision and think hard about getting as close to the core capabilities as possible. If you can get empowerment, end-to-end teams, self-organization and technical capabilities in place reasonably well, you will find that the actual need for cross-team coordination and alignment is already drastically reduced.

When you find that work is not flowing perfectly, or alignment is missing, consider the simplest possible solution that could bring you to the next level. You might be surprised by how much can be solved by simply having people meet in front of a portfolio board twice a week and how much additional coordination and alignment you get from a monthly meeting with key representatives from each team. You can choose to call it PI planning but you can also do it without synchronization of Sprints, Release Trains or having the entire teams present.

When practices and tools for scaling are discussed before core Lean Agile capabilities, you drastically increase the chance that you will scale something that did not need scaling or do it on top of dysfunctional processes and structures. As we all know, scaling has the full potential to magnify all existing organizational problems many times, and that is unfortunately what happens in many scaled "Agile" contexts.

So, next time you are about to scale, take a moment to reflect on your Agile vision. What are the core capabilities you must deliver successfully and how well are you set up to deliver on them? If you still need to scale, reflect deeply on what you cannot deliver within your current setup. Is it the inability to communicate a shared goal? Is it the inability to coordinate work toward that shared goal? Is it the problem of not delivering early and often? Only when you understand your direction and your Current Condition should you start to consider what specific scaling practices might help you reach your goal. You should be able to pinpoint exactly what the individual practice should help you achieve.

As we learned previously, most "problems" are not really problems at all if you match them to the end goal and, thus, they do not deserve our attention (Kahneman, 2013). If we apply 100 scaling practices without direction and without considering whether they will really help us overcome real Obstacles, we are very likely to introduce a large amount of overhead without any real results.

But that might be the very core issue here. To think deeply and reflect on both your direction and Current Condition, you must find your own path. That means acknowledging and dealing systematically with risk. I remember, 10 years ago, a program manager telling me that "Nobody was ever fired from choosing IBM". So, while it might be a huge risk to blindly apply the practices of SAFe, it is very secure from a personal perspective. Nobody will ever blame the consultant firm, the Agile Coach or director for choosing the practices of the most popular scaling framework on the market.

Back to my original point. I have nothing against Agile Scaling Frameworks, but I do have a problem with how they are applied. They represent a vast inspiration catalog of great ideas and we should really thank the inventors and contributors for making that catalog available to us in a way that is easily accessible. But using the detailed practices as the goal to strive for and with the argument "Then we have a common language for all roles, practices, events and artifacts" is problematic.

A last and funny twist is this: You can use Toyota Kata to implement SAFe-, Less- or Nexus-specific roles, events, tools and practices. You decide what a Process Vision should look like, and though any Toyota Kata practitioner would suggest that a Vision should be at a much higher level of abstraction, it is up to you to define your own. It is, therefore, possible to decide on a large part of SAFe practices as the actual Vision and to work systematically to implement them across teams and product management and portfolio levels.

Though it would not be my preferred approach, it would give you specific and measurable insights into the status of the implementation and you would get a systematic tool and approach toward dealing with all the Obstacles you are guaranteed to encounter when implementing a framework of that size. More aligned with the Toyota Kata mindset would be identifying aspects of SAFe, Nexus or Less as a Challenge and, thus, using them as a hypothesis to move one step closer to the Vision. You would need to include Challenge metrics from the Vision as well as framework-specific elements, but with the right combination, you could be getting the best of both worlds. I do not have personal experience doing it myself, so I will leave finding the right mix as an experiment for you.

If you have not bought my original argument and have already settled on SAFe roles, events and practices as the end goal, there is probably a good chance that Toyota Kata would be a great engine for driving your work in that direction.

Learning objectives and questions for real-life application of scaling Agile with Toyota Kata

In this chapter, we discussed the aspect of using Toyota Kata to scale Agile. Key learning objectives of this chapter include:

- Focus on core Agile/Lean capabilities before deciding to scale. You might find that you do not need to scale at all.

- Look at scaling frameworks like a toolbox. For each element of the toolbox, you choose to ask yourself, "How will this get us closer to our Process Vision?"

- When you encounter an alignment or coordination issue across teams, ask yourself, "What might be the simplest possible solution?" rather than "How many scaling practices can I use?"

- Know your Current Condition and Target Condition before attempting to scale. If you do not know where you are coming from and where you want to go, scaling practices will likely result in sub-optimal performance.

Before you continue, write your answers to the following questions to the best of your ability:

- What is the purpose of scaling?
- How do Toyota Kata and popular scaling frameworks fit together?
- What would your scaling toolbox look like?
- If you are already using specific scaling practices like Releases Trains, PI Planning, Integration Teams, portfolio Kanban Boards or something else, make a list of them and describe the purpose of each of them from the perspective of achieving a "smooth flow of customer recognized value".
- Building on the answer above, frame a Challenge that is a combination of framework-specific elements and Process metrics proving that you are also moving one step closer to the Vision.

Part 4. Using Other Models with Toyota Kata

In this part of the book, we look at how other methods and models support the use of the Toyota Kata framework and how Toyota Kata can be used outside the continuous improvement realm as an alternative to achieve product development goals. We will look at Value Stream and Workflow Mapping as tools to grasp the Current Condition and how a combination of Toyota Kata and the Kanban Method invented by David Anderson can support each other to achieve superior results. Each chapter can be read in isolation, so feel free to read them in any order you prefer.

21. Value Stream and Workflow Mapping

We have touched upon Value Stream and Workflow Mapping several times already. This chapter introduces the details and how you might use them in an Agile setting to understand your Current Condition and frame Challenges and Target Conditions. It is beyond the scope of this book to cover all aspects; entire books have been dedicated to that topic. It should, however, provide you with enough information to start using the principles.

Value Stream Mapping (VSM) is a technique used in Lean to define both the Current Condition and a Future State (Rother & Shook, 1999). To create a current-state VSM, you simply follow the flow of work and note the details of each process step, as well as the wait time between process steps. It may look something like this:

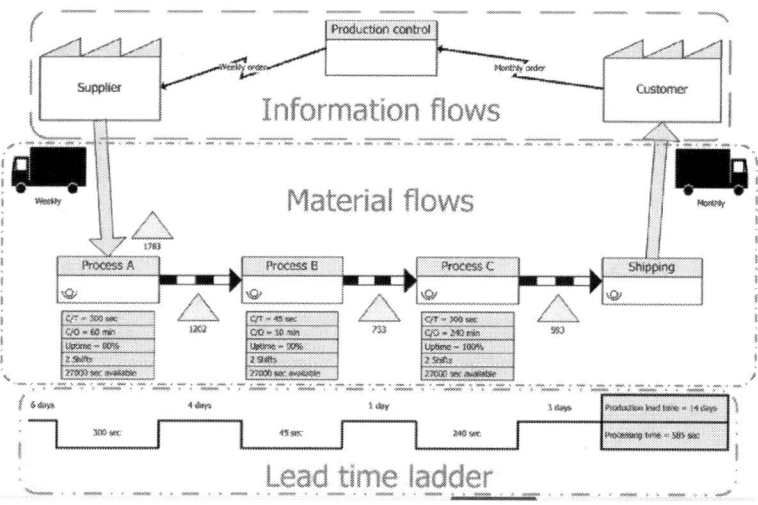

Figure 69: Standard Value Stream Map by Daniel Penfield,
https://commons.wikimedia.org/wiki/File:ValueStreamMapParts.png

As you can tell by the VSM above, the lead time is 14 days but the actual processing time is only 585 seconds or roughly 10 minutes. If we can eliminate wait time, it is, thus, possible to reduce lead time by 98.5% (if we assume that we have eight hours of work available every day – working in shifts, the consequence is three times bigger).

Using VSMs in the context of IT is not necessarily a problem. We also face the fact that our work items (e.g., User Stories) spend most of their time waiting. The key thing to understand is that to use it in an Agile context, you must keep it at the right level of abstraction. You are aiming for an overview and the goal is NOT to get all the details in place at this point. I have seen many examples of Lean consultants trying to use traditional manufacturing approaches in an IT context, aiming to cover all aspects of all work-item types. Due to the variability of the development process and the number of work-item types involved, it often ends up consuming huge amounts of time and generating very few actionable and useful insights.

In the worst cases, people try to sequence and standardize the workflow by representing it on a Kanban Board with policies like, e.g., "specification must be finished before development can start" or "test does not start until development is 100% finished", trying to force iterative work into a manufacturing-like sequence and moving away from Agility toward a more Waterfall type process. Some call that "Kanban" and I can easily remember the heated debates about how "Kanban" was trying to turn IT development into a non-iterative and fixed sequence of activities.

Fortunately, it seems that Kanban has recovered from that misconception, but this highlights an important aspect of the problem of using VSMs in an iterative setting. The historical "baggage" that the use of VSMs carry made some people coin the term Workflow Mapping (WM) instead.

Whether you prefer to use the term VSM or the term WM is not important; I will stick to the term VSM for readability. The importance lies in adjusting the approach toward fitting an innovation and knowledge work context. If you try to create a VSM by identifying each process step, and each time the work shifts from one person to another, you are going to end up with a lot of circular relationships and a lot of details. Instead, we use the notion of primary or dominant "knowledge discovery activities". It does sound a little "nerdy" but makes a lot of sense.

Looking at the flow of value in an IT context, you gradually add more knowledge as it goes from a vague statement of a user need to live working software in a production environment. But we all know that this is an iterative process in which multiple skills are involved in each step. Using the notion of "dominant knowledge discovery activity" provides us with the concept to get the insights we want without an obscure amount of details and internal loops. Here are a few examples of dominant knowledge-discovery activities:

- "Specification/Refinement" also involves coding, testing a technical spike, rough UX and validating a prototype with an end user.
- "Development" also involves testing, user feedback, design, UX, updating User Story descriptions and review.
- "Test" also involves fixing defects, updating User Stories and changing UX and design.
- "User feedback" also involves fixing issues, updating User Stories and changing UX and design.

The point is that as long as we recognize the iterative nature of each workflow step, we should not be afraid of talking about a dominant activity, as that can provide us with a lot of Process optimization

237

insights on where things are blocked, who is involved, how long it takes and the wait time between each step during which nobody is working on it.

Personally, I am not religious in terms of using the correct VSM notations. With one client, I spent an hour drawing a rough VSM with them as part of the training session. The director of the business unit was watching from the back of the room and came to me afterward, stating, "Six months ago we spent 14 days with a Lean consultant drawing up detailed VSMs of all our processes. What you just did in one hour was about 10 times more useful". But because they never managed to use the result of the 14 days, it does not take much to be 10 times better. Here are a couple of examples of Current State VSMs:

Upstream process

The interesting part of this VSM is that the upstream process spans multiple teams and systems. Some requests are initially handled by a service desk team and forwarded through email; other requests come directly via email from end users, while others are initially reported through a ticketing system called Cherwell. The details reveal that work is often missing critical information to be handled effectively, resulting in multiple extra cycles and blockers. Not until we started to visualize the end-to-end workflow and adding details did we understand the current situation well enough to set a clear Challenge and Target condition:

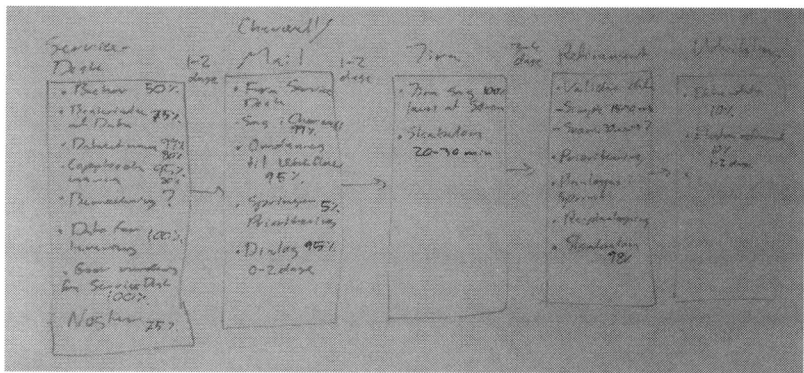

Figure 70: Upstream Value Stream Map example

Classical Scrum VSM

The following VSM is a typical example of a Scrum team. This was from the initial workshop and, as you can tell, a lot of numbers are still unknown (the parts with an underscore with no number above). That is typical, as we often need to investigate further as part of our Challenge refinement. Initially, this team had a hard time imagining a relevant Challenge, as everything seemed to be going well. The interesting part was that even though they had not fully clarified their Current Condition, it was

238

already clear that they had considerable gaps between their situation and the Vision of a perfect process:

- They did not assign business value to any work items, neither monetary nor using a score. It also turned out that they were in doubt about what the intended business value of their service was.

- No users or stakeholders were involved from the time things had entered the Backlog until the review meeting.

- Ninety percent of User Stories were identified by the team without being checked or validated with customers and real users before the result was presented at the review meeting.

- They had no idea how many User Stories were compliant with DoR before getting started but the number was presumed to be very low.

- Attendance at review meetings was, on average, 50%.

- Completed work items at review meetings were presented from a value-adding perspective in only 5% of all cases.

This might seem like a unique situation but data like this is very common once we start looking at the real Current Condition using VSM.

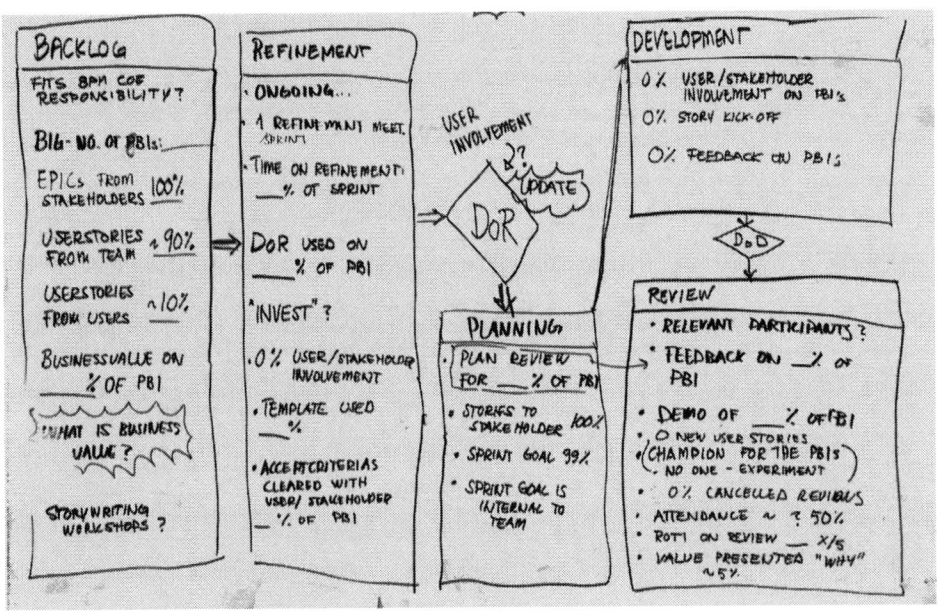

Figure 71: Scrum Value Stream Map example

Homework

Next is an example of what happens when the right people are not present to help establish the Current Condition. As previously explained, a Challenge preparation meeting became part of the roll-out concept. We would ask teams to make sure that the right people were present at this meeting to qualify the Current Condition in enough detail. Due to sickness or other unforeseen events, that was, however, not always the case and the result looked like the one below. (Each blue circle indicates something that will need to be explored further before the Challenge workshop.)

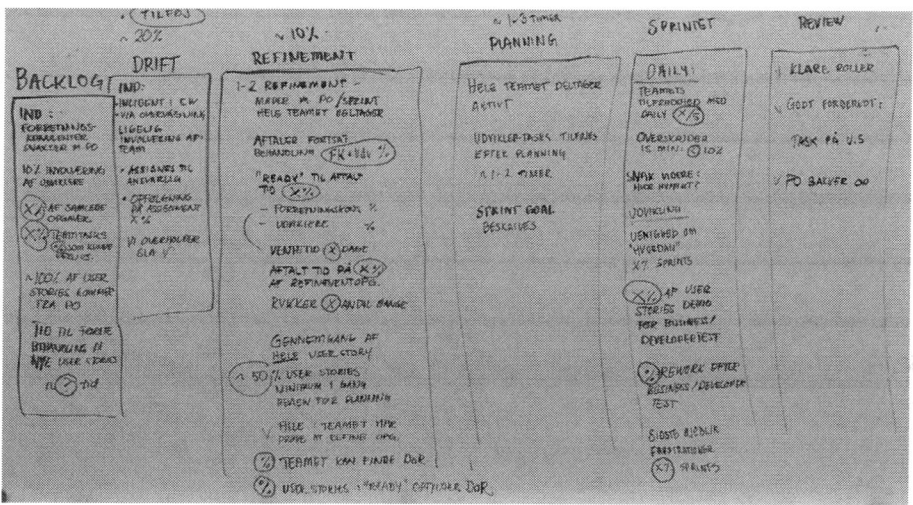

Figure 72: Value Stream Map showing missing information

Observations on using VSMs in an Agile context

In the beginning, many teams and Agile Coaches are often very skeptical. There seems to be a general notion that it adds unnecessary complexity and that the process is already well-understood. As mentioned, earlier feedback has, however, been very positive. In the case of Bankdata, they chose to offer a separate training session to teach the deeper aspects to the organization. After having used VSMs in the context of IT for the past 10 years, I am convinced that, done right, it delivers on some very important aspects and skeptics are often quickly turned into promoters:

- Even in teams that have worked together for a long time, there is sometimes surprisingly little agreement on the current process. A VSM provides a much-needed opportunity to get alignment across individuals and skill sets. Examples of misalignment include everything from branching strategies, code commits and how much test is needed to how much and how often end users should be involved and give feedback.

- As mentioned previously, end-to-end ownership for Process optimization is often poorly understood, even by the Process Leads who are supposed to be experts. Some might think

240

that the Product Owner is exclusively to blame when something fails in the "Upstream" part of the process or that the term "Process optimization" refers only to what is going on in the Sprint. Getting a shared overview of the process and talking about end-to-end Process optimization is a very valuable exercise.

- If we discuss abstract terms like feedback and T-profiles, you allow yourself to "pretty-print" the actual Current Condition and keep the notion that everything is perfect. A VSM forces you to put numbers on the details. It is often a huge surprise for people to find that, e.g.:
  - The Product Owner can prioritize only 30% of the Backlog according to what will generate the highest value, while 70% is prioritized to keep individual skill sets busy.
  - It takes an average of 37 workdays from starting refinement to reaching production for User Stories.
  - Seventy percent of all finished work has never been tested and validated by real users.
  - No engagement analytics exist to provide any kind of quantitative feedback.
  - The "stable velocity" fluctuates much more than they thought and is considerably lower (which could be the reason why they consistently start more work than they are able to finish).
  - Five critical areas of the code are worked on only by a single team member and T-profiles and collective code-ownership are probably closer to a dream than reality.

If we keep the VSMs at the right level of abstraction, they can be a powerful tool to truly understand the Current Condition.

Even at the right level of abstraction, we often end up with quite a lot of details on our Current State VSM. Once the topic of our desirable Future State Challenge has been chosen, we often create a simplified version of the VSM that includes only relevant details for that topic. It could be, e.g., any details relevant to "Test", "Deployment automation", "End-user feedback" and so on. Here is an example of a VSM focusing only on how work is entering the system and the process before it reaches "development":

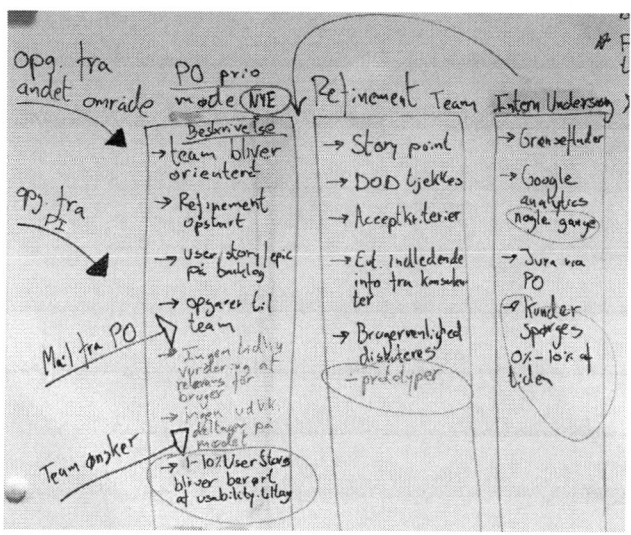

Figure 73: Value Stream Map showing how requests enter the system

Future State Value Stream Maps and why we stopped using them

Being brought up with Lean and the importance of Future State Value Stream Maps, I was heavily inclined to find a way to make that tool work in the context of IT, Agile and Toyota Kata. I have experienced the value of hands-on working with optimizing conference management and marketing teams, and though I had achieved some positive results in an IT context, I also reluctantly had to admit that it wasn't working as intended and that the benefit often did not match the effort put into creating them. Even before I worked with Kata, it seemed that despite my best intentions, the Future State map would have been easier to represent in a few simple sentences. In hindsight, I should have realized earlier that this was a good thing and not a bad thing; it is just another example of how easily we are tempted to focus on a specific tool instead of the purpose we are trying to achieve. If a Future State can be communicated in a few simple statements, why introduce the complexity of mapping that statement to a VSM?

I think I can provide a suggestion as to why the complexity of drawing the Future State VSM did not deliver on the value we intended. In Agile, we are often fortunate to have the entire Value Stream within a single team and, as previously mentioned, the dominant "knowledge discovery activities" are often at a level of abstraction above those you would identify in a manufacturing context. This means that we are rarely faced with a total redesign of the workflow on that level and, in the few cases in which we want to eliminate a step altogether, we can easily represent that in a single statement.

242

My initial assumption was that this was true only on the team level while at the department, area or organizational levels we could still benefit from Future State VSMs if we could find a way to use them correctly. But we discovered that an Agile context is very different from the manufacturing context, maybe even more so once you move above the team level. Fortunately, most Agile organizations have given up the notion of functional teams with lots of handovers. Therefore, a Value Stream simply does not exist at a higher level in the same way you would find it in a manufacturing company. Only for larger programs (scaled Agile), or in a functional structure, does it make sense to use the Future State Value Stream as a tool to communicate the desired flow.

My recommendation is, therefore, to use Current State Value Streams as an excellent tool to get the necessary insights but to frame Challenges as simple and quantitative statements.

I hope this chapter provided you with some insights into the value of using VSMs in an Agile context so that you can get a good picture of your Current Condition. It is important to keep in mind that it is only a tool and that you are free to find better and more effective ways of grasping your Current Condition.

Learning objectives and questions for real-life application of Value Stream and Workflow Mapping

In this chapter, we discussed the aspect of using Value Stream and Workflow Mapping to get a better understanding of the Current Condition and help frame Challenges and Target Conditions. Hopefully, you found it as valuable as the managers and teams working with Toyota Kata did. Key learning objectives of this chapter include:

- The concept of Value Stream and Workflow Mapping is very useful in an Agile context, but it is important to use it at the right level of abstraction. Use the notion of "primary knowledge discovery activities" and avoid trying to turn it into a sequential workflow.

- Getting a deep understanding of the Current Condition is essential to setting the right ambition level.

- Future State maps might make sense, but we have found them less useful in the context of Agile.

- Though people often believe they are aligned, Workflow Mapping will often reveal that this is not really the case.

- Understanding end-to-end Process optimization is not a skill that all managers or Process Leads possess and mapping the entire workflow has proven to be a great tool to catalyze the introduction of this concept.

Before you continue, write your answers to the following questions to the best of your ability:

- What is the purpose of using Value Stream and Workflow Mapping?

- What is a knowledge discovery activity and how does it differ from a traditional "process step"?

- Identify a primary work item type (e.g., User Stories) and try to draw a Workflow Map on a piece of paper. Put question marks and a red circle around it in places where you do not know the number or other details.

- Compare your Workflow Map with the Vision topics and list potential Challenge topics.

22. Toyota Kata and Kanban

We have discussed the use of Toyota Kata in an Agile setting, including the potential of an Agile vision and how you can take systematic steps in that direction through the Improvement Kata. But how does Toyota Kata fit with the Kanban Method for Process improvement? That is the topic of this section.

It is beyond the scope of this book to explain Kanban in depth, but a few details are needed to understand the potential of working with it in a Toyota Kata setting. Many think of Kanban as an Agile team method or an alternative to Scrum. Some even believe that Kanban is just Scrum with the Sprint is replaced by WIP limits. But though that is probably how 90% are using Kanban, that is not what David Anderson intended when he invented the method and it is not how it is taught and coached by Lean Kanban University, which is the official body behind the Kanban method.

Though difficult for people to grasp, Kanban is neither Agile nor a method for Software Development. Kanban has no roles or artifacts and Kanban does not favor cross-functional teams over functional silos. Kanban has no concept of a Product Owner or a Scrum Master and there is nothing in Kanban stating that Scrum is good or bad, effective or dysfunctional. Kanban is not limited to the team level but is designed for optimizing the service of the entire organization. All Kanban basically asks you to do is "start with what you do now" and use the six Kanban Principles to optimize flow. The fact that flow optimization will often make you more Agile because you will get faster feedback and build capabilities to inspect and adapt is another matter.

All Kanban uses are the following four principles and six practices for effective optimization of flow across all layers of the organization:

Foundational Principles:

- Start with what you do now.
- Agree to pursue evolutionary change.
- Initially, respect current roles, responsibilities and job titles.
- Encourage acts of leadership at all levels.

Core Practices:

- Visualize.
- Limit WIP.

- Manage flow.
- Make policies explicit.
- Implement feedback loops.
- Improve collaboratively, evolve experimentally (using models and the scientific method).

Those of us who started using Kanban when it was just getting some traction around 2008-2009 believed that it was simply a matter of time before Kanban would take over the world. The results we achieved far surpassed anything we had experienced before. Though Kanban wasn't Agile, we found that actual business Agility was achieved much faster because the focus was on optimizing flow and increasing feedback on the actual customer recognized value.

Instead of trying to force an existing structure to fit into predefined roles and practices, you could allow people to think about how they could achieve better flow and feedback on the things that really mattered. From the very beginning, Kanban allowed us to take an organizational view on optimization, which itself allowed us to move beyond the team level even before scaling frameworks became as popular as they are today. Unfortunately, that is not what happened. The world desperately needed an alternative to Scrum at the team level and specific emergent behaviors of Kanban turned out to be a perfect fit.

So, instead of releasing the huge potential of Kanban principles and practices, people decided that they needed a board with more workflow steps than the typical Scrum Board and the ability to move the Post-its or electronic tickets across without having to batch them into Sprints. Even from a true Kanban perspective, that would be a perfectly good place to start if teams and organizations would then continue to improve using WIP limits, policies and flow metrics to look beyond the individual team. Unfortunately, the rest of the Kanban method is rarely used in the majority of organizations and almost never beyond the team level. Even though you repeat the same message 100 times, people will still refer to Kanban as "the alternative to Scrum". You might say that the initial success achieved by what is now known as "Proto team-level Kanban" has become "real Kanban's" worst enemy.

But what has that got to do with Toyota Kata? It turns out that to drive further improvement with Kanban, you must develop a process of continuous focus on the Kanban principles and practices in all layers of the organization. The original idea was that the benefit of using those ideas would be so huge that it would happen naturally – but that is not what is going on in real life. It might be that it can be sustained for a while if an organization is fortunate enough to have a great Kanban coach but rarely for longer periods of time.

So, what can we do if we believe there is huge value in the Kanban principles, but we cannot find a way to continuously focus on them? It turns out that Toyota Kata might be a brilliant fit.

While I was doing the larger Toyota Kata initiative at Bankdata, I was simultaneously engaged in helping a medium-sized IT company in Copenhagen implement Kanban across the organization. They had really bought into the value of Kanban and already had some talented people with substantial knowledge. Having a lot of focus on Toyota Kata, I asked myself the questions, "What if we use the Kanban practices and principles as the Toyota Kata vision? What if we run Improvement Kata and Coaching Kata with the goal of striving for Process improvement using Kanban?"

So, that is what we ended up doing and the results were surprisingly positive. Naturally, we encountered all the usual problems associated with any kind of change (even evolutionary change), but the difference was that this time, a constant source of energy was being added to the system. Through Daily Kata and weekly Coaching Kata, people were constantly confronted with "true Kanban". It might be that a team had not yet built the capability to WIP constrain the entire workflow but had established a Challenge to get there and that would work systematically until the goal was reached. It might be that few teams initially had the capability to measure flow or even recognize what "flow of value" was but, again, there would be a constant focus on getting there. Toyota Kata was really making a difference and serving as an effective catalyst to implement true Kanban and not just a Kanban Board with a static visualization of work.

When I recently spoke to people who were part of the initiative, they mentioned Toyota Kata as the important catalyst that keeps bringing energy to the system. They had both moved on to a different company but had taken with them the general principles of Toyota Kata and were finding ways to implement it at the new workplace.

The nice thing about using the six Kanban practices as a vision is that they are high-level enough to be inspiring and long-term while still specific enough to set an actual direction. You might argue that they deliver on several very important aspects:

- When the six Kanban practices are actually used to drive improvement, they have proven to be able to deliver great results at all organizational levels and in all types of complex and complicated knowledge work.

- They are specific enough to set a direction while abstract enough to allow for local solutions and implementations details to be developed.

- They are easy to observe and, thus, it does not take much to make them measurable on both a Challenge and Target Condition level.

- You can always raise the bar. Starting with the simple goal of just applying the practices, the quality and ambition level of each practice can be increased. You might, e.g., start with WIP constraining a few elements of the workflow, then the entire workflow and then set goals to limit WIP further.

- All six practices are close to the core elements of Lean and, thus, are already perfectly integrated into the mindset from which Toyota Kata originates.

From the first time I heard about the Kanban Method in 2008, it resonated deeply with me. To say the least, it has been frustrating to see that the giant potential of Kanban has not been unleashed and that most teams and organizations claiming to use Kanban are stranded at a very basic level of static visualization of the workflow at the team level. Despite heavy investments in branding "real Kanban", Gartner still referred to Kanban as a team-level enabler for Agility in 2018. "Proto-Kanban", as this state is often called, is a natural and effective first step but not "Kanban". The real potential lies in using the practices as an improvement driver. I truly believe that the combination with Toyota Kata is a strategy that can finally get us there.

The Kanban Method is constantly evolving. Recent additions include the Kanban Maturity Model (KMM). Among other things, KMM identifies several more specific process capabilities that are associated with levels of organizational maturity and desired outcomes. Whether those can be turned into successful leading indicators of organizational performances or should be treated as experiments remains to be tested. It will be very interesting to follow this development in the coming months and years. For more information on KMM, see www.kanbanmaturitymodel.com/.

Learning objectives and questions for real-life application of Toyota Kata and Kanban

In this chapter, we discussed the aspect of combining Toyota Kata and Kanban to achieve superior results. Key learning objectives of this chapter include:

- Kanban remains one of the most misunderstood concepts. Many people still think of Kanban as Scrum without Sprints or simply the ability to pull one User Story at a time.
- Kanban is an improvement driver focusing on flow. This may lead to Agile organizational structures and processes, but it is not the goal.
- Toyota Kata is an effective framework for delivering on the true potential of Kanban and go beyond static Proto-Kanban implementations.
- If you are aiming for flow and feedback but have not settled on Agile principles, Kanban could be an effective way of framing the Vision.

Before you continue, write your answers to the following questions to the best of your ability:

- What are the four foundational principles and six core Kanban practices?
- How can Toyota Kata help deliver on the true potential of Kanban?
- Would Kanban be a great Vision in your company? Why or why not?

23. Using Toyota Kata for product development

So far, we have been discussing Toyota Kata purely as a process improvement drive. Sometimes, however, you find that a framework can be used successfully for things other than the original intention. Because some teams and organizations are starting to experiment with using Toyota Kata for product development, I will provide a quick introduction to the concept in this chapter. My own hands-on experience is limited to a single team context, and though books like "The Lean Enterprise" refer to cases at a higher level, it is safe to assume that the use of Toyota Kata for product development is still in the very early stages of innovators and early adopters.

I hope this chapter will provide enough basic knowledge to start experimenting with it on your own, but you should realize that some trial and error might be involved in getting it to work effectively. As of the time of this writing, "Escaping the Build Trap" by Melissa Perri has not yet been published but it is due later this year (2018) and should discuss this topic in more detail.

If you are familiar with the build-measure-learn loop introduced in Eric Ries' book "The Lean Startup" (Ries, 2011), you might already have noticed how closely Toyota Kata resembles this. That is not a coincidence because both represent the scientific approach in which hypotheses are continuously tested instead of relying on wishful thinking. But why is it relevant to introduce Toyota Kata in this setting when there are already so many Agile frameworks, tools and practices available that seek to address the same problem?

Addressing the real risk

Despite the best efforts, it has proven to be a difficult task to get teams and organizations to focus systematically on what seems to be the biggest risk of all in product development: namely, the inability to deliver successful features or products from a value-adding perspective. While we continue to add more objective metrics to better forecast delivery dates and budgets, we fail to provide more than guesswork to judge the actual value hypotheses of what we are building. As mentioned in the introduction, the Standish Chaos Report states that over 60% of all delivered features are rarely or never used by anyone, so though we talk a lot about "validating hypotheses", it seems we do not really get the point at all.

Despite talking about Minimum Viable Products and renaming User Stories "Hypotheses", we are still struggling as a community to bring value-risk to the forefront of our attention. That is probably because it is difficult not only to measure but also to accept the results of actual data.

I still clearly recall an experience a few years ago when a customer (typical client-supplier relationship) insisted on a "brilliant new feature" on the platform. The team and especially the UX designer doubted the value but the customer insisted. The team then argued that because the risk was high, they should build only the very core to make sure it showed signs of success before "gold-plating it" further. The customer thought that would be a waste of time given the clear potential and insisted on the full version, despite the longer lead time and higher risk. The team then suggested at least implementing some basic engagement metrics to judge the success. Those metrics were visualized and, not surprisingly, they were not anywhere in the ballpark of the predicted engagement.

Within the first month, 20 users (out of 5,000 active users) had clicked on the new features and two had clicked the result set that the feature produced (which you would need for deriving any value from using it). But instead of reacting to this very clear feedback, the team was asked to remove the data from the dashboard ASAP. I guess that qualifies as an action, too. This story is not a case against taking an outside-in perspective and listening to customers. The fact that it was a customer trusting his intuitive insights about the behavior of real users is purely a coincidence; it could just as well have been the UX designer or front-end developer making the same mistake. We all think we know much more than we truly do and that is why it is so critical to establish real quantitative feedback loops.

But how can Toyota Kata help if Lean Startup and other frameworks have not been able to turn our attention to the risk that matters the most in product development? I am not claiming that it is a silver bullet but one experience showed promising results.

Replacing the "Kanban Board" with the Toyota Kata "Product Improvement Board"

A few years ago, I was helping organize the adoption of Agile. Most teams were working within relatively stable domains enhancing several established products. One team, however, was working on a brand-new initiative. Despite being introduced to Lean Startup principles, they were still focusing on planning and implementing User Stories, and their Kanban Board did not look much different from the other teams' boards despite a different focus and domain.

During a meeting with the team, one of the team members suddenly exclaimed, "I think we should use Toyota Kata for this!" To be honest, the rest of us looked at him questioningly, sure that he had missed the basic difference between Product and Process improvement. We all told him how wrong he was until he burst out, "Guys! I get the difference, but we should use the Kata board for this and use the same approach. As long as we have a Kanban Board stuffed with User Stories, that is what we will focus on moving to "done" and not the risk we are really trying to address".

It was a classic case of "What you see is all there is". We agreed to try it out. Instead of focusing on User Stories, we focused on what we would observe if we had successfully validated our main risk of "does anyone want to use or buy this?" We asked questions like:

- How often should early adopters engage with the product?
- How many transactions should there be?
- How many different customers should it be installed at?
- How many CFOs should have agreed to a second meeting?

The main difference was that User Stories and initiatives were the LAST things to be discussed. They were added to the "Experiment Record" if and only if they would help solve an Obstacle and/or get the team closer to the goals they wanted to observe. User Stories were being treated as options and not a committed Backlog! Suddenly developers who had been focusing only on building a feature where busy discussing how they could make a simple mock-up that could be shown to the CFO of a potential client.

I really regret not taking a picture of the Product Improvement Board because some of the details are now becoming vague, but I will never forget how the whole dialogue changed and the focus was suddenly on value-risk and not on implementing just another feature.

Conclusion

I still think that more traditional Agile approaches are great when you are beyond the startup phase and your main product assumptions have been validated. At this point, you should have a functioning product and be able to continuously add features and measure the engagement and adoption rate of actual users. I also think that the transparency offered makes it many times easier to scale when you really need to do so.

I have seen and helped teams use tools like Kanban Boards in startups and some of those are now worth a lot of money. However, I have also seen how quickly they divert from addressing the real risk if constant attention is not given to validating the real hypotheses. My own experience applying Toyota Kata in the context of startups and new products is still limited but I truly believe that there is great potential to be found in the Toyota Kata way of framing goals and iteratively working toward them. Who knows? Maybe Toyota Kata will become the default approach toward both new and "old" product development in the future as we discover how much scientific thinking and real "value-risk" need to be brought to the forefront of our attention.

Learning objectives and questions for real-life application of Toyota Kata used for product development

Though not the core focus of this book, this chapter briefly introduced the aspect of using Toyota Kata for product development. Key learning objectives of this chapter included:

- Toyota Kata is, at its core, a framework for applying scientific thinking to setting goals and reaching them. These goals can also be framed from a product perspective.
- Scientific thinking implemented through Toyota Kata is very close to the Lean Startup concept of build-measure-learn.
- By using Toyota Kata for product development, we are focusing so much on the core principle of validating hypotheses that we might be able to finally break the typical anti-pattern of focusing on output before outcome in conditions of high uncertainty.

Before you continue, write your answers to the following questions to the best of your ability:

- What contexts would be a good match for using Toyota Kata for product development?
- What are the benefits and drawbacks compared to more traditional Agile approaches?
- Are there products or projects in your organization with which you would want to experiment using Toyota Kata for product development?

Part 5. Examples and Cases

If there is one single element people requested the most when we started scaling Toyota Kata in the wider organization, it was EXAMPLES, such as examples of the elements included in Challenges and Target Conditions to provide inspiration and a better understanding. Above all other examples, people requested actual metrics. People also requested cases so they could follow how those elements had been used in real life. The problem with cases, however, is that they take a long time to both read and write and, thus, fail to indicate the full range of possible applications. Therefore, we decided to split it in two: to provide cases and what we called "challenge and metric inspiration catalogs" separately. Because that split worked quite well, this book follows the same structure. This part includes a chapter containing in-depth coverage of the inspiration catalog, while we dive deeper into specific cases in the last chapter.

24. Vision, Challenge and Target Condition inspiration – including potential metrics

As I hope you have realized by now, our goals become more specific and concrete as we move from the Vision to the Challenge and Target Condition level. But seeing how this relationship can be translated into real-life examples of specific wording and metrics has proven to be a big help in adopting the mindset of Toyota Kata. This chapter includes a wide range of examples of Challenges and Target Conditions that point in the direction of our Agile Vision and their potential process metrics. The Agile vision presented previously serves as an overall structure when presenting the individual elements. Each part of the Agile Vision will be covered one by one. I attempted to include suggestions for relevant Outcome metrics for each process metric example, but it took up too much space and there was too much repetition. I will, therefore, leave it as an exercise for the reader to identify the expected Outcome of each leading indicator. Chapter 10 included a list of the most common Outcome metrics.

What I have included are the key personal benefits of establishing these capabilities as seen from both the CEO's and the team members' perspectives. From that, I am sure you can identify the personal benefits of the organizational layers in between. They are important because they clearly indicate why it is unlikely for anyone to want to game these metrics.

There is clearly some overlap between Vision elements as, e.g., automation is a key enabler of one-by-one flow, but because this is just an inspiration catalog, I will not spend time digging into the details of this overlap. Rather, I will simply put the example under the part of the Vision where it is most closely related. Note that the listed metrics are just examples; there are many aspects to, e.g., one-by-one flow and you are strongly encouraged to move beyond the inspiration catalog presented in this chapter. Remember that a Challenge is often related to a single vision theme but might span more than one underlying topic and often between two and five metrics.

Each included metric contains both a description, how to measure it, the unit and the metric cost. Metric cost is an indication of the expected effort in establishing both the initial Current Condition as well as updating it to visualize the trend toward the Target Condition. This is just an indication, as they can sometimes be obtained at close to zero cost from tools, while they might be incredibly expensive to collect manually. That is also why you will see that the cost of some metrics ranges from low to high.

I have included mostly objective metrics, as I am sure you are able to identify the subjective metrics that we use as a last resort, e.g.:

- Backlog quality score (1-5)
- Customer feedback quality (1-5)
- Outcome score (1-5)

You can read this chapter from beginning to end, though I suspect that most will find it more valuable to look up the specific topics of interest. You will probably find some to be overambitious (red zone) in your context, while some might seem so basic that you have a hard time imagining anyone not delivering on that capability already. They are just options, so use them if they make sense; use them as inspiration to find your own or anything in between.

Always releasable – all code, any time, fully automated on demand

This part of the Vision is the one that is most closely related to what has become known as continuous delivery capabilities. As you might recall, we included two key statements in the definition of this topic:

- It is never a technical decision to release. All code is continuously committed and always releasable, avoiding any kind of technical batching.
- Test and deployment are fully automated processes – no exceptions. Only with zero transaction costs of test, deployment and release can we fully get the benefits of small batches and one-by-one flow.

Because the authors of the book "Accelerate" did a wonderful job identifying many of the key process capabilities associated with success in this area, we have a long and qualified list of potential Challenge topics. Most have been validated, by actual research, as leading capabilities of organizational performance. Therefore, the grouping and wording of the metrics and topics listed below are inspired by the research presented in that book.

Why the CEO loves it:

- No cross-department blame games or finger pointing; releasing is never a technical issue
- Better predictability
- Less money tied in unrealized gains

Why team members love it:

- Less stress and anxiety
- Motivation from finishing work items
- Immediate feedback
- No manual repetitive work

Adding and mixing with our own examples, we ended up with the following list of Challenge topics and their associated metrics:

- Trunk-based development
- Fully automated deployment throughout the lifecycle
- Version control for all artifacts
- Continuous Integration
- Test automation and test data

Trunk-based development

Trunk-based development can be described as the capability to have fewer than three active branches in the code repository, with branches and forks having very short lifetimes (less than two days) before being merged into the trunk/master. This reduces merge problems and "code lock" periods during which no one can check in code or do pull requests due to merging conflicts, code freezes or stabilization phases. Trunk-based development can be regarded as a technical perspective on getting closer to one-by-one flow, as it also seeks to avoid the IT version of inventory (non-live code).

Potential Challenge and Target Condition metrics related to trunk-based development

Title	Description (why)	How to measure	Unit	Metric cost
Number of active branches	Feature branches that exist for days or weeks often result in complicated merges, high WIP and slow flow.	Count the number of active feature branches and/or their lifetimes.	#/time	low/medium
Frequency of commits or uncommitted code	Code should not stay on individual machines but should be committed at least daily to master or trunk to avoid the risk of merge problems and uncommitted code blocking progress if anyone gets sick or is out-of-office.	Count the frequency of commits and/or the amount of uncommitted code.	#	low/medium
Number of code locks or duration	Periods of code-lock when no one can commit or do pull requests should be close to zero because it drains capacity and motivation.	Count the number and duration of code-lock periods.	#/time	low/medium

Process Metrics table 1: Trunk based development

Example Challenges and Target Conditions:

- From 10 to 3 average active branches
- From 1 to 10 daily commits
- From 1500 to 400 lines of uncommitted code (technical WIP limit)
- From 20 to 5 code-locks per week with a duration above 5 minutes
- From 2 hours to 15 minutes average code-lock duration

Fully automated deployment throughout the lifecycle

This capability states that to deliver on the Vision, software should be in a deployable state throughout its lifecycle. This means that any quality issues are prioritized over working on new features. Fast feedback on the quality and deployability of the system is available to all team members, and when the system is not deployable, fixes are made quickly. The system can be deployed to production or end users at any time, on demand. Deployments are fully automated and do not require manual intervention

Potential Challenge and Target Condition metrics related to automated deployment:

Title	🗐 Description (why)	🗒 How to measure	🖊 Unit	💲 Metric cost
Number of manual deployment steps	Fully automated deploy to all environments is a key part of continuous delivery and an effective Agile team. All manual steps should be removed to minimize transaction cost and enable more frequent releases.	Count the number of steps in deployment that have not yet been automated.	#	low
Staged roll-outs	Gradually exposing your User Stories to increased amounts of traffic is an excellent way of reducing risk and getting fast feedback – safe-to-fail!	Count the number of points where traffic can be increased. You can also count the percentage of work items that are exposed to two or more points of increasing traffic when deployed.	#/%	low
Threshold warnings	Threshold warnings are a great way to automate feedback on KPIs and react proactively to any changes (potentially automatic rollback).	Identify key performance parameters (e.g., response time, CPU usage, memory usage, etc.) and count how many of those are monitored and displayed and/or can trigger an automatic rollback.	#	low
Time to fix	One thing is getting feedback while another is reacting to feedback from failing commits or deploys.	Measure the mean time to recovery from identifying a failing build, test or deploy and until the issue is fixed.	Time	low (automatic)
Technical debt – Code analysis (clean code)	A wide range of Static Code Analysis tools are on the market. They provide the means to analyze code on several parameters related to all aspects of code quality and security.	The score is provided by Code Analysis tools.	score	medium
Deployability	Keeping the system in a deployable state throughout the development cycle enables fast feedback, flexibility, low risk and fast time-to-market.	How many days per week or hours per day is the system in a deployable state?	#/%	low/high
Deployability recoverability	How long it takes to bring the system back to a deployable state could be a strong indicator of how seriously you take keeping the system in a deployable state.	Measure the time to recovery. Can be brought to almost zero if the system automatically rejects any changes that cause a problem with deployability.	time	medium
Deployment time or effort	If deployment requires either much effort or calendar time, we are unlikely to do it often, as the transaction cost is too high. This delays the receipt of feedback on both product fit and quality.	Measure the calendar time and/or effort used to deploy a new version to production.	time/man-hours	medium
Who can deploy	True continuous delivery means that we have moved beyond deployment as a technical issue. Ideally, this means that everybody with deployment privileges can deploy new versions to production environments.	Count the groups or number of people who can deploy new versions.	#	low

Process Metrics table 2: Fully automated deployment throughout the lifecycle

Example Challenges and Target Conditions:

- From 21 to 2 manual deployment steps
- From 1 to 5 steps in staged roll-out gradually increasing traffic from 1-5 early adopters to all users
- From 0 to 4 threshold warnings that are visualized and monitored, including CPU usage, memory usage, system response time and number of log-ins
- From 0 to 4 threshold breaches that trigger automatic deployment rollback, including CPU usage, memory usage, system response time and number of log-ins
- From 70 minutes to 5 minutes average time to fix broken builds
- From 67 days to 5 days of technical depth (SonarQube)
- From 1 to 5 out of 10 workdays in a deployable state
- From 9 workday to 1 workday average time to bring the system back to a deployable state
- From 7 hours to 1 hour deployment time
- From 1 person to 10 people who deploy to production (including at least one customer)

Version control for all artifacts

This might seem like a very specific topic for a Challenge but the ability to provision environments and build, test and deploy our software in a fully automated fashion from information stored in version control is not a simple matter. Most Agile teams have their application code under version control but fail to include all production artifacts, including application configurations, system configurations and scripts for the automating build and configuration of environments. This makes them fragile because these artifacts are as complex as the application code in a modern continuous delivery setup. If a problematic change cannot be easily rolled back, the entire delivery setup is at risk and might delay test, development, deployment and feedback.

Though not easy, this topic is often included as part of a Challenge involving more continuous delivery capabilities.

Potential Challenge and Target Condition metrics related to version control:

Title	Description (why)	How to measure	Unit	Metric cost
Artifacts under version control	Having all artifacts in version control is a key element of establishing continuous delivery capabilities. That includes application code, system configuration, application configuration and scripts for automating build, deployment and configuration.	Count the number of your types of artifacts or the percentage of code in version control.	#/%	medium
Time to provision new environments	Being able to provision all types of environments automatically from version control makes it much easier to test and deploy, as new environments can be created and destroyed as they are needed with various configurations.	Measure the time it takes to provision new environments.	time	low
Manual steps in provisioning new environments	As an alternative to the metric above, you can instead measure the number of manual steps to provision a new environment.	Count the number of manual steps involved in provisioning new environments.	#	low

Process Metrics table 3: Version control for all artifacts

Example Challenges and Target Conditions:

- From 1 to 6 elements under version control (adding system configuration, application configuration, scripts for automated build, scripts for automated deployment and configuration files)
- From 2 hours to 1 minute average time to provision new environments
- From 32 to 0 manual steps in provisioning new environments

Continuous Integration

You might argue that basic Continuous Integration capabilities are the first steps toward any kind of continuous delivery setup. All code is checked in at least daily, and each check-in triggers a set of tests to discover serious regressions, which developers fix immediately. The Continuous Integration process thus creates packages that are later deployed and released.

Potential Challenge and Target Condition metrics related to Continuous Integration include:

Title	Description (why)	How to measure	Unit	Metric cost
Speed of CI build	If feedback is slow, you are likely to generate long wait times after each commit or people stop paying attention to the result.	Simply pull the number from your CI tool.	seconds	low
Validity of CI build result	CI builds are an excellent way to discover problems early but only if it shows actual results you can trust.	Count the number of red builds that were actual red (indicated a problem with the code) and match it with the total number.	%	medium
Time to fix	One thing is getting feedback; another is reacting to feedback from failing commits or deploys.	Measure the time to recovery from identifying a failing build, test or deploy and until the issue is fixed.	time	low

Process Metrics table 4: Continuous Integration

Example Challenges and Target Conditions:

- From 15 minutes to 2 minutes running the entire CI build
- From 50% to 85% real red builds (indicating a problem with the code)
- From 45 minutes to 5 minutes average time to fix a broken build

Test automation and test data

I might have chosen to cover this under the basic Continuous Integration capabilities but because test capabilities involve several specific aspects and metrics, I chose to deal with it separately. As part of a continuous delivery setup, we aim for all tests to run automatically and continuously throughout the development process. Tests find real failures, and unit and acceptance tests are run against every commit. Research shows that the most effective setup is one in which developers are primarily responsible for the creation and maintenance of automated test suites and can run them on their workstations, while testers focus on exploratory testing against the latest builds (Forsgren, Humble, & Kim, 2018).

Potential Challenge and Target Condition metrics related to test:

Title	Description (why)	How to measure	Unit	Metric cost
Manual regression test	A large number of manual regression tests can be an impediment because we are likely to release/deploy less often due to the transaction cost.	Count the number of remaining manual regression tests or the time used to run them.	#/time	low
Code coverage (aut. test)	Tools exist to measure the Automatic test code coverage on most platforms and can provide fast feedback on quality problems. Be careful, though! Code coverage does NOT tell you if you have written usable tests – ONLY if the code has been touched by the test.	Use the automatic test code -coverage tool to measure.	%	medium
Speed of running test suite including manual tests	If running the test suite is a matter of days and not seconds or minutes, you are unlikely to be able to deploy often. This slows flow and feedback.	Measure it manually or get it from the test tool.	Time	Low/medium
Tested programs /modules	Because not all teams can measure code coverage automatically, the percentage of tested programs/ modules is a better and cheaper leading indicator to collect in terms of test quality.	Count the percentage of tested programs/modules. If one work item touches five programs/modules and only one of those are tested. that counts as 20%.	%	medium
Root cause analysis and fixes	A quick fix can be tempting to solve an immediate problem (reboot, etc.), but expensive in the long run, as it will likely reoccur.	Count the number or percentage of the root cause analysis performed and root cause fixes.	%/#	low
Test data	Having relevant test data and being able to require it on demand increases flow.	Count the percentage of work items in which test data does not impede the test.	%	low
Time to fix	A failing test is valuable only if the information is acted upon.	Measure the time from when a test fails until it is fixed, manually or from CI or test tool.	time	low/medium

Process Metrics table 5: Test automation and test data

Example Challenges and Target Conditions:

- From 153 to 40 manual regression tests
- From 4 man-days to 5 man-hours to run the manual regression test suite
- From 20% to 45% code coverage

- From 20% to 50% average tested modules/programs
- From 0 to 10 defect root cause analyses per week
- From 0 to 5 root cause fixes per week
- From 40% to 80% of work items not impeded by missing test data
- From 1 hour to 5 minutes average time to fix failing test

Empowered, self-organizing teams

This element of the Vision deals with the organizational capability to delegate decision authority to the team level to foster engagement and the ability to inspect and adapt on both the Product and Process levels. It also includes the ability and empowerment to make coordination a shared responsibility among team members. That is why we included these two statements in the Vision:

- Self-organization is the only way to effectively handle the complexity involved in innovative work across skill sets. Trying to coordinate the work of others results in information bottlenecks and uninformed decisions.

- Empowerment makes it easy to respond to Process and Product feedback. Once a high-level strategy is decided upon, the empowerment to make all necessary Product and Process changes to deliver on that strategy belongs to the team. That includes empowerment to identify user needs and decide how to implement them.

Why the CEO loves it:

- Ability to focus on strategy
- Operational issues are handled locally
- Less administrative overhead

Why team members love it:

- Autonomy – no puppet masters
- Ownership
- Ability to influence the process and product

But "talk is cheap" and to establish potential Challenges around the concepts of self-organization and empowerment, we must be able to observe how this is done in real life. I have grouped these metrics and behaviors under the following topics:

- Product decision authority
- Technical decision authority
- Self-organization

Product decision authority

In Scrum, this capability is often implemented through a Product Owner role but from an Agile perspective, it is not about identifying a person but making sure that Product decision authority is delegated to the place where the actual work is done. If a Product Owner fits in your situation, great. You are free to include it in your Challenge wording but remember that from the perspective of the Vision, the important part is not the person but the capability. For this section, I define "product decision authority" as the ability to identify and prioritize which user needs to support and to what ambition level to support the strategic direction, hopefully including feedback from multiple end users and stakeholders but still a team-level responsibility.

Note that in the case of our Agile vision, we are not including the strategic decision authority to be delegated to the team level. Instead, we are aiming for teams to be able to decide how they will fulfill the strategic direction that has already been defined. When reading the suggested metrics below you should, therefore, do it from the perspective that the following type of decisions have already been made at the strategic level (including how to measure whether a team is successful): "entering the Chinese market", "compliance with GDPR ", "offering a new type of loan to people age 18-25" and "moving product X to a modern platform".

In terms of numbers, they are often surprisingly low in larger organizations. This is often a sign that only the more mechanical aspects of an Agile organization have been implemented.

Potential Challenge and Target Condition metrics related to product decision authority:

Title	Description (why)	How to measure	Unit	Metric cost
Work item identified by the team	A true cross-functional team is not just being spoon-fed with User Stories by an external party. They engage with end users and perform market research to identify business needs.	Count the number of completed, started or planned work items where the team identified the need. Match against the total number.	%	low
Work item prioritized by the team	Even if the team is responsible for identifying needs, they are still seriously impeded if they cannot act on feedback and change existing priorities,	Count the number of completed, started or planned work items where the team prioritized the need. Match against the total number.	%	low
Ambition level decided by the team	If external stakeholders or customers get to decide the scope and ambition level for each work item, the Agile team will not be able to inspect and adapt on the work item level.	Count the number of completed, started or planned work items where the team set the ambition level. Match against the total number.	%	low
Change authority	The ability to make changes to the system (including changes that affect other teams/systems) without requiring permission from a central authority has proven to be a lead indicator of organizational success.	Count the percentage of previously completed changes that affected other systems/teams where the team had the authority to do it relying only on internal peer review.	%	low

Process Metrics table 6: Product decision authority

Example Challenges and Target Conditions:

- From 0% to 20% of started work items identified by the team
- From 40% to 80% of started work items prioritized by the team
- From 0% to 40% of finished work items where the ambition level is decided by the team
- From 20% to 50% of completed changes relying only on internal peer review

Technical decision authority

A key part of Agile is the ability for a cross-functional team to decide HOW they want to solve a business need. That includes anything from the design of the user interface to how the actual code should be written. It also includes what tools to use and the choice of frameworks and programming languages. Many Agile organizations do have a platform team offering standard tools for, e.g., monitoring, deployment and testing but if technical decision authority is truly delegated to the team level, it is a team decision as to whether to use that platform or not. A great side effect of such a strategy is that the platform team will need to provide a solution that is better than what is offered through open-source or other vendors and will need to stay competitive to stay alive (showing they are "fit for purpose").

Potential Challenge and Target Condition metrics:

Title	Description (why)	How to measure	Unit	Metric cost
Technical decision authority	To work as a self-organizing team and effectively iterate that the team needs decision authority in terms of how to implement business needs on the technical platform.	Count the percentage of previously completed or prioritized work items where the team had sufficient technical decision authority.	%	low
Tool decision authority	Research shows that organizations in which teams are free to choose their own tools perform better than their counterparts.	Count the percentage of tools in the tool stack that were chosen by the team (including design tools, test tools, process tools, IDEs, etc.).	%	low

Process Metrics table 7: Technical decision authority

Example Challenges and Target Conditions:

- From 30% to 60% of completed work items where the team had full decision authority to decide "how" – including design, UX and code
- From 0 to 2 tools chosen by the team

Self-organization

Self-organization is at the heart of Agile. To some organizations, it has now become a standard working pattern to the extent that it would be meaningless to look at it as a prospective Challenge, but to organizations that have just embarked on their Agile journey or have never moved beyond Agile mechanics, it could very well be part of an ambitious Challenge.

There are many ways to define a self-organizing team. The simplest way I have found to describe it is by imagining a prioritized list of user needs. If should be a shared team responsibility to find out who will work on what and in what sequence the top priorities should be started, as well as to coordinate and collaborate to complete the items until they are validated in production. From the opposite perspective, it is not a self-organizing team if a project manager, team lead or lead developer assumes special responsibility for choosing who should work on what and in what sequence as well as for coordinating the work of finishing it. A Product Owner type role might decide on the prioritization, but the self-organizing team can choose which sequence will start the top priorities.

Potential Challenge and Target Condition metrics:

Title	Description (why)	How to measure	Unit	Metric cost
Self-organizing the start of work	Typical traditional project management responsibilities start with the delegation of work. Therefore, this is the first point to check on whether we have moved toward a more modern and effective team setup.	Percentage of started work items for which it was a shared team responsibility to decide who should work on it.	%	low
Self-organizing the coordination of work	Once work has started, it is essential that it be a shared team responsibility to coordinate and communicate to avoid a single person becoming an information bottleneck.	Percentage of finished work items for which only team members working on it took part in coordinating the work.	%	low

Process Metrics table 8: Self-organization

Example Challenges and Target Conditions:

- From 0% to 50% of started work items for which it was a shared team decision responsibility in terms of who should start work.
- From 20% to 60% of finished work items for which only team members working on it took part in coordinating the work.

Stable end-to-end teams with 100% allocation

Though it has more to do with the organizational structure, this is also an important aspect of an Agile organization. As we stated in the Vision:

- Bring the work to people – not people to the work. It takes time for people to learn how to coordinate and collaborate effectively. Average team churn is measured and kept below an officially communicated threshold (e.g., 25% per year). Zero-percent churn is not a good goal, as it implies a static structure that is unable to adapt and attract new talent.
- There is no need for external experts or help from other teams to turn vague user needs into working functionality. End-to-end teams reduce coordination overhead because the entire Value Stream is found within a single team.
- Bringing work to people and having stable teams makes sense only if people are not allocated to several teams. One-hundred-percent allocation of team members is key to long-term effectiveness and fast flow.

So, what might this look like on the Challenge level? Though I have experienced the result of self-selecting teams myself and would strongly encourage you to adopt it at some scale team, structure remains a management responsibility in most organizations. In the few cases in which some aspect of self-selection occurs, it is often within a single department where, e.g., 20 existing employees are asked to form three teams and divide the development, operation and maintenance of future and existing products among them.

Therefore, most of the topic of stable end-to-end teams with 100% allocation is often a Challenge on the management level. But not exclusively. Part-time team members and people being moved around have huge consequences with respect to team effectiveness, and though it might officially be a management responsibility we have seen teams taking on the Challenge and doing everything they possibly could to influence it – with success.

Why the CEO loves it:

- Better predictability
- Simple capacity overview
- Execution power
- Transparent funding

Why the team members love it:

- Clear prioritization
- End-user value ownership (purpose)

- Less stress and task-switching
- Less administrative waste and interfaces

The aspect of end-to-end teams also has a product and technical dimension, as you will see in the following Challenge topics:

- Stable teams
- End-to-end teams
- 100% allocation
- Loosely coupled architecture

Stable teams

As mentioned previously, a stable organizational structure is needed for Toyota Kata to be successful. But stable teams are also necessary for Agile to work. "Individuals and interactions", as written in the Agile Manifesto, is called out for us to remember to respect that people are not just man-hours in an Excel spreadsheet. They need to learn how to work together and, try as we might, there is no single solution that works across all teams. Therefore, it is essential that we provide an environment in which individuals are given the chance to learn how to collaborate and become true and effective teams. It is sometimes surprising to learn that even organizations that consider themselves Agile with stable teams still have an average team churn of over 50% per year (less than 50% of team members have been part of the same team for a year).

This Challenge topic is typically found at the manager level and metrics typically cover several teams, departments or areas. Remember that 100% stability might be a sign that the organization is no longer adapting to match market demands or teams are no longer getting inspiration from the "outside", so be careful setting the bar too high.

Title	Description (why)	How to measure	Unit	Metric cost
Team churn	Stable teams are the basis for effectiveness because it takes time for people to learn how to work together and achieve high performance.	Count team churn. How large a percentage of team members have been part of the team for one, two, three, six months or longer?	%	medium
Average tenure of team members	How long have team members been part of the same team? Visualizing this can provide a great source of information on a global level.	Track how long each team member has been part of the same team.	time	medium/high
Average tenure of teams	How long teams exist is a great indication of the ability to avoid project teams and work toward product streams.	Measure the tenure of each team (individual team members might have changed).	time	medium

Process Metrics table 9: Stable teams

Example Challenges and Target Conditions:

- From 30% to 10% team member churn in the next month
- From 50% to 15% team member churn in the next two months
- From 70% to 25% team member churn in the next six months
- From 3 to 4 months average tenure of team members
- From 4 to 6 months average tenure of teams

End-to-end teams

The aspect of the cross-functional Agile team is one of the most important and misunderstood concepts. At the very core, it is about creating an organizational structure to minimize dependencies through product-oriented and cross-functional teams. Teams are structured around the product and not component teams or technical layers of the application. Each team has the capability to deliver end-to-end value without the need to involve other teams or external specialists. Sadly, this is often not given enough attention, both as a continuous improvement focus and when initially forming the Agile teams. Because it seems easier to keep the original structure of the organization, the "Agile teams" are sometimes just functional teams that have now adopted a different way of work. But the potential to minimize dependencies and act swiftly to changing customer needs and feedback is still lost in handovers and interfaces.

Remember that the Vision of an entire organization fitted to the structure of end-to-end teams delivering value to the company's real end users, without introducing component teams or any kind

273

of internal dependencies, is an ideal Future State. Thus, the goal is to move closer to that goal but do not expect to reach it.

Potential Challenge and Target Condition metrics include:

Title	Description (why)	How to measure	Unit	Metric cost
Work items completed without outside help	If work items cannot be completed without outside help, it is not an end-to-end team. Lowering this number should decrease dependencies and increase effectiveness.	Count the percentage of work items the team has been able to finish without help from other teams and match it with the total number.	%	low
Component vs. Feature/Product teams	End-to-end teams that can deliver end-user functionality without depending on deliveries from other parts of the organization support flow, feedback and adaptability.	Count the ratio between teams that are primarily component (delivering mainly to other teams) and feature/product teams (delivering to end users).	%	low

Process Metrics table 10: End-to-end teams

Example Challenges and Target Conditions:

- From 10% to 50% of work items finished without external help
- From 80% to 50% component teams

100% allocation

This Challenge is often very valid, as it addresses one of the biggest problems when an organization is moving from a traditional functional setup to an Agile organization with cross-functional teams. In an organization with functional silos, each person is typically assigned to many project "teams" at the same time. This is quite natural, as work is brought to the people, various projects are competing for the same skill sets and it is hard to get a full overview of the number of projects in progress and the workload of individuals. Aiming for 100% allocation across all skill sets in a team is a worthy but ambitious Challenge, as it drastically reduces the coordination overhead, provides an environment for true teams to emerge and minimizes stress on individuals.

When you identify your Current Condition, it is important to remember that we are not interested in blame games. Sometimes an ambitious step is going from 10% fully allocated team members across five teams to 40%. Do remember that it is often the case that a single Agile team is responsible for more than one product (you-build-it-you-run-it structure), so it is not necessarily a bad thing that a single team member might work on more than one product during a workweek.

As you have probably already realized, Challenge and Target Condition metrics are pretty straightforward:

Title	Description (why)	How to measure	Unit	Metric cost
Team allocation	Part-time team members are ineffective, as they must spend extra time keeping up to date and are more prone to stress and task-switching.	Either count the percentage of 100% allocated team members or the average number of teams per person.	%/#	low

Process Metrics table 11: 100% allocation

Example Challenges and Target Conditions:

- From 10% to 50% team members allocated 100% to a single team
- From 3.5 to 1.5 average teams per person

Loosely coupled architecture

But the issue of end-to-end teams is not only a matter of hiring the right people and structuring the organization from a product perspective. End-to-end means that you have all capabilities within the team to deliver value to real end users. Yet that matters little if platforms and systems are not set up to let teams work independently on their products from a technical perspective. Borrowing some of the wording from the book "Accelerate", we might state it like this:

"Teams can deploy applications on demand, without requiring orchestration with other services. We have a loosely coupled architecture that allows teams to work independently, without relying on other teams for support and services, which enables them to work quickly and deliver value to the organization".

This is a typical example of a Challenge that will often benefit from being launched as an organization-wide Catch-ball, as it requires changes both to the overall structure as well as in how the individual teams work. Note that dependencies on shared technical platforms and closely coupled architecture are not the same as the topic of a cross-functional team. Shared technical dependencies will still exist no matter what subject matter expert you add to the team.

Potential Challenge and Target Condition metrics include:

Title		Description (why)		How to measure	Unit	Metric cost
Independent deploys (organization level)		The percentage of teams or products that can be deployed independently is an important indication of the effectiveness of the technical architecture.		Count the percentage of teams (and/or their products) that can deploy independently without the need to coordinate with other teams or centralized functions.	%	low
Independent deploys (team level)		The percentage of work items or products that a team can deploy independently is a good leading indicator of their ability to inspect and adapt.		Count the percentage of work items or products that can be deployed independently of other teams and products.	%	low

Process Metrics table 12: Loosely coupled architecture

Example Challenges and Target Conditions:

- From 1 to 5 products that can be deployed independently
- From 5 to 15 teams that can deploy independently
- From 20% to 50% of work items that can be deployed independently of other teams and products

Small batches (MVP, MVF), always outside-in approach

In his book "The Principles of Product Development Flow" (Reinertsen, 2009), Don Reinertsen makes an excellent point:

"The most dangerous of all batch size problems is the tendency to pack more innovation into a single product that is truly necessary".

This is such an important statement that I have included it in pretty much every conference presentation and training material on the subject. Essentially, this means it is not enough to minimize the number of items in progress if those items are still too big. This also ties nicely with the Lean Startup concepts of Minimum Viable Products (MVPs) and Minimum Viable Features (MVFs). If it takes us years to develop the first "Minimum Viable Product", we will never achieve business agility even though we might have focused extensively on feedback loops and not committed ourselves to a fixed scope. Fast time-to-market is essential, and it is hard to claim agility without it. But we can reap the benefits of faster time-to-market only if we have managed to take an outside-in and customer-centric approach on both the product and feature levels, as we can validate little from a purely technical solution. That is why we included the two following statements in the Vision:

- New enhancements, features and products represent the smallest possible vertical slice and are deployed all the way to production within one day (enhancements), three days (features) and one month (new products) to reduce cycle time and risk and get early feedback.

- All estimated, tracked and visualized work is relevant and prioritized from an end-user perspective and the flow of those items is the only real measure of progress. Only work items representing end-user value count and each work item includes a hypothesis of the actual monetary value!

Why the CEO loves it:

- Business Agility

- Less money tied in unrealized gains

- Lower risk

- Customer focus

Why the team members love it:

- No "marathon" projects

- Customer focus

- Daily progress

- Outcome focus

How this can be translated into actual Challenges is discussed under the following three headlines:

- Minimum Viable Products
- Minimum Viable Features
- Outside-in perspective

Minimum Viable Product (MVP)

The term MVP was popularized by Eric Ries in his book "The Lean Startup" (Ries, 2011). He defines an MVP as the "version of a new product which allows a team to collect the maximum amount of validated learning about customers with the least effort".

In terms of understanding the use of "Minimum Viable Products", we must frame "vertical slice" in a slightly different way, as we are not always interested in including all technical layers to validate our most important assumptions on a product level. Instead of thinking about technical layers of a system, the "vertical slice" becomes the smallest possible version we can create that allows us to validate the biggest risk with real end users.

Using the term MVP outside the context of startups, I have found it helpful to look at it from a risk perspective. We want to build the smallest possible version that can help us learn and validate whether we should spend more money heading in that direction. Thus, an MVP is about buying information as cheaply as possible to validate assumptions. In one context, the biggest risk might be engagement, and we can validate that with a prototype that looks like the real product from an end-user perspective. However, the "backend" and business logic is handled by manual work in the background. In another case, it might be time-to-market, as a competitor has already launched a successful version and protecting the market share will depend mostly on cycle time. In this case, a prototype will be useless, as engagement has already been validated. Instead, we must focus on what core features to include to avoid customers leaving.

If you are launching a new type of product in a new market, you are addressing a much different risk than if you are developing a product like others in your portfolio within a market in which have been operating for 10 years. While an initial prototype that can't scale beyond one or two users will make perfect sense in one context, it can be a waste of time in the other. That also means that the concept of an MVP changes within the same context. Once you have validated engagement risk through a prototype MVP, the risk has changed, and you now move on to validate conversion risk or scaling risk depending on your context.

Second, regardless of the context, if you can reduce scope by 50% you are almost guaranteed to reduce budget risk, schedule risk and complexity by considerably more than that. Even if you should opt for a traditional stage-gate model to implement it, you will still achieve more business agility.

Setting up a Challenge around the concept of an MVP often requires minimizing the scope needed to validate your biggest risk. A rule of thumb is that you should consider yourself in trouble if you cannot launch your MVP in fewer than three months and preferably much sooner than that. The Continuous Delivery capabilities like "staged roll-outs", introduced in the previous section, can help support this, as it drastically reduces the consequence of being wrong by gradually making the MVP available to more users.

Remember that once your product is "live", you should strive to deploy each finished feature in production when it is finished (one-by-one flow). Some use the term "Minimum Business Increments" (MBI) to describe the process of adding to the MVP after it is launched.

Potential Challenge and Target Conditions metrics include:

Title	Description (why)	How to measure	Unit	Metric cost
Minimum Viable Product (MVP)	Finding the creativity to slice new product initiatives into the smallest possible first version is key to getting feedback early and validating the riskiest hypotheses.	Count the number of items or story points included in the first release.	#	low
Validating the hypothesis	Being able to validate the main hypothesis is essential for a successful MVP. This metric fails to deliver on our goal of a high metric update frequency but remains important.	Do you have quantitative metrics that enable you to validate the success of the MVP?	yes/no	low
Projected cost of first release	Converting the labor cost into dollars and showing that you are spending less on the first release is sometimes more effective than relative effort estimates like story points.	Calculate the forecasted cost of the first release.	$	medium

Process Metrics table 13: Minimum Viable Product (MVP)

Example Challenges and Target Conditions:

- From 150 to 90 work items in the first release – MVP (without changing the size or merging them)
- From 2,500 to 1,300 story points in the first release – MVP

- From 0 to 3 visualized metrics (engagement, conversion rate, churn)
- From $2,500,000 to $1,800,000 projected cost of first release (using the same calculation)
- From $300,000 to $150,000 average investment in first release (organizational perspective)

Minimum Viable Features (MVFs)

MVFs work in much the same way on the feature level as MVP does on the product level. If we want to build a culture of Lean product development, we must learn to slice new features so we can test and validate our assumptions in days and not weeks. We do not want to build a Rolls-Royce if a Micro Car is enough to solve the end-user need. The important thing is to keep a strict outside-in perspective on all metrics associated with this and not fall into the trap of thinking that we have truly validated our hypothesis by simply building one technical layer or a written specification. Work items should be able to provide feedback from real users through vertical slices.

But learning to slice features vertically is a difficult skill to master. You will find literally hundreds of blogs, books and articles on the subject, which are all great input for Toyota Kata experiments. But you should, however, be aware that though most suggest an outside-in and customer-centric perspective, not all live up to that promise. So, watch out for techniques that focus more on making work items small and less on validating end-user hypotheses. Otherwise, you might find yourself building a horizontal slice and not a feature. Note that while it does not make sense to use cycle time on a product level as a leading indicator, it is often possible on the feature level if throughput is high enough.

From a Challenge and Target Condition perspective, we might validate our capability to do this by using these types of metrics:

Title	Description (why)	How to measure	Unit	Metric cost
Minimum Viable Feature effort	Slicing User Stories into small vertical slices of end-user valuable functionality is key to flow, feedback and effectiveness.	Count the average size of work items in story points (or your chosen unit of estimation). Also, consider counting the percentage of work items in your largest acceptable story point bucket.	#/%	low
Minimum Viable Feature cycle time	Slicing User Stories into small vertical slices of end-user valuable functionality is key to flow, feedback and effectiveness.	Count the average cycle time from starting work on a work item until it is "done".	#/%	low

Process Metrics table 14: Minimum Viable Features (MVFs)

Example Challenges and Target Conditions:

- From 22.5 to 12 average story point size of work items (keeping an outside-in focus)
- From 20% to 5% large-size work items
- From 13 to 5 days average work item cycle time

Outside-in perspective

The topic of keeping outside-in is crucial but often not given enough attention as part of being an Agile team. If we do not take an outside-in and customer-centric approach toward everything we do, we might simply be performing a charade including various Agile roles, events and practices but essentially delivering nothing of real value in the wrong order and with no real feedback and ability to inspect and adapt. That is also why Challenges within this topic have been among the most popular, as it is at the very heart of the capabilities we want to build and the culture we want to create. One important aspect to note is that if the flow of the most important work items from a customer or end-user perspective is the only real measure of progress, that also influences how we are set up to deliver on that from a team perspective. We cannot reprioritize the sequence of work to fit specialist skills without diluting that concept.

User Stories have become the standard way of communicating end-user needs in the Agile community, as they offer a simple and adaptive way of capturing conversations from an outside-in perspective. It is beyond the scope of this book to cover User Stories in detail but one of the key features is the format "As a <type of end user> I want to <action> so that I <benefit>", which should guarantee an outside-in focus on all work items (Cohn, 2004). Some teams have, however, adopted the format but misunderstood the concept and start the User Story descriptions: "As a Team member..." or "As a Product Owner..." and thereby turn an outside-in format inside-out. If you find yourself in such a situation, this might be a great challenge for you.

Let us have a look at the many interesting Challenge and Target Condition metrics found in the area of an outside-in perspective:

Title	Description (why)	How to measure	Unit	Metric cost
End-user-focused work items	The percentage of planned, started or finished work items that are relevant from an end-user perspective. This shows how good we are at taking an outside-in, customer-centric approach.	Count the number of planned, started or finished work items that will result in real value to end users.	%	low
Order of business priority	If you cannot solve things in order of business priority, you are likely not ideally balanced as a team or simply optimizing for output over outcome.	Count the percentage of items that were finished in order of highest business priority.	%	low
T-profile/knowledge sharing score	If teams are not able to solve work items in order of business priority, growing a broader T-profile could be a strong lead indicator in terms of achieving better flow or ability to start work in the right order.	Identify the domain, skill or technical area where bottlenecks occur. How many team members can do either all work in that area or the easiest work in that area?	#	Low
Percentage of operation/ maintenance a team member can handle on his/her own	T-profiles are important to be able to handle operation/maintenance during holiday periods and avoid unnecessary internal interruptions. Thus, the ability to handle it without having to ask for help can be a good leading indicator. It is important to stress that the end goal is typically not 100% and that it is not a personal problem, but a team effort to get there.	Count the number of issues individual team members can complete on their own and match with the total. They should feel OK doing it alone!	%	low
Prioritization by business value	The amount of work prioritized by business value (can be a simple score) shows that you are not solving things in random order but taking an outside-in perspective.	Count the percentage of work items that are assigned business value and prioritized accordingly.	%	low
Monetary value hypothesis	Being able to assign a hypothesis of monetary value for individual work items is a very strong leading indicator of process maturity and an outside-in perspective. Consider using frameworks like Cost of Delay.	Count the percentage of planned work items that are assigned a hypothesis of monetary value.	%	low

Process Metrics table 15: Outside-in perspective

Example Challenges and Target Conditions:

- From 15% to 60% of work items relevant from an end-user perspective
- From 40% to 80% of work items fixed in order of business priority
- From 1 to 2 team members who can complete 4 out of 5 "loan" features in the t-module
- From 1 to 4 team members who can complete 1 out of 5 "loan" features in the t-module
- From 3 to 5 team members who can handle 4 out of 5 operation and maintenance issues
- From 10% to 80% of planned work items prioritized according to the business value score
- From 0 to 20 work items assigned a Cost of Delay per week in USD

One-by-one flow (Limit WIP)

One-by-one flow is arguably the closest we get to core Lean Process optimization. You might be excused for thinking that it presents limited possibilities for optimization in an Agile setting. But if we look more closely at the capability to effectively finish one feature before starting a new one and limiting the number of work items in progress, it presents a surprisingly big perspective on optimization. Essentially, it is by getting closer to this that we can harvest the full potential of all the other elements of the Vision. It is essential to stress that one-by-one flow is a principle we apply through the entire Value Stream. It is not one-by-one flow in "development" or "test".

We cannot complete a large batch of analysis and we cannot release 100 work items in a single batch and claim to have one-by-one flow. One of the problems we face in knowledge work is, however, that work is not visible. We cannot walk down the production floor and see all the inventory and work in progress. It is "hidden" on computer disks and in people's heads and, therefore, we often need to deliver on some aspects of the Vision theme of "Visual Management" to work effectively with this topic.

Why the CEO loves it:

- Ability to quickly react to market feedback

- Less money tied in unrealized gains

- Lower risk

Why the team members love it:

- Avoiding analysis paralysis

- Stop starting, start finishing

- Less stress and task-switching

There is a reason that "Focus" is part of the five Scrum values, but it is one thing to talk about it and another thing to provide an environment in which you deliver on it and achieve smooth flow. I think you will find a few surprises among the potential Challenge and Target Condition metrics, as it includes the ability to defer details, handle bottlenecks and avoid unscheduled work.

We look at the one-by-one flow from the following three perspectives:

- Focus
- Work in Progress (WIP) limits
- Smooth and level flow

Focus

Teams and team members can focus on finishing started work and are not interrupted by changing priorities, expedites or meetings. That enables fast flow and, thus, the priority of not-started-work can be changed and adapted continuously without causing stress, demotivation or task-switching. Expediting unscheduled work is expensive and we should, therefore, reserve it for the few items that truly deserve this treatment. Unfortunately, that is not what happens in real life due to misguided advice on "customer service", habits and choosing the easy path. Thus, focus and the ability to finish one thing before starting a new one is a strong leading indicator of increased effectiveness in these situations.

But focus is not limited to the work items displayed on the Kanban or Scrum Board. It is also the scheduled and unscheduled meetings and events. One of the Challenges we have seen offering the most return on investment in terms of both productivity and team member happiness is the ability to create time for uninterrupted work in the team.

Potential Challenges and Target Condition metrics for focus include:

Title	Description (why)	How to measure	Unit	Metric cost
Expedites	Expedites or irrefutable demand must be solved now and cannot wait for existing work to finish. That is the opposite of a pull system and causes slow flow, less throughput and stress.	Count the number of expedited or alternative items that should not have been expedited but were.	%/#	medium
External interruptions	Teams that are constantly interrupted are less effective and prone to stress. A key element of focus is protecting the team from external interruptions.	Count the number of external interruptions per team or team member.	#	medium
Periods of uninterrupted work	A high number of periods (e.g., 2.5 hours) during which team members can focus on started work without being interrupted by changing priorities or meetings is a strong leading indicator of effectiveness.	Count the number of periods during which each team member can focus on started work without being interrupted by meetings or changing priorities.	#	low
Changes to priority of started work	If people are not allowed to finish started work because of changing priorities, work becomes stressful and ineffective.	Count the number of weekly/daily changes to priorities of already-started work.	#	low

Process Metrics table 16: Focus

Example Challenges and Target Conditions:

- From 10 to 0 "fake" expedites per week
- From 4 to 2 average external interruptions per team member per day
- From 1 to 6 periods of 3 hours of uninterrupted work per day per team (without unscheduled work, meetings or external interruptions)
- From 5 to 1 changes in priorities of started work per week
- From 10 to 2 expedites per week

Work In Progress (WIP) limits

In Kanban systems, a limited number of work permits (Kanbans) are used to make sure that we cannot start more work than we have proven able to finish (Anderson, 2010). That creates a pull system in which instead of pushing work, the system pulls work at its actual capacity. In IT, we often visualize our work permits by setting a limit on how much work can be introduced into the individual columns on the Kanban or Scrum Board. If there are two work items in the "Development" column and the limit is three, we have a work permit to pull one more work item into that column.

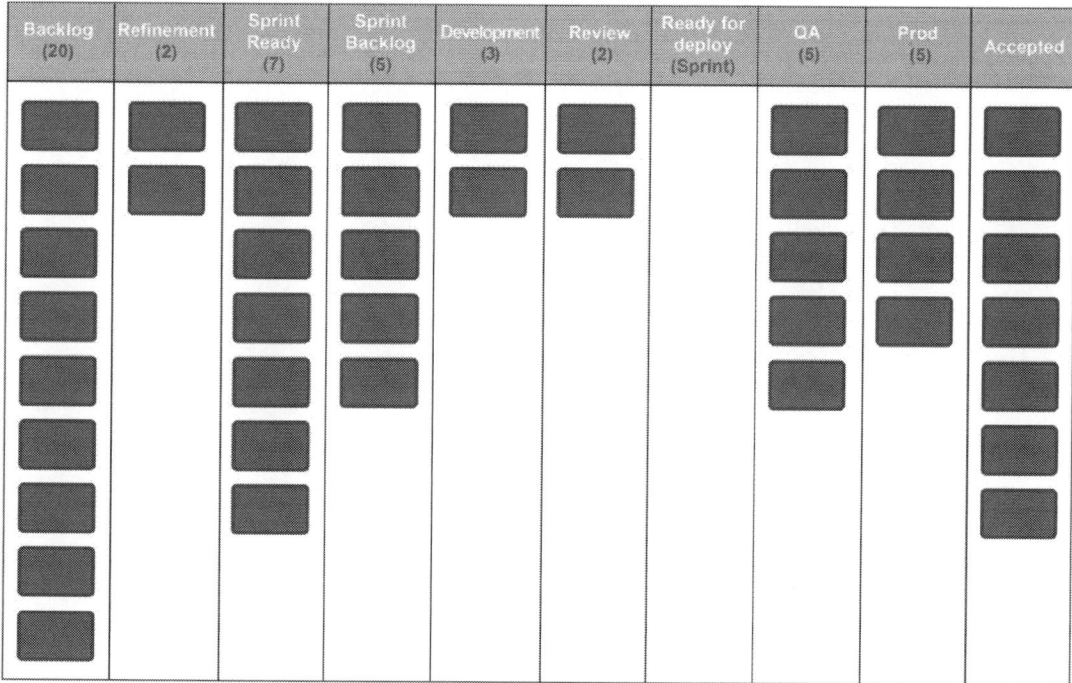

Figure 74: Kanban board with Work In Progress Limits

Using Work In Progress limits is an incredibly simple and powerful mechanism, as it forces us to focus on finishing work rather than starting work even when we run into blockers and problems. But not only is it a powerful way of balancing the system and creating smooth flow and effectiveness, it is also a powerful way to drive Process improvement. The active use of setting and lowering WIP limits will reveal obstacles to higher flow, and we can remove these obstacles through Process improvement. Thus, WIP limits drive Process improvement, increase throughput and make constraints visible in the system.

Even though the simple and powerful principle of setting and continuously lowering WIP limits can be a major improvement driver, it remains one of the most misunderstood and unutilized aspects of improvement in IT and Agile settings.

Here are a few examples:

- WIP limits are set but blocked or paused work is not counted against WIP – basically eliminating the purpose of using WIP limits.
- WIP limits are set on the subtask level but not on the level of value adding work items (e.g., User Stories). Thus, we can keep pushing work into the system without being forced to finish any customer-recognized value.
- WIP limits are set but ignored when broken. I have experienced teams in which a WIP limit on a single column had been broken and ignored for over six months.
- WIP limits are set but increased as soon as blockers or other problems occur. Used like that, it has nothing to do with a "limit"; the number is simply a count of in-progress items.
- WIP limits remain static and though they are not broken, neither are they used to drive Process improvement.
- WIP limits are applied only to the "development" part of the workflow and both upstream and downstream processes are not included. This means that you can complete a traditional waterfall requirement specification phase or do a Big Bang release to production without receiving warning signals. To be a true pull system, WIP limits must be applied to the entire Value Stream, including the "fuzzy frontend" and the deployment to real users.

The last point above is especially important, as that is where it becomes difficult. We must deal with both the inability to defer details and to do real Agile risk management through early and frequent releases. I have unfortunately seen quite a few teams and organizations work with WIP limits but include only the "easy" parts. That way, they could keep their existing waterfall model but still pretend to be Agile. Combining Toyota Kata with the principle of WIP limits has proven to be incredibly powerful. This should not come as a surprise, as this combination is one of the main reasons for Toyota's success in the last 60 years. With this combination, WIP limits are given the constant attention they need to become effective and there are great Challenge and Target Condition metrics to work with:

Title	Description (why)	How to measure	Unit	Metric cost
Amount of Work in Progress (WIP)	Limiting WIP can be a strong leading indicator of increased effectiveness because it exposes bottlenecks and drives Process optimization. It is not limited to "development" work and should be applied to both upstream and downstream processes.	Count the number of work items or story points in progress. For individual workflow steps or across (Con WIP).	#	low
WIP limited part of workflow	WIP limits on just "development" work do not ensure a pull system. Bottlenecks can also form in upstream and downstream processes.	Count the number of workflow steps; count how many of those have associated WIP limits.	#/%	low
WIP limit compliance	WIP limits are not effective if they are broken.	Count the number of times that WIP limits are broken and/or the duration.	#	low

Process Metrics table 17: Work In Progress (WIP) limits

Example Challenges and Target Conditions:

- From 10 to 6 maximum number of work items in "test" column
- From 35 to 20 maximum number of work items in "specification, development and test" columns (con-wip)
- From 1 to 5 columns with Work In Progress limits
- From 5 to 0 times WIP limits are broken per week (without increasing the limit)

Smooth and level flow

Even with small batches and WIP limits in place, we must actively manage for smooth and level flow to make one-by-one flow result in optimal performance. Smooth and level flow basically means that once work has started, it is not blocked or placed on a waiting queue at any time during "execution". Rather, it flows smoothly from started to being validated in production. Nor is workload unstable and the system is never pressed or stressed beyond its current capabilities.

Doing this effectively includes both the use of bottleneck-handling, commitment points and flow metrics. Surprisingly to some, level flow sometimes includes the capability to increase WIP and even set limits for a minimum inventory as we strive to smooth flow across skill sets and cadences. Teams are often surprised when they realize that they must increase WIP and even set up explicit buffers of inventory, but that is because we are aiming to protect bottlenecks against starvation or the fluctuation of throughput in upstream processes. It is beyond the scope of this book to cover the aspects of bottleneck strategies, but I strongly suggest that you read books like Don Reinertsen's "Principles of Product Development Flow" (Reinertsen, 2009) or David Anderson's "Kanban" (Anderson, 2010) if you want to dive deeper into the subject.

An important aspect of flow is knowing when to start counting – when does the "clock" start? We often call this the "commitment point" and define it as the place in our flow where work items are no longer considered "options" but where work has started with the intention of finishing it as soon as possible. Knowing your "commitment point" is also important in terms of expectation management, as we must clearly communicate the difference between options and committed work items both internally and externally. Here is a visual example of how this is not always the case:

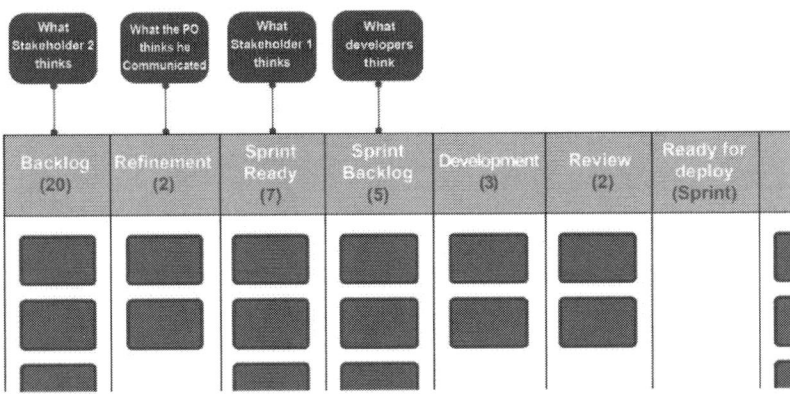

Figure 75: Kanban Board showing different commitment points

Examples of Challenges and Target Condition metrics include:

Title	Description (why)	How to measure	Unit	Metric cost
Blocked items	If the percentage of work items that are blocked during execution is high, it could suggest a serious flow problem, and solving it will likely result in both higher throughput and increased predictability. We typically include only external blockers.	Count the number, percentage or average blocked duration of started work items that are blocked.	time/#/%	medium
Flow efficiency	Work should flow. Flow efficiency describes the relationship between wait time and work time. If a work item is worked on for one hour but it takes four hours to complete, flow efficiency is 25%.	A pragmatic approach is to divide the total sum of available work hours by the total sum of the lead time (in hours) of finished work items (for a specific period).	%	medium
Process cycle time	Cycle time on the end-to-end process remains one of the most powerful indicators of flow. If the current cycle time is too long to be used as a lead indicator, the cycle time of an individual process step (e.g., test or deployment) can be used.	Measure the time from start to finish.	Time	Low/medium
Stakeholder response time	In Agile, we do not specify everything upfront and, thus, we rely heavily on close customer collaboration. If we cannot get the answers we need when we run into problems, we will likely start to detail everything upfront or ask our customers to "lock down" requirements in a traditional requirement spec.	Simply count the hours/ days from asking a question until stakeholders provide an answer that unblocks the work item.	time	medium
Number of "Ready" items	Some teams suffer from not having enough work ready, which indicates an unbalanced workflow. As a result, work items are blocked due to missing clarifications or the fact that people are idle. Because this is quite specific, it is often found at the Target Condition level and should not be the only metric.	Count the number of work items or story points in "Ready".	story points /#	low

Process Metrics table 18: Smooth and level flow

Example Challenges and Target Conditions:

- From 50% to 20% of work items getting blocked for over 3 hours by external problems during execution
- From 5% to 20% flow efficiency
- From 5 days to 1 day average blocked time
- From 10 to 2 blockers on average per week
- From 6.5 days to 2 days average stakeholder response time to unblock work
- From 1 to 5 average work items in "ready column"

Visual Management – full transparency

Transparency is a core element of Agile, as we seek to cause problems to surface early and manage risk through fast feedback. To do that, we make sure that both the progress of work and the system health are visualized. Not only do we use time and effort making the invisible visible but we strive to make it easily accessible to all interested parties. Therefore, we used the following statement in the Vision:

- Full visual transparency in terms of system health and the status and progress of all ongoing work. Available to all interested stakeholders – nothing hidden.

At this point, you might just imagine a Scrum or Kanban Board, and though they are both visual and add transparency, this topic is both deeper and broader than that. It includes visualization of the entire value stream and system health as well as the collection and visualization of the related data on flow.

Why the CEO loves it:

- Transparent and honest status

- Proactive decisions

- Overview

- Better forecasting

Why the team members love it:

- Overview

- Proactive decision-making

- Honest and open dialogue

- Better coordination

We will cover the associated metrics and example Challenges of Visual Management under the following headlines:

- Flow of work visible through the value stream
- System health is monitored, displayed and checked
- Data-driven optimization, planning and predictability

Flow of work visible through the Value Stream

Visualization of workflow is at the very core of Visual Management; we want the flow of work to be visualized from business needs all the way through to customers and end users. Visual displays such as Kanban Boards should be used to organize and track the flow of value through the entire Value Stream to coordinate and manage work effectively in a single place. To make sure that we keep an outside-in approach, all tracked work items should be relevant from an end-user perspective and include a clear statement of the customer/end-user value hypothesis.

Challenge and Target Condition metrics include:

Title	Description (why)	How to measure	Unit	Metric cost
Prioritization channels	There should be only one place to look to see the priority of planned work if you want to align a team toward a shared goal and avoid stress and conflicting priorities.	Count the number of places you should look to find the full amount of work-to-be-done (planned work).	#	low
In-Progress visualization places	There should be a single space where all ongoing work is visualized to achieve pull, coordinate work effectively and avoid task-switching, stress and conflicting priorities.	Count the number of places you must look to track ongoing work.	#	low
Visualized workflow steps	All workflow steps should be visible to achieve total transparency and end-to-end optimization. That includes all workflow steps from starting as a vague idea and to validated in production.	Create a high-level Value Stream Map of your current end-to-end process and count the steps during which ongoing work is visualized.	#/%	low
Percentage of visualized work	How much of your work is visible can be a strong leading indicator of working on the right priorities, the amount of task-switching and the ability to identify blocked work and bottlenecks.	Track the amount of invisible work (local mailboxes, walk-ins, phone calls, Post-its on the desk, etc.) against visible work.	%	medium

Process Metrics table 19: Flow of work visible through the Value Stream

Example Challenges and Target Conditions:

- From 6 to 1 places where work items are prioritized and visual
- From 5 to 2 places where in-progress work is visualized
- From 50% to 80% of all work visualized
- From 4 to 9 workflow steps visualized

293

System health is monitored, displayed and checked

We often tend to limit our view on visualization and transparency to the capabilities to visualize the actual flow of work and communicate progress clearly to internal and external stakeholders. But visualizing system health is at least as important, as it enables us to react proactively to any problems before it results in a major customer or end user facing issues. Thus, system health monitoring and visualization help us build the capability to have an integrated feedback loop that ensures we do not focus only on the number and quality of individual features but also on the entire system. Inspired by the wording from Accelerate, 2018 we state:

We create and maintain visual displays showing key quality, productivity and system health metrics. These visual displays are available to both team members, managers and customers, and metrics are aligned with operational goals. System health is monitored, using threshold and rate-of-change warnings, to enable us to preemptively detect and mitigate, e.g., performance problems.

Challenge and Target Condition metrics include:

Title	Description (why)	How to measure	Unit	Metric cost
Time spent on operation and maintenance	Time spent on maintenance and operation could be a leading indicator that users cannot find out how to use the system (not intuitive) or that many incidents are reported (low quality).	Pull the numbers from the time-tracking system.	%/hours	low
System health monitored and displayed	Monitoring and displaying system health are key parts of continuous delivery and DevOps because they make essential data available to teams, leaders and stakeholders and enable proactive action before things go wrong.	Identify relevant system metrics (e.g., CPU, memory, response time) and quality metrics (incidents, defect rate) and count how many are visualized to the team and stakeholders.	#	low
Threshold warnings	Identifying threshold warnings for system health metrics indicates that you have considered acceptable service levels. Automatic rollback is the next step.	Count the percentage of identified system metrics that have threshold warnings. Consider extending with the ability to trigger automatic rollbacks.	%	low

Process Metrics table 20: System health is monitored, displayed and checked

Example Challenges and Target Conditions:

- From 8.5 to 2.5 hours per day spent on operation and maintenance (without increasing the number of unresolved items)
- From 1 to 4 system and quality metrics visualized (including CPU, memory, response time and defect rate)
- From 0 to 2 system and quality metrics with threshold warnings
- From 0 to 1 system and quality metrics that can trigger an automatic rollback
- From 0 to 2 system and quality metrics that influence decisions

Data-driven optimization, planning and predictability

The use of data for planning and expectations management offers an honest and transparent alternative to wishful thinking and overoptimistic deadlines as well as full transparency in terms of how effectively work is flowing through the system. Thus, using data for transparency and visibility serves the primary purpose of being an active driver of Process improvement and expectations management.

Before diving into this specific topic, it is very important to realize that you must make sure that other capabilities are in place first. One of the most common misconceptions is that you can use historical data to make future predictions in any context and get a useful result. That is, unfortunately, not true.

If you find yourself in a situation with highly unstable WIP, in which flow is neither smooth nor level or in which team members are switching teams and projects constantly, your throughput or cycle time data will probably not be very useful for forecasting. In such a situation, you should instead focus exclusively on using data to indicate whether you have brought the system under control and leveled flow. We often refer to a situation in which these capabilities are in place (stable WIP, smooth flow etc.) as a system that is under control. In those cases, using historical data for forecasting and expectations management can be highly valuable. We might state it like this:

We use cycle time, WIP, defects and throughput data to improve the flow and predictability of customer value through our Value Stream. Based on that data, we use probabilistic forecasting to realistically align expectations with key stakeholders through a standardized and customer-centric interface (not process).

Title	Description (why)	How to measure	Unit	Metric cost
Collecting data types for optimizing flow	Flow and quality data provides valuable insights and can help guide improvement initiatives. It includes: Cumulative Flow Diagrams (CFD), cycle time, flow efficiency, started vs. finished, throughput and defect rate.	Count the types of data you want to collect for different work item types (e.g., User Stories and Incidents). Consider extending with a count on your ability to use that data.	#/%	medium
Probabilistic throughput and cycle time forecasting	Once you can collect data, you can use it to visualize future trends. Measuring this capability is often binary so we often end up with a subjective score.	Rate your ability to visualize and communicate probabilistic throughput and cycle time trends, e.g., 10th, 50th and 90th percentiles.	score (1-5)	low

Process Metrics table 21: Data-driven optimization, planning and predictability

Example Challenges and Target Conditions:

- From 0 to 3 data types collected and visualized (cycle time, throughput, blocked time)
- From 1 to 3 in ability to use probabilistic throughput forecasting displaying 10th, 50th and 90th percentiles 4-20 weeks into the future (subjective score from 1-5)
- From 1 to 3 in ability to use probabilistic cycle time forecasting of defect fix time, displaying 10th, 50th and 90th percentiles (subjective score from 1-5)

Continuous qualitative and quantitative customer and end-user feedback

Feedback is at the very essence of Agility, as it is essentially the capability that makes it possible for us to inspect and adapt. Thus, feedback capabilities are already part of many of the topics we have already covered as, e.g., visual management is a key enabler of feedback on the health of our process and our ability to provide adequate expectations management. Closing the feedback from customers and end users is, however, such an essential part of Agile that it deserves its own topic.

Without this type of feedback, we can very well be delivering on most of our Agile vision but failing to work in a truly iterative manner. We might pretend to inspect and adapt with full team-level authority but if our feedback loop does not extend beyond our own opinions, we risk:

"...building a beautiful cathedral in record time. Except that the users didn't need a cathedral, they needed a camper van".

This is what Henrik Kniberg states in his popular YouTube video "Agile Product Ownership in a Nutshell". The book "Accelerate" deals explicitly with this topic; mixed with our own wording, we ended up with the following, as you might recall from the Vision statement:

- We continuously seek customer feedback and incorporate this feedback into the design of our products. We validate new products and features by performing user research from the very beginning of the process lifecycle. We do qualitative studies and collect real-time data on quality and usage against new deployments to real users. Developers have access to real users and user data, to enable flow and feedback.

Feedback is, thus, not just about counting the number of defects. It is about being able to find out if we have truly delivered customer and end-user recognized value. To quote Russell Ackoff once again (Ackoff, 1994):

"Quality ought to contain the notion of value not merely efficiency ... There is a difference between efficiency and effectiveness. Quality ought to be directed at effectiveness. The difference between efficiency and effectiveness is the difference between knowledge and wisdom".

If nobody uses our products or if it takes 10 times longer than necessary to complete a workflow, quality is still poor even if there is not a single registered "defect".

Why the CEO loves it:

- Transparency
- Outcome focus (bottom line)
- Measurable results

Why the team members love it:

- Purpose
- Close collaboration
- Value-driven
- Informed decisions

I will deal separately with quantitative and qualitative feedback in the topics below. There is naturally an overlap but because there is a large tendency to mix them up and an even larger tendency to totally ignore the quantitative part, I found it valuable to separate them.

Example Challenges and metrics of feedback will be covered under the topics of:

- Continuous qualitative feedback
- Continuous quantitative feedback

Continuous qualitative feedback

With the extensive focus on close customer collaboration and end users, it is often surprising to see how little actual feedback some "Agile" teams get from customers and end users. This is especially true in larger organizations where asking questions to team member like "When did you last speak to a real end user?" or "When did you last watch a real end user using the system you are building?" are often given the response "never" or "more than six months ago". This is sad from the perspective of "inspect and adapt" and the ability to build products that users truly like. It is also sad from the perspective of productivity and joy of work. We are much more purpose-driven than we think and removing the link to the people who use and appreciate what we are building is also crucial from a productivity perspective (Pink, 2011). When that link is missing, we not only build something of less value, we do it at a slower pace and with the risk of higher employee churn.

A funny side effect of having teams and team members who are not delivering on this capability is that they often find the need to replace it with something else. I have seen this so many times that I am convinced it is a general tendency. Essentially, they replace value and feedback with other things like chasing story points or arguing about who is to blame for missing a Sprint goal. I have also seen the opposite, in which managers complain that teams do not seem to care enough and that they seem indifferent to missed deadlines or their Sprint Goal. Essentially, the real problem is that the organizational setup has removed one of the main drivers of productivity. As Daniel Pink states in his famous book on motivation and productivity:

"Humans are not just slower, smaller, better smelling horses and thus we need to move away from simplified carrot and stick notions of human productivity".

Potential Challenge and Target Condition metrics include:

Title	Description (why)	How to measure	Unit	Metric cost
Useful verbal feedback	The percentage of completed work items in which the team gets useful verbal feedback from stakeholders/end users is a strong leading indicator that you are talking to the right people about something relevant and that they are listening.	Count the number of work items in which you got useful verbal feedback and match it with the total number.	%/#	low
Touchpoint with real end users	It might seem overly simplistic to set a Challenge that includes something as narrow as a touchpoint with a real user. But in situations in which there is no interaction at all, any kind of touchpoint with a real end user could be a valid goal.	Count the number of touchpoints per day/week. Any kind of conversation counts.	#	low
Qualitative feedback	Sometimes we talk about customer representatives as if they were the actual users. However, getting feedback from actual users is very different from talking to a proxy. It might include observation as well as interviews	Count the percentage of work items in which feedback from real users was part of the process.	%	high

Process Metrics table 22: Continuous qualitative feedback

Example Challenges and Target Conditions:

- From 10% to 60% of work items with valuable verbal feedback from real end users
- From 0 to 1 verbal touchpoint per day with real end users
- From 0 to 2 observations of real users using the system per week

Continuous quantitative feedback

Building the capability to use quantitative metrics to get feedback is something that is often discussed but unfortunately not always implemented in real life. We have all heard about companies like Amazon, Netflix and Spotify, in which each team has a clear responsibility and can measure the engagement of each individual feature, taking proactive action if numbers are not as expected. In the book "Lean Enterprise", a quote from a former senior manager at Amazon states that Amazon removes between 60% and 90% of all new features and enhancements because they are not moving the metric they were supposed to move in the right direction. They do that because they realize that most of the cost of IT is not developing a feature but maintenance and operations during its lifetime.

For organizations without this type of feedback loop, we might ask ourselves how much of their money is spent maintaining features or entire products that should have been removed instead. We read about those companies and we agree that we should do something like that, but next time a new feature is deployed, we have magically forgotten it and rely solely on intuition and qualitative reviews with customers or end users.

Setting a Challenge to build a true capability to both collect, visualize and use quantitative data is not easy, as you will face the fact that not all metrics are good metrics. It might be harder than you think to accept that not all your great ideas are successes.

Challenge and Target Condition metrics include:

Title	📄 Description (why)	📐 How to measure	Unit	💰 Metric cost
Adoption time	The goal of Agile is not to make software available. The goal is that real users should use it to solve real problems. Short adoption time indicates a fast feedback loop. It is relevant mostly in B2B, non-SAAS scenarios.	Measure the average time from when a version is available until it is in active use.	time	high
Adoption rate	Focus on the number of versions or features instead of the time. In B2B, non-SAAS scenarios, it is not unusual for customers to resist new features or versions which increase complexity and reduces instant feedback.	Count the number of finished work items or versions that are not in use by all customers.	#	Low
Quantitative feedback	Having quantitative metrics in place to measure the engagement and success of released features enables proactive decision-making.	Count the percentage of released work items for which usage data is tracked and/or displayed/ used.	%	high/ low (if automated)
Hypothesis testing	If we do not know what we expect and how to measure it, how will we judge whether it was worth the time and effort?	Count the percentage of work items with established criteria for success on the actual effect/value/ engagement and the ability to measure it.	%	medium/ high
Cost of Delay (CoD) hypothesis	Similar to the metric above but specifically targeting the use of CoD.	Count the number or percentage of work items with assigned Cost of Delay in monetary value.	%/#	low

Process Metrics table 23: Continuous quantitative feedback

Example Challenges and Target Conditions:

- From 50 to 70 User Stories in real use at the customer (currently 40 User Stories in "done" that are not in use)
- From 40 days to 10 days average time from placing a User Story in "done" until it is in use by least 1 customer
- From 0% to 20% visualized quantitative engagement data on finished User Stories
- From 0 to 5 User Stories with visualized quantitative engagement data
- From 0% to 20% of User Stories with identified metrics for outcome success

Strategic alignment

The last part of our vision deals with strategic alignment. I saved it for last because in many ways it is different from the other potential Challenge topics we have covered so far. It also represents a potential danger, as focusing on alignment too soon can yield suboptimal results. In our vision, we described it like this:

- Highly aligned, loosely coupled. At all organizational levels, people can identify how their "service" is contributing to the overall success and how it is aligned with the strategic direction. Without a strategic direction, iterative development can become a buckshot approach.

- Funding is transparent, dynamic, outcome-focused and based on unbiased financial modeling.

But this comes with a strong word of warning. Research shows that companies need to focus on optimizing delivery before alignment (https://sloanreview.mit.edu/article/avoiding-the-alignment-trap-in-it/). Surprisingly, highly aligned but inefficient organizations perform worse than do those that are less aligned and less efficient. But not only are they doing worse, they are also unable to do better because being closely aligned with strategic business goals makes it very difficult for them to make room for improvement. Ideally, Toyota Kata should be a strong remedy for this but what is known as "the alignment trap" is very real. Thus, initially, you should be careful focusing on alignment.

Why the CEO loves it:

- To stay competitive, it is necessary to link Strategy to actual execution power.
- If teams are working on many small things but failing to deliver on organizational strategy, disruption is right around the corner.
- Boards and shareholders are not paying attention to the individual items but on the ability to deliver on the strategic direction.

Why team members love it:

- The "purpose driver" is one of the most important aspects of employee satisfaction and productivity.
- Reactive problem-solving on 100 fragmented User Stories feels more like being part of a sausage factory than doing frontier work to succeed as a company.
- With end-to-end teams, you quickly become an island in the organizational sea. Feeling like part of a bigger whole increases motivation and lowers employee churn.

We will deal with example Challenges and metrics on strategic alignment from three perspectives:

- Aligning teams toward shared organizational goals
- Aligning teams that need to collaborate to achieve a shared result (scaled Agile)
- Dynamic funding aligned with unbiased outcome goals

The first two perspectives share the notion of "loosely coupled, highly aligned" but in particular the scaled context does provide us with some specific constraints. The last point deals specifically with striving for mature strategic alignment based on unbiased risk and funding.

All of Chapter 20 and one of the cases in Chapter 25 focus on scaling, so I will deal only briefly with it from a Challenge and Target Condition perspective.

Alignment toward organizational goals

It is not that we do not want to delegate decision authority to the team level in an Agile setting. It is not that we are not big fans of end-to-end teams that can make decisions based on feedback and use it to inspect and adapt. But we can easily run into problems if 100 teams are going in separate directions without anyone paying attention to the broader picture. While "command and control" has proven unable to deal effectively with complexity and uncertainty, loosely coupled but unaligned organizations also face problems when they are unable to deliver on strategic visions. The most obvious signal of this taking place is when directors complain that the organization is delivering a lot of "stuff" but is unable to deliver on the strategy that they believe is needed for the organization to flourish and survive in the long term.

Essentially, that is what we mean by the term "highly aligned, loosely coupled". We have already dealt extensively with "loosely coupled" in the previous sections on end-to-end teams and technical architecture, so this section will focus on "highly aligned".

So, what is highly aligned and how can we set up Challenges and Target Conditions that will get us closer to it? Examples are found below but bear in mind that these metrics are often relevant as organizational Catch-balls and not necessarily driven by team-level improvements (though they can be).

Potential Challenges and Target Condition metrics include:

Title	📖 Description (why)	📠 How to measure	📏 Unit	💲 Metric cost
Link to customer journey	If work items are linked to the customer journey, you are likely to have considered which customer touchpoints you are optimizing and which fit with the overall strategy.	Count the percentage of work items with a link to customer journey touchpoints.	%	low
Team members aware of strategy	If all team members can clearly explain the current link to the strategy, it is a good indicator of alignment.	Count the number of team members who can clearly explain how the current focus links to the overall strategy.	#	low
Link to organizational strategy	If work items can be linked to the overall strategy of the organization, it is a good indicator that such a strategy exists, is communicated in a way that makes sense and is actively used to influence prioritization.	Count the percentage of work items that have a direct link to the overall organizational strategy.	%	low
Aligned budget	Money talks, and one of the simplest indications of aligned strategy is the percentage of the budget used to deliver on strategic goals.	Count the percentage of the budget supporting strategic goals.	%	medium

Process Metrics table 24: Alignment towards organizational goals

Example Challenges and Target Conditions:

- From 10% to 50% of User Stories linked to customer journey touchpoints
- From 20% to 70% of team members aware of current work items' link to organizational strategy
- From 30% to 65% of work items linked to organizational strategy
- From 2% to 10% of the budget supporting strategic goals

Cross-team collaboration on shared products

We did everything possible to avoid the complexity of scaling. We fought hard to not introduce the overhead of having to coordinate and align several teams on a shared goal, but we failed. Sometimes there is no way around scaling when products simply cannot be delivered by a single team or just a few teams relying on informal coordination and communication (see Chapter 20). In this section, we will look at the leading indicators of effectively aligning and coordinating work across several teams. Ultimately, we are seeking to handle the remaining dependencies between teams, departments and external parties as proactively as possible without unnecessary complexity interfaces and delays.

As we also discussed in Chapter 20, you might find inspiration in the catalog of specific practices made available by scaling frameworks, but from a Toyota Kata perspective, they are only means to an end. You should find that most of the Strategic alignment examples from the previous section are also highly relevant in a scaled context and that, basically, all other elements of the Vision will make it easier to handle work in a scaled context.

Specific Challenges and Target conditions include:

Title	Description (why)	How to measure	Unit	Metric cost
Cross-team dependencies	If cross-team dependencies are handled proactively, we should still be able to experience a smooth flow of value.	Count the percentage of work items that are blocked during execution due to cross-team collaboration issues.	%	low
Work items integrated in the shared product	Not being able to integrate features in the shared solution escalates merge problems to the cross-team level.	Count the number of work items that are not integrated in the cross-team.	#	low
Cycle time to shared integration	Delaying integration is a dangerous strategy in a scaled setup. Measuring cycle time to integrating work items in the shared solution can be a strong leading indicator.	Measure the cycle time from starting work until fully integrated into the shared solution.	#	Low/ medium
Component vs. feature teams	Also included in a previous section. Dividing teams according to product and not functional skills is essential in a scaled setup.	Count the number of component vs. features teams.	#/%	low

Process Metrics table 25: Cross-team collaboration on shared products

Example Challenges and Target Conditions:

- From 50 to 10 blockers per week across all teams
- From 250 to 125 User Stories not integrated into the shared solution (not jeopardizing throughput)
- From 48 to 20 days User Story cycle time
- From 8 to 4 component teams

Dynamic funding aligned with unbiased outcome goals

As with the other two topics concerning strategic alignment, funding is usually not a team-level issue. Writing this book, I went back and forth on whether this topic should be part of the Vision. It is, after all, a specific topic and aligned funding processes should ideally follow naturally from delivering on the other capabilities. There is, however, so much power in money that we can seriously limit our ability to deliver on the rest of our Process improvement goals if funding is still tied to old-fashioned waterfall models with yearly budgeting cycles. The worst part is that it happens almost secretly, and it is not until you dig deeper that you recognize how many flow problems are tied to a dysfunctional funding process.

Teams might, e.g., be struggling to adopt the capability of working with Minimum Viable Products because the funding process is not set up to handle dynamic requests. It is difficult to establish one-by-one flow, work iteratively and delegate decision authority because funding requires detailed upfront specifications. Recall the previously introduced analogy of designing a house from a systems thinking perspective: If we do not change the way funding is done, we risk optimizing the individual rooms without having an overall structure to support it. If there is no roof, even the most perfectly designed kitchen will not make much difference.

It is, therefore, necessary to align funding with our Agile mindset of small batches, outcome focus and fast feedback. Interestingly, according to Douglas Hubbard, the cost of development has very limited information value when managing the risk of a new project, whereas not delivering the expected business value is a much greater economic risk. Yet most organizations focus primarily on cost.

Note that we are not trying to standardize the actual funding process. That will be context-specific. From a Vision perspective, the essential part is that core capabilities in terms of how money is distributed to individual initiates are aligned with the strategic direction and the Agile capabilities presented in the previous sections. How you do this is up to you.

Specific Challenges and Target conditions include:

Title	Description (why)	How to measure	Unit	Metric cost
Funding decisions aligned with strategy	Does strategy influence actual decisions? The number of funding decisions that are directly linked to strategy is a strong leading indicator of alignment.	Count the percentage of funding decisions or the budget that can be traced directly to delivering on the current strategic goals.	%	low
Dynamic funding	How often funding decisions are made can be a good lead indicator of the dynamic nature.	Count the frequency of funding decisions (above a de minimis amount).	#	low
Funding tied to expected outcome	If funding is not tied to a specific expected outcome, organizations have a tendency to focus solely on cost, scope or time, not only for new initiatives but also the cost of help desks, etc.	Count the percentage of funding decisions with an expected and measurable outcome in terms of business value.	%	Low
Validation of outcome success	The former metric makes sense only if the outcome hypothesis is actually validated.	Count the percentage of funding decisions in which actual business outcome was validated against the hypothesis.	%	high

Process Metrics table 26: Dynamic funding aligned with unbiased outcome goals

Example Challenges and Target Conditions:

- From 1 to 6 funding evaluations per year
- From 5% to 20% funding decisions that include expected business outcome metrics
- From 0% to 10% funding decisions in which actual business outcome is validated

Final notes on Challenge and Target Condition inspiration catalog

I hope this rather long chapter gave you insight into the many ways of establishing process capabilities that are aligned with your overall vision, as well as the associated metrics. If you read this chapter front to back, I am impressed. If you dove into the specific topics of interest, I hope you found what you were looking for. In the next chapter, we will cover five cases of building those capabilities in real life and the iterative and experimental nature of the Toyota Kata framework.

Learning objectives and questions for real-life application of the Challenge inspiration catalog

Being that it is an inspiration catalog rather than an introduction to new elements of the Toyota Kata framework, I hope this chapter provided you with the following insights:

- Example Challenges and Target Conditions can provide needed inspiration when looking toward the desirable Future States that will make the biggest difference.
- Specific examples are among the most important aspects of moving from high-level theoretical concepts to the ability to use Toyota Kata in real life.
- Each vision topic includes multiple Challenge topics.

Before you continue, write your answers to the following questions to the best of your ability:

- List two or three Challenge topics that you think will have the biggest potential in optimizing your own process. Why did you choose them?

25. Cases

In this chapter, we will look at some specific cases of applying Toyota Kata in real-life situations. Real life is always a bit messier and things do not always go as planned, but I also hope to demonstrate to you that with a clear direction and a systematic focus on reaching valuable and measurable results, applying Toyota Kata does not have to be that complicated. To condense the points and maximize the outcome of reading the cases, I have taken the liberty of merging the results of more than one team/context in some of the example cases. Many have been working with the same topics, and to present each point separately would make the chapter twice as long without adding to the learning outcome.

Case 1: Blocked work

This case deals with a team-level Challenge. The team in question had recognized a significant gap between their current process and the ideal state of a smooth and level flow. Diving deeper into their Current Condition, they found more specifically that:

- 50% of all started User Stories were blocked for one workday or longer.
- The average blocked time was four-and-a-half days.
- That 60% of those blockers were waiting for clarifications from Subject Matter Experts (SMEs) at the customer's side.
- It took an average of 5.5 days for SMEs to respond.
- Due to work being blocked, they had a total of 18 User Stories in progress at the same time.

From this data, they framed the following Challenge:

Title: Improve throughput and cycle time through reduction of blocked work

Effect:

- From 23 to 32 average story points per week
- From 22 to 10 workdays average cycle time for User Stories

Process:

- **From** 50% to 90% of User Stories completed without blockers
- **From** 4.5 to 1.5 workdays average blocked time
- **From** 18 to 9 maximum number of User Stories in progress (WIP limit)

There are several interesting aspects included in this Challenge. First is that they chose not to include the response time from SMEs, leaving the amount of unblocked work and lowering WIP as the two major leading indicators. There would have been nothing wrong with setting a goal to lower the response time but it would have narrowed the solution space, which they were not prepared to do at that point in time. Second is that two leading indicators were overlapping – if you reduce the amount of blocked work, you likely have a lower WIP and if you explicitly set a lower WIP, that will force you to unblock work. That is perfectly fine – both are aligned with the overall Vision and both leave lots of creative solution space.

At the Improvement Kata Planning meeting, the team framed their first Target Condition like this:

Target Condition Focus: SME response time and quality

Target Condition	Current Condition
Outcome metrics • 27 story points per week	**Outcome metrics** • 23 story points per week
Qualitative observations • Flow • Getting something done • Engaged stakeholders	**Qualitative observations** • Frustration • Stress • Stop and go work • SME's do not understand the consequence
Process metrics • 80% first-time answers good enough to un-block work • 2 days average SME response time	**Process metrics** • 20% first-time answers good enough to un-block work • 5.5 days average SME response time

Figure 76: Target condition and Current Condition, SME response time and quality

As you can tell, the team decided to use the first four weeks focusing exclusively on lowering the response time from SMEs. It is not uncommon for the Target Condition metrics to be at a lower level of abstraction than those stated on the Challenge level. The important thing is that it points directly to the Challenge. In this case, we should expect both average blocked time as well as the percentage of blocked items to decrease. But it does limit the solution space, as with a Target Condition like the one above we are, e.g., not focusing on the quality of incoming work (upstream).

The results of the first Target Condition looked like this:

Outcome metrics:

- From 23 to 30 average story points per week

Process metrics:

- From 5.5 days to 3.5 hours average response time from customer 1

- From 5.5 days to 2.4 days average response time from customer 2

- From 20% to 65% of first answers good enough to unblock work

The most successful experiments included:

- Obstacle: No visibility into the status and ownership of questions/clarifications
  - Setting up a "Clarification" Kanban Board in Jira with columns "Identified", "Asked" and "Answered" tagging relevant SMEs
- Obstacle: Lack of SME ownership – no urgency or consequence if the response is delayed
  - Official agreement of 48-hour response time limit; if only one customer has answered on time, the other customer must accept that response.

The second Target Condition looked like this.

Target Condition Focus: Customer 2 response time and ready to flow

Target Condition	Current Condition
Outcome metrics • 12 workdays cycle time	**Outcome metrics** • 18 workdays cycle time
Qualitative observations • Flow • Engaged SMEs	**Qualitative observations** • Stop-and-go work • SMEs are still not close enough
Process metrics • 1 day average response time from customer 2 • 90% of work deemed "ready to flow"	**Process metrics** • 2.4 days average response time from customer 2 • 70% of work deemed "ready to flow"

Figure 77: Target condition and Current Condition, Customer 2 response time and ready to flow

During their first Target Condition, the team learned that they were able to seriously decrease the response time from the SMEs, but also that they had greater success with one customer compared to the other. They also learned that another reason for work getting blocked was that items were started though not "ready to flow". "Ready to flow" simply means that you expect to be able to finish them without major blockers or wait time. As you can tell, the team is, therefore, now turning their attention to the upstream part of the process while keeping a focus on customer 2's response time.

The results of the second Target Condition looked like this:

Outcome metrics:

- From 18 to 13.5 average cycle time (workdays)

Process metrics:

- From 2.4 days to 6.5 hours average response time from customer 2
- From 70% to 95% ready to flow

The most successful experiments included:

- Obstacle: Customer 2 is still not committed and does not understand the consequences
  - o Official escalation of problems if 48-hour response time is not met
  - o Categorizing questions as "Not urgent – 48 hours" and "Urgent – 24 hours"
- Obstacle: We discover too late that work items are not ready to flow
  - o Set a minimum WIP limit of 5 work items in "ready column"
  - o Brief daily evaluation of ready queue after Stand Up

After one more Target Condition, the team had delivered on pretty much their entire Challenge and more:

Effect:

- 37 average story points per week (goal was 32)
- 10.5 workdays average cycle time for User Stories (goal was 10)

Process:

- 95% of User Stories completed without blockers (goal was 90%)
- 5.5 hours average blocked time (goal was 1.5)
- 9 maximum number of User Stories in progress (goal was 9)

The results were great and no doubt this team was much better off after finishing this Challenge than they were before, when they suffered from demotivation stress and slow flow. They got one step closer, but there were also other paths that they discussed but chose to disregard. Here is a list of what they chose not to do:

- Focusing on internalizing the knowledge of the SMEs upon which they were relying for clarifications in the team so they could avoid the dependency altogether
- Getting decision authority to make decisions on their own if SMEs did not reply

Both were considered but judged to be either not a good idea or in the red zone.

Case 2: Automation

Sometimes things are so obvious that you wonder why they took so long. In Agile, we are not big fans of heavy manual work that could be done much faster and more efficiently by computers. That is why full automation is included in our Vision. It is not that the team in question did not realize this. Every day, they were spending over 2.5 hours manually gathering information from various systems, putting it together in an Excel sheet and distributing it to customers to be compliant with risk regulations. They had made several attempts to improve the process through retrospective SMART goals, but their actions had either been unsuccessful or not been carried out at all due to the ever-present Daily Whirlwind. Besides draining their capacity to do other work, the situation was also seriously affecting their enjoyment of work, as they hated the entire procedure. When asked them about their ideal Future State, they were very quick to reply, "One click of a button – fully automated!" From looking at their Current Condition, they quickly gathered the following simple data:

- 150 minutes gathering data, attaching business numbers and sending it to customers

From this data, they framed the following Challenge:

Title: Automate!

Effect:

- From 8 to 0 data errors due to manual mistakes

Process:

- **From** 150 minutes to 0 minutes of effort

This Challenge includes some interesting aspects. First, they chose to not state an expected Outcome of higher throughput. The reason was that in a 7 people team freeing up 2.5 hours every day is "only" a 5% improvement and throughput variability is much higher than that.

At the Improvement Kata Planning meeting, the team framed their first Target Condition like this:

Target Condition Focus: Automating data collection

Target Condition	Current Condition
Outcome metrics • 4 data errors per week	**Outcome metrics** • 8 data errors per week
Qualitative observations • Freedom • Motivated to go to work • Working on things that matter	**Qualitative observations** • Frustration • Hating it • Not value-adding
Process metrics • 0 minutes spent daily gathering data	**Process metrics** • 40 minutes spent daily collecting data

Figure 78: Target Condition and Current Condition, Automating data collection

As you can tell, the team decided to use the first four weeks to focus exclusively on automating the first part of the manual process. Being only 40 minutes out of the 150 minutes, that might seem less than ideal, but without automating this, it would be impossible to automate the next step of attaching business numbers.

The results of the first Target Condition looked like this:

Outcome metrics:

- From 8 to 8 data -errors per week

Process metrics:

- From 40 minutes to 0 minutes used on data collection

The most successful experiments included:

- Obstacle: Only one person on the team can automate
  - Experiment: Protecting that one person from all other work he did not need to do to free up time for automation
- Obstacle: Collecting data automatically through interface in Excel
  - Experiment: After several failed attempts, a Google search revealed a solution that worked.

Because they managed to finish only the final parts of the automation just before the end of the Improvement Kata, the desired outcome of a few data errors could not be validated.

The second Target Condition looked like this.

Target Condition Focus: Automating business numbers

Target Condition	Current Condition
Outcome metrics • 0 data errors per week	**Outcome metrics** • 8 data errors per week
Qualitative observations • New work • Engaging • Working on things that matter	**Qualitative observations** • Repetitive • Booooring • Not value-adding
Process metrics • 0 minutes spent daily attaching business numbers	**Process metrics** • 110 minutes spent daily attaching business numbers

Figure 79: Target Condition and Current Condition, Automating business numbers

The results of the second Target Condition looked like this:

Outcome metrics:

- From 8 to 2 data-errors per week

Process metrics:

- From 110 minutes to 10 minutes used on attaching business numbers

The most successful experiments included:

- Obstacle: Numbers in inconsistent format from different sources
    - Experiment: Developing a middle layer to act as a shared interface
- Obstacle: Not all numbers available
    - Experiment: Automatically generating a list of unassigned numbers to be handled manually

As you can tell from the numbers, they did not deliver on their Target Condition but they got close. After two Improvement Kata, the 150-minute job is down to an average of 10 minutes. It took another Improvement Kata to finally bring it down to a one-click, fully automated procedure. First and foremost, the joy of work was much improved. When they are presented with this case, many people often remark, "But why didn't they do this months ago? They should have easily been able to do this

315

as part of their retrospectives." or "Shouldn't it just have been a User Story on their Product Backlog?"

We have heard the same arguments in many other cases, but perhaps the interesting fact is that before, they tried and failed, while now they succeeded; the result made a real difference. If we can successfully deliver on the capabilities we want with Toyota Kata, if we find the process of doing so to be engaging, if it motivates us to set even more ambitious goals … well, it is probably less interesting to ask why we were not successful before. I would suggest that some key factors are at play in this case:

- The process of automating the procedure was highly iterative with lots of failed experiments. Had those experiments been planned as part of a two-week retrospective focus, it would have taken many iterations to reach the result. Probably, attention would have drifted to another subject before success was achieved.

- Longer term Process improvement initiatives are often not prioritized when matched against end-user features on a Backlog. They are blown away by the Daily Whirlwind or forced to be so narrow and specific that they are not able to deal with the iterative nature of improvement.

Case 3: "Catch-ball" – Engaging the management hierarchy to restart continuous improvement

This case is not my own experience but was provided by experienced Lean/Agile consultant Adam Light from SocioTech Advisors. He describes the use of Toyota Kata in an organization in which Agile improvement had plateaued. He illustrates the adoption of a "Catch-ball" pattern with ongoing coaching relationships between layers in the management hierarchy. The example also shows how an outside coach can partner with a senior leader to introduce the Improvement Kata and Coaching Kata to an organization.

Getting started

In the IT organization of a mid-sized industrial company, the Director of Applications was responsible for approximately 15 Agile teams, each developing or supporting specific back- or front-office systems. The cross-functional Agile teams included testers, and each team had a definition of "done" that covered testing. But before releasing anything to production, a separate integration test team ran additional tests across the applications delivered by the various independent teams.

Members of the individual Agile teams reported to application managers, each of whom was responsible for applications to serve a specific business unit or department. The QA manager reported to the director, as did the manager of the Scrum Masters, who was also the owner of the Agile Software Development Lifecycle (SDLC) and responsible for Process improvement.

Five years after adopting Agile, many of the Product Owners and internal customers who were among its early champions were becoming dissatisfied. Following a honeymoon period, critics once again grumbled that IT was unproductive and that releases didn't arrive predictably. The Scrum Masters and their manager acknowledged among themselves that they had stopped changing and achieved a new status quo. They felt stuck!

Worst for the manager of the Scrum Masters were the whispers among the Scrum Masters and many team members who said that, by protecting their individual turf, he and his peer managers were preventing the application group from serving customers better. The whispers hurt because they rang true!

The Director of Applications had heard the whispers too, and he committed himself and his management team to practicing the Improvement Kata and Coaching Kata. An external Toyota Kata coach was paired with the director as a "second coach," meaning that her job was to help the director learn to coach the managers who reported to him.

Initially, the director and second coach were paired together to begin coaching two members of the Applications management team. The QA manager worked with the integration test team and the manager of Scrum Masters worked with one of the development teams. Both teams identified initial Target Conditions directed toward the Challenge of shortening the average cycle time to release a feature from eight to five weeks.

Development Team – Initial Target Conditions

When the manager/coach sat down with the development team to examine the Current Condition and set the first Target Condition, the team struggled at first. Because the contents of each release varied, they were not confident they could reach a goal of reducing the average release delay. Eventually, somebody suggested using the "5 Whys." This led to the breakthrough that the Obstacles to reaching the Target Condition would be different depending on which components of the application the team was trying to release.

Challenged by their Coaches to focus on a single obstacle for one release type, the team zeroed in on the observation that releases often waited for several days until a system administrator for the Integrated Voice Response (IVR) system could be scheduled to conduct an after-hours release. Upon this realization, the development team decided to set a Target Condition focus on the IVR release process.

Target Condition	Current Condition
Outcome metrics • 7 weeks cycle time	**Outcome metrics** • 8 weeks cycle time
Qualitative observations • Focusing on specific components may be a way to subset the problem!	**Qualitative observations** • Different components are released in different releases depending on the features they contain.
Process metrics • 6 days average IVR release cycle time • 0 manual steps in IVR releases	**Process metrics** • 8 days average IVR release cycle time • 10 manual steps in IVR releases

Figure 80: Target Condition and Current Condition, IVR release process

With almost-daily coaching, the manager and the development team proceeded to automate key steps of IVR releases. Each time they completed a step, they recorded the effort as one row on their Experiment Record. In the first two steps, the team discovered the limits of available knowledge. They found that they could not understand the release process without consulting an expert administrator. Then they discovered that the development environment wasn't configured identically to the production environment.

At the end of their first Target Condition, the team had a proof of concept that they predicted would reduce delays for IVR releases by an average of over three days. It took the team a second target condition to validate the improvement by observing and measuring which releases were shortened and by how much, as well as how the time savings affected the average release time.

The director and second coach then created a "Success Card" next to the Improvement Board to celebrate the learning that had occurred. They made a special point of not emphasizing the technical aspects of the automation. Rather, they focused on the realization that the problem had been broken down and that an incremental improvement had been made and measured in a relatively short time.

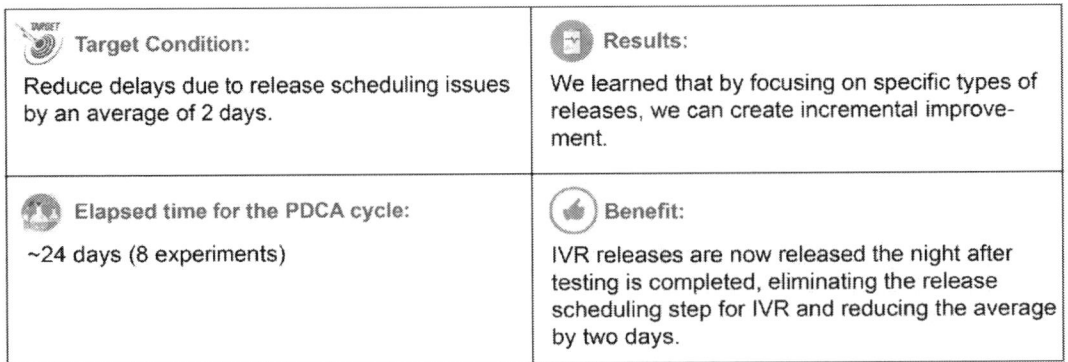

 Target Condition: Reduce delays due to release scheduling issues by an average of 2 days.	Results: We learned that by focusing on specific types of releases, we can create incremental improvement.
Elapsed time for the PDCA cycle: ~24 days (8 experiments)	Benefit: IVR releases are now released the night after testing is completed, eliminating the release scheduling step for IVR and reducing the average by two days.

Figure 81: Success Card, release scheduling

Integration Test – Initial Target Conditions

Meanwhile, the integration test team chose to address a troublesome impediment: Their test environments were frequently unavailable, which caused them to lose work time. The team's work required running a variety of complex end-to-end tests across multiple systems and applications in the enterprise. Their work could, therefore, be blocked whenever a test environment for one of those many systems wasn't up and running.

Examining data from recent incidents, they found a variety of examples. In one case, the test team mistakenly filed a series of defects when a network upgrade caused the intermittent availability of several servers. In another case, an unscheduled upgrade to their defect-tracking system prevented them from using it for six daytime hours. There were so many apparent causes of downtime, the team couldn't decide where to start!

At this point, the director – who was simultaneously coaching the application development team as described above – explained how that team had succeeded by focusing on an obstacle for just one type of release rather than trying to address all release obstacles at once. Taking inspiration from this example and reminded of their overall Challenge to shorten average release time, the integration test team and their Process Owner decided to focus on eliminating downtime during application installs to the test systems.

Because the complicated installs required the participation of multiple individuals from more than one team, they typically had to be scheduled ahead of time. This meant that downtime during installs was a big cause of lost time. If the problem couldn't be resolved and the participants couldn't all wait around, they'd have to re-schedule the install for the next day or later. Also, there was a consensus that changing the culture and treating the test environments more like production environments in terms of service level and downtime would improve availability overall. The integration test team set their first Target Condition as: "System is always available for planned installs."

Target Condition	Current Condition
Outcome metrics • 7 weeks cycle time	**Outcome metrics** • 8 weeks cycle time
Qualitative observations • Everyone who might make changes will need to avoid install times.	**Qualitative observations** • Downtime and lack of availability are caused mostly by uncoordinated changes to various parts of the test system.
Process metrics • System is available 100% of the time we schedule an install to the test environment.	**Process metrics** • System is available 73% of the time (8 out of 11) we schedule an install to the test environment.

Figure 82: Target Condition and Current Condition, System is always available for planned installs

The test team's first experiments to reach their target condition ended in failure. They attempted to create and distribute a new planning and notification procedure to all IT groups. After spending several days crafting the procedure, and over a week trying to implement it, the effort died when members of several IT groups identified good reasons why the procedure was unworkable.

Through this failure, the team learned three lessons. The first lesson was that they didn't have all the knowledge necessary to solve the problem and that they had to bring in participants from the groups that were making changes to the test environments. The second lesson was that aiming for 100% availability in the first Target Condition was setting the bar too high. While many causes of downtime could be eliminated by scheduling around release windows, not all causes would be addressed, so availability would not reach 100%. They had to qualify the Target Condition further. The third lesson was that they had to make experiments shorter to get feedback earlier and reduce the risk of overall failure. With these lessons learned, the integration test team was able to reset and achieve a new Target Condition.

Process Mapping

Once the director had worked with each of the managers to practice the Coaching Kata through one Target Condition cycle, the outside coach provided training that included an introduction to batches and queues and a module on Value Stream Mapping. As part of the class, each manager and their team produced Current Condition process maps for their own work. Then the two groups worked to combine their process maps into an end-to-end visualization.

Facing the combined block diagram, the second coach suggested that the class walk a recent User Story through the combined process from end to end. This exercise produced an important insight. When viewed at a high level, the two groups were following one continuous process, but at a slightly more detailed level, they were not tracking the flow of value throughout.

Once the development team completed a User Story in their current Sprint, they moved the story into a "ready for integration testing" stage in the work tracking system. This satisfied their internal definition of "done". The development team saw their value as delivering User Stories, but they couldn't deliver them all the way to the user, so they had defined "done" as delivery to the integration test team.

Then, when the integration test team began their Sprint, they built a release package by consolidating work from multiple teams into a larger batch. The integration test team saw their value as preventing problems by regression testing the interactions between enterprise applications. They did not focus on new functionality and did not track individual features created by the development teams. The two teams agreed to add a new stage to their combined process map that represented a previously invisible queue between them.

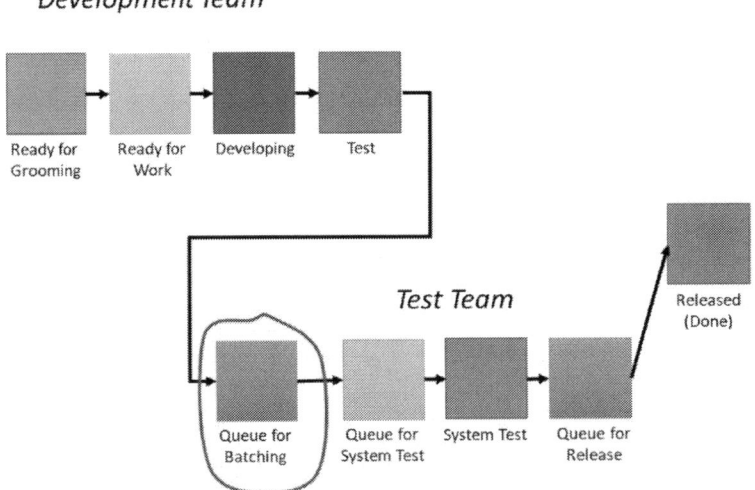

Figure 83: Cross team Value Stream Map

An organization-wide challenge

Seeing the combined process map, the director could immediately envision a Future State Challenge toward which he wanted to lead the entire organization. He envisioned seeing every team across the organization focused on delivery of value all the way to the end users. He wanted to measure department productivity according to the cycle time of User Stories, and he wanted everyone to feel responsible for preventing regression defects.

In short, the director wanted his managers and all the teams to measure success according to the bigger picture shown by the combined process map. Achieving this challenge would require expanding coaching from the advance group of two teams to include the other Agile teams that delivered work through the integration test process.

The managers who had been the first Kata Coaches continued working with their teams. The director continued to coach these managers toward specific Target Conditions, but now their coaching discussions focused on reaching the overall department Challenge. As the managers worked with each team separately, they continued to work on obstacles that lay within the team's span of control. But their Target Conditions were now explicitly aligned with the overall Challenge. They had moved from local problem-solving to end-to-end optimization toward a desirable Future State.

Scaling up coaching to increase its reach

The director and the second coach could now initiate Coaching Kata relationships with the managers of other development teams that delivered applications into the shared integration test process. Using what he had learned with the first two teams, the director was able to begin coaching new manager/coaches and teams, with the second coach acting as an advisor. As with well-run Agile transitions, the organization gradually became less dependent on the external coach.

Case 4: Scaled Agile context

This is a different case compared to many other examples of applying Toyota Kata, as it neither represents a traditional Catch-ball nor is limited to the team level. It involves the context of successful optimization of a program with about as many constraints to flow as you can imagine. If you are interested in the details of the case beyond Toyota Kata, they can be found on my blog at AgileUpgrade.com, titled "Taking a Look Under the Hood – Successful Implementation of Lean and Agile Principles in a Large Program". As I want to use this case to provide an example of the effect of going through multiple Challenges on a program level (and not use 15 pages to describe it), I will not dive into the details of the individual Target Conditions in this case but instead will provide examples of goals, results and experiments at the Challenge level.

I was hired as a Lean/Agile consultant to help get the program off to a good start. When, as a consultant, I am starting in a new context or organization I am always very aware that I am on what Henrik Kniberg refers to as "Mount Stupid" (also known as the Dunning-Kruger effect) in his 2015 conference presentation (Knibert & Roost, 2015) .

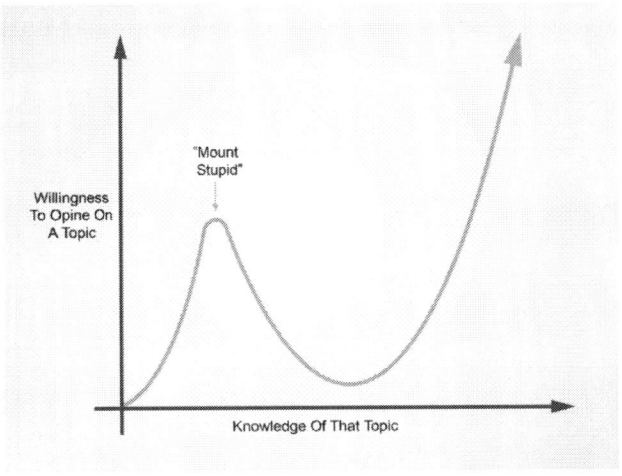

Figure 84: Mount stupid (also known as the Dunning-Kruger effect), adapted from http://www.smbc-comics.com/?id=2475

You think you have seen it all before and you already have the remedy to fix all the problems. The only problem is that you don't! So, avoiding jumping to conclusions during the initial learning phase is crucial. No two contexts are the same, and even if they look the same, people are different. What might be crucial in one context matters little in another, and despite our deep desire for a silver bullet, no such thing exists in the world of Complex Adaptive Systems. So, though I really wanted to jump right in and start "fixing stuff", I forced myself to spend the first two weeks speaking to program managers, Scrum Masters, Products owners and program support to get a picture of the Current Condition. It looked something like this:

- 4 months since the program was initiated
- High dependency on an external off-the-shelf platform configured by a third-party vendor
- "Front runner" team had focused on writing specifications
- Recently scaled to 7 teams working on 7 separate Backlogs
- Shared goal but no actual alignment between teams (not aligned, tightly coupled)
- No delivered features
- 2 teams delivering end-user features, 5 component/functional teams (tools, infrastructure, business analysis, test, integration)
- Shared deadline but not yet supported by estimates or analysis
- No identified Value Stream
- Scrum mechanics implemented in all teams running 2 week Sprints
- Strong focus on MVP but still a major undertaking to get the first release deployed
- Tactical decision authority not delegated to the team level

The first Challenge

Looking at the Vision, there were serious gaps; "not aligned, tightly coupled" with no visualization of the program Value Stream spells problems in any scaled context in which effective alignment and coordination are arguably some of the most important capabilities. This was clearly demonstrated by the fact that the tool team was building support tools that none of the other teams were planning to use. I have no doubt that some participants expected me to jump right in and help the individual teams with their retrospectives, Sprint planning meetings and Backlog refinements. However, having gotten a better understanding of the Current Condition, I found that it made little sense to put a lot of effort into optimizing Scrum Sprints in the individual teams, as a higher throughput might simply increase the current alignment problems.

Instead, we set up the following Challenge:

Title: Alignment, Visualization and Outside-in focus

Process metrics:

- From 0 to 7 teams aligned toward a common goal
- From 0% to 100% of epic-level work items visualized and aligned toward the common goal at the portfolio level
- From 0 to 7 teams understanding their role in the Value Stream.

324

- From 2 to 4 "feature teams"

- From 10% to 80% of User Stories representing value to other teams and end users

Why not set a Challenge to eliminate more of the component teams and move toward end-to-end teams across the entire structure? We did consider this but judged it to be in the "red zone", as it would break the change capacity of the program. Therefore, we opted for the more evolutionary approach of getting closer to the goal. You might also wonder why no outcome metrics were included. The simple answer was that we failed to find a current condition on either cycle time, throughput or quality because nothing of real end-to-end value had yet to be produced.

The results of the first Challenge looked like this:

Process metrics:

- From 0 to 7 teams aligned toward a common goal

- From 0% to 100% of epic-level work items visualized and aligned toward a common goal at the portfolio level

- From 0 to 7 teams understanding their role in the Value Stream

- From 2 to 4 "feature teams"

- From 10% to 65% of User Stories representing value to other teams and end users

We delivered on almost all aspects of the Challenge and results were dramatic in terms of teams starting to work together. Instead of status meetings, people were now discussing coordination and alignment issues and working out how to solve them. A surprising side effect was the amount of local decision ownership that teams started to take because they now understood their role in the Value Stream and knew the end goal. As with anything, in a program context, things are never as easy as you believe but ultimately several successful experiments provided us with the results we wanted:

- Obstacle: Teams do not understand the flow of value (and what value is)
  - Experiment: Illustration of Business analysis, service (component) vs. features teams

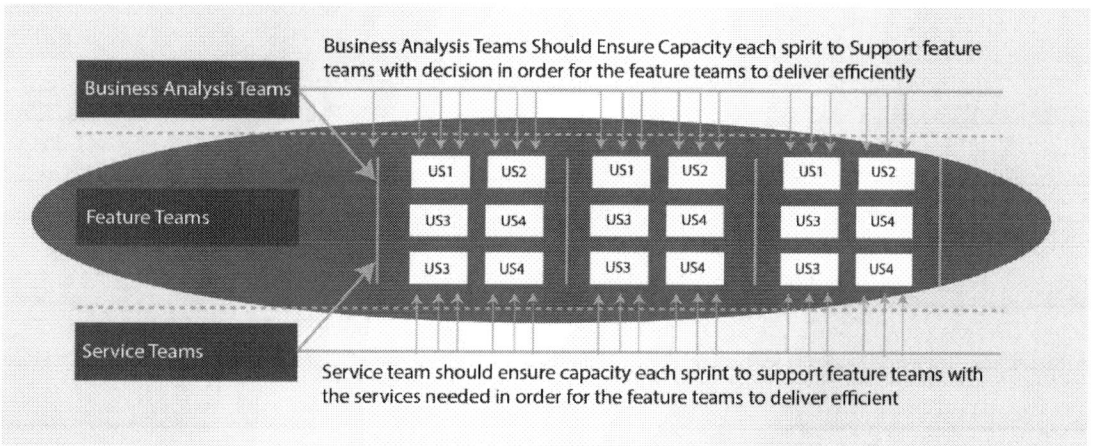

Figure 85: Illustration of cross team collaboration

- Obstacle: Mapping epics and dependencies
  - o Experiment: Story map workshop with representatives from all teams

Figure 86: Story Map

- Obstacle: No shared place to visualize flow and dependencies
  - o Experiment: Using a giant wall next to the team rooms

Figure 87: Portfolio board

- Obstacle: Blockers and dependencies surface too late
  - o Experiment: Representatives from each team meeting twice a week in front of the portfolio board to discuss flow problems (NOT STATUS!)

- Obstacle: How do we split the "product" to fit 4 "independent" feature teams?
    - Experiment: Workshop with experts on the third-party product and internal architecture team to learn from previous experiences and the internal and external technical architecture
- Obstacle: Teams are not aware of their service and who their customers are; "User Stories" are just internal activity lists and not customer-focused
    - Experiment: Workshop with Product Owners and key SMEs from all teams to understand "outside-in" focus and identify customers (internal and external depending on team)
    - Experiment: Meeting with all Product Owners to go through their Backlog one week before Sprint Planning meeting

The second Challenge – Agile forecasting

With value starting to flow and aligned teams, we were able to turn our attention to other desirable capabilities. There were still important gaps between our Vision and Current Condition, and with a shared deadline to get the MVP released, it was time to consider the capability of transparent and data-driven forecasting and minimizing the consequences of being wrong.

We framed the second Challenge like this:

- From 0 to 4 feature teams using probabilistic forecasting and visualizing results weekly
- From 0 to 4 teams having a plan to minimize the consequence of failure

With close collaboration and coordination between the teams, we were not nervous in terms of their ability to surface internal program bottlenecks and coordinate the work on the specific epics. Therefore, we chose to focus only on the forecasts of the four feature teams, as their ability to deliver would cause any problems in meeting the shared deadline to surface (i.e., any issues with product or service teams would be reflected in the feature teams' ability to deliver).

The result of the second Challenge looked like this:

Process metrics:

- From 0 to 4 feature teams using probabilistic forecasting and visualizing results weekly
- From 0 to 3 teams having a plan to minimize the consequence of failure

This almost but not quite delivered on the Challenge. One team wasn't able to come up with a plan to minimize the consequences of failure, as they found themselves struggling with unfortunate issues like team churn. As with the first Challenge, we experienced successful and unsuccessful experiments. The ones that worked included:

- Obstacle: Jira cannot do useful probabilistic forecasting
  - Experiment: Building on an Excel spreadsheet using a bootstrap algorithm found online to visualize the 10th, 50th and 90th percentiles

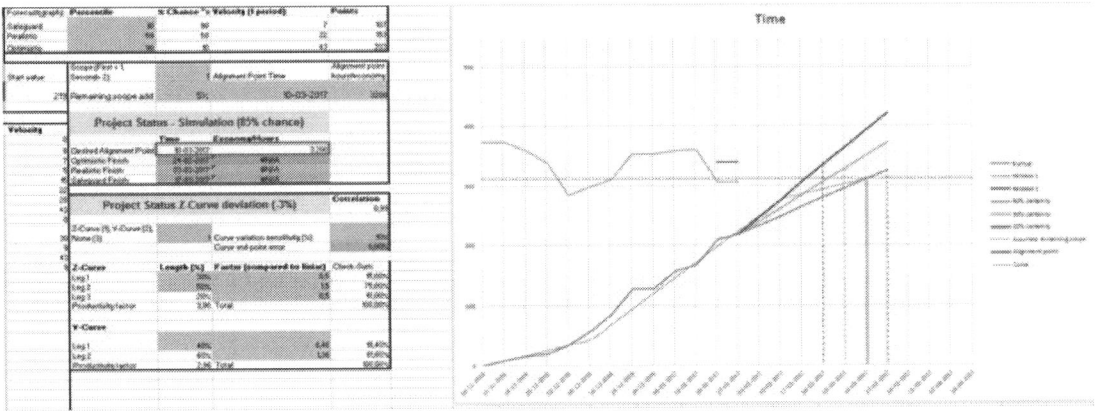

Figure 89: Probabilistic Forecasting in Excel

- Obstacle: Backlogs are not estimated
  - Experiment: Rough t-shirt size estimation in story points using techniques from "how to measure anything" to estimate the cost of 1 point
- Obstacle: Teams cannot find out how to use the spreadsheet and they keep messing up the formulas
  - Experiment: Have each team send the weekly throughput numbers and centralize the reporting work
- Obstacle: How do we help teams minimize the consequences of failure?
  - Experiment: Workshop with teams to find creative solutions (3 out of 4 teams reprioritized their Backlogs accordingly to optimize for lower total risk)
- Obstacle: Distribution of outcomes is unrealistically wide for two teams
  - Experiment: Adjust the update cadence to throughput cadence of teams

We released the first MVP successfully despite the entire world around us expecting us to fail, and we did it almost without the need for panic and overtime. We continued building on top of our current capabilities in the coming months but to avoid another 10 pages of description of this case, I will simply provide an overview of what happened next:

Unfortunately, the second release included new areas of the third-party product we were integrating, which meant we were forced to reorganize teams and scale the organization to fit the product structure. Therefore, the theme of the third Challenge became "Empowered, stable, end-to-end teams" for the next release. Unfortunately, we succeeded with only 80%. For the fourth and final Challenge (before I left the program), we focused on building the process capabilities of "deferring details and strategic alignment" because we found teams planning too far ahead at a too-detailed level as well as a missing alignment of the strategic focus. (Actually, a consequence of having a much better end-to-end team setup was that teams were now able to work so independently that the shared result lost focus.) Successful experiments in this regard involved a PI planning type event as well as a fixed cadence of alignment meetings every four weeks.

After I left, the program kept experimenting and adopted elements of Nexus to get an even better flow. It was still far from perfect, and if you read the case study (Boeg, 2015) on my blog www.agileupgrade.com/blog I am sure you will find that there were more constraints in this program than what most people experience in their entire careers. But despite this, we managed to consistently move closer to the Vision and build capabilities that, despite problems, got the program to a place where the second release was also successfully launched, much to the delight (and surprise) of sponsors and customers.

Case 5: Visualization

Nothing demonstrates as clearly as this case that a clear and simple Challenge aligned with the overall Vision can produce great results through hard work. The team in question felt so overloaded with work that the initial thought of taking time out of their capacity to start using Toyota Kata made the team members protest loudly. Their Scrum Master insisted, however, and reluctantly the rest of the team agreed to show up for the initial workshops and training sessions.

Trying to draw a VSM of their process in a workshop revealed a serious problem – nobody knew what was going on. Essentially, they would try to plan a Sprint Backlog but personal requests, expedites from the manager, support system tickets and changes of priorities would ensure that they often worked on something completely different. When they were asked, "Where do you go to look for the highest priority to work on?", their answer included 7 different places. The follow-up question "How do you decide what to start working on, then?", produced answers that included "gut feeling", "the one who asked the nicest or yelled the loudest", "personal preference" and "I have no idea". The question "So, what are you working on now?" revealed that nobody really knew, that work could be stopped, put on hold or simply forgotten in multiple ticket systems, on personal Post-its or on the Scrum or Kanban Board. (Yes, they had both.)

It was clear that mapping the Current Condition in more detail would only reveal that it was a process out of control, with little overview and consistency and a high potential for stressed-out team members. When going through the Vision, we asked ourselves the simple question "If within the next two to three months you could have any capabilities you want, what would they be?" The answer was clear and immediate: "We want one input channel where work items are prioritized, one place where ongoing work is visual and the ability to finish work before we start new work items".

From this, they framed the very simple but effective Challenge:

Title: Visualization and pull

Outcome metrics:

- From 6 to 12 story points per week

Process metrics:

- From 7 places to 1 place to see the priority of planned work

- From 5 places to 1 place to see in-progress work

- From 0 to ? work-in-progress limits on all workflow steps

The cool thing about this was that as soon as we started discussing it, the atmosphere in the room changed. The entire team went from disengaged and wanting to get back to the ever-growing pile of work to active participation, engagement and commitment. They were able to visualize how much better it would be to come to work and how much more they could do if they could deliver on this Challenge. Only one team member seemed skeptical and voiced the opinion, "But haven't we talked about this many times before? Why do you think it will be different this time?" Fortunately, the rest of the team was now so committed to the idea that their reply was swift: "Because this time we are not going to be just talking. We are going to focus on it every single day until we get there!"

At the Improvement Kata Planning meeting, the team framed their first Target Condition like this:

Target Condition Focus: One prioritized list, using the right in-out channel

Target Condition	Current Condition
Outcome metrics • 8 story points per week	**Outcome metrics** • 6 story points per week
Qualitative observations • Overview • Clear and aligned priorities • Working on the most important thing	**Qualitative observations** • Total chaos • Task switching • Stress, stress, stress – everything is important
Process metrics • 1 place to see the priority of planned work • 90% of requests through the right input channel	**Process metrics** • 7 places to see the priority of planned work • 30% of requests through the right input channel

Figure 90: Target Condition and Current Condition, One prioritized list, using the right in-out channel

As you can see, the team decided to use the first four weeks to focus exclusively on building the capability to visualize priorities in a single place and educate customers to communicate with the team through the right channels. You might be excused for thinking, 'That is simple', but I am sure you recognize the difficulty of doing this continuously in a world where tools are not integrated, customers do not know which input channel to use and people have been used to getting personal favors for years.

The results of the first Target Condition looked like this:

Outcome metrics:

- From 6 to 10 story points per week

Process metrics:

- From 7 places to 1 place to see the priority of planned work

- From 30% to 70% of requests through the right input channel

Though quite a few experiments failed, the most successful included:

- Obstacle: In the team, we do not agree on "the right input channel"
    - Experiment: 1 sheet of paper posted in the team room and on the door explaining what to use for different requests
- Obstacle: Support ticket tool does not integrate with process tool
    - Experiment: Script to automatically create User Stories when tickets are opened

- Obstacle: Personal favors
  - Experiment: Explaining that it causes stress and poor performance and showing them how to use the right input channel
- Obstacle: Old habits
  - Experiment: Honestly (and blame-free) documenting each time we do not follow the policy and start working on, e.g., an issue from a personal mail. Reviewing yesterday's count at standup and visualizing the result on the team wall

After the first four weeks, throughput had increased by almost 70% and team members were ecstatic. I participated in their next Improvement Kata Planning meeting, where they declared that even if they stopped there, the work so far with Toyota Kata had put them on the positive side of the J-curve. Great!

For their next Improvement Kata, they decided to focus on visualizing in-progress work in a single place and assign WIP limits to the entire workflow

The second Target Condition looked like this.

Target Condition Focus: Visualizing in-progress work

Target Condition	Current Condition
Outcome metrics • 12 story points per week	**Outcome metrics** • 10 story points per week
Qualitative observations • Overview • Clear and aligned priorities • Working on the most important thing	**Qualitative observations** • Overview lacking • Task switching • Stress, stress, stress – everything is important
Process metrics • 1 place to see in-progress work • 7 workflow steps with WIP limits	**Process metrics** • 5 places to see in-progress work • 0 workflow steps with WIP limits

Figure 91: Target Condition And Current Condition, Visualizing In-Progress Work

The result of the second Improvement Kata looked like this:

Outcome metrics:

- From 10 to 13.5 story points per week

Process metrics:

- From 5 places to 1 place to see in-progress work

- From 0 to 7 workflow steps with WIP limits

As with the first Target Condition, they had both successful and unsuccessful experiments. The ones that worked included:

- Obstacle: We do not know our workflow steps (the number in the Target Condition wasn't there initially)
  - Experiment: Workshop with Agile Coach identifying the main "knowledge discovery activities"
- Obstacle: What is the right WIP limit to start with?
  - Experiment: Starting with 5 and adjusting the first week
- Obstacle: WIP limits are broken
  - Experiment: Each day at Stand Up, evaluate whether broken WIP limits are too aggressive or are we "pushing"?
- Obstacle: Where should we visualize work?
  - Experiment: Testing Scrum Board and Kanban Board in Jira in parallel for five days (Kanban Board won)
- Obstacle: We forget to close support tickets in the support tool when they are moved to "done"
  - Experiment: Extend script to close ticket automatically in the support ticket system
- Obstacle: Not all work is visual, as we are still doing "secret favors"
  - Experiment: The one who has done the most will bring cake on Friday (based on honesty)
  - Experiment: Update the number of "secret favors" daily and visualize the trend (based on honesty)
- Obstacle: We like the quick fix of "expediting" a support ticket so we break the WIP limits even when things are not urgent
  - No successful experiments so far....

Having gained experience working with and not breaking WIP limits, they focused their third Improvement Kata on lowering the WIP limits across the Value Stream to surface bottlenecks and avoid push. At that point, they had more than doubled their throughput and were much happier going to work. We included this case in our training material to show that great Challenges do not have to be complicated to formulate. We thought that the topic of the Challenge and the Current Condition were unique to this team. After all, most teams in the organization had been working with Scrum and

334

Agile for one or two years and should have been familiar with the concepts of focus and visualization. However, we were very surprised to find that many teams were experiencing the same issues. The team from the case was overwhelmed with requests to visit and for other teams to have a look at what they were doing. Fortunately, they welcomed the chance to "show off".

Learning objectives and questions for real-life application of Toyota Kata cases

From this case chapter, I hope you got the following insights:

- Toyota Kata Challenges are not limited to a single category. They can span organizations and programs or just a single team or manager.
- Challenges do not have to involve advanced Lean flow metrics to be effective.
- There are a lot of other effective lead metrics besides process cycle time.

Before you continue, write your answers to the following question to the best of your ability:

- What are the most important points you learned from reading the five case studies?

26. Conclusion and final notes

I hope this book provided you with insights into applying Toyota Kata successfully in the context of Agile IT organizations. There is a huge untapped improvement potential, but dedication and discipline are required to unleash it and we must recognize the importance of developing effective improvement drivers at both the team and management levels. Team-level optimization is great if you have managed to create end-to-end teams that cover all the Value Streams, but in scaled contexts or functional departments, there is a chance that it will have no effect at all. Even with end-to-end teams, many constraints and obstacles to flow and feedback are often organizational in nature. That is why we must engage managers at all levels in driving continuous improvement.

Because I wanted you to recognize how the different elements of Toyota Kata support each other and form a "whole", I purposely waited to present this last and final point until the very end. Through this book, we have been introduced to several concepts that are all part of the Toyota Kata framework and the Starter Kata:

- Establishing an Agile Process Vision
- Assigning measurable goals to Process improvement initiatives on the Challenge and Target Condition level
- Coach/Learner relationships enacted through the Coaching Kata
- Working iteratively with Process improvement through experiments and hypotheses
- Clearly assigning Process improvement responsibility to Process Leads and managers

We have also introduced several specific tools and practices to help support the framework:

- Rating of current Agile capabilities using 1- to 5-point scales and clear statements from the Process Vision
- Value Stream Mapping
- Meta-Kata maturity scores
- Challenge and Target Condition inspiration catalog

They do form a framework in which each element supports each other to make the total value bigger than the individual parts. However, should you find yourself in a situation in which you are able to apply only individual tools and principles, nothing should stop you from doing that. Even without the other parts, establishing a clear Agile vision will help create shared ownership and increase the chance of people pulling in the same direction. Coaching Kata-like sessions are highly likely to improve the effect of your existing improvement work, and measurable leading indicators will help you deliver on your goal in a way that is both more fun and more effective. Naturally, I recommend that you try to apply the Starter Kata to the best of your ability but if that is not possible, do not let that discourage you from benefitting from the individual elements.

I also hope that you have learned that culture and habits are changed by doing actual work differently and not by reading books and PowerPoint slides. That is equally true for Process improvement and the way we approach product development. It is not enough to talk about continuous improvement; you must do improvement daily, the same way that talking about a customer-centric mindset has no effect if your work items are defined from an inside-out perspective.

This book ended up being longer than I originally intended. This wasn't simply because I was unable to write shorter sentences but also because there are many more layers to effective improvement than meets the eye. You do not realize this before you try to put it in writing and are forced to reflect on the many aspects and learning points. This was made very clear by the feedback I received from the many reviewers who took the time to provide me with valuable feedback and who asked for clarifications on topics and details that I had taken for granted.

If you have questions, comments or feedback or need assistance with Toyota Kata, Kanban, Scrum, Agile or Lean in the context of knowledge work, do not hesitate to contact me.

Best regards

Jesper Boeg

Email: agileupgrade@gmail.com

Mobile: +45 51542820

Skype ID: j.boeg

LinkedIn: linkedin.com/in/jesperboeg

About the Author

Implementing Agile and Lean principles in the context of innovation and IT has been Jesper's work and passion since 2006. He enjoys difficult challenges and is constantly seeking new ways to deliver great solutions and make work simpler, easier and more enjoyable for everybody involved.

Jesper works with the entire value stream from C-level to individual teams. He enjoys both the job of aligning senior management on the company's Agile direction, building a team of internal change agents and hands-on implementation. Jesper is known for being to the point and unafraid to bring difficult matters to the table; but with a smile and humor as a key enabler. Jesper has worked with all size companies from small Startups to large corporations and hands-on in almost all possible roles. That includes a position as VP of Agile and Lean Process Excellence at the software development and consulting company Trifork. Jesper is now the owner of AgileUpgrade.com focusing on leading Agile and Lean change initiatives. He regularly speaks at local meetups and Agile and Lean conferences.

Bibliography

Ackoff, R. (1994). *YouTube.* Hentet fra https://www.youtube.com/watch?v=OqEeIG8aPPk

Ahlstrom, P., & Modig, N. (2012). *This is Lean: Resolving the Efficiency Paradox.* Rheologica Publishing.

Anderson, D. J. (2010). *Kanban: Successful Evolutionary Change for Your Technology Business.* Blue Hole Press; 3.8.2010 edition .

Boeg, J. (2015). *Taking a look under the hood – Successful implementation of Lean and Agile principles in a large program.* Hentet fra agileupgrade.com: http://agileupgrade.com/taking-a-look-under-the-hood-successful-implementation-of-lean-and-agile-principles-in-a-large-program/

Cappelli, P., & Tavis, A. (2018). HR goes agile. *Harward Business Review.*

Cohn, M. (2004). *User Stories Applied: For Agile Software Development.* Addison-Wesley Professional; 1 edition .

Covey, S. (2015). *4 Disciplines of Execution.* Simon & Schuster Ltd; UK ed. edition.

Covey, S. R. (2004). *The 7 Habits of Highly Effective People: Powerful Lessons in Personal Change.* Free Press; Revised edition.

Doidge, N. (2007). *The Brain That Changes Itself: Stories of Personal Triumph from the Frontiers of Brain Science.* Penguin Books; 1 edition.

Forsgren, N., Humble, J., & Kim, G. (2018). *Accelerate: The Science of Lean Software and DevOps: Building and Scaling High Performing Technology Organizations.* IT Revolution Press.

Hiatt, J. (2006). *ADKAR: A Model for Change in Business, Government and Our Community.* Prosci Learning Center Publications.

Hubbard, D. W. (2009). *The Failure of Risk Management: Why It's Broken and How to Fix It.* John Wiley & Sons; 1st Edition edition.

Humble, J. (2018). *The problems with agile at scale.* Hentet fra LinkedIn: https://www.linkedin.com/learning/lean-technology-strategy-running-agile-at-scale/the-problems-with-agile-at-scale

Kahneman, D. (2013). *Thinking, Fast and Slow.* Farrar, Straus and Giroux.

Knibert, H., & Roost, L. (2015). *GOTO 2015 • Is SAFe Evil?* Hentet fra YouTube: https://www.youtube.com/watch?v=TolNkqyvieE

Knight, S. (2010). *NLP at Work: The Essence of Excellence.* Quercus, 2010.

Mann, A., Stahnke, M., Brown, A., & Kersten, N. (2018). *2018 State of DevOps Report.* Hentet fra https://puppet.com/resources/whitepaper/state-of-devops-report

Münster, M. (2018). Hentet fra https://mortenmunster.com/motivation-er-overvurderet-goer-i-stedet-disse-4-ting/

Nicole Forsgren, J. H. (2017). Forecasting The Value of DevOps Transformations. *DORA.* Hentet fra https://devops-research.com/roi/

Pascale, R., Sternin, J., & Sternin, M. (2010). *The Power of Positive Deviance: How Unlikely Innovators Solve the World's Toughest Problems.* Harvard Business Review Press; 1St Edition edition.

Pink, D. H. (2011). *Drive: The Surprising Truth About What Motivates Us.* Riverhead Books.

Reinertsen, D. G. (2009). *The Principles of Product Development Flow: Second Generation Lean Product Development.* Celeritas Pub.

Ries, E. (2011). *The Lean Startup: How Today's Entrepreneurs Use Continuous Innovation to Create Radically Successful Businesses.* Currency; 1 edition.

Rother, M. (2009). *Toyota Kata: Managing People for Improvement, Adaptiveness and Superior Results.* McGraw-Hill Education.

Rother, M. (2018). *The Toyota Kata Practice Guide: Practicing Scientific Thinking Skills for Superior Results in 20 Minutes a Day.* McGraw-Hill Education; 1 edition.

Rother, M., & Aulinger, G. (2017). *Toyota Kata Culture: Building Organizational Capability and Mindset through Kata Coaching.* McGraw-Hill Education; 1 edition.

Rother, M., & Shook, J. (1999). *Learning to See: Value Stream Mapping to Add Value and Eliminate MUDA.* Lean Enterprise Institute; 1 edition.

Shpilberg, D., Berez, S., Puryear, R., & Shah, S. (2007). Avoiding the Alignment Trap in IT. *MIT Sloan Management Review.*

Snowden, D. (u.d.). Hentet fra Cognitive-edge: https://cognitive-edge.com/

Standish Group Chaos Report. (2014).

Stout, L. (2012). *The Shareholder Value Myth: How Putting Shareholders First Harms Investors, Corporations, and the Public.* Berrett-Koehler Publishers; 1 edition.

17566902R00185

Printed in Great Britain
by Amazon